"With a compelling and rigorous critical lens, Jan Baars uncovers the humanly destructive effects of neoliberalism and its 'humanist' intellectual apologists. He demonstrates clearly how popular narratives of social science, philosophy and popular culture are logically and empirically flawed, and how they have served to legitimate neoliberalism's rise and its continued expansion while naturalizing or otherwise ignoring and obscuring the harmful impact its policies have on individual life chances and aspirations."

Dale Dannefer, *Case Western University, author of* Age and the Reach of the Sociological Imagination

"This superb book illuminates, more clearly than any other, the profound relationships among capitalism, neoliberalism, poverty, inequality, and aging. Baars cuts through the misconceptions about healthy aging by showing how the very rich have exploited old people in the quest to accumulate capital. Through a wide range of data and other startling information, the book documents the ways that neoliberal policies prop up global capitalism but deeply hurt people as they age. As a sociologist and medical practitioner trying to care for old people, I often have faced the disastrous conditions that this book describes. But until reading the book, I never fully understood the political-economic sources of patients' suffering. The book's revelations point to a need for fundamental social transformation if we are serious about improving health and quality of life for people as they age."

Howard Waitzkin, MD, PhD, *Distinguished Professor Emeritus, Sociology and Health Sciences, University of New Mexico*

"A bold and original critique of the impact of neo-liberal policies in widening inequalities and undermining social rights. Drawing on his commitment to critical scholarship and a passion for social justice, Jan Baars provides a comprehensive account of the way in which neo-liberal policies have drastically reduced security for the middle and working class in the US, and for disadvantaged older people in particular. He demonstrates how the experiences of older citizens provide a powerful illustration of the operation of social inequalities – and the way these shape health inequalities – over the life course. Jan Baars concludes his book by arguing for a new moral vision of the life course, one guided by considerations of social justice, equity, and mutual respect between citizens."

Chris Phillipson, *Professor of Sociology and Social Gerontology, University of Manchester*

Long Lives Are for the Rich

Long Lives Are for the Rich is the title of a silent ominous program that affects the lives of millions of people. In all developed countries disadvantaged and, especially, poor people die much earlier than the most advantaged. During these shorter lives they suffer ten to twenty years longer from disabilities or chronic disease. This does not happen accidentally: health inequalities – including those between healthy and unhealthy life styles – are mainly caused by social inequalities that are reproduced over the life course. This crucial function of the life course has become painfully visible during its neoliberal reorganization since the early 1980s. Studies about aging over the life course, from birth to death, show the inhumane consequences as people get older. In spite of the enormous wealth that has been piled up in the US for a dwindling percentage of the population, there has been growing public indifference about the needs of those in jobs with low pay and high stress, but also about citizens from a broad middle class who can hardly afford high quality education or healthcare. However, this ominous program affects all: recent mortality rates show that all Americans, including the rich, are unhealthier and dying earlier than citizens of other developed countries. Moreover, the underlying social inequalities are tearing the population apart with nasty consequences for all citizens, including the rich. Although the public awareness of the consequences has been growing, neoliberal policies remain tempting for the economic and political elites of the developed world because of the enormous wealth that is flowing to the top. All this poses urgent questions of social justice. Unfortunately, the predominant studies of social justice along the life course help to reproduce these inequalities by neglecting them. This book analyzes the main dynamics of social inequality over the life course and proposes a theory of social justice that sketches a way forward for a country that is willing to invest in its greatest resource: the creative potential of its population.

Jan Baars is Professor of Humanistic Gerontology at the University for Humanistic Studies in Utrecht, and Emeritus Professor of Philosophy of the Social Sciences and the Humanities at Tilburg University, The Netherlands. Jan's previously published books include *Aging and the Art of Living*, and co-edited volumes *Ageing, Meaning and Social Structure: Connecting Critical and Humanistic Gerontology*; *Aging, Globalization and Inequality*; and *Aging and Time: Multidisciplinary Perspectives*.

Aging and Society

Edited by Carroll L. Estes and Assistant Editor Nicholas DiCarlo

This pioneering series of books creatively synthesizes and advances key, intersectional topics in gerontology and aging studies. Drawing from changing and emerging issues in gerontology, influential scholars combine research into human development and the life course; the roles of power, policy, and partisanship; race and ethnicity; inequality; gender and sexuality; and cultural studies to create a multi-dimensional and essential picture of modern aging.

Aging A–Z
Concepts toward Emancipatory Gerontology (2019)
Carroll L. Estes with Nicholas DiCarlo

The Privatization of Care
The Case of Nursing Homes (2020)
Pat Armstrong, Hugh Armstrong et al.

Age and the Research of Sociological Imagination
Power, Ideology, and the Life Course (2021)
Dale Dannefer

When Strangers Become Family
The Role of Civil Society in Addressing the Needs of Aging Populations (2021)
Ronald Angel and Verónica Montes-de-Oca Zavala

Safeguarding Social Security for Future Generations
Leaving a Legacy in an Aging Society
W. Andrew Achenbaum

Long Lives Are for the Rich
Aging, the Life Course, and Social Justice
Jan Baars

For more information about this series, please visit:
https://www.routledge.com/Aging-and-Society/book-series/AGINGSOC

Long Lives Are for the Rich

Aging, the Life Course, and Social Justice

Jan Baars

Routledge
Taylor & Francis Group

NEW YORK AND LONDON

Designed cover image: ©shutterstock.com

First published 2024
by Routledge
605 Third Avenue, New York, NY 10158

and by Routledge
4 Park Square, Milton Park, Abingdon, Oxon OX14 4RN

Routledge is an imprint of the Taylor & Francis Group, an informa business

© 2024 Jan Baars

British Library Cataloguing-in-Publication Data
A catalogue record for this book is available from the British Library

Library of Congress Cataloging-in-Publication Data
Names: Baars, Jan, author.
Title: Long lives are for the rich : aging, the life course, and social
justice / Jan Baars.
Description: Abingdon, Oxon ; New York, NY : Routledge, 2022. |
Series: Aging and society | Includes bibliographical references and index.
Identifiers: LCCN 2022061684 (print) | LCCN 2022061685 (ebook) |
ISBN 9781032492025 (hardback) | ISBN 9781032491967 (paperback) |
ISBN 9781003392590 (ebook)
Subjects: LCSH: Older people--Social conditions. | Older people--
Economic conditions. | Poverty--Health aspects. | Equality--Health
aspects. | Social justice. | Social policy.
Classification: LCC HQ1061 .B236 2022 (print) | LCC HQ1061 (ebook) |
DDC 305.26--dc23/eng/20230119
LC record available at https://lccn.loc.gov/2022061684
LC ebook record available at https://lccn.loc.gov/2022061685

ISBN: 978-1-032-49202-5 (hbk)
ISBN: 978-1-032-49196-7 (pbk)
ISBN: 978-1-003-39259-0 (ebk)

DOI: 10.4324/9781003392590

Typeset in Bembo
by Taylor & Francis Books

Contents

Figures

Preface

My interest in aging has been inspired by indignation. As a young professor at the Free University of Amsterdam in my late thirties, I was challenged in 1985 to join a research group on aging. As I had already been teaching quite passionately sociological theory and social philosophy for over 15 years I followed my first impulses to explain extensively that this move could not be expected from me. To defend this position I began to read recommended 'state of the art' articles about aging. Most publications seemed to me like tales about another, deeply problematic species. As a young boy I had always been attracted to older people; I liked especially their friendly quietness and clarity. As a student I had rented a room from an older couple who were approaching their eighties. They did have some difficulty climbing the steep stairs of the old Amsterdam house but seemed quite normal to me and were interesting to talk to, having lived, for instance, through the First World War, the Spanish Flu, the roaring twenties, the Great Depression, the rise of National Socialism, the Second World War and the post-war reconstruction. And they were still following present developments with interest.

Many questions arose from reading the research articles about aging: did the lives of all these 'elderly' turn around diseases? Did they all, or most of them, live in homes for the aged? Why the silence about the others? Did society push older people into care trajectories as soon as they had been defined as 'old'? Why did the age related definition of being 'old' change to '50+', following the policies of early retirement of the mid 1980s? Did this increase the realm and importance of the gerontologists? What might be the consequences of all these scenarios of miserable and costly decline for the ways in which young adults were advised to see their futures? I began to doubt some of the motives behind the governmental investment in gerontological research in a society that was only beginning to learn that it should be 'lean and mean'; urging gerontologists to innovate care arrangements so that they would be 'better and cheaper', leading to a 'win–win' situation for all. The pressure was on with no time to lose in the face of demographic disaster.

Without looking for it, I had found a subject of study of high human interest and social relevance, besides my continuing passion for social theory and social philosophy. My questions resonated among a broad audience but appeared difficult to digest for the Dutch gerontological establishment of the mid 1980s. My involvement in aging studies would have been short-lived had I not met colleagues from abroad who shared my main concerns such as Dale Dannefer, Chris Phillipson, Alan Walker, Matilda and Jack Riley. The circle of engaging colleagues rapidly expanded to include Andy Achenbaum, Vern Bengtson, Bob Binstock, Tom Cole, Carroll Estes, Martin Kohli, Victor Marshall, Rick Moody, Paul Stein and others. Thanks to these and other colleagues my intellectual exile turned out to be a blessing in disguise as it opened up a world of intense discussion with inspiring colleagues. In spite of our somewhat dissident agendas the annual scientific meetings of the *Gerontological Society of America* provided an invaluable platform to share and discuss a diversity of questions and approaches. I have especially good memories from the period that I chaired GSA's *Humanities & Arts Committee* on its mission for a stronger inclusion of the humanities in aging studies.

Meanwhile, many European countries had come further under the spell of neoliberal policies that were initially advanced by the US president Reagan. As these policies worked so well for big corporations there was huge pressure to use these approaches also for public domains such as education, worker's rights, health care, pensions, or income policies. Top corporate executives came to be seen by governments as experts on the question 'how to run a society?' In The Netherlands, for instance, an expert group on industrial policy, chaired by the former Shell CEO Gerrit Wagner became very influential. Initially, its task was merely to advise the Dutch government on industrial policy but its recommendations were soon applied to other forms of policy. The main message of this new 'industrial *élan*' was contained in his slogan: 'Don't back the losers, but pick the winners!'

This new spirit of corporate America leading the way to a supposedly better world contrasted with my cherished memories of Martin Luther King who received a honorary doctorate at The Free University in the first year of my academic study. This great little man also spoke of an American vision: a dream of mutual respect and social justice that inspired many people around the world. Such considerations were erased from the budgetary scenarios that were meant to remodel social policies over the life course.

Four decades of neoliberal policies are now behind us; they have led to a population that has become increasingly divided into 'winners' and 'losers'. The growing group of politicians who are recently voicing concern about these destructive divisions and the poverty of public sectors such as health care, education or public transport can hardly be surprised: these have been the targets of the corporate-political *élan* of the last four decades. Out of concern for political stability there have more recently been doubts about the consequences of austerity policies, leading occasionally to more support for the population in times of crisis. But the deeply problematic and divisive societal model that has been implemented for decades will not easily be changed as it has increased the grip of the most powerful political and corporate elites on society. A developmental model that began in the US has negatively impacted most developed countries; its extreme consequences can also most clearly be seen in the US which makes this an issue of international concern.

Over the last years the urgency has grown to address more elaborately the consequences of this deeply problematic and divisive societal model from a perspective of social inequality and social justice. It is illuminating to see this through the lenses of longitudinal life course research as this demonstrates that much of what is usually seen as *natural* processes of growing up and growing older may not be so natural after all. Distributions of opportunities, disease, careers, even long or short lives are actually heavily influenced by unequal circumstances along the life course, beginning with very early life; even during gestation. Divisive 'for profit' policies have deepened the gap between those who profit from the marketed services that they or their families can afford and those who cannot. Such inequalities in life chances become more manifest as people get older. Abandoned citizens see their chances to flourish wane and will eventually question whether this society with its 'democratic institutions' is also meant for them.

What divides and unites us

Long Lives Are for the Rich is a book about *social inequalities* between people. Such inequalities are not mere *differences*. All people are different from others: discrimination is the morbid practice to turn differences, for instance, of skin color, culture or gender *into* social inequalities. The nasty characteristic of social inequalities is that they exclude certain groups of people from opportunities or even life chances. Why should we oppose such practices? The answer is that all these very different human beings are *inherently equal*, giving them rights to equal respect, equal opportunities to flourish and equal life chances. In short: granting them equal citizenship. A mere *declaration* of equality, however, does not settle the issue as long as there are still serious forms of social inequality. Speaking of an equal dignity of human beings is a normative principle – not an empirical statement – that should lead to criticism of the problems and suffering that are plausibly caused by social inequality instead of covering them up by solemn declarations that 'all men are created equal'.

This principle of equal dignity of human beings can, however, remain rather abstract if it cannot be related to personal experiences. Apart from offering an excellent window on the development of social inequalities over the life course, studying human aging also offers a window on this fundamental equality of people, beyond all the differences between them. When we speak about subjects like finitude, time or vulnerability in the *experiential* context of aging, the focus is on what human beings *share* with each other. They are equal in confrontation with these unfolding conditions and the questions they bring with them. Such processes are *personally* experienced, giving the understanding of aging an experiential basis that is different from an *objectifying* empirical approach. Although personal experiences of growth, development, loneliness, happiness, sadness, loss or death are thoroughly colored by social and cultural contexts that does not erase the personal character of these experiences. The personal experience that one is getting older, looking back on the years that have flashed by, traveling into a time horizon that becomes shorter than one used to take for granted, can also give a feeling of deep connection with other human beings. This has indeed been one of the elements of transmitted forms of wisdom.

In my work on subjective experiences of living in time, in contrast to the time that is measured and imposed on our experiences I have tried to articulate some dimensions of such personal experiences. One of the leading questions of *Aging and the Art of Living* (2012) was how we can enrich our thinking about human aging as an art of *living in time* by learning from ancient and modern thought about cosmological, scientific and personally experienced forms of time. To address what unites us as human beings we need such a *social-existential* approach to aging.

To flourish in our personal lives, however, we are also dependent on structural preconditions regarding, for instance, housing, education, income, work or health care that have a profound influence on personal lives. Many problems that confront people as they get older are not universally shared but consequences of unequal life course trajectories. The aggregate dynamics and consequences of social structures and culture, however, cannot be adequately explained from personal experiences but have to be monitored from a macro perspective. To do this we need a *social-structural* approach as applied in *Long Lives Are for the Rich*.

The well being of citizens, however, remains a source of critical interrogation of the structural arrangements they are confronted with. Their human *dignity* requires that societies respect them and create the necessary preconditions of their participation as equal citizens. The *social-existential* and the *social-structural* approach are both necessary: they presuppose each other and neither of them can be reduced to the other. In this way *Long Lives Are for the Rich* can be seen as a companion volume to *Aging and the Art of Living*.

Acknowledgements

I am very grateful to Carroll Estes for her enthusiastic support over the years, from the very beginning to the final version. And to Dale Dannefer and Chris Phillipson for their clarifying and inspiring comments on the manuscript in different stages of its development. My special thanks to Dean Birkenkamp for his solid support over the years, to Kristina Wischenkamper for improving the text, and to Sarahjayne Smith for coordinating the production process. I am infinitely grateful to Carolina, my family and friends for their enduring support.

Introduction

The neo-liberal turn against a supportive life course and the US as its tragic champion

'… for people age quickly in misfortune'.

(Homer Odyssey. 8th century BC)

Somewhere in the last decades many developed countries have taken a wrong turn with ominous consequences. Wealth has been growing steadily but it is not trickling down, as has been an often repeated promise since Reaganomics, but sucked upwards by a small powerful economic elite. Moreover, the accumulated wealth is mostly highly unstable financial capital, floating through Wall Street in apparent isolation from its consequences for small businesses and jobs on Main Street, creating implosive bubbles, permanent insecurity and recurrent crises. The consequences of these processes raise concerns in all developed countries as the majority of their political and economic elites have been tempted to follow a developmental model that has been forcefully backed up by the US. I will just mention growing social inequality; a weakening middle class; continuing inequalities of healthy life expectancy of up to twenty years; growing mistrust in economic and political elites who have orchestrated these developments.

The US figures in this story not only as the breeding ground of this developmental 'neoliberal' model but also as the country where the consequences have crystalized most clearly. The majority of the US population have been suffering from this harsh model and I can only hope that critical analyses may help to turn developments in a more humane direction and that the economic and political elites of the US and other developed countries stop following this model even though they have been its primary beneficiaries. Recently many critical publications have addressed 'neoliberalism' but little focus has been placed on a life course perspective, despite the ominous results of this developmental model being demonstrated quite clearly in a life course perspective of aging from birth to death. This study will show that, eventually, deepening social inequality over the life course will threaten the health and well being of the *whole* population, including the most wealthy. Moreover, the forces of social inequality are tearing the country apart.

DOI: 10.4324/9781003392590-1

One would expect these destructive implications of deepening social inequalities to lead to intensive debates about urgent questions of social justice. However, the predominant debates in the US about social justice over the life course and, especially about the ways in which these societal divisions are gradually but painfully taking shape as citizens are getting older, have ignored these inequalities. As will be discussed in chapters 5 and 6, these debates about social justice over the life course are caught in a straight jacket of uncontextualized 'individual responsibility', 'wholesome markets' – as if they are the embodiments of social justice – and misleading 'generational clashes'.

What I have referred to above as 'the wrong turn' began to gain momentum in the US at the beginning of the 1980s and soon became a model – loosely called 'neoliberal' – for further development of rich Western countries. In stark contrast to its accumulated wealth there is much poverty and a worrisome growth of socioeconomic insecurity for large parts of the middle class. This wrong turn is, however, not an accidental mistake; it wouldn't have continued for over four decades if it hadn't produced major benefits. But we need to ask: what benefits and for whom? What appears to be 'a wrong turn' is a consequence of a reductionist model of societal development that has been extremely profitable for the political and economic elite, which explains its attraction for similar elites in other developed countries, in spite of its devastating effects on major parts of the population.

There are, however, important differences in the magnitude of the damage that is done to these populations. In countries where the social rights of citizenship have been less damaged, and citizens have not as much been reduced to producers and consumers, the damaging effects of the neoliberal model have been mitigated. Unfortunately, as will be discussed more elaborately in the following chapters, this has not been the case for the US, although this country has been seen as the ideal or even inevitable model for the future of developed countries. Its population has been suffering the full brunt of a developmental model that has been dominant since the early 1980s. I will give some brief examples that will be discussed more elaborately in the following chapters. Because the differences in indicators such as life expectancies may seem small it should be noted that it is easy to underestimate their significance. The *US Center for Disease Control and Prevention* estimates that the elimination of all cancer deaths – which would be a huge step in improving population health – – would increase life expectancy by only three years. So, seemingly small differences in these expectancies really amount to serious inequalities.

First, the richest, technologically most innovative country of the world, spending extremely high amounts of money per capita for health care is dramatically falling behind other OECD [Organisation for Economic Cooperation and Development] countries in *life expectancy*. Although the

US remained close to the OECD average in the decades after the Second World War, after 1980 this development has been deteriorating rapidly. In 2018 American men and women could expect to live 5.18 and 5.82 fewer years than Swiss men and Japanese women (Ho 2022).

Second, in recent years the US has had a higher *infant* mortality rate than most other OECD member countries, ranking 33 out of 38. If they were included in this ranking, even the best performing US states, such as Massachusetts and New Hampshire with 3.9 deaths per 1,000 live births in 2019 would come in at rank 27. Mississippi, with an infant mortality rate of 8.6 deaths per 1,000 live births is off the chart with twice the OECD average.[1]

Third, according to recent research by The *Commonwealth Fund*,[2] in comparison with women in other OECD countries, women in the US have the highest rate of emotional distress, and they experience the greatest burden of chronic illness. Moreover, maternal mortality rates are highest in the US and its female citizens have the highest rates of skipping needed health care because of cost.

These are comparisons between the population, children and women of the US with those of other countries without taking notice of differences and inequalities *within* these populations, where advantaged women and children are doing much better than their disadvantaged counterparts. Even these poor averages still hide and embellish situations of extreme misery. The title of this book *Long Lives Are for the Rich* refers to such inequalities in (healthy) life expectancies within countries. It is an international disgrace that in all developed countries citizens with the lowest socioeconomic status have a shorter life expectancy than those with the highest socioeconomic status. Most developed countries – in spite of their neoliberal policies – have during the last four decades continued to extend life expectancies of their populations, although the most disadvantaged still die relatively young. Contrary to such slow improvement the inequality in life expectancies *within* the US population has *increased* over the last decades. Whereas the difference between the life expectancies of those with the lowest and highest socioeconomic status in 1982 was 3.7 years, this had almost doubled to 7.2 years in 2019 (Barbieri 2022).

Moreover, the most disadvantaged have a much shorter *healthy* life expectancy: the number of years they can be expected to live without a burdening disease or disability. In all the rich OECD countries disadvantaged people die earlier, moreover, after having suffered ten to twenty more years from chronic disease than the most advantaged. I have called this shameful phenomenon the *Perverse Longevity Gap*. Still, between 2010 and 2019 almost all OECD countries experienced a growth in healthy life expectancy of their population; in Japan, for instance, there was an increase from 73 to 74.1 years. At the same time, the perverse longevity gap between the materially and culturally advantaged and the disadvantaged grew smaller.

To avoid the impression that the US is framed negatively by comparing it only with the best performing country, it should be noted that the US has been the *only* OECD country that has experienced a decrease in *healthy* life expectancy over the decade since 2010: from 66.7 to 66.1 years. Only two underdeveloped countries demonstrated such as decrease: Yemen and Venezuela. These countries have been confronted respectively with an ongoing civil war and a decade-long humanitarian crisis.[3] The dynamics of social inequality in the US are leading to a situation where we can no longer see any winners. Recent mortality rates in the US are showing that *all* Americans, *including the rich*, are unhealthier and dying earlier than citizens of other developed countries.

For a long time, the US took pride in doing well in life expectancy at age 85 – generally, an age category populated by the most advantaged – but since 2010 things have declined further so that *the US population was in 2018 worst off at just about every age* (Barbieri 2022; Ho 2022). To put this in perspective: if the other peer countries were to freeze at their present levels and the US suddenly began to grow its life expectancies at the pace of the best performers, it would still take 14 years to catch up with the average of its peer countries. Catching up with the world leaders would take more than 20 years (Ho 2022). Realistically, the US will not come anywhere near these levels in the coming decades. Consequentially, the population of the richest and most powerful country in the world faces a continuing worsening of its prospects to live – in comparison to citizens of other countries – a reasonably long and healthy life. That *Long Lives should* only be for *the Rich* has turned out to be a self destructive program, raising urgent questions of social inequality and social justice over the life course. Even when the rich – short for the most materially and immaterially advantaged citizens – somehow do manage to live longer, there is a price to be paid for the extreme inequalities that will continue to divide the nation.

This raises the complicated question: what is going on in the US that it finds itself in such a position? These developments are neither inevitable nor do they happen accidentally: as can be plausibly demonstrated *health* inequalities are mainly caused by *social* inequalities that are reproduced over the life course. In spite of the enormous wealth that has been piled up in the US for a tiny percentage of the population, there has been growing public indifference about the needs of those in jobs with low pay and high stress, who live in ill maintained houses and neighborhoods, unable to afford marketed services in early childcare, education or health care. The US health record trails far behind other high-income countries, despite spending far more than any other country per capita on health care. Investing more in health care without improving the infrastructure of the life course (see Ch.7) will not help to improve these dreadful circumstances. The health care system is chronically overburdened with problems it cannot solve in the clinic.

In a country where high quality education, health care and other forms of support are marketed it has a huge impact when incomes are falling behind rising costs of living. Between 1980 and 2014 the average income of the bottom 50% of workers in the US 'grew' from $16,000 to $16,200. Over the same period the incomes of the top 1% grew from $428,000 to $1,305,000 (see Ch.1). Over the last years the incomes at the bottom of the pyramid have somewhat improved but it would be farfetched to speak of a reduction of income inequality. It does not help that much of what used to be dignified work – for many the only source of income and respect – has become precarious, lost its status and is hardly rewarded. In the self pro-claimed 'land of equal opportunity' prospects of children are more depen-dent on the income and wealth of their parents than in other advanced countries. Those born at the bottom are likely to remain there without any prospect of a better future even when they have had much more education than their parents, adding the status frustration of not being able to do what they are trained for. The chances of making it, Horatio Alger-style, from a childhood in poverty to an adulthood in affluence are lower in the US than in other nations. Although opportunities have never been equal in the US – nor have they been equal in other countries – now they seem to have shrunk to the equal opportunity to be *told* that you can become whatever you want and that the sky is the limit.

The champion of neoliberalism seems to have decided that *Long Lives should remain a privilege for the Rich*. This is the silent program behind the neoliberal organization of the life course in the US that is leading to dee-pening divisions in its population. In a life course perspective the inhumane consequences become painfully visible as people get older. Most of the materially and culturally advantaged, who are wealthy, highly educated and not subjected to discrimination will live relatively long and healthy lives. They may also face difficult years as their lives come to an end but overall 'old age' can be a time of reaping the fruits of accumulated resources. By contrast, for most of the disadvantaged, the middle years will already be hard as chronic disease and material problems begin to accumulate. Age-related arrangements for those who make it into 'old age' such as Social Security and Medicare (cf. Estes & DiCarlo 2019) will give them much needed support but are simply too late to prevent the accumulation of bodily and mental insults that lead many of them into early chronic disease and early death. In contrast, age based entitlements, pensions and (healthy) life expectancies tend to be more favorable for those who enjoyed advan-taged positions all along.

This does not imply that this program has been intentional. Partly it is systemic: a dismal confluence of different processes, such as the market-ization of education, protection, support or care, leading to cumulative disadvantages for those who have already been disadvantaged from the very start of their lives. But also it comes from an overemphasis on individual responsibility and public indifference, possibly fed by the assumption that a supportive infrastructure of the life course would be a bottomless pit. 'Social inequality' does not only refer to a situation at a particular moment but also to ongoing processes in which an unequal society is being reproduced over time. The organization of the life course plays a major role in this reproduction as it creates, protects, neglects or destroys the structural and cultural preconditions that are necessary for education, work, retirement or health care to function well for all citizens. This poses the question of how the life course can be organized in such a way that such pathogenic situations for disadvantaged citizens can be avoided or mitigated as much as possible.

This deeply rooted combination of public indifference and individual responsibility has even been reproduced in predominant theories of social justice over the life course. The general conclusion of these theories is that society should avoid throwing money into a 'bottomless pit' to keep people alive who have already lived 'a long life': citizens who have already become 70 or 75 years of age or even those who have survived into 'old age'. In other words: long lives are meant for those who can afford it.

However, as these consequences are becoming more and more obvious it is hard to see how large parts of the population will ever be able to benefit from this developmental model. This is extremely worrying because it is an illusion to think that democracy can function well or even survive when basic needs of the population are not respected. In their book *How Democracies Die* Levitsky and Ziblatt (2018) discuss two threats to democracy: a military coup and a democratically chosen leader who turns into an authoritarian leader. These are certainly major threats but democracies are also undermined by a neglect of structurally caused social problems that further erode social rights that are rightly seen as the responsibility of democratic governments.

Citizens need to commit themselves to realizing whatever they want, such as a family, a long and healthy life, an inspiring career, a good house or clean air. But governments need to take responsibility for the necessary preconditions: the solemn proclamation of equal opportunities does not make them any more realistic. Inspite of the promises, expectations and hopes of citizens of sharing in the wealth that has been amassed in their economies, so that they might improve the quality of their lives, the situation of too many of them is, in reality, deteriorating. The most wealthy country of the world is increasingly falling behind its peer countries because it is even less willing to invest in its greatest resource: the creative potential of its population.

'Wholesome' markets and the myopic fog of individualism

Over recent years there has been no shortage of critical discussions about 'neo-liberalism': a quite contradictory and opportunistic political orientation with impressive differences between its 'theory' and its political practice, for instance, with regard to its celebrated 'free market'. The strategy to enlarge the global growth of oligopolistic corporations and the fortunes of their beneficiaries was not invented by neoliberalism. In *The Myth of Capitalism: Monopolies and the Death of Competition* (2018) Jonathan Tepper and Denise Hearn tell the story of how, in a few decades, America has gone from an open, competitive marketplace to an economy where a few very powerful companies are increasingly dominating the playing field. This transition, however, is not as clear cut as it may seem. In 1968, when many young people had hopes for a better world, Baran and Sweezy published *Monopoly Capital. An Essay on the American Economic and Social Order* in which they already showed that the assets and incomes of large multinational corporations exceeded those of many nations. This tendency, however, has grown beyond expectation.[4]

In many critical retrospective analyses of the neoliberal turn there has been little attention paid to the problems in the US economy at the end of the 1970s. It is plausible that the reduction or readjustment of some market regulations did play a constructive role in increasing productivity. This, however, does not legitimate the deregulation of all markets. Moreover, the financialization of the economy has shifted the focus of investors to quick returns so that manufacturing and productivity in the US have actually been declining (Stiglitz 2015; Phillips 2006). As the years went by, the severe consequences of a heavily lopsided developmental program have become more and more obvious. The long term implications of the political changes at the beginning of the 1980s justify speaking of a demarcation or transition to a new 'neoliberal' mix of preexisting tendencies that are undermining the well being of the majority of the population. One of its main social coups has been to brake away from the project of a supportive life course (see Ch.1) that had gradually become a priority since the Second World War. This breakdown of an institutionalized public responsibility for the well being of the population has become one of the divisive errors of the neoliberal turn of capitalism. The wealth of a small group with its huge private consumption and investments has become so enormous that the US GDP *per capita* has been one of the highest in the world, but its distribution over the population falls short on all counts.

In the context of this inquiry about social inequality and social justice over the life course, 'neoliberalism' is first of all an ideology (in the broad sense of a set of ideas and interpretive frames that support and legitimize the policies of the most powerful forces in a society) that serves to legitimate the concentration of wealth and to cover up political responsibility for the well being of the population. Many don't want to discuss 'neoliberalism' anymore because it would be unclear what the term might refer to. It is, indeed, a new *hybrid* kind of ideology: an opportunistic mix of principles of ideas or principles that are easily abandoned as soon as the dominant interests decide against them. Such flexible opportunism should not be rewarded by avoiding discussion of 'neoliberal' strategies. Instead of reviewing the debates on neoliberalism or contemporary capitalism I will briefly characterize what has struck me during the research for this book as typical of the policies that have undermined the well being of the populations of the developed countries since the late 1970s. The neoliberal policies may be contradictory and diffuse, but the main pattern is clear enough.

Neoliberalism's target is the growth of wealth for a small international elite by expanding successful enterprises and corporations into global monopolies or, at least oligopolies, far beyond the boundaries of classical 19th or early 20th century capitalism. In order to make this possible, obstructing laws and regulations have to be removed, corporate tax and wealth tax reduced. The ideological message to the general public is that they have to wait until all boats will be lifted by the rising tide of booming profits. The justification of these policies is not based on a consistent theory; it proceeds with flexible opportunism, appealing to traditional values such as family, the hard working individual, or patriotism without much concern for broken families, the working poor, or the social cohesion of society. There are, however, two typical complementary slogans.

The *first* slogan propagates the individual responsibility for the citizens' societal fate. The uncontextualized 'individual' is praised for his success that would be his merit and his alone. The less elevating flipside of this eulogy of the individual's omnipotence is the message that the individual's failure would be completely his own fault. This moral narrative has a long history in American culture in the context of a work ethic that made more sense when there was more reward in hard work, at least for racially privileged men. The praise and blame of the uncontextualized individual has been intensified and spread to an international audience in the form of a self-help culture which has done its share to cover up a worrisome neglect of public responsibilities. As will be documented in the following chapters, this slogan of individual responsibility stands in flagrant contrast to empirical evidence that the health prospects of many citizens are already darkened by such disadvantages as malnutrition or lacking health care in early childhood, dire family circumstances and educational opportunities. Upward social mobility has declined dramatically over the last decades so that the status of the parents has become the most reliable predictor of the future positions of the children (see Ch.1). It has become extremely difficult for a large part of the population to reach a form of material security that used to be taken for granted by a broad middle class.

The *second* slogan idealizes the dynamic enriching qualities of the 'free' and 'wholesome' market where 'individuals' compete with each other under fair and equal conditions. This slogan stands in flagrant contradiction to the politics of protecting big corporations with their monopolies and oligopolies, that are not only fiscally privileged but also bailed out when in trouble: policies of public support have shifted from citizens to corporations.

Inclusionary ideas such as 'society' or the 'common good' are seen as obsolete because those individuals who are willing to work will be taken care of by the markets. Those, however, who are not successfully participating are seen as a public burden that cannot be discarded because they are still formally citizens, but they are not seen as individuals with promising potentials that should be invested in. There appears to be a solid conviction that these problems cannot be solved by governments. Trying to do this would even send a wrong message to lazy people (see Ch.1). The course is set on a reduction of public funds and public investment to a political feasible minimum, a suffocation of social policy, and a residualization of public responsibility in a broad sense.

The claim of the American philosopher Nozick, made infamous by the British Prime Minister Thatcher (see Ch.1), that there is 'no such thing as society' is illustrative of the strategy to block any perspective that would go beyond 'individuals' and their responsibilities. This 'eclipse of society' (see Ch.7) serves a political purpose: from a perspective that transcends the individual the nasty consequences of the wholesome markets for certain categories of individuals might be critically exposed. It has become a popular political strategy to answer such criticism by pointing out that experiments to cancel markets and distribute resources by other mechanisms have failed, so that there would be no alternative for 'the market'. The crucial point, however, concerns the question of where markets can be trusted to distribute resources efficiently, without harming public interests and where markets should be supervised and regulated. In many cases markets may be efficient in allocating resources but this does not mean that the health care system or public transport should be left to the 'blissful' mechanisms of 'the market'. Besides articulating this crucial problem of the neoliberal developmental model, a macro-perspective on the larger society might also reveal the growing interdependence between the interests of a large part of the political elite and those of big corporations. Without such broader contextualization we are caught in a myopic fog where we can only see 'individuals' who are taking care of their interests on markets like everybody else. Even the crucial distinction between an individual and his or her public office becomes blurred: a matter of personal character or opportunity. It comes as no surprise when a US president uses his public office to advance his individual interests: he is merely doing bluntly what has secretly become normal.

Public Indifference, alienating bubbles and irresponsible elites

One of the most serious consequences of this quasi self regulatory process is a *public indifference: a neglect of the structural preconditions of a good society*. Typical of such structural preconditions or 'public goods' is that these cannot be directly arranged by individuals such as the material infrastructure of bridges, highways, or internet connections. They are the primary responsibility of governments that need to be monitored and held accountable by their citizens. In this book I am primarily concerned with the structural preconditions of a life course which should support citizens in developing their potentials during their lives. In other words: the *social and moral infrastructure of the life course* (see Ch.7). This includes income protection for all citizens, free or affordable access to health care, good working conditions, adequate pensions, safe and healthy housing. The public indifference regarding the preconditions of the populations' well being has led to deepening social inequalities and increasing health inequalities within the US, also in comparison to peer countries. Health inequalities are the aggregated result of indicators such as life expectancies and mortality rates that can be seen as indicators of the populations' well being over the life course. This well being or not so well being of the population is heavily influenced by social inequalities of resources and respect (see Ch.3 and 7).

The structural preconditions of a good society do not have to be perfect but they should not be left with indifference to 'the free play of the market' or the responsibility of the uncontextualized 'individual'. They need to be subjects of public debate and responsibility; monitored and improved in the awareness that major structural problems like 'the working poor', inequalities in access to high quality education and health care or a lack of integration of older people in society breed problems that become more difficult to solve as time goes by. The danger, even for a democracy, is that public indifference will itself become structural: evading responsibility on the side of political elites, who are kept in power by those who precariously profit from this situation and by the political apathy of disadvantaged citizens which explodes occasionally in unfocused or erratic protest.

It didn't help that many of the economic and political elite began to be contained by their golden bubbles as they amassed their wealth, losing touch with a society where unknown problems were accumulating for unknown others. However, 'Democracy does not require perfect equality, but it does require that citizens share in a common life', as Sandel (2012, p. 203) has commented. The neoliberal slogans about the uncontextualized individual and the profitable markets encourage a stunning public indifference among the dominant political and economic elite regarding the well being of the population. During the last decades we have witnessed the alienation of a large part of the rich political elite from the population whose interests they are supposed to represent; having lost, in their comfortable bubbles, any feeling with the problems most citizens have to face on a daily basis. The Commerce Secretary Wilbur Ross, for example, tried hard but couldn't understand how federal workers could get into financial problems if they would miss a paycheck for the second time as a result of the 2019 government shutdown (see Ch.1). The yellow vest protests in

France erupted after millions of those who are struggling to survive in this rich country were confronted, again, with the French Government's inability to even imagine the situation of these citizens as it increased fuel taxes after having substantially reduced wealth taxes.[5] In the UK thousands of ordinary citizens were heavily fined – up to a thousand Pounds and more – for breaking lockdown rules while members of the political elite were partying. They trusted that the police would avoid to knock on their doors, assuming that those who make the rules don't have to follow them, having become used to getting away with such behavior. That some of them have been fined does not change the pattern of which there are many telling examples. Following the rules they helped to create can apparently become a matter of minor importance for those who rarely meet people who have to take these rules seriously.

The US as a problematic ideal for developed countries

In this book I will document the negative consequences of neoliberal policies for the well being of the population mainly with results from life course research about the US population, put in profile by a comparison to other OECD countries. This is, however, not so much a book about the US but, rather, about the consequences of a neoliberal policy model that has become most dominant in the US since the early 1980s. Given the status and power of the US it has been seen by many outside the US as the ideal model for further development of affluent countries, especially after the fall of the Berlin Wall. The political preference for highly concentrated private wealth for a few versus wide spread public poverty and misery for many, has gained much popularity among the political and economic elites of most developed countries. As the main proponent of neoliberal policies showed an impressive growth of GDP other governments were eager to follow its example. For decades the policies of the US have been propagated by the multinational corporate elite and by transnational organizations such as the IMF or the World Bank as the only way to more prosperity or even as an indisputable condition for support.

The problem here is to extract a Weberian 'ideal type' of neoliberalism from the *consequences* of this opportunistic model, as it has been functioning within a societal context that is much more complex than this ideal type. Whenever I visit the US it never fails me to impress me with its diversity, dynamic energy, resourcefulness and openness. The problem is not the US as a population with an immense potential for creativity and innovation. Moreover, many communities, churches or charity organizations demonstrate that solidarity and compassion are very much alive. Part of the complexity is that a large minority of the population is clearly opposed to the neoliberal ideals.

Many commentators have been worried for a long time about the ways in which the US fails to take care of its citizens and its public infrastructure in a broad sense, putting all cards on the increasing wealth of a small minority that uses its considerable influence to consolidate a problematic model. True, many middle class citizens have also been able to profit as shareholders from this accumulating wealth, but their economic positions have become more insecure as they have been pushed into positions of risk taking entrepreneurs in highly volatile markets. There is a major internal contradiction between the magnificent resourcefulness and thriving diversity of the US on the one hand and on the other hand the rigid determination that the country's public sector has to become lean and mean to survive the global competition where 'every individual' needs to fight for himself. Bridges need to collapse, roads need to fall apart, large areas of land need first to be flooded with loss of lives and drinking water needs to become brown and toxic before something is done in dramatic emergency mode. The country appears to have been highjacked by political and economic elites that are geared to accumulate wealth for a few with little consideration for the well being of the larger population. The US represents the most advanced implementation of the neoliberal turn of capitalism and its problematic outcomes are becoming extremely worrying. As we shall see in the next chapters, it remains difficult to see how the lives of the majority, and eventually the whole population, might benefit from this developmental model. The world champion of neoliberal policies is even increasingly falling behind its peer countries in many ways that are important for the population's well being.

This does not mean that there are no major health inequalities in other OECD countries. One of the most solid findings in public health research in developed countries is the fact that people with a relatively low level of education, occupational status or income tend to be doubly disadvantaged: not only do they have shorter lives, but many of these fewer years are spent in ill health. This perverse longevity gap has been found in all developed countries ranging between 10 to 20 years' difference in years that are free from chronic disease or disabilities. Although the welfare states of North Western Europe continued to offer more support and protection along the life course, the lives of large parts of their populations have also become more precarious (e.g. on income support, job protection, pensions) because of the undeserved admiration of their political elites for the neoliberal developmental model with its continued emphasis on reduction of public responsibilities. The devastating effects of the widespread austerity policies of most OECD countries in the aftermath of the Financial Crisis can be seen as a clear statement that the well being of the population does not rank high when the interests of dominant actors are at stake (Krugman 2015; Loopstra et al. 2015, 2016a; McKee et al. 2012).

However, the unfavorable trends that have been observed in the US, especially in the aftermath of the 2008 Financial Crisis have not, at least not to the same degree, been found in Europe. The governments of European nations have been more hesitant to reduce their public budgets as they encountered more political resistance from labor unions and political parties. Generally, countries with higher social transfers and universal health care show smaller health inequalities. In most OECD countries there is less unequal access to high quality education and health care. Social policies and programs supporting citizens across the life course are still more comprehensive than in the US, ranging, along the life course, from early education and child care programs via more employment protection for those in early adulthood and midlife to better housing and income transfer programs for those in old age. Still, due to the establishment of neoliberal policies, most countries of the developed world have seen growing numbers of citizens who used to have secure positions declining into chronic socioeconomic insecurity. Grave social inequality is not the exclusive product of neoliberal policies. The crucial point remains, however, that these policies have continued to accumulate and concentrate outrageous wealth in the hands of a few, while impoverishing public funds that could have been used to reduce inequalities and grow productivity, creativity, and well being in a broad sense.

Protest and nostalgic nationalism

Among the populations of developed countries there has been much unorganized and unfocused political protest, apathy, cynicism and lack of trust in the political establishment. Most likely, a lack of perspective to improve the situation of too many citizens plays a major role in this discontent. Nevertheless, most Western societies have persisted in following a course towards a further intensification of inequalities. Many citizens have lost their patience listening to the stories of how they would share in the growing wealth, after this particular crisis was over, whilst seeing their situations worsening. The lack of convincing positive perspectives is leading to increasing polarization with a nostalgic twist. In his *Evil Geniuses. The Unmaking of America* (2020) Kurt Andersen argues that there has been a long extended stagnation in the US, with movies, music and fashion being caught in a nostalgic loop. It is, indeed, telling that some of the most influential political movements are looking backwards: *Make America Great Again* is just the most advertised example of many populist slogans heralding a heroic return to old times when the country was not yet flooded with problems from 'others'. The preference for the past instead of the future is also at the heart of the Brexit battle cry '*Taking Back Control*'. These slogans evoke a nostalgic nationalism that defeats itself because it diverts attention away from the very developments that invite the escapist dreams of returning to old times. Moreover, the consequences of nationalism are usually increasing antagonism between citizens of the same nation combined with a political climate in which political discussion is starved because it would be useless to discuss with your enemies and not necessary to discuss with your friends.

Lack of material resources is not the only reason for the slow disintegration of democracy. Other sources of discontent are lack of respect and inclusion of discriminated citizens (race, gender, age), but also of productive but illegal immigrants. In the US, *Black Lives Matter* movements have protested against continuing denigration and violence from police officers who are incapable of seeing African, Asian or Native Americans and Latinx as equal citizens who deserve to be respected. Given its long tradition of integrating immigrants the US might have become a role model for a future world of international migration and mobility. The present situation is still far from such inclusion. One more reason to emphasize the importance of equal citizenship (see Ch.7).

The mutual heuristic value of aging and social inequality

In a moral perspective it may be said that a society shows its face in the way it respects, takes care or neglects its most vulnerable citizens of all ages. As human lives are finite, a more or less extended period of extreme vulnerability will usually be inevitable as a life approaches its end. This means that there is an inherent connection between aging and vulnerability although we need to avoid identifying people above a certain age as incapable or frail (see Ch.4 on compassionate ageism). The consequences of social inequality become gradually more visible as people get older: birth cohorts are not becoming more homogeneous over time but more and more heterogeneous. To appreciate this more fully we need to pay attention to 'selective mortality' (see Ch.2) and continue to acknowledge those who are already dead as members of their birth cohorts because inequalities along the whole life course prevent many disadvantaged people from reaching 'old age' at all.

There is a relationship of mutual heuristic value between aging and social inequality that has been explored over the last decades by proponents of *Critical Gerontology* (Baars et al. 2006; see Ch.5). On the one hand, social inequality can explain much of the differences and inequalities in health or resources that develop between older citizens of the same age. As will be discussed in Chapter 3, longitudinal life course studies have shown how social disadvantage can already weigh heavily on conditions of gestation and early childhood with long term health consequences for later life. Similarly, conditions after early childhood, in education or employment can mitigate or deepen earlier disadvantages. On the other hand, experiences of older citizens have great heuristic value for understanding how social inequality eventually works out over the life course.

The constitutive influence of inequalities of resources and respect along the life course for situations in later life has consequences for aging studies. Beginning to study 'aging' after people have reached a relatively advanced age will come too late to fully understand their situations or to prevent their problems. The dominant restriction of aging studies to the study of people above a certain age (such as 65+) blocks understanding why certain problems occur so disproportionately in the later life of specific groups and, especially, why there are major inequalities between people of the same ages. Many of the problems older people are confronted with, are not caused by 'old age' but are the cumulative effects of processes that have developed over the life course. The emerging possibilities to follow people as they are growing up and older opens possibilities to reflect back from later life to childhood circumstances, opening a source of growing insight in what could and should be provided by the infrastructure of the life course (see Ch.7). The educational system, the legal system, health care, social care, income support, or retirement provisions should also protect the opportunities of those citizens who cannot afford marketed services.

A part of gerontology or aging studies will still focus with good reasons on issues that are more common or even specific for later life. But it usually remains clarifying to put the experiences, situations or problems of older people in a broader life course perspective. If we want to understand the impressive inequalities between older citizens of the same age we cannot afford to underestimate the influence of the social context, including the ways in which the life course has been organized.

Neoliberalism and 'underdeveloped' countries

It should not be forgotten that the neoliberal turn has also had important consequences for global inequalities. Many reports have shown how unbalanced, to put this euphemistically, these developments have turned out to be as the richest 1% possess more wealth than the rest of the planet and the dynamics of wealth concentration have still not been reversed; on the contrary.[6] I will, however, restrict myself to a discussion of the consequences of the neo-liberal developmental ideal for developed countries, especially the US, with a grim reminder that the chances to live a long life are still much less in many other countries although some indigenous counties in the US come pretty close to the worst life expectancies on the planet (see Ch.3).

Criticizing the neoliberal developmental model also implies questioning the assumption that the developed countries would know from their advanced perspective what a desirable development would look like. Moreover, it remains awkward to generalize about countries that are as complex and different as, for instance, Kazakhstan, India, Iraq, Zimbabwe or Brazil. We have become used to talking about developmental targets for underdeveloped countries but tend to neglect the question what developmental ideals might be, even for so-called developed countries. Adopting a more responsible model of development for these countries might also improve the situations of the so-called underdeveloped countries by inflicting less harm on them. These questions can hardly be silenced by a proclamation of the 'End of History' (Fukuyama 1992) or evoking the fall of the Berlin Wall that would have proven that the only way forward would be identify 'free democracies' with 'free markets' which would guarantee fair and equal opportunities for all.

What society do we owe each other?

In the final chapter I will argue that feasible opportunities for equal citizenship should be taken seriously as a desideratum of social justice and be implemented in the moral and social infrastructure of the life course. This is not the same as proclaiming that equal opportunities are already a reality while justifying, at the same time, growing inequalities because individuals would only need to grasp their opportunities. In contrast to, for instance, income equality, the basic right to equal opportunities – limited by the inevitable contingency of human life – to live a long and healthy life, not having to die prematurely from avoidable causes has been acknowledged by most developed countries. Therefore, most of them have universal health care. In reality, however, these opportunities are still far from equally distributed; this is true for all developed countries but health inequalities have become most extreme in the US. In order to implement these rights, so that they do not remain abstract ideals, they have to be supported by institutions that take care of generating and distributing opportunities to all citizens over the entire life course. In the course of this book I will present arguments and empirical evidence to support the suggestion that health inequalities are both part and indicators of the long-term effects of social inequalities, while social inequalities are closely related to unequal opportunities to participate in society and develop one's potential. To understand someone's societal fate merely as the cumulative results of her individual decisions or choices hides the structural and cultural processes that support or undermine the well being of citizens.

Although governments cannot solve all societal problems and much must be done by citizens at different levels and in changing configurations, governments have to create and protect the preconditions of citizenship. Many of these have been insufficiently developed or even demolished over the last decades. Amidst all the things that need to be changed to face the multiple crises of the present it should not be forgotten that the wealth of a nation – and of the world – lies in the development of its population. The flourishing of a nation and its citizens depends to a large extent on the availability of high quality education, good work, high quality health care, sufficient pensions, and healthy living conditions from early childhood to later life. In accomplishing this, the organization of the life course and its infrastructure of resources and respect play a crucial role.

Notes

1 https://www.americashealthrankings.org/explore/health-of-women-and-children
2 https://www.commonwealthfund.org/publications/issue-briefs/2018/dec/womens-health-us-compared-ten-other-countries
3 https://www.who.int/data/gho/data/themes/topics/indicator-groups/indicator-group-details/GHO/life-expectancy-and-healthy-life-expectancy
4 https://www.globaljustice.org.uk/news/69-richest-100-entities-planet-are-corporations-not-governments-figures-show/
5 Piketty T. 'Gilets jaunes' et justice fiscale. http://piketty.blog.lemonde.fr/2018/12/11/gilets-jaunes-et-justice-fiscale/
6 https://www.credit-suisse.com/about-us/en/reports-research/global-wealth-report.html

Chapter 1

From a supportive to an entrepreneurial organization of the life course

Overview

This first chapter presents a historically contextualized interpretation of the neoliberal reorganization of the life course since the early 1980s. Although the US had begun to organize a supportive life course – much later and much less well funded than other affluent countries – this was replaced by an entrepreneurial organization of the life course. The strong urge for individualization from the 1960s and 1970s was given a neoliberal spin by reducing public support, forcing social activities into marketed forms, and convincing citizens that competition in markets would be the highway to individual freedom, self actualization and unlimited consumption. In reality, however, big corporations have become the center of political concern while individual citizens have to work harder and are losing support, protection and high quality education or health care if they cannot purchase these on the market. Even, or especially, the most vulnerable are pushed into entrepreneurial positions. Helped by this lean and mean reorganization of the life course the majority of workers and their families have not made any material progress since the early 1980s and much of their savings have been depleted or become insecure by imploding financial bubbles that were first blown up by irresponsible political and economic elites. These elites have a much greater chance to be bailed out by taxpayers' money and most of them will be much richer when the dust has settled down. At a time when the vast majority of seemingly equal 'individuals' are at the mercy of structural forces beyond their control, the uncontextualized 'individual' is still presented as in full charge of his life if he would only commit himself. This is supported by narratives of the entrepreneurial life course such as 'choice biography' and in admonitions to display your 'authenticity' on social media to advance your chances of being successful. Before presenting some concluding remarks on the entrepreneurial life course there is a comparison of Adam Smith's version of liberalism with its degenerated contemporary form which has led to a society in which citizens can participate at their own risk. Which is a dreadful thing to say about a society.

DOI: 10.4324/9781003392590-2

The rise and fall of a supportive life course

It may be useful to clarify what is meant by the concept of 'life course' in contrast to other concepts that have been used in discussing similar subjects. One of them is the traditional idea of a *life cycle,* referring to a fixed sequence of irreversible stages in life such as early childhood, adolescence, adulthood and old age. Often this concept is applied in a perspective in which birth, maturation, reproduction and death repeat themselves over several generations. Popular examples are the historic pictures of the 'wheel of life' or the staircase of ages. Typically modern, by contrast, is the concept of a *biography:* a narrative about a specific individual who develops as a person as she grows up and older. Contemporary biological and psychological studies predominantly use the concept of a *life span* to refer to developmental processes from their genetic predispositions to old age.

Over the last decades there has been an ongoing discussion about the relationship between life span and life course perspectives (Silverstein et al. 2012). Depending on the theoretical context in which they figure, the differences between the two concepts are, however, not always clear-cut. In this book I will generally use the concept of 'life course' referring to the interplay of structural and cultural forces with institutional arrangements that generate and distribute opportunities and constraints for citizens during their lives. On the one hand, the life course has a general structure: all citizens can expect to be confronted with institutions that regulate, for instance, subsequent phases of education, followed by work and retirement. Such a general structure of lives over time can be used to anticipate and plan ahead or to structure retrospections. On the other hand, the supportive functions of institutional arrangements have become very unequal as parts of these are marketed so that their services only become fully available if citizens can afford them. This is not only a matter of resources but also of mutual respect: to make participation in society fully possible it is not only crucial that citizens receive sufficient resources, such as income, education and health care of a high quality, but also that they are respected as equal citizens.

There have always been life course policies, in some form or another, as each society has to plan for the future in the awareness that those who presently rule, work, care and educate will have to be replaced by others who must be cared for, trained and prepared to fulfill their future tasks. Similarly, social inequalities have played a major role throughout history and have tended to be reproduced by the way the life course was somehow organized, with quite different perspectives for children from poor versus powerful families. In 19th century Europe, however, a new societal phenomenon came up: bureaucratically implemented life course policies at a *national* level that were meant to increase productivity and mitigate workers' poverty in 'old age'. The institutionalization of the life course (Kohli 1986) implied that laws were being developed granting each citizen certain rights and obligations in the context of a life course model, such as the right and obligation to be educated for a specified number of years and the right to receive a pension after having reached a certain age or having worked for a specified number of years. Childhood, adulthood and old age became officially defined as age-related phases with specific rights and obligations so that the labor market, especially, would function optimally.

One of the main reasons that these developments began to take shape in the 19th century is that this was a period in which enormous wealth began to be accumulated by the captains of industrial capitalism while at the same time workers and their families were suffering severely. Whereas in earlier centuries riches were accumulated by exploiting far away colonies, now the exploitation became more directly visible in the miserable conditions of workers at home. As a result of revolutionary pressures and social criticism from Socialist, Humanist and Christian politicians and thinkers, more egalitarian policies gradually gained momentum. During the last decades of the 19th century we can see the gradual emergence of social laws that were meant to give minimal protection to those who could barely survive under the harsh conditions of industrial capitalism. Typical problems were poverty, child labor, illness from miserable living conditions, unemployment, disability, early death, and extended poverty for those who survived into old age (Baars 2012, ch.1). The identification of 'being old' with 'being poor' figures in many of the first laws that begin to regulate state support for older people during the late 19th and early 20th century: instead of providing a pension that would guarantee a decent minimum income, the aim of the early social policies was merely to help older people to survive.

The basic plan behind the new life course policies was to gradually improve the productivity of the working population by obligating children to attend school and offering exhausted workers some hope that they could, one day, retire. The political strategy behind Bismarck's 1889 pension policies was to give the politically most strongly organized workers a reason to remain loyal to the state as they could look forward to enjoying some material support in an 'old age' that only very few of them would live to see as the first pensions would only become available for those who reached the age of seventy years. The regulations that were developed to address these issues were built on chronometric age and changed the meanings of 'age' and 'aging' in the transition from traditional contexts to bureaucratic and scientific contexts (see Ch.6; Baars & Visser 2007; Baars 2010, 2016).

Over the last century and a half, protective life course policies have been implemented, albeit in different forms and tempo, in all developed countries, with the US typically lagging behind most peer countries. In England the 1847 *Factory Act* already aimed at restricting working hours of women and children while in the US 'oppressive child labor' was only declared illegal by the 1938 *Fair Labor Standards Act*. In 1935 a *Social Security* program was established following the adoption of public pension schemes by other

Western nations, albeit not without a racial twist (see Ch.3). These policies reflected Franklin Roosevelt's *New Deal* that was intended to respond to the market failures of the Great Depression (Binstock 2010).

Caring for old parents, grandparents and older people in communities has often been seen as a practical challenge but also as a moral obligation. Initially, the income transfers benefitting older people remained rather poor until the 1950s when the governments of the Western nations gradually began to develop more generous pension schemes. The strong economic growth and full employment of the reconstruction years provided a material basis for a further inclusion and protection of the working population resulting in a materially more supportive life course. As a result, the workers, who were in high demand during the reconstruction years, could feel somewhat relieved of their material obligations towards older family members. Still, for many people, especially in the UK and the US, pensions remained hardly sufficient to survive, leaving many older people in miserable circumstances. This was reflected in extremely concerned publications such as Harrington's *The Other America* (1962) or *The Poor and the Poorest* by Abel-Smith and Townsend (1965), and Robert Butler's 1975 Pulitzer awarded *Why Survive? Being Old in America.*

During the 1960s and well into the 1970s there have been important improvements of pension schemes and other collective provisions helping older citizens to continue to live their lives and participate in society, while at the same time helping the economy by supporting consumption. Slowly, the US made up for some of its retardation in social policy. In 1965 it enacted several programs to support people along the life course, such as *Medicaid* and *Medicare*. Together with *Social Security* these long term programs were built on the trust that future populations would continue to fulfill what has often been called the 'intergenerational social contract', taking turns in paying for and receiving entitlements. In comparison with other affluent countries US pensions have, however, been stingy; moreover, the implementation was often fraught with racism (see Ch.3).

The implicit cultural ideal or 'normal' model of the life course was that heterosexual lovers would marry at a young age and remain married for the rest of their lives; the wife would stay at home to take care of the children and the household, while the husband would continue to work as the principal breadwinner. Employment contracts typically affirmed the loyalty of workers encouraging them to stay their working life with the same employer who would provide them with a pension so that they could retire at a fixed age. Many low educated white males enjoyed a good income in industrial work and, as pensions gradually improved, they could look forward to a 'carefree old age' if they lived long enough.

Undoubtedly, this short portrayal of the first decades after the Second World War downplays the many problems that people were confronted with in these years; a tendency that has become all too visible in contemporary forms of nostalgic nationalism. Nevertheless, although the general standard of living was relatively low there was a general trust, at least among the white part of the population, that they would be able to find good work, gain sufficient income, and that their children would have better lives. Increasingly, citizens seemed to agree with each other about the timetable of the life course. Dennis Hogan (1981), for instance, investigated the changes in the transition to adulthood (leaving school, entering the workforce and marrying) for American men born between 1907 and 1952. He found a steady decline in its duration: whereas the first cohort took 18 years to complete this transition, this had declined to 8 years for the youngest cohort. These were indications that the life course was becoming increasingly standardized; moreover, its phases and transitions were increasingly seen as 'normal' and 'natural'. Interestingly, the dominant interpretation has been that this standardization should be seen as a loosening of economic constraints and an increase in individual choice (e.g. Modell 1991; Dannefer 1984).

This was not quite the view of the many Baby Boomers and other cultural dissidents of the 1960s and early 1970s. The protective policies that were built around the 'normal' life course of the white male working head of the family, were increasingly seen as continuing millennia old ethnocentric and patriarchal traditions in which the male head of the family remained the center of intergenerational concern (Baars 2012). This gave little protection and support to those who deviated from this model and could even make life more difficult for them. Black people, for instance, were excluded by design (Dannefer, Gilbert & Han 2020). Rigid convictions about what would be 'normal' or even 'natural' neglected the dignity of women, ethnic minorities, immigrants or gay people. The cultural foundations of this life course model began to be challenged as a result of the Civil Rights movements, the student protests, and the rejuvenation of the feminist movement during the late 1960s. There was a strong cultural urge to reorient and reorganize the life course because it privileged white heterosexual males.

Meanwhile, there was a strong conviction that growth towards greater material prosperity would continue; the 1973 Oil Crisis was for many a first sign that such prospects could not be taken for granted. As Meg Jacobs describes in her book *Panic at the Pump: The Energy Crisis and the Transformation of American Politics in the 1970s* (2017) two oil crises at the beginning and the end of the 1970s shocked a country that was used to consuming gas like water, driving gas guzzlers with oversized 8 cylinders because they sounded great. Moreover, changing ideas about what a desirable life course would look like – especially for women – brought birth rates rapidly down from their high post-war levels, drastically changing the demographic situation that had been one of a large population of workers bearing the costs of caring, in a broad sense, for a relatively small group of older people. It became clear that in the future the large cohorts of the post-war Baby Boom would have to be supported by a smaller than expected basis of young people and workers who had already their own children to take care of. For many, it seemed inevitable to change the 'intergenerational contract' that was at the heart of the moral and social infrastructure of the life course.

Many of the Baby Boomers had little appetite to continue the existing intergenerational social contract as they wanted to break away from the oppressive social bonds of the post-war 'normal' life course. Especially among young highly educated people there was a gradual but steady transition away from traditional loyalties and social cohesion towards a greater flexibility of life styles, leading to a broader palette of personal relationships over the life course:

- Rising symmetry in sex roles, rising female education levels, and greater female economic autonomy
- Falling numbers of people who get married, with rising age at first marriage
- Postponement of having children; increasing mean ages at parenthood and fewer children than would be necessary to replace the population
- A rise in divorce, including early divorce
- Declining numbers of those who remarry
- Rising numbers of those who have children outside of marital bonds such as cohabiting couples or single mothers
- Rising numbers of those who don't have children at all
- A gradual recognition of same-sex relationships
- Multiple partnerships or a 'serial monogamy' over the life course with the result that children may have several parental figures and a greater variety of relatives.
- A growth of LAT relationships and forms of cohabitation, before, after and instead of marriage

Underlying these changes, often typified as the *Second Demographic Transition* (Kaa 1987), there was a growing interest in the pursuit of what became popular as 'individual autonomy' and 'self-actualization'. Whereas the increasing standardization of the life course in the first half of the 20th century had been interpreted as an increase in individual choice the following de-standardization has also been seen as a increase in personal control and individual choice (Settersten & Ray 2010). For many less advantaged citizens, however, the de-standardization of the life course meant that opportunities for personal control over one's life declined with increasing precarity on the labor market. The answer to the de-standardization appeared to become 'everyone for himself, according to his own unique wishes in a land of endless opportunities'. The decline of supportive institutions has especially hit the most economically insecure and socially vulnerable (Huang 2021).

The broader tolerance of different life styles has also led to a rising disengagement from civic and community-oriented networks, trade unions and political parties. As many emancipatory movements had ignited in protest against racial and gender discrimination they tended to remain focused on identity politics while the vital connection between, on the one hand, mutual respect for singular identities and, on the other hand, sufficient material resources and equal opportunities in education, the labor market and old age received less attention (see Ch.7).

The neoliberal turn and the pseudo-individualization of society

From the beginning of the 1980s the Reagan presidency (1981–1989) acted in favor of a developmental program that promised to give society a boost by unleashing free markets and reducing public responsibilities to a politically bearable minimum. While the US had begun, since the *New Deal*, to extend support and protection of its citizens in their basic needs and opportunities, this development ground to a halt and began to be reversed.

One of the most problematic consequences of the neoliberal turn has been a gradual individualization of all problems that might arise for citizens, even when these problems were clearly the result of changes far beyond their influence. As if the withdrawal of supportive policies along the life course would make individuals automatically independent and well equipped to thrive in an even more strongly marketed society. A fundamental ideological step was to portray any theory that might challenge this view because of its consequences for society as rubbish. Margaret Thatcher famously denied the very existence of such a thing as 'society': there would only be individuals who are trying to take care of themselves on a 'free' and, therefore, apparently 'fair' market. At the time, she echoed Robert Nozick's attack on Rawls' theory of social justice in his 1974 book *Anarchy, State and Utopia:*

> There are only individual people. Different individual people, with their own individual lives. Using one of these people for the benefit of others, uses him and benefits the others. Nothing more. What happens is that something is done to him for the sake of others. Talk of an overall social good covers this up. (Intentionally?).
>
> (33)

The idea that taxes might support the public good or help those in need is interpreted by Nozick to imply that taking something from somebody for the sake of others is to use this person unrespectfully: '*He* does not get some overbalancing good from his sacrifice, and no one is entitled to force this upon him – least of all a state or government that claims his allegiance' (33).

Those who fail to succeed would only have themselves to blame. With an eye on these developments the Danish sociologist Esping-Andersen (1999) singled out the US as the closest embodiment of *Homo Liberalismus* –

although I will argue below that *Homo Neo-Liberalismus* might have been better – whose ideal would be to pursue his personal welfare: 'The well-being of others is their affair, not his…. His ethics tell him that a free lunch is amoral, that collectivism jeopardizes freedom, that individual liberty is a fragile good, easily sabotaged by sinister socialists or paternalistic institutions' (p. 171).

This neoliberal model of development received a strong welcome in the US, probably because it was also an amplification of trends and ideologies that have long been vividly present in its history. The uncritically acclaimed 'American Dream', the assumption of equal and limitless opportunities for all, combined with the idea of individual responsibility for one's fate have facilitated the acceptance of the idea that society should primarily be seen as a 'free market'. In this context there have also been references to American or even Anglo-Saxon 'exceptionalism': the idea that the US or the UK are inherently different from other nations because of their histories or even their 'DNA'. Such narratives of national or regional exceptionalism are popular in many countries and can be a touristic asset, but become a fundamental problem if they turn into blind spots that block a realistic view. This obviously serves those in power. As Alston (2017) has rightly commented, instead of realizing its founders' admirable commitments, today's US has proved itself to be exceptional in ways that are shockingly at odds with its immense wealth and its founding commitment to human rights.

When civil and human rights have been debated in American politics this has, however, usually led to their further individualization. From a communitarian position Mary Ann Glendon has argued in her *Rights Talk: The Impoverishment of American Political Discourse* (1991) that the forceful overemphasis on individual 'rights talk' has impoverished American political discourse and eroded the social foundations of individual freedom. This diagnosis is basically confirmed by Alston (2017), who criticized the US government for persistently denying that human rights would also imply social rights, although this has been affirmed in important treaties such as the *Universal Declaration of Human Rights* which the US has signed and often insisted other countries must respect (see Ch.3 and Ch.7; cf. 'Human Rights' in Estes & DiCarlo 2019). The US has shown special interest in the human rights of political dissidents in other countries, in cases where they are imprisoned without a fair trial, tortured or even murdered. That is in itself undeniably important, but this critical attention for human rights looks away from US sore spots like Guantanamo Bay, and avoids social rights when looking inward. International human rights law recognizes a right to education, a right to healthcare, a right to social protection of those in need, and a right to be free from discrimination because of race or gender. Such fundamental rights are not fulfilled by granting a large part of the population only formal or minimal access.

Fading perspectives for the celebrated 'hard working individual'

In his 1952 book *American Capitalism*, the liberal economist John Kenneth Galbraith described what he saw as the secret to the country's success. The nation had a political economy that worked to generate robust levels of steady economic growth. He stressed the importance of countervailing powers – trade unions and consumer groups bargaining with the nation's businessmen – all under the watchful eye of Washington politicians who remained alert to monitor and stabilize markets. Without this system, he wrote, 'private decisions could and presumably would lead to the unhampered exploitation of the public or of workers, farmers and others who are intrinsically weak as individuals' (p. 167).

The positions of hard working citizens suffered a major blow when the labor unions, one of the last counter weights in the new power play were effectively weakened by forceful interventions such as Reagan's infamous breaking of the air-traffic controllers' strike of 1981 in which he banned 11,359 strikers from federal service for life. Moreover, the union that had called the strike, the *Professional Air Traffic Controllers Organization* (PATCO), was decertified. PATCO was dominated by Vietnam War-era veterans and was, paradoxically, one of the very few unions to endorse Reagan in 1980. His brutal repression put public sector workers on the defensive and led to a revival of strike breaking. According to Joseph McCartin, who documented the strike and its aftermath in his 2011 book *Collision Course: Ronald Reagan, the Air Traffic Controllers, and the Strike That Changed America*, this was a game-changing event in American labor relations.

Such policies put an end to the earlier politics of countervailing powers and from that moment on, Galbraith's 'watchful eye of the Washington politicians' was guided by an intimate bond between the country's political and economic elites that would prove to be lucrative for both sides. The general public was persuaded to believe that deregulating markets, supporting corporations and lowering taxes would lead to more investments, a trickling down of wealth and good jobs so that citizens would be able to afford private insurance for remaining hazards such as disease or disability. Thus all hard working citizens, the state, the corporations and their elite were freed, not only from useless fiscal burdens, but also from a neoliberal bogey: the perverse incentives of the welfare system that would only deepen the misery of the poor. At the beginning of the 1980s conservative think tanks such as the *Manhattan Institute* were promoting the idea that the continuation of poverty, especially among black families, would actually be the result of President Johnson's *War on Poverty*. The anti-poverty programs would discourage work efforts and promote idleness. They would reward and encourage a lack of personal responsibility: the basic problem would not be not poverty but anti-poverty policies. With a large public relations campaign by the Manhattan Institute, George Gilder's *Wealth and Poverty* (1981) and Charles Murray's *Losing Ground: American Social Policy, 1950–1980* (1984) were pushed as media sensations and became influential best-sellers. In 1986 Lawrence Mead followed with his *Beyond Entitlement: The Social Obligations of Citizenship* arguing that welfare recipients should be obligated to work (see also Ch.2). Other think tanks like the *Heritage Foundation* or the *American Enterprise Institute* joined the efforts with thousands of mainstream media articles dripping the idea that poverty was a result of cultures and behaviors that lacked individual responsibility (cf. Lewis 1966).

The short term troubles hard working citizens might encounter in getting a good job, health care or other services should be seen as signs of future prosperity as the country had to go through a deep cleansing transformation by 'wholesome' markets. At the end of the long tunnel there would be light because, eventually, the accumulated wealth would trickle down and lift all boats. In this way, the US society would flourish again as a society of hard working people and heroic entrepreneurs inspiring their fellow citizens to follow their lead or otherwise face the consequences of their laziness. America would return to its former glory of the 'shining city upon a hill whose beacon light guides freedom loving people everywhere', as Reagan put it.

But how did the celebrated hard working citizens fare under the neo-liberal regime? This is a complex question with many different aspects and changing numbers for subsequent years, but the general pattern of a dramatically increasing inequality is clear. Between 1980 and 2014 the average *income* of the bottom 50% of workers in the US has 'grown' from $16,000 to $16,200. Over the same period the incomes of the top 1% grew from $428,000 to $1,305,000 (Piketty, Saez & Zucman 2016). The sad balance is that the bottom half of the working population has seen their incomes decline over the last 40 years while the incomes of the top 1% have grown 300%. Another indicator, the *wealth* gap between America's richest and poorer families more than doubled from 1989 to 2016. In 1989, the richest 5% of families had 114 times as much wealth as families in the second quintile ($2.3 million compared with $20,300). By 2016, this ratio had increased to 248, a much sharper rise than the widening gap in income. A comparison with the 'wealth' of the poorest 20% is not possible because this is usually zero or negative.[1] Piketty and Saez (2014) have shown that across multiple measures of income, the income share of the bottom 90% was quite stable during the post-Second World War period up to the beginning of the neoliberal turn and markedly greater than the period prior to 1940. While the income share of the top 1% was 10% of total pre-tax income in 1980, this had doubled in 2014. During the same period the share of the bottom 50% fell from 20% to 12% (see Figure 1.1).

Wealth at the top has become so massive that the US GDP per capita is still relatively high which might give the impression that its citizens would

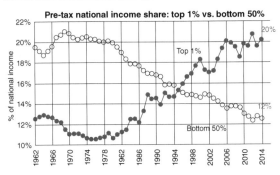

Figure 1.1 Share of pre-tax income by income group.
Source: from Piketty, Saez & Zucman 2016.

be better off than in other countries. Under these conditions it makes hardly sense to speak of average income. The outcomes of these politics of income distribution are staggering: the top 1% is swallowing the part of the national income that used to go to the bottom 50% of the whole population. The shining city upon a hill has been invaded and occupied by the extremely rich and powerful. Because the most wealthy invest heavily in hiding important parts of their income and wealth, these figures most probably underestimate their actual share. Moreover, this is not a situation where the majority enjoys sufficient resources while a minority is extremely rich: poverty rates[2] are much higher in the US in comparison with other high-income countries: the US poverty rate stood in 2017 at 17.8%, while Germany (10.4%), Sweden (9.3%), Switzerland (9.1%), France (8.3%), and Denmark (5.8%) scored much lower on this scale of shame.[3]

For the majority, work in the US has become not only less rewarding in terms of income but also more stressful. The screws have been tightened over the last decades: instead of turning higher productivity into more possibilities for leisure and quality time with families and friends, weak unions and poor protection laws have encouraged employers to force employees to work more hours or lose their jobs. In the name of boosting the unregulated flexibility that would be so essential to be successful on markets, numerous individuals who depend on the labor market for their income have been forced into short term contracts exposing them to risks that were formerly absorbed by their employee status. Even the most vulnerable on the labor market have been forced into the position of an entrepreneur, who is active on the market at his own risk. Unchecked by labor unions and protective regulations, the bargaining position of workers on the labor market has been weakened, giving employers more freedom to fire them without compensation, leading to lower income, more insecurity, and socioeconomic survival stress. In the same fashion, pension reforms have been introduced, forcing many older workers to work as long as they possibly can and to take more investment risks in building their pensions (see Ch.4).

Besides such retrenchment policies, changes resulting from globalization and technological innovations such as robotics, digitalization or artificial intelligence have had a major impact on the temporal stability of the labor market. Work has become more precarious and careers less predictable over the life course. For young people it has become less clear what kind of professional training they will need in the future and older workers face a heightened chance that the market demand for one's fine tuned experience suddenly disappears. Moreover, the enterprise where one used to be employed may suddenly be bankrupt or taken over by another corporation that employs mainly workers in low-wage countries.

Standing (2012) has developed a class theory based on the distribution of societal insecurity and the growth of precarious employment. At the top of his model resides the *plutocracy* of the richest 0.001%, followed by a larger elite of *millionaires* and a well positioned *salariat* with strong employment security and an array of non-wage forms of remuneration. Going down the social gradient these relatively secure material positions are followed by what he calls *proficians*: workers, often in small businesses, who are project oriented, entrepreneurial and multi-skilled. They tend to do well as long as they are able to surf the waves of the neoliberal economy but their lack of security and protection still makes them vulnerable and burnouts may be the price they have to pay for their possibly exciting but also exhausting way of life. Even more insecure are the representatives of the traditional manual labor force, the *proletariat*, who have not yet been thrown out of their industrial jobs. As the proletariat slowly diminishes in size, their position as the most disadvantaged group is taken over by the *precariat*. They can be seen as the poorer version of the *proficians*: working from one unprotected short term, part time job to another they bear the brunt of the flexibility that is dictated by the unleashed labor market. They are moving in and out of jobs that give little meaning to their lives, living in chronic uncertainty as if they have lost their citizenship and have migrated to a harsh unwelcoming society (see Ch.7; Osnos 2021).

Unpredictability and flexibility can be exciting for those whose work is in high demand, and many forms of work – especially in well paid positions – bring agreeable intellectual, entrepreneurial, emotional, or artistic challenges, and some of these can be so satisfying that many people would prefer not to retire from their work. For others, however, the flexibility of the labor markets is less inspiring. When working in short term contracts even a short illness of oneself or a family member becomes stressful and every stagnation or crisis will hit you with full force. Work and schedule precarity (see Ch.2) have become widespread features of the labor market as employers have gradually transferred more of the risks and uncertainties of doing business onto workers and their households. This has not only resulted in lower pay and more insecurity but also in a more general erosion of job quality that is usually not included in income statistics such as a loss or a major reduction of benefits like retirement plans, paid holidays and health insurance. And in between jobs they will be busy with applications, new qualifications, filling out forms, and hoping for support from bureaucrats who may hold them responsible for their situation, as persons who are lacking initiative or work ethos. Publications such as Murray's *Coming Apart: The State of White America 1960–2010* (2012) show that such moralistic individualizing approaches continue to be firmly defended in American public discourse.

According to regular monitoring of the OECD, income inequalities continue to be greater in the US (followed by the UK) than in other 'high-income countries'. Research on wealth is much less available, although wealth remains crucially important in many ways, for instance, as a buffer against unexpected adversity. Lacking such a buffer implies being at immediate risk in case even a short term income loss would occur, which can be an extremely stressful perspective. The US is not only the champion of income inequality; behind this more easily visible layer, the accumulation of wealth continues. Profits from capital, especially from shares, are much higher than income from work and they are even more unequally distributed (Wolff 2002).

Much flexibility and mobility – but not upward

Given these distributions of income in a broad sense, what are the chances of climbing from a disadvantaged position upward? For decades, a majority of Americans have been able to climb the economic ladder by earning higher incomes than their parents. These improving conditions are known as upward mobility, and form an important part of the American Dream. However, although job mobility has gone up, upward social mobility has gone down. As early as 2003, in his *Unequal Childhoods: Class, Race and Family Life*, Lareau showed how parents' social class predicts children's school success and their further life chances. In 2016 researchers from Stanford, Harvard and Berkeley published 'The Fading American Dream: Trends in Absolute Income Mobility Since 1940' (Chetty et al. 2016a), assessing whether the US was living up to its idealized self concept by estimating rates of 'absolute income mobility': the fraction of children who earn more than their parents. Although this is a limited understanding of 'equal opportunity', this focus on income is central to the American Dream. After the neoliberal turn, absolute income mobility has fallen dramatically across the entire income distribution, with the largest declines for families in the middle class. Between 1947 and 1973, the typical family's income roughly doubled. But since 1973 median family income has increased by only 20%, while income inequality has increased and upward social mobility decreased. In comparing the chances of the 1940 birth cohort with those of the 1980 cohort it appears that the middle-class has taken the largest hit. Whereas those born in 1940 had a 93% chance of earning more than their parents at age 30, the chances for the 1980 birth cohort have fallen to less than half.

Figure 1.2 is based on the research by Chetty et al. (2016a) and shows the decline of upward social mobility as a decline in the percentage of people earning more than their parents, in the form of a comparison between cohorts born between 1940 and 1980. It shows a consolidation of the trend towards increasing economic inequality by restricting upward income mobility.

Some middle class Americans are still managing to pull themselves up into the next income bracket, but fewer people from the lower- and middle-classes are climbing the economic ladder. The overwhelming impression from several research projects is a so-called 'stickiness at the ends': children

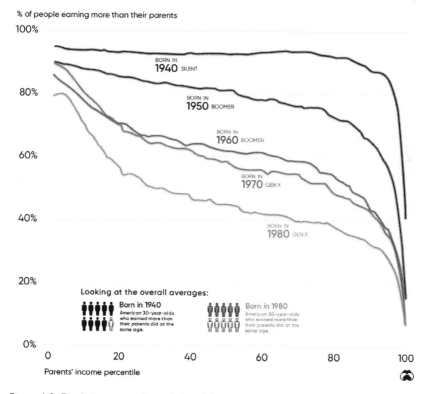

Figure 1.2 Declining upwards social mobility in cohorts born 1940–1980.
Source: https://www.weforum.org/agenda/2020/09/social-mobility-upwards-decline-usa-us-america-economics/.

born to parents with income on the bottom rung of the ladder are highly likely to remain in the bottom rung in adulthood. Those born to parents on the top rung are very likely to stay at the top. That children from the top quintile may not be able to earn more than their wealthy parents is not the most urgent message of this figure. More importantly, only 6% of children born to parents at the bottom make it to the top quintile of the income and wealth distribution in adulthood (Haskins, Isaacs & Sawhill 2008). Even when some of them succeed in freeing themselves from their disadvantaged situations so that they can participate more fully in society, this does not mean that the general structure of inequality of opportunities has changed. We may applaud another hero of the 'American Dream' but this treacherous ideology suggests that opportunities are equally available for all citizens, when in fact, the chances for upward social mobility have always been unequal and they have been reduced even more drastically since the beginning of the neoliberal turn.

However, according to a Gallup Poll of July 2019[4] 70% of the American population hold on to the view that the American Dream would be personally achievable. A solid majority believes in the message of equal opportunities for all citizens but even so, they should be concerned about a large minority of almost 30% who told Gallup that even by working hard and playing by the rules, the American Dream would be unattainable for them. This minority has grown from a quarter to a third of the population since Gallup last asked Americans this question in 2009. Moreover, women aged 18 to 49 were significantly more likely than older women – and men in all age groups – to say that even by working hard and playing by the rules, the American Dream would be unattainable for them in their lifetime.

The reality appears to be that in the self proclaimed 'land of equal opportunity' prospects of children are more dependent on the income and wealth of their parents than in other advanced countries. Those born at the bottom are likely to remain there without any prospect of a better future although they may have had much more education, adding the status frustration of not being able to do what they have trained for. The chances of making it, Horatio Alger-style, from a childhood in poverty to an adulthood in material comfort are lower in the US than in other nations. The American Dream is in better shape in Canada with 13,5% probability that a child born to parents in the bottom fifth of the income distribution will reach the top quintile (Chetty et al. 2014; Corak & Heisz 1998). Nearly half of the variation in wages of sons in the US can be explained by looking at the wages of their fathers at the same age. That compares to less than 20% in relatively egalitarian and tuition-free countries like Finland, Norway and Denmark. The story of the US is similar to that of the UK, where over half of the judges, MPs and CEOs of UK companies attended expensive private schools, while around one third of children live below the poverty line.

The profitability of crises and the waning of public responsibilities

Studies such as the annual *Credit Suisse Global Wealth Report* have shown that the gradual recovery since the Financial Crisis has disproportionately benefited the wealthy with less recovery, if any, for those with lower incomes. This unbalanced recovery has led to another increase in wealth inequality, especially of the top 1% versus the rest of the population. At this point the comment might be that crises are just a rare and unfortunate short term incident in a society that is becoming more and more prosperous; a specific crisis may hit some unfortunate cohorts particularly harsh for some time but would remain an exception. However, it appears more realistic to acknowledge that more or less severe crises are becoming a more frequent phenomenon so it is likely that each birth cohort will go through several crises.

Small and large crises have become systemic, much like earth quakes and volcanic eruptions are part of the geological system with the major difference that crises are usually the bitter fruits of indifference or extreme risk taking in chasing short term profit. Moreover, the increasing speed of market transactions tends to create havoc on markets increasing the risks of unintended consequences; just like expanding traffic of persons and animals around the globe leads to rising risks of pandemics that are already spreading around the globe before they are even noticed.

The global economy has become a ring of fire: interconnected slumbering volcanoes in Asia, Europe and the US are increasingly put under pressure because the risks bring huge profits for a small global elite. Crises are at the same time highly probable and unforeseeable: you know they will come again but you don't know when and what they will look like. We have seen a number of major economic crises in the last two decades: the *Asian financial crisis*, the *European sovereign debt crisis*, the *US Subprime mortgage crisis*, the *Financial Crisis* and the *Covid-19 crisis*. Meanwhile more temporally extended crises are steadily unfolding, such as the long term undermining of democracy by neoliberal policies, and the long denied climate crisis which has now forced itself on the agenda through the intensification of 'familiar' catastrophes such as droughts, hurricanes, wildfires and floods.

The recent Financial Crisis has shown that the financial elite is openly playing with fire: they know about the risks but continue to inflate them as long as they are profitable. When strategies and calculations explode in front of them, they are the first to know, so they trust to have time enough to escape from the disaster zones, flying away in their private jets to the tropical beaches where they have hidden their fortunes, while the large population will be overrun by a pyroclastic flow that will burn through their resources. In case of imminent bankruptcy they will try to let tax paying citizens pick up the bill for their irresponsible behavior. In the process of rebooting the economy, huge quantities of cheap money will probably be created pro-claiming, again, that this will stimulate productive investment, but which actually has the effect of driving prices of houses, shares or commodities up far beyond their intrinsic value, creating new bubbles that are set to explode in a new crisis.

It has usually taken some years for total billionaire wealth to get back to the levels they enjoyed before a crisis or recession. However, this recovery process was accelerated during the Covid-19 pandemic when the US gov-ernment began to hand out trillions of dollars to support the economy. According to a report from the *Institute for Policy Studies*[5] the billionaire class added another $308 billion to its wealth in four weeks. In the same period in which 26 million people lost their jobs, the richest 1% profited from loopholes in a $349 billion bailout meant to save hard-hit small businesses. Big companies managed between 18 March and 22 April 2020 to bag more than $600 million in forgivable loans before the funds ran out adding 10.5% to the wealth of America's plutocrats. The researchers conclude that in July 2021, 16 months after the formal beginning of the pandemic lockdown, the combined wealth of 713 US billionaires had surged by $1.8 trillion, a gain of almost 60%. The total combined wealth of US billionaires increased from $2.9 trillion on 18 March 2020 to $4.7 trillion on 9 July 2021. Those at the apex of the wealth pyramid appear to be eminently positioned to take advantage of any crisis or chaos.

It would be too easy to blame these major inequalities in gains versus losses on these crises, while assuming that our societies are basically in order. Gains and losses are also unfairly distributed when the system seems to work well: crises tend to lay bare the destructive constitutive dynamics of the system which protect the most wealthy and hit the most vulnerable. Even short-term stagnations demonstrate this structural logic. Although the 2018/2019 Government shutdown lasted only 35 days, it demonstrated not only the socioeconomic vulnerability even of those with relatively solid positions, but also the estrangement of the political elite from the daily situation of the population they are supposed to lead and take care of. One of the extremely rich members of the Trump administration, the Commerce Secretary Wilbur Ross tried hard, apparently, but couldn't understand how federal workers, crucial for many critical functions in keeping society safe, could get into financial problems if they were to miss a paycheck for the second time as a result of the 2019 government shutdown. Why did they not just access their savings? He added that the economic ramifications of the shutdown – the fact that 800,000 workers were not getting paid – were barely a blip on the US economy's radar. If, hypothetically, the workers never got their back pay, 'you're talking about a third of a percent on our GDP; so it's not like it's a gigantic number overall'.[6]

Ross's blunt statements aroused widespread indignation about this dis-regard for the social vulnerability and potential poverty levels among those who might appear to have a steady job. According to research from the *Center for Retirement Research* at Boston College,[7] right after this incident, 40% of Americans would struggle to come up with even $400 to pay for an unexpected bill or they would have to resort to even more credit card debt. Such unpaid credit card balances are high-interest loans, bringing huge profits to credit card companies. The average interest rate had at the time risen to almost 18%, compared with 12% a decade ago, in spite of the fact that on the financial markets' interest rates have been sinking dramatically over that same period of time. The deregulation of the financial sector has led to extreme profits from predatory lending and abusive credit card practices resulting in extreme payments to those at the top, leaving the less well positioned 'individual' at the mercy of merciless financial corporations.

Pampering shareholders and abandoning stakeholders

The emphasis on share value appears not only to dissociate financial markets from what has been called the 'real economy', leading to precarious financial bubbles, but also to dissociate the owners and managers of big corporations from their responsibilities. The neoliberal developmental program for rich countries puts too few barriers in the way of large multinational corporations in case they act without moral, social or ecological scruples. In a strange way, many of these multinationals seem to have become a source of national pride, although they spend fortunes looking for tropical islands to pay as little in taxes as possible, even when corporate taxes have already been forced downwards, as governments compete with each other in the international arena to receive a minimal percentage of the outrageous profits.

Although neoliberal politicians have declared that lowering corporate and high income taxes is crucial because it makes it possible to invest a larger part of the profits and results in more productivity and good jobs, the share of the profits used for long-term investments or to increase the pay of the workers below the executive level have been declining. Besides taking disproportionate salaries and bonuses out of the corporate resources, even in the absence of any profits, growing parts of profits have been channeled into share buyback programs, thus increasing share value. In 1970 only 10% of profits were paid out to shareholders whereas this had increased to 70% in 2015.[8]

Much has been invested to peddle the idea that it doesn't matter that those at the very top gain enormous amounts of money because one cannot overrate the work of those who create work and prosperity for the whole nation. The general public in the EU has, sometimes successfully, protested against outrageous salaries and bonuses; the usual answer to silence the critics has been that the proposed salaries and bonuses were already much lower, even a fraction of what has become 'normal', that is 'market conform' in the US. These extreme incomes, however, may also buy advantageous influence on politicians, undermining the social cohesion of a society, creating parallel worlds of rich and powerful people who rarely meet people with modest incomes and have no idea what their daily lives actually look like. Stiglitz (2015) has effectively debunked the ideology that those at the top of the corporations are heroic entrepreneurs who fully deserve their salaries and bonuses while those who are ungratefully questioning their geniality have no idea what these heroes are going through every day. Warren Buffett, who can hardly be accused of anti-capitalist sentiments, has also repeatedly complained that executive compensation in the US is drastically out of line with performance.

There remains the important moral issue of whether exercising rights of enterprise should not go together with responsibilities of its owners and managers to all who are more or less affected directly by their actions: stakeholders such as consumers, workers or the residents they share the environment with. Those who have the right to take decisions that affect the lives of others should be held accountable for their actions if these lead to damage or destruction, such as pollution, contaminating water or emitting toxins into the air. This moral responsibility goes beyond the acceptance of legal consequences such as paying fines, for instance, for illegal dumping that are small compared to the profits that are made by doing this but also in comparison to the damage that is done to the environment.

This implies not only that shareholder value must be balanced with the interests of stakeholders but that the last need to weigh heavier. Stakeholders typically have a long-term interest in the company's role in the preservation of public health, care for the environment, income security and protection against life course hazards such as unemployment, disability and illness. Sadly, the Rhineland Stakeholder model that has for a long time been predominant in parts of North Western Europe such as Germany and The Netherlands, has come under threat from the liberal Anglo-American Shareholder model, as a result of economic neoliberalization induced by the European Union (Soederberg, Menz & Cerny 2005; Bieler & Morton 2001). During the 2020 Davos Meeting the *World Economic Forum* apparently discovered the merits of the stakeholders approach, even though it had been fighting this for many years. The coming years will show whether such statements announce substantial improvements or whether they are just the next move in the defensive strategies of the international political and economic elite.

One important aspect of the ideological function of the principle of individual responsibility for one's fate is to evade public responsibilities. This evasion has two contradictory sides: it maximizes the responsibility of disadvantaged people for their problems and minimizes the responsibility of those in power. When those in power are personally held accountable for the consequences of their actions, or lack of these, they suddenly become tin soldiers: small helpless individuals with awful memories who are caught in a system that could apparently not be challenged. While market forces play an important role in the neoliberal turn of capitalism both Nobel laureates Joseph Stiglitz (2015) and Angus Deaton (Case & Deaton 2000) have argued forcefully that politics has shaped those market forces. According to their analyses, the severe inequality in the US was a choice of the country's leaders: a consequence of their policies, laws and regulations. Politicians are accused of misusing public office, and the corporate elite of evading its responsibility for the broader society: 'Our story of American distress is that, at a time when working people were increasingly vulnerable to automation and trade, politicians and corporations, instead of working to cushion the harm, seized the chance to benefit themselves, redistributing upward from labor to managers and shareholders' (Case & Deaton 2000, p. 260).

Although the neoliberal turn was also a turn towards more global expansion it would be too easy to see the process of globalization as the source of all evil. The attempt to define the globalizing world as a lawless jungle, discrediting transnational and multilateral institutions and their attempts at regulation serves important interests. It frees national governments from their responsibilities because they would be unable to control processes within their borders. Even when the necessity of international regulations, such as the reduction of harmful emissions is acknowledged, the neoliberal approach dictates that it would be foolish to lose a competitive edge by not waiting for others to move first. To survive, corporations and societies alike have to become lean and mean. It is, however, too easy to declare that the accumulation of wealth for some and insecurity or even poverty for many is the inevitable product of international capitalism for which there can be no alternative. Increasing social inequality is much more than unfortunate collateral damage of an otherwise benign free market capitalism: it is also a symptom or proof of policy negligence, where for decades, shortcuts such as deregulation, tax reductions and monetary policies have come instead of structural reform, creative investment and responsible public health policies. Instead of increasing productivity, monetary stimuli and quantitative easing tend to create financial bubbles. And, as we have seen in the aftermath of the Financial Crisis, when they burst the richest will eventually have become even richer while the large majority of the population is still suffering the consequences. Neoliberal policies increase the risks of crises and endanger the lives of a large part of the population by leaving them vulnerable and unprotected in spite of promises of a better future as the growing wealth will eventually trickle down. What has successfully trickled down is the trickle down ideology. It would be better, for practical as well as moral reasons, to invest in a well funded life course infrastructure (see Ch.7).

Private wealth and public poverty

Evading taxes may seem like a good idea but poor public resources can have nasty consequences. That solidarity amongst US citizens still exists is demonstrated when they are confronted with the undeserved misery of others. Their response tends to be 'charity': giving money to those who deserve their support. If there are no other arrangements charity is, of course, vitally important because without free meals or beds, many poor people would have no possibilities to survive. Given a lack of public funds to address social misery the call for charity is certainly honorable, but it also has important limitations. First, it is often arbitrary and prone to shifting popular and mass media sentiment. Second, because it is *my* money that goes to others, a punitive tendency is readily attached to charity, and there is usually a much stronger indignation about charity or welfare cheats than about tax cheats: 'people who are merely trying to keep their own money'. While welfare frauds and tax frauds are both equally bad, the public support for government agencies that fight tax evasion is much smaller than for those who go after charity or welfare fraud (see Ch.2). Third, and most importantly, political calls for charity tend to be combined with a neglect of the structural causes of the misery that charity organizations are trying to relinquish. The clients of soup kitchens and night shelters are increasingly not only the unemployed or poor older people, but even employed people who work for outrageously low pay, where the word 'minimum' does not refer to a socially acceptable minimal income but to the lowest hourly pay that is on offer.

Social charity initiatives are no solution, for instance, to the problems of their homeless clients: many of them will most likely suffer early disability and an early death. Roncarati and colleagues (2018) conducted a 10-year cohort study of 445 unsheltered homeless adults and found that the mortality rate for the unsheltered homeless was almost 10 times higher than the mortality rate for the adult population of Massachusetts. It was also three times higher than for a similar cohort of homeless adults who were primarily sleeping in shelters. The health problems of these homeless people were primarily treatable chronic conditions such as HIV, heart disease and substance use disorders. Wolch and Dear (1993) who studied homelessness in Los Angeles have called such conditions 'malign neglect'. A major obstacle to the development of more humane responses to these problems is a lack of public funding. The sharp contrast between the minimal taxes that are paid by immensely wealthy multinational corporations and the impoverished conditions right outside their main offices has already led to public tensions and protest. Moreover, it has been estimated that as much as 6 billion dollars go from the *Supplemental Nutrition Assistance Program* to support workers in poverty. According to a study by the *Government Accountability Office* millions of full-time workers rely on federal health care and food assistance programs.[9] Some of the biggest and more profitable companies in the US such as Walmart, McDonald's and Amazon train workers to apply for such benefits since their wages are so low that these workers would qualify. In other words, US taxpayers are forced to subsidize these economically thriving corporations to keep the wages at or below the bearable minimum.

Narratives of the entrepreneurial life course

Loosened from its embeddedness in more traditional forms of social cohesion and mutual support, the neoliberal 'individual' has been blessed with the ambivalent honor of being praised as the source of infinite possibilities. According to the accompanying ideology, opportunities and challenges will be fairly distributed along the life course thanks to the impartial operation of free markets so that success ultimately depends on the individual's determination, willpower and hard work. The neoliberal deconstruction of the life course and its construction of 'the individual' appear to be inspired by the ideal of the heroic entrepreneur who ventures out into the world at his own risk, to gather as much profit as he can. The problems he encounters would merely be challenges that help to bring out his best qualities. Even in the case of bankruptcy he would discover inside himself the individual resilience to begin anew, relying on his resources to invest again in new exciting plans so that he will succeed in the end. The flipside is, however, that any failure must be regarded as primarily caused by the individual: he must have made the wrong choices or failed to fully commit himself.

This heroic individualization is hardly adequate for entrepreneurial activities as the resources that are needed for successful enterprise are not merely inner determination but also, for instance, training opportunities or material resources, and these are very unequally distributed in society. It is even more inadequate – not to say destructive – as an ideal for citizenship. The individualization of society amounts to its denial as a broader constitutive context for individuals and families, which restricts or enlarges their opportunities. This denial has helped to hide the structural backgrounds of social problems and the broader implications of policies. The uncontextualized principle of individual responsibility has effectively become an ideological mantra to evade public responsibility for structural problems, legitimating moral judgments in which people's situations are seen as outcomes of individual choices or decisions, neglecting their positions in structural and cultural processes of inequality (see Ch.3).

Narrative I: Choice biography

Many influential authors, such as Anthony Giddens (1991), Zygmunt Bauman (2000), or Ulrich Beck (1992), have highlighted the fluid character of contemporary society, emphasizing that individuals are overwhelmed with choices rather than being confronted with a regulated life course. In the not so distant past it was, indeed, more common to stay in the place where you were born and to follow traditional patterns such as your father's profession or the life long marriage between the male head of the family and the obedient housewife. Contemporary society confronts especially its well off citizens with many choices that have major implications for their future lives: from education to primary relationships, from types of work to places to live. This is where theorists such as Giddens, Beck, and Bauman are partly right: individuals have to choose and must assume the consequences of their choices. However, the balance between restriction and enablement is not the same for everyone. For those in advantaged positions societal contexts are more enabling; for the socioeconomically disadvantaged these contexts are more restrictive. A large part of the population can neither choose the education they would prefer for their children, nor choose modest but good work, or a good house in a safe environment. The choices they have are limited by the options that are available but they still have to face the consequences as if they would have chosen them freely.

There is an important ambivalence in these theories that can also be found in Giddens' concept of the 'trajectory of the self' and Beck's theory of reflexive individualization (Beck 1992; Giddens 1991; cf. Baars 2006). The basic phenomenon they try to articulate in these theories is that individuals must make their own decisions without being able to rely on traditions or authorities (Beck & Beck-Gernsheim 2002). This *moral* condition of 'individualization', which is basically a combination of an abundance of choices and a moral uprooting, has, however, become mixed up with an *empirical* interpretation suggesting that every individual would be equally blessed or overburdened with the opportunities to construct her or his life. The moral evaluation that every individual must decide and act on his own cannot, however, support the conclusion that the individual is in fact 'the architect of his or her life': the options that one may choose from are distributed quite unequally.

The lasting popularity of perspectives that emphasize the dominance of such a 'choice biography' in contrast to a former 'standard biography', especially beyond sociological theory, in 'self help' programs and media discussions of life course policies is striking. It seems ironic that at a time when societies have become overwhelmingly complex and unpredictable, individuals would be more strongly enabled than before to choose their biographies. Moreover, the assumption that the standard biography tends to be socially determined whereas the choice biography seems to float in abstract realms of individual freedom overlooks societal pressures and unequal support. Generally, the idea that one would be able to construct one's biography is an attractive self-concept; especially when presented as the opposite of a more traditional standard biography in which people were obligated, or took it for granted, to follow standards that were laid out for them. The idea of a choice biography implies the alluring suggestion that, as a critical consumer, it is important to resist others who could prescribe how one is supposed to live. Hence the pressure is to individualize ways to dress or to present yourself in daily life, preferably using brands that underline your individual life style. It is not hard to see a widely shared deep craving to be respected as a unique person in a seemingly individualistic society.

In a society in which a free market is presented as the realm of freedom, the illusion is cultivated that everything can be bought and that choices are unlimited for those who can afford them and are, therefore, regarded as successful. However, even in rich Western countries many people are just trying to survive in situations that leave them little choice. The critical idea that humans should be respected in their fundamental rights and capacities to choose freely must not be confused with the actual possibilities of exercising this capacity, otherwise the idea of autonomy loses its critical edge and will fit all situations alike (see Ch.7). Probably, the main reason that the idea of a chosen biography has gained so much support is the ideological role it plays in the restructuring of social protection that has been taking place in many Western countries. Terms such as 'modernization' or 'flexibility' serve the same strategic purpose: to shift risks that were formerly assumed by governments or corporations to 'individuals'. The flip side of the chosen biography is an individualization of risks that are in no way produced by the individual. Nevertheless, she will be held fully responsible for her situation: when she runs into trouble, the message will be that she should have chosen differently.

Structurally or culturally constituted inequalities are individualized in the sense that they are framed as the results of bad individual choices, neglecting structural limitations that hit vulnerable families, children and older people who remain puzzled how to improve their situations by making better choices. It's like saying 'study harder and your problems will soon be over' to a child when her neighborhood is unsafe, her family is struggling to survive and her school is also unsafe and lacks resources. Or to say to a poor older person that she should have made other choices in her life than caring for others in her family and that, therefore, her stressful life of insufficient resources is the fruit of her choices. In evading and neglecting these problems the emphasis on the choices and decisions individuals make during their lives has turned into an ideology that serves especially the interests of the political and economic elite who have, indeed, more to choose.

Narrative 2: The need to display authenticity

Another life course ideology has been the paradoxical result of certain cultural trends that became popular in the 1960s and 1970s. Especially in large cities and institutions for higher education young Baby Boomers opposed the social, economic and political establishment, being inspired by neo-romantic versions of authenticity with an emphasis on nonconformist expression and spontaneity. This powerful cultural force was driven by the large birth cohorts that were challenging the existing views of a 'normal' life course. Crowded university campuses became the centers of an explorative youth culture which distanced itself from the hierarchies and bureaucracies that would frustrate freedom, sex and creativity. As they sang with Bob Dylan that the times were changing they wanted to break away from of an 'old' world that would also be the world of 'older' people; basically everyone above the age of 30 years.

More established citizens were worried by much of this. According to Daniel Bell's 1976 *The Cultural Contradictions of Capitalism* the spread of aesthetic creativity and impulsiveness, beyond the realms of artists, would lead to a new hedonistic morality that would conflict with the requirements of capitalism. However, as a stunning paradox and further proof of the flexible tenacity of capitalism, these desires for authenticity and self realization have been functionalized to rejuvenate capitalism (Honneth 2012). Contemporary management concepts emphasize non-hierarchical relations, brainstorms, enthusiasm, inventiveness and 'out of the box'-ness. Every organizational demand should be seen as a professional and personal challenge. The CV should read as a personal adventure, just like a visit to a shopping mall or any other exquisite spending opportunity promises to be a profound experience.

Presenting yourself authentically has become a professional and personal asset with a need for advertising personal feelings, experiences and skills on social media as if there were a general panic to be left behind and not to figure in success stories. In this process, individual authenticity tends to be transformed into an openness to embrace external demands that may with all their exhausting restlessness lead to further excitement and, maybe, even success for those who know how to play the system. Especially for younger people, the willingness to take on new challenges at their own risk has become crucially important as protected positions have come increasingly under threat. Meanwhile, the life course consequences are serious: the demands for authenticity transform ideals of individual self-realization into legitimations of the systemic environment, justifying the dismantling of social protection within organizations. To insist that you and your family need social protection would amount to confessing that you don't trust your own creativity and resourcefulness to overcome any problem.

The result of such structural uncertainty is an undermining of loyalties from all sides. Professional experience does not tend to accumulate but to lead to a sequence of dispersed and quickly outdated achievements so that seniority status in work tends to lose its grounds. The informal, quasi personal and non-hierarchical culture of leadership emerges in the behavior of the boss who slaps you on the back in a friendly way and fires you an hour later without any compensation. These processes are turning 'self-realization' into a barren system of demands in which individuals are more likely to suffer than to prosper. Those who cannot participate in this flexible world of virtual careers may, however, be even worse off. A tragic transformation has taken place: the commodifying tendencies that were intended to be challenged by romantic ideals of authenticity have been strengthened by them. Privacy and intimacy are being exposed and exploited because, if presented well in social media, they might enlarge the chances to become successful or even famous.

The neoliberal amputation of liberalism – The demise of the individual and the return of plutocrat aristocracy

At the core of neoliberalism is a stated belief in the wholesome effects of free markets on all sectors of society – introducing deregulation of financial as well as labor markets, privatization and marketization of public services, tax reductions and welfare cutbacks in order to unleash the full force of the market (Harvey 2005; Saad-Filho and Johnston 2005). The famous economist Adam Smith has often been cited as the great predecessor of neoliberalism but this is a serious amputation of his work. Understandably, he was overwhelmed by his discovery of markets as a reality *sui generis* with remarkable mechanisms of distribution without an individual regulator pulling the strings. Not kings or the nobility were to thank for prosperity or meeting demands with supply but markets. Smith's trust in the beneficial workings of the market for all has proven to be naïve, but his primary concern was the common good: 'the great society of mankind' as he would call this (1759/1982, p.229). This relationship between the common good and markets – a basic problem in Smith's economical theory as well as in contemporary society, should have been developed in the direction of distinguishing and monitoring where markets are adequate to further the common good and where they are disruptive. Although the question what the 'common good' might be in any situation deserves to be hotly disputed, it should not be cast aside. It remains crucial for social formations at any level, from family, community to society. Concern for a common good appears to be completely lost in contemporary neoliberalism. Its main multinational agents are only after enlarging their own power and profit, embracing any country wherever they have to pay fewer taxes, inviting a race to the bottom. The neoliberal political practice has been to protect the wealth of the extremely wealthy, thus betraying Adam Smith's fight for a common good instead of the supreme good of aristocratic – now plutocratic – privilege.

Secondly, Smith sought to combine self-interest with altruism, compassion and concern for the opportunities to participate in society as a respected citizen.

> 'It is not from the benevolence of the butcher, the brewer, or the baker that we expect our dinner, but from their regard to their own interest' (Smith, 1776/1976, p. 119).

This most famous quotation from his work has been taken out of context, to mean that 'greed is good'. Smith trusted that the wealth created by the market would 'extend(s) itself to the lowest ranks of people.' (1776/1976, p. 115)

He went, however, beyond the admonition to wait for the wealth to trickle down. Not only in his 1759 *Theory of Moral Sentiments*, but also in his 1776 *Wealth of Nations* he pointed out that 'creditable people, even the lowest order', should be supplied with the necessary material goods but also with the type of goods a person 'would be ashamed to appear in public without' (1776/1904 Book Five, 2, IV). According to Smith, people need sufficient resources to survive but *also* to be able to participate in society as a respected and equal citizen (see Ch.7).

Thirdly, there has been a major change in approaching 'the individual'. The basic political movement in classical liberalism has been to emancipate 'the individual' – short for non aristocratic citizens – from repressive lords and masters and to guard their freedom from oppression and exploitation. In neoliberalism this *moral call* to respect and support the autonomy of individuals has been transformed into the claim that all individuals *are in fact* autonomous in the sense that they can be held accountable for their societal position (see Ch.7). Subsequently this appeal to the autonomy of citizens is misused as an alibi to undermine all public arrangements that are necessary to protect and further their autonomy and well being. Moreover, the emancipatory idea of a struggle against repressive governments has been twisted and turned against public goods – such as the common good of universal healthcare – as if these would put 'hard working citizens' in a collective straitjacket blocking, moreover, progress by eliminating the competition that would be the only way to an optimal supply of goods. The marketization of care in the form of, for instance, for profit hospitals or nursing homes would be 'cheaper and better'.

Better for whom? Nobel Prize laureate Kenneth J. Arrow had already argued in 1963 quite convincingly that health care cannot be subjected to a free market without major damages, and later Nobel Prize laureates Angus Deaton and Joseph Stiglitz have basically come to the same conclusion. High quality health care as well as education have become the privileges of those who can afford them. Those who cannot – as will be documented in the next chapters – face a major reduction of their chances to participate in society and to live a reasonably long and healthy life. Whereas big corporations are protected, the cherished 'individual' is confronted with an oligopoly of information and surveillance in the hands of a small technocratic elite who know much more about how to influence and manipulate the population than those who would dare to challenge them. The prefix 'neo' means that basic emancipatory ideas from classical liberalism have been transformed and used as an ideology: a constellation of ideas, slogans and practices that serve to hide and protect the interests of a small but very wealthy and powerful elite.

The entrepreneurial life course – concluding remarks

The supportive life course that was slowly but steadily built up in the US has increasingly come under threat since the neoliberal turn. Much of the social protection and support that was gradually built into the life course during the first decades after the Second World War has been taken down under the neoliberal verdict of being outdated and blocking progress. The decision to give free rein to 'the market' and even elevate it to a model for policies in general had grave consequences for institutions that were meant to distribute opportunities more equally over the population or to protect vulnerable citizens. The privatization and marketization of public services have especially been pushed ahead in sectors that are not known for their profitability in the short term perspective that tends to dominate economic and political decision making. The result of the transformation of public goods into marketed services has been that these services will benefit mainly those who can afford them and fail to reach those who need them most.

Although all citizens will be confronted with the neoliberal arrangements of the life course, it will affect them not only differently but in deeply unequal ways, making it easy for the wealthy, difficult for many of the middle class and practically impossible for large groups of disadvantaged citizens to enjoy high quality education, find well paid work, receive optimal health care and live well as retirees. Citizens who are born into wealthy families with good houses in safe neighborhoods will also have to make efforts to realize their dreams, but for other groups of citizens such opportunities are hardly available from the very beginning of their lives.

One of the most destructive consequences of the neoliberal turn is that support and protection of citizens have been drastically reduced while structurally produced insecurities and risks have grown. In a time when economic and financial macro developments have overpowering effects on individuals' lives, they are told that they are exclusively responsible for their lives and that the sky would be the limit if they would only be fully committed to becoming successful. Criticizing this view does not mean that individual responsibility and prudential choice are not important: they are. But they are also limited because they presuppose that people have feasible options to choose from and can reasonably be assumed to know the consequences of their choices. Somebody who, as a young man in the 1960s, made the prudential choice of taking a job in mining or shipbuilding may find out some decades later that his refined expertise has lost its value on the labor market where he is, moreover, discriminated against as an 'older worker' and becomes chronically unemployed like countless others in his community. The same has happened to numerous workers who have been laid off as a result of other structural changes in the economy. We can hardly say that such citizens have been irresponsible and should carry the full burden of their 'autonomous decisions' (see Ch.7). The neoliberal answer might be, with Wilbur Ross, 'access your savings!' or to point out that, fortunately and for the benefit of all, the market offers excellent solutions for unemployment risks: enormous opportunities arise for insurance companies as soon as governments retreat from their tasks to guarantee basic security over the life course.

Freeing markets from regulations does not automatically lead to opening up opportunities for all citizens. The idealized free market has failed to secure, let alone improve, the lives not only of the poorest but also of the positions and future perspectives of a large part of the middle class. Instead of material security and mutual respect only the 'trickle down' ideology is trickling down telling the disadvantaged to wait until this particular crisis is over and their boats will be lifted with the rising tide of progress. Advantaged citizens, by contrast, are more likely to experience that structures help them ahead as high quality education or health care are readily available for them or because cultures of discrimination work to their advantage, even if they don't agree with them.

The opportunistic neoliberal ideology of the 'free market' has produced bizarre paradoxes. As welfare for disadvantaged citizens and their families was reduced, corporate welfare increased, securing corporations' existence by granting them billions in bail outs and tax reductions. As Medicaid benefits were limited, Big Pharma received billions of dollars. While the victims of their financial speculations were left to perish as armies of expensive lawyers marched in to foreclose on mortgages and evict people from their homes, banks received billions. In a bizarre acknowledgement of these problems income tax cuts were introduced to take care of those who don't gain enough to pay taxes or have even lost their income.

The appeal to 'the individual' serves to superficially equalize all citizens: whatever their circumstances or public responsibilities, they are only 'individuals' trying to take care of themselves and their families as best they can. It is only the extreme consequence of the idea that citizens are basically competitive individual entrepreneurs when a US president uses his office to advance his individual interests and those of his dynasty: he is merely doing what everybody is supposed to do. The common good shrinks to cheering on national representatives in sports events like the Olympic Games or unifying behind the military and Commander in Chief in times of war.

The uncontextualized idea of 'the individual' hides from view that this idea has been modeled after the ideal of the entrepreneur who takes risks investing his capital: material and immaterial resources such as education and training, however, do not come from 'being an individual' but usually from having an advantaged position in society. The laudation for the citizen as an energetic independent entrepreneur makes disadvantaged citizens individually responsible for overcoming structurally produced problems such as bad education, insufficient qualification for the labor market, or discrimination. As all individuals should be able to succeed on the 'free and fair market' any remaining social problems must be caused by dysfunctional individuals who must either change their ways or be regarded as hopelessly unfit for society. Consequentially, when all 'normal' citizens are seen as entrepreneurs who venture ahead in life, taking calculated risks and assuming full responsibility for their successes and losses, the protective and supportive functions of the life course lose their grounds: who wants a 'nanny state' when you are a successful entrepreneur who is dashing forward with a dazzling life?

The entrepreneurial reorganization of the life course has to an important degree been the result of policies that did not have the life course as their specific target, such as deregulation of the labor market, taxation policies, the marketization of social care or for-profit health care. However, even when there are no explicit policies regarding the whole life course, these processes do not happen at random: powerful structural forces reproduce a harsh unequal society and the ways in which the public infrastructure of the life course has been demolished plays a crucial role in this reproduction (see Ch.7). The general effect of these processes is that further concentration of wealth is guaranteed, while negative effects are scattered away from the wealthy center to the periphery, and systemic life course risks are explained away as consequences of individual choices. Although the material wealth is piling up in corporations and amongst a very small minority of citizens, the system of income redistribution appears to be geared to giving them even more.

This painfully increases social inequality: although more miserly than in most other peer countries, the project of a supportive life course in the US aimed at supporting and protecting the most vulnerable citizens, including disadvantaged older people. As the vulnerable positions of disadvantaged older people are usually the result of accumulating disadvantages over the life course, supporting them is not just a matter of policies for 'old age': the whole organization of the life course is implicated. The life course functions as a mechanism of reproducing an unequal society by sorting people from childhood on into unequal trajectories. Although this does not lead to complete determination, the relatively low degree of upward social mobility, and the steady expansion of those who are excluded from socioeconomic security testify to the problematic nature of this life course organization.

The entrepreneurial view of society as a constellation of free and fair markets amounts to one of the worst things one could say about society: that everybody participates in it at his or her own risk. As we shall see in the next chapter, these risks are very unequally distributed, leading to stark differences in what may generally be called health inequalities: the life expectancies of the rich are much higher than those of the less advantaged. Especially the number of years they can expect to live in good health show a gap, up to a staggering 20 years. Eventually, however, the neoliberal undermining of society will also undermine the life expectancies of the most privileged. The quest for probable causes leads away from the popular assumption that it all depends on someone's genes or individual life style.

Notes

1 https://www.pewresearch.org/social-trends/2020/01/09/trends-in-income-and-wealth-inequality/#:~:text=In%201980%2C%20the%2090%2F10,%2C%20an%20increase%20of%2039%25.
2 The ratio of the number of people whose income falls below the poverty line and the total population; the poverty line is here taken as half the median household income.
3 https://www.statista.com/statistics/233910/poverty-rates-in-oecd-countries/
4 https://news.gallup.com/poll/260741/americans-american-dream-achievable.aspx
5 https://inequality.org/billionaire-bonanza-2020-updates
6 https://www.vox.com/2019/1/24/18195782/wilbur-ross-shutdown-workers-loans-food-banks
7 https://crr.bc.edu/wp-content/uploads/2019/07/IB_19-11.pdf
8 See the Purpose of the Corporation Project website. http://www.purposeofcorporation.org/en/news/5009-behind-the-purpose-of-the-corporation-infographic
9 https://www.gao.gov/products/gao-21-45

Chapter 2

Long lives are for the rich ... until this backfires

Overview

In the first decades after the Second World War the supportive life course organization led to slowly rising life expectancies of the US population. As a result of the implementation of the entrepreneurial life course since the early 1980s the improvement of life expectancies has further fallen behind those of other high income countries and finally ground to a halt. Meanwhile, health inequalities have increased, both within the US and in comparison with its peer countries. After documenting these regressions the chapter continues by following the traces upstream, trying to understand how health inequalities originate from social inequalities. The usual focus in life course studies on socioeconomic resources is broadened to include respect, denigration and discrimination as dimensions of social inequality. The health care system appears to play only a minor role in solving health inequalities, but reducing its public services without adequate structural change would particularly hit the most disadvantaged. Moreover, there are still policies to exclude disadvantaged citizens from health care and even after having gained access to the clinic they may be confronted with racial discrimination or ageism. Next, it will be argued that good or bad health cannot sufficiently be explained by good or bad health choices and that structural and cultural backgrounds need to be taken into account. Approaches to the Covid-19 pandemic have given many examples of myopic biomedical diagnoses, by neglecting the pre-existing conditions of a materially unequal and discriminatory society. Following the traces upstream has provided an answer to the much debated question: does bad health cause socioeconomic inequality or is it the other way around? The chapter closes by summing up the impossible position of the health care system, being faced with a structural overload of health problems that could largely be prevented by addressing their causes outside the clinic.

The implosion of the entrepreneurial life course

The Population Reference Bureau in Washington DC proudly announces that '*The increase in U.S. life expectancy is a public health success story*'.[1] Fortunately, the

DOI: 10.4324/9781003392590-3

business of producing triumphant one-liners has not yet replaced scholarly work. Such work allows us to get an overview of the development of life expectancies and, generally, health inequalities since the neoliberal turn, with an emphasis on a comparison of the US with other rich countries that have been following – some more, some less – its example.

But why are life expectancies or health inequalities so important? Nobody should need to be healthy to be fully respected as a citizen, nor would I maintain that a healthy life would per se be a good life or that being in good health is the ultimate purpose in life (see my *Aging and the Art of Living*). But health does have a particular value for citizens because it is crucial for being able to do what one aspires to do, including the ability to care for others, to work and participate fully in society. Ill health means potential suffering, disability, and possibly early loss of life. It may seem that chances to be and remain healthy are a matter of good or bad luck, in genetic predispositions as well as during somebody's life, but this would be too simple. Luck certainly plays a role but what is sometimes called 'luck' is often the outcome of good or bad circumstances that make it more likely that the good luck (!) of being born in a harmonious and wealthy family is followed by the 'good luck' of a good education, good jobs and a long healthy life. In contrast to the slogan of equal opportunities the neoliberal society respects privileged birth; it is less supportive for those who do not have resourceful backgrounds. Moreover, socioeconomic positions play a huge role in the ability or inability to absorb bad luck. An important objection against claiming that 'luck' would be the determining factor in our lives is that this obscures the driving forces behind it and what we can and should do to improve the ways in which we live together (see also Ch.6).

There are major differences in opportunities to live long and in good health and such differences are important from a perspective of social justice because optimal health is widely regarded as one of the most fundamental citizen's rights, that should be equally distributed to all citizens. This idea has led in most Western countries to systems of universal healthcare that are meant to secure that every citizen, no matter how poor or rich, will have the same opportunities to live a long and healthy life. Unfortunately, it is not as simple as that. In this frame of thought, health care functions as a way to *repair* damage which represents only a part of what public responsibility for a population's health is about. A soon as we know that bad health in later life can be caused by conditions in early life, from gestation to kindergarten and, later, by bad working and housing conditions or toxic environments, we need to search upstream. As we investigate the upstream causes of the downstream fall-out in the health care system it will turn out that health care, although certainly indispensible, is not the ultimate answer to health inequalities. But it certainly doesn't help when health care remains unaffordable for many citizens.

The health care system is overridden by fundamental social inequalities. Life expectancies can be regarded as indicators of more general health inequalities, which are part and indicators of the long term consequences of social inequalities of resources and respect. Among the population of the US these inequalities have grown significantly over the last decades, also in comparison to other developed countries.

How well or how badly did the US perform in increasing the life expectancy of its population since the neoliberal turn?

A *first* way to answer this question is to compare the life expectancies of the US with the average scores of other developed countries (Barbieri 2022; Ho 2022[2]). From a baseline in 1959 when life expectancy for the US population was 69.9 years, there has been reasonable progress in the 1970s to begin to advance more slowly in the 1980s. In 1982, life expectancy at birth in the US was 70.8 years for men, 78.1 years for women. This was just a little below the average of the peer countries: 72.0 years for men and 78.4 years for women. However, between 1982 and 2019 life expectancies at birth in the other OECD countries developed more favorably making the gap with the US larger by the year. This stands in stark contrast to the fact that the US continued to have the highest per capita health care spending in the world; a stunning paradox that I will discuss below. On average life expectancies in the other countries increased from 72.0 to 80.1 years for men and from 78.4 to 84.9 years for women, an increase of 8.1 and 6.5 years respetively. The US did much worse: over these years life expectancies had only grown to 74.9 and 81.8, falling behind the OECD average by 3.5 years for men and 3.1 years for women. Moreover, the average life expectancies of the peer countries hide important differences between these countries. In 2018, American men and women could expect to live 5.18 and 5.82 fewer years than the world leaders, Swiss men and Japanese women (Ho 2022).

In the decade between 2008 and 2018, life expectancy in the US increased by only 0.78 years for men and 0.89 years for women. Before the neoliberal turn the US experienced life expectancy levels that were far higher than the worst-performing peer country. In 1961, for example, life expectancy at birth in the US was 7.07 and 8.21 years higher than that of Portuguese men and women, respectively. In 2019 this situation has been reversed. American citizens could expect to live considerably shorter than those in the worst performing peer countries: men 1.78 years shorter than Portuguese men; women 1.42 years shorter than British women (Barbieri 2022). To put this in perspective I recall the *CDC* estimate that the elimination of all cancer deaths – which would be a huge step in improving population health – would increase life expectancy by only three years.

The following thought experiment provides a sense of just how far the US remains behind (Ho 2022). Oeppen & Vaupel (2002) have calculated that best-practice life expectancy over the last century and a half has been an increase by about 2.5 years per decade. If we froze all other countries at their current life expectancy levels and assumed the US would be able to increase its life expectancy at such a rate it would take about 14 years to catch up with the average of its peer countries. To catch up with the world leaders would take more than 21 years for men and 23 years for women. Without a drastic change, the population of the richest and most powerful country in the world faces a continuing worsening of its prospects to live – in comparison to citizens of other countries – a reasonably long and healthy life.

So far, we have discussed average scores of populations, with the usual distinction between scores for men and women. To answer the general question of this section we need, *secondly*, to examine such averages more closely as they are notorious for hiding differences *within* the population that might be more important than the average overall score. Underlying the developments of life expectancies and, more generally, health inequalities there are plausible causal connections with socioeconomic inequality. Many studies have shown that people of higher socioeconomic status (SES; usually indicated by income and/or education) typically have better health, lower mortality rates, and higher life expectancy than those with a lower SES (e.g. Lynch et al. 2004; Elo 2009). As discussed in Chapter 1, income and wealth have increasingly been concentrated in the upper reaches of their distribution while decreasing shares went to working and lower middle class individuals. Over the last decades, the majority of the population (those below the top 20% of the income distribution) experienced economic stagnation or decline combined with declining health. As a result of these and other developments, the US mortality gap is not only widening between the poorest 25% and the richest 25% but also between the richest 25% and the 50% in the middle (Evans, Wolf & Adler 2012).

In the US socioeconomic inequalities have become larger in comparison with other wealthy countries while the US has also seen an intensification of health inequalities (Avendano et al. 2010; Okonkwo et al. 2021). There are even widening socioeconomic inequalities in US childhood mortality (Singh & Kogan 2007). These differences in life chances are becoming more extreme: the US life expectancy gap between the richest and poorest 1% of its own population rose between 2001 and 2014 to more than 14 years for men and 10 years for women (Chetty, Stepner & Abraham 2016). Since 2014 life expectancies among US citizens of lower socioeconomic status have been dropping so much that they outweigh small improvements among advantaged groups (Hendi 2015, 2017; Woolf and Schoomaker, 2019).

Barbieri (2022) has compared the development of age-specific death rates and life expectancy between the US counties in relation to the socioeconomic inequalities between them since 1982. The counties were classified into 10 socioeconomic categories. In 1982 life expectancy for men at birth ranged from 68.8 years in the lowest SES decile to 72.5 years in the highest decile. For women in 1982, it ranged from 77.2 to 78.8 years. So, in 1982 the gap between the lowest and highest deciles was 3.7 and 1.6 years respectively. This internal gap in life expectancies between US counties had increased in 2019 to 7.2 years for men and 5.8 years for women (73.0 years versus 80.2 years for men and 78.7 versus 84.5 years for women.)

Although we see in many other developed countries similar relationships between socioeconomic status and health, health inequalities are most severe in the US, especially for those in midlife, with the UK only a little behind. Research on the relationship between socioeconomic status and health in the US and England among persons in late middle age found that in both countries, people of lower socioeconomic status had significantly higher rates of diabetes, hypertension, heart attack, stroke, lung disease, and cancer than those with higher SES. Still, people in the US had significantly higher rates of disease than those in England across all socioeconomic groups. Banks et al. (2006) showed that Americans in the highest wealth quintile had poorer health status than their English counterparts despite benefiting from a much steeper economic gradient. This all adds up to a rather shocking balance: if the US had the same mortality rates and the same remaining years of life at given ages as its peer countries in 2019, a total of 446,400 deaths would have been averted in the US: 274,687 for men and 171,713 for women. All of these decedents would have collectively lived an additional 14.5 million years (Barbieri 2022; cf. Preston and Vierboom 2021 and Marmot's exemplary estimate for England in Ch.7).

The 10% of the US population with the lowest socioeconomic status contributed in 2019 almost one fifth of the total number of years of life lost (18% for men, 19% for women). The 50% most deprived Americans contributed 69% for men and 70% for women to the total number of years of life lost by the US compared to peer countries (Barbieri 2022).

A *third* way to contribute to answering the question 'How well or how badly has the US performed in increasing the life expectancy of its population since the neoliberal turn?' is to look at age-specific death rates. In 1982, the difference in life expectancy at birth in the US was entirely attributable to higher mortality at ages younger than 70 years. At the beginning of the neoliberal turn death rates were already considerably higher for American young adults (ages 20–35 years) compared to their age peers in other OECD countries. In 2019, this situation had become worse: death rates for these young adults had risen further and spread to surrounding age groups. The 20% of the most socioeconomically disadvantaged between ages 20 and 40 experienced death rates that were about four times higher than OECD average. Of all Americans in their mid-20s death rates were nearly three times higher than the average of their age peers living in other high-income countries. Deaths from drug overdose, firearms, and car accidents play a large role in these exceptionally high numbers (Ho 2022; Barbieri 2022; Preston & Vierboom 2021).

Over the four decades since the neoliberal turn of capitalism the US has basically continued this unfortunate tradition of neglecting disadvantaged young adults and the midlife population (see sections below). There has sometimes been a tendency in American gerontology to celebrate the relative high life expectancies of US citizens aged 70 years and older. Over the last decade, however, this advantage has practically vanished. At the moment this book was written it was not yet possible to oversee the Covid-19 pandemic in its full consequences. The most recent research shows, however, that the drop in US life expectancy in 2020 was the largest since Second World War (Heuveline & Tzen 2021). Although most countries showed a reduction in life expectancy in 2020, New Zealand, Taiwan, and Norway saw a gain in life expectancy while there was no change in Denmark, Iceland, and South Korea. Out of 37 countries the US experienced – after Russia – the second strongest decline in life expectancy: almost two years (Islam et al. 2021). One of the most disturbing aspects of the pandemic in the US has been the disproportionate harm it has caused racially marginalized groups. Black, Hispanic, and Asian people suffered substantially higher rates of infection, hospitalization, and death compared with White people (see also below).

In recent years the decline of life expectancies has become visible in all age groups and at all wealth levels: even the life expectancies and mortality rates of most wealthy US citizens, especially women, have fallen below the average levels of the their socioeconomic peers in other OECD countries. It has become doubtful whether American men and women of 85 years and older have continued to maintain an advantage in life expectancy over the worst-performing peer country (Barbieri 2022; Ho 2022). Given the chances for disadvantaged citizens to die relatively early, the majority of people who reach such high ages can be expected to be wealthy or otherwise advantaged. They do deserve to get the support and care they need. This should not lead to overlooking a major moral problem that is produced by the present organization of the life course: *those who live shorter have to endure more miserable years*. This is what I have called the *perverse longevity gap*. The most disadvantaged, poor and mostly low educated are confronted, not only with *more* chronic disease but also with a much *earlier* onset of chronic conditions, such as cardiovascular disorders, diabetes or chronic lung disease, than the highly educated (Crimmins & Cambois 2003; Elo 2009). The disadvantaged are doubly disadvantaged by shorter life expectancy and more years spent in ill health.

This brief confrontation with the destructive consequences of the neoliberal turn in social policies over the life course will be completed by discussing two more problems. First, *selective mortality*, a mechanism of inequality that grows in importance as cohorts get older and secondly that grim disruptive tendency of the entrepreneurial society to rip apart the middle ground of society: undermining the position of the *middle class* and, more generally, shortening the lives of those in *midlife*. Finally, there will be a short note on *Millennials* in the US and their struggle to find their way in an unsupportive society, unless they can rely on their families to help them ahead.

Selective mortality: the presence of those who are already dead...

The tendency of socioeconomically advantaged people to live longer and in better health than the disadvantaged is a phenomenon that can be seen in all developed countries. Generally, differences within birth cohorts increase as their members get older (see Ch.3), and without adequate social protection these differences will lead to growing social inequalities within these cohorts. Life expectancies and mortality rates are strongly connected with social inequalities such as unequal socioeconomic status: the higher somebody's socioeconomic status, the higher her life expectancy in comparison with her age peers. This is the reality behind the title 'Long lives are for the rich'.

The long tradition in the US of having relatively good life expectancies for people aged 70 years and older must be seen against this background. This does not imply that the US would be especially kind and supportive to older people, but that a disproportionate number of the more disadvantaged are already dead before they have a chance to become old. As Crimmins and others (2011) have observed, among those older than 70 years, mortality scores in the US used to be relatively good; surviving to old age is where the US performs poorly. The reasons behind this are relatively clear: if social inequalities are allowed to grow without much intervention, the most vulnerable will die early while the most advantaged will live relatively long and healthy because they can afford to buy whatever they need to live well, including social support, education and health care. This relative advantage of the oldest population in the US in comparison with the oldest in other developed countries has practically disappeared. But that doesn't mean that the health expectancies of less advantaged US citizens have become higher.

Celebrating relatively high life expectancies of people with ages of 70 years or older should go together with mourning those who did not make it to live that long. This awareness of *selective mortality* also changes the understanding of the development of cohorts over the life course. The effects of social inequality over the life course is underestimated when we look at cohorts of older people without remembering those of the same cohorts who did not survive to older ages. In passing over this selective mortality the destructive effects of social inequality along the life course are played down by the idea that in the long run, all social tensions will be harmonized so that social inequality is becoming even more irrelevant as people get older. Moreover, as many of the disadvantaged will not survive into 'old age' there will be more wealthy people among the oldest cohorts than among the general population.

One of their most strongly advocated views on the position of older people in the entrepreneurial society is to point out that older people, who are generally supposed to be wealthy and intolerably advantaged compared to 'the young', are no longer of any productive use so that their lives should be prevented from becoming a long extended burden on society. The nasty consequences of such ageist convictions – that have especially been propagated by those who plead for *Generational Equity* (Ch.6) – in terms of social policy will hit especially the most vulnerable because the well off are more able to help themselves. As a result the disadvantaged may get even fewer chances to reach 'old age' in good health. Another form of glossing over the facts of increasing inequalities as people get older, is the 'age as leveler' hypothesis: health inequalities among older people would not be important because, eventually, every one of them will be confronted with declining health so that the health inequalities within the cohort will flatten out. This hypothesis is incorrect because it is not age but illness that leads to mortality differences and the chances to become severely ill are unequally distributed (Hoffmann 2011; Crystal and Waehrer 1996).

Of course, in the long run we will all be dead but this does not in any way diminish the importance of health inequalities along the life course. In the almost 40 years that I have been involved in aging studies I have heard a steady repertoire of popular wisecracks or quasi-deep observations about the nature of human aging to mystify the long-term effects of inequality, poverty or neglect: 'well, aging comes with problems'; 'it's not easy for any of us'; 'some have better genes than others'; or 'anyway, in the end we all die'. Even more unpleasant are remarks that those who have been hit by disruptive developments beyond their control, such as the disappearance of whole industrial sectors without compensation for the loss of jobs 'should have made better choices'.

Tearing apart the middle ground: middle class and midlife

The destructive developments of the last decades have undermined the proud self awareness that the US still has a broad middle class, with little internal inequality, composed of citizens who are not rich but who can feel economically secure. Now, many have to live with the permanent danger of sliding down into worse conditions. Thanks to the establishment of neoliberal policies most developed countries have witnessed the growth of the numbers of citizens with a permanently insecure socioeconomic position.

A large part of the middle class experiences more or less constant socioeconomic survival stress as they do not feel secure in a society that is increasingly being modeled as a high risk market. Numerous citizens who desperately sought to improve the living conditions of their families were seduced to buy homes with disastrous consequences. Especially residents of lower-income and minority neighborhoods, who were targeted by lenders for high-interest sub-prime mortgages during the financing frenzy that preceded the 2008 collapse, lost their homes to foreclosure. Savings for a rainy day or for retirement have been severely reduced or have even completely gone although the dependence on such savings has increased with rising insecurity about future income and pensions (see Ch.4).

The midlife population, usually defined as the population between the ages of 55 and 64 years, used to be one of the most affluent age groups as they could reap the fruits of their work, with less economic pressure from their children. This allowed them to gather resources for their lives in retirement. Since the neoliberal turn this has become increasingly problematic for many people who are confronted with a destructive confluence of societal pressure and premature functional decline. The changing position of midlife with its steady decline of meaningful opportunities to participate in society was already a central theme in Matilda Riley's theory of the life course in the 1990s (Riley, Kahn & Foner 1994). Since then, the situation has worsened. According to research by Bosworth, Burtless and Zhang (2016) income inequality within the midlife population increased by a third from 1979 to 2012. In the following years, from 2010 to 2017 midlife adults experienced the largest increase (6%) in mortality. To put this in perspective: mortality rates were also rising in other developed countries during the flu season of 2014/15. In these countries the victims were predominantly older people above the age of 65 years. In the US, however, the growth in mortality hit especially the midlife population, overbidding an already regrettably long trend.

There is a strong connection between unemployment – together with bad working conditions and social insecurity one of the main problems in midlife – and early death, even controlling for pre-employment health or the use of stress palliatives such as tobacco and alcohol. Even the wives of the unemployed risk dying much younger than married women in more stable socioeconomic positions (Gerdtham & Johannesson 2003). Bleak economic prospects such as chronic unemployment lead to desolation and feelings of abandonment: it has been estimated that a 1% increase in US county unemployment rates is associated with a 3.6% increase in opioid deaths (Ruhm 2019). Especially those without college education have seen a dramatic decline in the availability of well-paying, stable jobs with good health and retirement benefits (Crystal 2018). Several studies suggest that unemployment has been a particularly difficult experience for low educated whites, resulting in bitter disappointment and discouragement of those who used to think they enjoyed a privileged racial status (see Ch.3; Case & Deaton 2015; Cherlin 2018).

Midlife has increasingly become a battle ground with increasing death rates and suicide rates, especially for disadvantaged groups. Until the age of

45 years the differences in comparison with the rest of the population tend to be relatively small but above that age the disadvantaged begin to die more frequently. Economically left behind, many of them are suffering under the cumulative pressures of living in a severely unequal society. Being a member of a lower socioeconomic class in a society with extreme social inequalities leads to shame, distrust, and other forms of burdening emotions, which can have direct physiological effects on health (see below), as well as indirect effects when stress leads to smoking or other health undermining behavior (Kawachi et al. 2010; Hao & Farah 2020).

In such situations there is a growing risk of giving in to substance abuse and opioid addiction. Many countries have over the last decade seen an increase in people dying from drug overdose but this epidemic has been much worse in the US. Personal responsibility has its place but it would be shortsighted and counterproductive to discard the structural pressures that put people in situations with an overdose of socioeconomic survival stress. To be able to act responsibly in challenging situations requires a supportive infrastructure of the life course (see Ch.7) in order to protect the basic well being of citizens. Extreme social inequalities in material and immaterial resources put particular groups of citizens throughout the life course in living and working conditions that are oppressive instead of supportive. Such conditions produce not only stress but also depression, together with the risk of being denigrated because the victims would lack the personal commitment, resilience or competence to rise above their problems. It shouldn't come as a surprise that countries with greater social inequality appear to be more susceptible to phenomena such as drug overdose epidemics (Ho 2017).

In his 2021 book *Empire of Pain: The Secret History of the Sackler Dynasty* Keefe has captured the moral perplexity about a health care system that failed to free itself from the fangs of a large scale corporate corruption which operated with a shocking indifference about the health consequences. Case and Deaton have in their 2020 book *Deaths of Despair* accused an irresponsible pharmaceutical industry and a dysfunctional health care system of being responsible for the many opioid deaths in the US. To liberate the opioid market for pharmaceuticals as a 'free market' has made this a magnet for rent seekers, inflating costs instead of controlling them. This has cleared the way for the destruction wrought by *OxyContin*, a drug twice as powerful as morphine; developed and patented by Purdue Pharma and aimed at anyone who suffered from pain. Purdue claimed the new slow-release drug was less addictive than other opioids, persuading doctors and other professionals to overcome their 'opioidphobia' as it was approved by the *Food and Drug Administration* without, however, properly testing the company's claims. Forcefully trying to silence critical voices by corrupting the protection that justice extends to those who are unjustly discredited, these practices could go on for too many years. Eventually, it has been estimated that more than

450,000 Americans died as a result of various opioids, of which *OxyContin* was the bestselling. These deaths of despair have not happened anywhere near this scale in other countries; Case and Deaton conclude that people's lives have been sacrificed to corporate profits (p. 259). From Keefe's grim epic of the Sackler family we can also gain a perspective on the ambivalent role of American philanthropy and charity (cf. Ch.1 and Ch.7) to leave public responsibilities to wealthy individuals, some of whom have gathered fortunes at the costs of those they choose to treat with small parts of it.

Besides drug abuse, for many middle-aged people suicide seems the only way out: although suicide rates have come down somewhat from their extreme numbers in 2018 (14.23 per 100,000 individuals), these rates are still well above global average of 9 per 100,000 citizens. These averages need, again, a further differentiation: the highest rates were among disadvantaged middle-aged white men and young adults. White males accounted for 69.68% of suicide deaths in 2020 but suicide rates continued to be disproportionally high under American Indian and Alaska Native populations. The increase in mortality rates for midlife males has been caused by a combination of rising suicides, alcohol-related diseases and drug overdose as a result of wide spread misuse of prescription opioids. Women also experienced an increase in midlife mortality caused by fatal drug overdoses, alcoholic liver disease and suicide. The excess adult mortality reflects both 'deaths of despair' linked to substance use and suicide, and a stagnation in the treatment of cardiovascular disease among those without high school education (Stein et al. 2017; Case & Deaton 2017).

Inequality has risen less among the older population than among the middle aged because older citizens are receiving government transfers. However, even if incomes have become sufficient to live well in old age, this does not the cure the health insults that have been accumulated over many decades. Disadvantaged older people may fare better as soon as they receive Social Security and Medicare but their health histories are often not so good. These health inequalities severely reduce the redistributive goals of the Social Security system.

Millennials' early socioeconomic survival stress

Increased income inequality, rising student debt, tighter mortgage rules, higher home prices, less access to pensions, and stagnating upward social mobility have created a perfect storm, most evident in the US, holding back wealth accumulation and career development from millennials (Brandmeir, Grimm, & Holzhausen 2015). Of particular concern are the indications in recent data that growing socioeconomic inequalities will, again, most likely be accompanied by growing health inequalities, reflecting the excess mortality and morbidity of despair noted in many communities that have undergone reversals of economic fortune.

A large US healthcare insurance company has recently published an alarming report about the health of millennials based on data from more than 41 million of its clients (Blue Cross Blue Shield 2019). Besides concern about the economic consequences in terms of productivity loss and health care costs the report expresses deep worry about the health conditions of this 'generation' (see Ch.6 about the use of this term). According to the report Millennials (born 1981–1996) are seeing their health decline faster than the previous 'Generation X' (born 1965–1980) as they get older. This extends to both physical health conditions, such as hypertension or high cholesterol, and to behavioral health conditions, such as major depression and hyperactivity. Without intervention the authors of the report foresee mortality rates of this generation climbing up by more than 40% compared to Generation X-ers at the same age with a concentration in areas that are struggling economically. Growing income inequality can easily lead to a vicious cycle of even greater prevalence of health problems.

A key concern of the report is 'behavioral health': rapid upticks in conditions like depression, substance abuse, and hyperactivity. Between 2014 and 2017 alone, prevalence of major depression and hyperactivity among millennials was up roughly 30%. Moreover, accidental deaths, which include overdoses, and suicides were the cause of 60% of the deaths among 25–29 years old in 2017. In 2002 those two causes accounted for less than half of all deaths in the same age cohort. Such changes in 'behavioral health', however, are not happening at random. Millennial health declines are concentrated in areas of grave economic problems that have already led to worse health outcomes compared with previous cohorts, but might further negatively influence their economic prospects leading to even more health problems.

Accumulating private wealth and public indifference

We didn't zoom in on the socioeconomic differences in health and life expectancies in other developed countries but we should not forget that also in these countries, wealthy, highly educated people tend to live longer and healthier than the less advantaged. Kröger, Pakpahan and Hoffmann (2015) conclude in their systematic review of research on the causes of health inequality that one of the most solid findings in public health research is the fact that people with a relatively low level of education, occupational status or level of income tend to live shorter lives *and* have a higher prevalence of disease. These inequalities in health have been found in the US and in all European countries; usually amounting to a 10 to 20 years' difference in disability-free or healthy life expectancies (Singh and Siahpush 2006; Mackenbach et al. 2018; Head et al. 2019). The *perverse longevity gap* – or the social gradient in healthy life expectancies – turns out to be an international phenomenon but there are still major differences in severity.

From the early 1960s Japan had the smallest differences in income among all industrialized countries with corresponding smaller differences in health. Following the Japanese implementation of neoliberal policies, however, there has also been an increase in socioeconomic inequality in this country resulting in increasing health inequalities between those who are well off and those who are less advantaged (Reich & Shibuya 2015).

Although the welfare states of North Western Europe continued to offer more support and protection along the life course, the lives of large parts of their populations have also become more precarious because of the undeserved admiration of their political elites for the neoliberal developmental model with its continued emphasis on reduction of public responsibilities. In practically all European countries inequalities in mortality have deepened from the early 1980s through the 1990s (Mackenbach et al. 2003). In European countries lower socioeconomic groups are worse off than higher socioeconomic groups for mortality and morbidity, including subjective appraisal of health (Mackenbach et al. 2018). Generally, welfare regimes in many European countries did contribute to the reduction of *income* inequalities, but not as much to the reduction of *health* inequalities. Johan Mackenbach (2012) a prominent researcher of health inequalities, especially in European countries, has called this the paradox of the modern welfare states.

This does not mean, however, that these developments are identical to those in the US. According to Mackenbach and colleagues' (2018) research of the period 2002 to 2014 covering 350,000 survey respondents in 27 countries, mortality declined not only among the high educated but *also* among low educated men of Eastern and Western Europe, resulting in a narrowing of health inequalities. Research into trend interruptions as a result of the impact of the 2008 financial crisis showed that declines in self-assessed health affected the low and high educated equally. There was no discernible short-term impact of the crisis on health inequalities at the population level. The main pattern in Western Europe remains one of stagnation or slow lengthening of life expectancies of the poor and the low educated, while the lifespans of the highly educated are developing more favorably. However, Mackenbach concludes that the unfavorable trends that have been observed in the US, especially after the 2008 financial crisis, have not been found in Europe.

So, not only is the inequality in life expectancy and mortality rates between groups with a different socioeconomic status larger in the US than in its peer countries, even the most advantaged groups in American society have *worse health* than their counterparts in other high-income countries (Avendano et al. 2010; Banks et al. 2006; Ho 2022). The proud declaration of the Population Reference Bureau that the increase in US life expectancy is a public health success story reads like an ad for a product that wouldn't pass consumer scrutiny. Although there has been monumental growth of life expectancies in most countries over the last century and a half, the sad conclusion must be that since the neoliberal turn the wealthiest country in the world has done much worse than other affluent countries. Even some much poorer countries have been doing better in supporting and protecting their citizens than the immensely rich US society.

As Barbieri (2022) notes, whatever 'the type of disparities' investigated, the early 1980s appears to have marked a turning point, initiating divisive trends in survival within the US population and across communities. Since then, the US's previously small lag in life expectancy behind other high-income countries has started increasing. The phenomenon has generated some alarming reports, such as the 2021 report *High and Rising Mortality Rates Among Working-Age Adults* by the National Academies of Sciences, Engineering, and Medicine.

The US stands out as a worrisome example because it has enormous wealth but fails to invest this in the well being and future of its population. Like the initially admired hero in a Greek tragedy it gets increasingly pressed down by the *hubris* of its self-centered political and economic elites. Disrupting loyalty and social cohesion, neoliberal politics have reversed the expansion of a protective and supportive life course that began with the New Deal and continued after the Second World War until the neoliberal implosion gave new energy to a ruthless concentration of wealth. The supportive functions of the life course infrastructure have been downgraded while established patterns of productivity and wealth creation for citizens have been uprooted without adequate compensation or promising perspective, putting millions of people out of respected jobs and into economic hardship. Even the majority of the working population – not the weakest group in society – is not adequately protected. When their services are suddenly not needed anymore, as may occur in any crisis or pandemic, their existence can be abruptly threatened leaving them no other options than cutting into their financial buffers and pensions or appealing to food banks and other forms of charity. A long trend to reduce inequality in life chances has been reversed during the last decennia. A large percentage of its citizens have fallen victim to developmental ideals that, although presented by their beneficiaries as an ongoing success story, look to others more like a gradual breakdown of society.

Following the traces upstream – health care system and society

A downward slope of stressful disrespect

Usually the socioeconomic and health inequalities that have been discussed are framed in terms of behavior: Americans would behave poorly, not only in inappropriately using drugs but also in smoking, eating, lack of exercise and violence. That is supposed to be the reason why the health status of the poor and the uneducated are worse than in other countries. The key question remains, however, *why* a large part of the American citizens behave in ways that are detrimental to their health and well being.

An important approach to explain such major differences in life expectancies as we have seen above has developed from pioneering research on the relation between health inequalities and social, or rather, occupational status. This relation has extensively been explored in a longitudinal research project on the health of more than 10,000 Whitehall civil servants that started in the mid 1970s, conducted by Michael Marmot and colleagues. One of the initial intentions of this research project was to study whether and how the highly stratified environment of the British Civil Service affects the health of the people working there. One of the most astonishing outcomes was that those who were lower in the hierarchy would sooner get a disease and also die earlier than those in the next grade; and this continued to be the case over the six major grades of the hierarchy. After retirement civil servants in the lowest grade showed an increase in mortality of 86% compared to the highest grade (Marmot and Shipley, 1996). These findings led to many further questions: how to explain these extraordinary findings?

A first way to find answers was to look at possible differences in the health behaviors of civil servants according to their hierarchical status. It turned out that the civil servants in the lowest employment grades were indeed more likely to show many of the behavioral risk factors for coronary heart disease such as smoking, reduced leisure time, and lower levels of physical activity. Taken together with other risk factors such as a higher prevalence of underlying illness, higher blood pressure, and shorter height these risk factors accounted, however, for no more than 40% of differences between the civil service grades in cardiovascular disease mortality.

What about the other 60%? The answer from Marmot and his colleagues that came up after many years of research was that this 60% were caused by socially generated, especially occupational stress. This unequally divided stress load was probably also behind much of the behavioral risk factors that made up the other 40%. For some of us this may sound counter-intuitive as we may tend to think – or are led to believe – that those with the most decision-making responsibilities have the most stressful lives. Yet the conclusion was that the lower someone is in the chain of command, the less control he has over his daily working life with stress as a result. In other words: stressors of demand and control appear to be institutionalized in hierarchies. Not having to take orders on how to perform a task, or when to do it, tends to lead to a lower heart rate, less hormonal stress, and lower blood pressure than being told how and when to execute orders.

During the many years – in fact, several decades – of the Whitehall project much attention was given to the negative effects of stress on the human body. In the Whitehall project low control at work appeared to be linked to low heart rate variability and raised cortisol levels. These stress pathways can easily lead to the *metabolic syndrome*: a clustering of medical conditions such as abdominal obesity, high blood pressure or high blood sugar, associated with the risk of developing cardiovascular disease and type 2 diabetes. In many developed countries, especially in the US, about a quarter of the adult population have this metabolic syndrome, with racial and ethnic minorities being particularly affected.

Such observations already indicate the possibility of a much broader relevance of what merely seemed to be an interesting study of a peculiar, typically British old-fashioned occupational culture. And indeed, the occupational, or 'social gradient in health' as it has been called, is not a phenomenon confined to the British Civil Service: it has been found throughout the developed world. Of course, there is an ongoing discussion about many important aspects of this research, and studies in the US have focused more on income differences than occupational status. The general pattern, however, has been confirmed in many studies. For instance, in a large prospective study Wolfson and colleagues (1993) tracked half a million Canadian men and compared their average income between the ages of 45 and 65 with their mortality rates from age 65 to 70. The researchers found a clear gradient, with men in each income bracket being less likely to die than those in the brackets below them. A research project in Sweden (Erikson 2001) showed that persons with a PhD had lower mortality than those with a master's degree, who had lower mortality than those with a bachelor's degree, and so on down the educational hierarchy. Such differences are not a matter of poverty and pose many intriguing questions: why would people with a master's degree tend to die earlier than those with a PhD? Do we underestimate the long term effects of such things as status or (self)respect?

Brian Barry observes in his *Why Social Justice Matters* (2005) that most researchers tend to neglect that for a majority of workers paid employment is a form of servitude they have to endure on a daily basis. In contrast to the positions that academics tend to be in, many jobs are boring, don't invite creativity, they are paid badly and require subservience to superiors. Moreover, there is a particularly bad influence on health coming from the rapidly growing gig economy. Barbara Ehrenreich's (2001) participative research into the impact of the 1996 *Welfare Reform Act* on the working poor in the US gives a taste of the brutal conditions and minimal pay in a variety of jobs: 'What surprised and offended me most about the low-wage workplace … was the extent to which one must surrender one's basic civil rights and – what boils down to the same thing – self-respect' (p. 208).

Most people would like to be proud of their work, for instance, because it would make a meaningful contribution to society. Many low-wage workers do make such a meaningful contribution but do not receive the respect they deserve. To have a bullshit job, as David Graeber (2019) has called this, is even worse. It is to know that your daily efforts make no difference; in fact, to stop doing them might make the world a better place. Since bullshit jobs make no economic sense, Graeber argues, their function must be political (see Ch.2). Together, such different forms of devaluing dignified work have led to an enormous deterioration in the quality of lives of tens of millions of workers: working long hours, on more than one job, having to accept changes in shifts, without decent breaks or any flexibility to care for children or ill relatives. It appears that the old ideology of a 'free contract' on the labor market is alive and well at the cost of the most vulnerable workers who have to accept the lowest possible pay while accumulating stress with devastating health consequences. The bullshittification of tasks has also entered otherwise meaningful work such as medical practice, psychotherapy, education, nursing or home care as managers with little heart or knowledge for these professions claim that productivity would be largely improved by analyzing detailed reports about what workers have actually been doing.

Notwithstanding the importance of occupational status for respect and self-respect, there are good reasons to broaden the attention for social sources of stress beyond the work place. There is growing evidence that prolonged stressful experiences of socioeconomic adversity and social status along the life course can accumulate and negatively affect the functioning of biological regulatory systems that are crucial for health in later adulthood (Gruenewald et al. 2012; Wilkinson 2006). In investigating almost 25,000 people from 52 countries in Asia, Europe, the Middle East, Africa, Australia, and North and South America, Rosengren and others (2004) from the global *Interheart Study* extensively demonstrated that psychosocial stressors in a broad sense are independently associated with coronary heart disease. Not only stress at work but also stress at home, financial stress or stress from discrimination reduce the abilities to confront and endure the major life events that inevitably take place during the course of life, enlarging the risk of, for instance, heart attacks. From their research on the pervasive influence of poverty on physiological, psychosocial, self-regulatory processes and socio-emotional adjustment Evans and English (2002) conclude that all these processes are compromised by prolonged exposure to the stress of economic disadvantage.

The cumulative effects of socioeconomic survival stress at hormonal and cellular levels

In situations of stress, hormones such as epinephrine and norepinephrine are released from the adrenal medulla and the nervous system, as part of the fight-or-flight response, to prepare the body for action. However, with repeated activation of the stress response systems, these mechanisms become inefficient, resulting in a so-called 'allostatic load' on the body's systems.

This allostatic load is often used as an index of overall physiological dysregulation. It can contribute to the development or progression of a broad range of pathological processes, including cardiovascular disease, obesity, diabetes, susceptibility to infection, cancer, and accelerated senescence. It has been shown to increase even in very young children if they are exposed over long periods of time to burdening situations (Douthit 2006; Evans 2003; Evans & Kim 2007). Much research confirms the cumulative risk hypothesis suggesting that experiences of prolonged socioeconomic adversity will accumulate across the life course in the form of higher levels of allostatic load having a negative impact on multiple biological systems in later adulthood. This may help explain some of the lower (healthy) life expectancies we have discussed before.

In the almost 50 years that have gone by since the early Whitehall investigations numerous research projects have been undertaken leading to a more differentiated understanding of the ways in which social inequalities tend to shorten the life expectancies of disadvantaged people. More recent approaches have also focused on the ways in which daily stresses affect the body at a cellular level. As biological indicators of the ways in which socially induced stress impacts the body at a cellular level *telomeres* have drawn particular interest. This type of research has been developed in biological studies on the ways cells are changing as humans and mammals are getting older, leading in 2009 to the Nobel Prize for Elizabeth Blackburn, Carol Greider and Jack Szostak.

Telomeres cap the ends of chromosomes in order to protect them. They have been compared to the plastic tips on the ends of shoelaces, as they protect the chromosomes from falling apart and from sticking to one another. Telomeres shorten with each cell division to the point where chromosomes become functionally impaired, threatening health through a higher risk of infection and chronic disease. As people get older their telomeres will inevitably shorten but not for everyone at the same rate; depending on their situations and ways of living there are even important differences between identical twins. Confronted with the growing diversity between older adults of the same age much recent research has focused on using telomere length as a measure of biological rather than chronometric age (see Ch.4).

Over the last three decades Arline Geronimus has initiated research about the relationship between health and social inequality. Early on she was confronted with the rather shocking fact that the health of women who are in perpetual struggle with stressful circumstances, such as the daily experience of racism and social injustice in its many forms, already begins to deteriorate in young adulthood (1992; cf. 1996). Since then, Geronimus and her team have gathered evidence that the rate of telomere shortening may help to explain why those with limited access to resources and chronic exposure to stress face early onset of chronic disease. One of the research projects investigated people living in impoverished neighborhoods of Detroit (Geronimus et al. 2015). As they were working with a community-based participatory research group the researchers were able to draw blood samples and to gather detailed community survey responses from the participants. In that way they were able to combine state-of-the-art laboratory and social scientific research with local insight.

The studied population consisted of an ethnically heterogeneous population of poor African-Americans, people of Mexican descent and Whites. As earlier research had suggested that telomere length differed between racial and ethnic groups the Detroit project was eminently situated to explore this further as these different groups were living in the same or proximate areas, subject to similar environmental, economic and political disadvantages. Social inequality was operationalized as the difference between the poor and non-poor (moderate-income).

The results showed that both poor and non-poor black people had similar telomere length, which was explained by the fact that poor and non-poor African-Americans mostly lived in close proximity and were exposed to similar stressors, for instance, from racial discrimination. Surprisingly, the Mexican poor had longer telomeres than the non-poor, which was explained by the fact that many of the poorest of this group had recently immigrated and lived together in supportive enclaves. The non-poor of Mexican descent, however, were often born in the US and struggled much more with their stigmatized identity. Finally, the difference between poor and non-poor whites was dramatic, with the poor showing significantly shorter telomere length.

It appears that stress plays an important role in explaining health inequalities and that pressures and lack of support from the social context play a major role in the generation of stress. The example of the Mexican poor demonstrates the crucial importance of mutual support to share and mitigate the effects of shared discriminatory processes. Stress levels are not merely a matter of individual attitudes as the relaxation industry would have it. The cumulative biological impact of being chronically burdened with socially structured stressors appears to increase health vulnerability and to shorten life expectancy. Occupational stress is only part of the story: socially generated stress also comes from insufficient pay, from polluted and unsafe neighborhoods, racial discrimination or poor possibilities to give your children a good education.

In the following chapters I will, therefore, go beyond approaches that focus one-sidedly on material resources to explain social inequalities and acknowledge, besides resources, the crucial roles of discrimination and mutual respect (see Ch.3 and Ch.7). Both resources and respect are necessary to satisfy what Marmot has called the 'fundamental human needs for autonomy and to be integrated into society' (2006, p. 1304). Autonomy cannot be seen as something that is given with being human or becoming an adult: a society must play its role in enabling its citizens to *become* and *remain* autonomous, through, for instance, high quality education, rewarding work and democratic political institutions (see Ch.7).

This calls for a more supportive life course; all the more because the neoliberal turn in many developed countries has not only led to an erosion of many clear occupational hierarchies but especially to the loss of solid, secure positions such as those of the Whitehall civil servants. Stable occupational hierarchies are giving way to diffuse and unstable but steep social slopes. Below the extremely wealthy top, the boundaries between those who are fighting to survive and those who are doing well can shift very quickly. Besides the risks from participating in a labor market of flexible unprotected jobs there is also the risk of sliding downward if there is no adequate support in case of crises. In the US even an inadequate health insurance can offset a downward cascade that cannot be overcome. The ways in which contemporary developed societies have been reorganized under neoliberal influence support especially those who are well off, as they can buy the marketed services they need to educate their children or handle their problems. They also reap more of the health benefits that come from rewarding forms of social participation. As a consequence their chances of living long and healthy are quite different from those who cannot afford these services.

More on the perverse longevity gap

Health inequalities represent most visibly the long term consequences of broader social inequalities between the most advantaged and the most disadvantaged groups in society. The inequalities that matter, however, do not only exist between the top and the worst off but also between the intermediate layers. A large comparative study on middle-aged and older people in the US and England has demonstrated the distribution of disability and death according to wealth, instead of income, as has been the case in most research on socioeconomic status. Makaroun and colleagues (2017) built on two large longitudinal studies of nationally representative cohorts of community-dwelling older adults: the US *Health and Retirement Study* and the *English Longitudinal Study of Aging*. In both countries two age groups were investigated: a 'younger cohort' consisting of 6,233 US respondents and 4,325 English respondents aged 54 to 64 years and an 'older cohort' of 5,940 US respondents and 3,274 English respondents aged 65 to 76 years. The reason for taking the age of 65 years as a distinction between the two age groups is that around this age most safety net programs begin.

Makaroun and colleagues asked the following question: are different levels of wealth associated with different rates of death and disability in older adults in the US and England? Prior research on smaller groups of respondents (Bond Huie et al. 2003; Menchik 1993) had already found a strong inverse relationship between wealth and mortality; now, the risk for disability has been included in the project. To answer the research question all respondents were followed over 10 years, between 2002 and 2012, and grouped into five layers or 'quintiles' of wealth.

The main finding was that in both countries mortality and disability increased as wealth decreased. In the US, participants of the younger cohort who belonged to the poorest 20% (the lowest wealth quintile: ≤ $39 000) had a 17% mortality risk and 48% disability risk over 10 years, whereas in the highest wealth quintile (> $560 000) participants had a 5% mortality risk and 15% disability risk. In other words, for the poorest 20% the chances of dying or becoming disabled were three times higher than for their age peers from the wealthiest 20%. In England the inequality in mortality turned out to be even four times higher: participants of the younger cohort belonging to the 20% with the lowest amount of wealth (≤ £34,000) had a 16% mortality risk and 42% disability risk over 10 years, whereas the richest 20% (> £310,550) only had a 4% mortality risk and 17% disability risk.

For the older cohort (65 to 76 years) the mortality and disability risks were of course higher in an absolute sense, but the relative chances between the poorest and richest 20% of becoming disabled or dying remained approximately the same. Furthermore, although the age of 65 years heralds the beginning of many social support programs in both the US and England, there was no evidence to suggest that the wealth-associated inequalities changed after the age of 65 years. Another remarkable conclusion that can be drawn from this body of research is the absence of major differences between populations of the US and England in the relationships between wealth on the one hand and disability and mortality on the other hand. Something one would expect with the drastically different health care systems in these countries, where England has universal access to health care, and the US still lacks such a system.

The most shocking conclusion, however, appears to be that the chances of becoming disabled were relatively high, even for the younger cohort, if they fell into the poorest quintile. The consequences of disability in this group must be disproportionately heavy and difficult to endure. An important part of their lives is lost in the perverse longevity gap: its members are likely to spend a large part of their already shorter lives as disabled persons, while their wealthy age peers don't suffer as much from disabilities and will probably live much longer. Moreover, they are least able to mobilize the needed financial resources that would help them to adapt to their disabilities by hiring private help, making practical modifications at home, or acquiring technological assistance to improve their mobility.

Although the most disadvantaged typically experience the worst health, those with intermediate income or education levels also tend to be less healthy than the most affluent or most highly educated (Braveman et al. 2010; Minkler, Fuller-Thomson & Guralnik 2006). Studies of socioeconomic inequalities in health expectancies have generally found that these exceed socioeconomic inequalities in life expectancy, suggesting that inequalities have a stronger impact on the quality rather than the quantity of remaining life. In other words, the social gradient in healthy life expectancy or disability-free life expectancy – as in the research of Makaroun and colleagues – is steeper than for life expectancy. So steep is the first social gradient, in fact, that the lowest groups at age 45–64 tended to have illness rates comparable to higher socioeconomic groups aged 65 and over. The more disadvantaged tend to live shorter, and during these shorter lives they have to endure more miserable years as their health expectancies tend to be very short. Those, however, who are more advantaged have fair chances to live long and healthy lives.

Figure 2.1 provides a clear example of this pattern. The most deprived live almost ten years shorter but their health expectancies (indicated by the darker horizontal line) are almost twenty years shorter than the most wealthy, or as Marmot puts this: the least deprived.

On top of the evidence that there are major differences in life expectancy for people with different socioeconomic status, Marmot demonstrated that

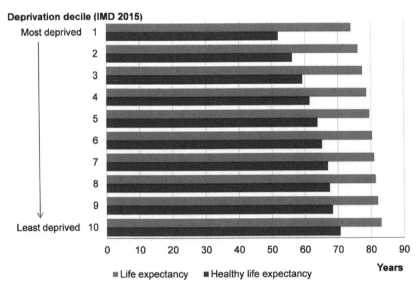

Figure 2.1 Life and healthy life expectancy at birth England 2013–2015.
Source: from *Health profile for England. A report combining Public Health England (PHE) data and knowledge on the health of the population in England in 2017*. Published July 13, 2017. https://www.gov.uk/government/publications/health-profile-for-england.

these differences become even worse when people live in parts of the country that have particularly been hit by the neoliberal abandonment of formerly important industrial regions such as North East England. From 2001 to 2003, 700 out of 100,000 men between the ages of 24–64 years with a low socioeconomic status living in North East England died, whereas this number dropped to less than 200 for those with a high socioeconomic status living in the South West.

Health care: inequality of resources, access and treatment

Universal access to health care does not solve health inequalities ... But 'I wouldn't be here today if it were not for the NHS', Stephen Hawking

One of the surprising conclusions of the Whitehall project and, for instance, the comparative Makaroun study has been that access to health care plays such a relatively minor role in explaining health inequalities. Because of England's *National Health Service*, inequality in access to health care – still a problem in the US – was ruled out as a possible cause of the social gradient. As Marmot (2001) concluded, neither health behaviors nor access to health care explain much of the socioeconomic health gap. That specific problems in the way the NHS is functioning would explain the social gradient was also unlikely because most of the other developed countries where the social gradient has been confirmed also have universal access to medical care. However, the US may produce a similar social gradient in health inequalities, but it is also a steeper one than in most other developed countries where welfare state support has been less demolished.

The ability of the health care system to improve the health of a population appears to be modest; the crucial point is not to become ill and these chances are far from evenly distributed: they are to an important degree the result of political choices. According to House & Williams (2003) the contribution of health care to the rising life expectancies over the last 250 years should not be overrated in comparison with, for instance, improvements in sanitation, working conditions, living conditions in the cities or education. With its present overemphasis on treatment of disease rather than 'upstream' prevention, interventions from the health care system are too little and too late to change the health trajectory of those who need this most.

In fact, access to medical care has been estimated by McGinnis, Williams-Russo and Knickman (2002) to account for only 10% of avoided preventable mortality in the US. However, to exploit these findings about the minor role of access to health care in comparison with more structural causes to reduce public spending on health care, without exploring better ways to invest in population health, would only aggravate health inequalities. Such a reduction would worsen the access of disadvantaged groups to necessary treatment and still not improve their situations. It would make more sense to invest in prevention in a broad sense, addressing the structural causes of social inequality such as socioeconomic insecurity, unhealthy working, and living conditions.

When Stephen Hawking travelled to Washington to receive the *Medal of Freedom* from President Obama, an American newspaper used him – wrongly assuming that he was a US citizen – as an example to highlight the deficiencies of the *National Health Service*'s 'socialized medicine': 'People such as scientist Stephen Hawking wouldn't have a chance in the UK, where the National Health Service would say the life of this brilliant man, because of his physical handicaps, is essentially worthless'. Representing countless unknown people, Hawking's clear response was: 'I wouldn't be here today if it were not for the NHS' (*The Guardian*, 11-8-2009).

But universal access to health care does not imply that the health care system remains outside of the fabric of social inequality. This also affects the actual use of free access to health care: in spite of Britain's NHS, disadvantaged groups make much less use of, for instance, medical prevention programs. Several studies have shown that women from ethnic minorities in Britain make less use of cervical screening than white women. They are more likely than white women to say that they are not at risk or they are scared of what might be found, or embarrassed or fearful of being seen by a male doctor. Moreover, in areas with more sickness and death, general practitioners have more work, longer waiting lists, less hospital support, and inherit more clinically ineffective traditions of consultation than in the healthiest areas. In disadvantaged regions hospital doctors shoulder heavier case-loads with fewer staff and equipment, more obsolete buildings, and suffer recurrent crises in the availability of beds and replacement staff. Such trends have been typified by Hart (1971) as the *inverse care law*: the availability of good medical care tends to vary inversely with the need of the population served; a law that has assumed new relevance in the context of the Covid-19 pandemic (Hainey & Katikireddi 2020). So, not merely a formal but a real equality of access to health care remains an indispensible ingredient of a good public health system. 'Universal health care' is a complex program that can be executed in different ways that will have real consequences. Yet, it appears that even if it were to treat all citizens equally well, health care would still be just one of the many needed answers to health inequalities.

Health care spending in the US

Apparently, many still think that the US health care system is the best that money can buy, at least for those who can afford its services. Yet, the US scores very low on maintaining and improving the health of its citizens, compared to other OECD countries and even to countries with much less wealth – at this point one might hesitate to say 'less developed' countries – such as Costa Rica or a large region like Kerala, India. In spite of their low economic resources these countries and regions have more favorable health indicators because they have made long-standing societal investments in education, social safety nets, and prevention-oriented medical care (Evans 2008).

Regarding outcomes there are several studies which document that US citizens have poorer health than those of other high-income countries; as we have seen above even the most advantaged tend to have worse health than their peers in other affluent nations. According to the 2016 WHO Global Healthy Observatory the US had the highest percentage of adults who were overweight or obese at 70.1%; the range for other countries was 23.8–63.4%. Based on the large US *Health and Retirement Study* and the *English Longitudinal Study of Ageing* Choi and colleagues (2020) conclude that both countries show a substantial health gap between midlife adults (55–64 years) with low income versus those with high income. The health gap between those from the bottom 20% and the top 20% of the income distribution, however, was significantly greater in the US than England. For most measures, the health of US adults appeared to be poorer than that of their peers in England, both for those from the lowest and the highest end of the income distribution. From 2017 into 2020 Emanuel and colleagues (2020) compared the performance of the US health care system on process, outcome, and patient, as well as life expectancy with Australia, Austria, Canada, Denmark, Finland, France, Germany, Japan, the Netherlands, Norway, Sweden, and Switzerland. They found that the US health care system underperformed on nearly every metric. The US ranks behind every country on causes of preventable mortality that could have been addressed by health system interventions. The researchers mention explicitly infant mortality; maternal mortality; five-year survival of patients with colon cancer, breast cancer, or childhood acute lymphocytic leukemia; and 30-day age-standardized case fatality after acute myocardial infarction. The health outcomes of white US citizens living in the 1% and 5% richest counties are better than those of average US citizens but not consistently better than those of average residents in many other developed countries.

Irene Papanicolas and colleagues (2018) have made an elaborate comparison of health care spending and results in the US versus those of 10 other high-income countries (United Kingdom, Canada, Germany, Australia, Japan, Sweden, France, the Netherlands, Switzerland, and Denmark). According to their findings the US in 2016 spent 17.8% of its gross domestic product on health care whereas spending in the other countries ranged from 9.6% (Australia) to 12.4% (Switzerland). The US spends more than $3.5 trillion per year on health care, 25% more per capita than the next highest-spending country: Switzerland, a country with a higher GDP per capita than the US. In spite of these large amounts of spending, life expectancy in the US was the lowest of these countries at 78.8 years while the other countries scored much better with 80.7–83.9 years. On the other side of the border the Canadian population could expect to live around four years longer. Infant mortality, also, turns out to be the highest in the US with 5.8 deaths per 1,000 live births in contrast to 3.6 per 1,000 for all 11 countries.

What causes this extravagant health care spending in the US with such mediocre results? Papanicolas and colleagues conclude that the drivers of spending over 2016 were, first, managerial costs, adding up to 8% in the US versus a range of 1% to 3% in the other countries. And second, pharmaceutical costs, where spending per capita was $1,443 in the US versus a range of $466 to $939 in other countries. Salaries of physicians and nurses were also higher in the US; for example, generalist physicians salaries were $218,173 in the US compared with a range of $86,607 to $154,126 in the other countries. Expensive managers and Big Pharma drive up the costs of health care in all developed countries but especially in the US they appear to have found lucrative markets.

I have earlier referred to Stiglitz, Warren Buffett and others who have concluded that too much from the wealth at the top does not come from or lead to productive investment, so that actual productivity growth remains low. Big Pharma, with its huge oligopoly and monopoly profits, presents a case in point. A recent investigation into the operations of the biggest pharmaceutical companies such as *Johnson & Johnson, Novartis* and *Pfizer* over the years 2000–2018 shows that they have been expanding their debt to be able to pay high dividends (quadrupled in 18 years) to their shareholders who are also indulged by share buybacks. These strategies reduce investment in their own research which they are seeking to compensate by scouting for promising start-ups and patents (Fernandez & Klinge 2020). Wouters (2020) has undertaken extensive research on other 'investments' that are made by this remarkable Big Pharma complex – that is supposed to further the health of citizens – notably its lobbying expenditures and campaign contributions. Between 1999 and 2018 the pharmaceutical and health products industry in the US ranked first for federal lobbying expenditures: $ 4.7 billion out of a total of $ 64.3 billion over the 20-year period. Wouters and other investigators before him have documented how the lobbying budgets have gone up when important decisions had to be made, for instance, in the drug pricing reform of 2019. Meanwhile, for the large pharmaceutical industries these political transactions have been extraordinarily profitable; for them, the money appears to be well spent. Moreover, there is the phenomenon of the 'revolving door': former legislators and regulators assuming excessively paid lobbying positions for the industries they know very well from their monitoring activities. The result of these strategies is that many important drugs have become so expensive that they only benefit those who have the privilege of optimal health insurance.

Figures of health care spending per capita are misleading. The large sums that are spent on health care disproportionally benefit those who are well off, which adds even more health advantages to those that flow from their socioeconomic position, while numerous disadvantaged people don't even have access to proper dental care.

In their 2020 book *Deaths of Despair and the Future of Capitalism* Anne Case and Angus Deaton conclude that the US health care system is a disaster: for the harm it does to health and because it is draining the livelihoods of Americans to make a rich minority richer. Big Pharma is reaping enormous profits from addictions and from pricing strategies that deny ordinary citizens access to decades old medical advances. Changing this health care system may, however, be extremely difficult because the healthcare lobby is one of the most powerful in Washington. However, according to Case and Deaton the problem is not finding enormous amounts of money: the amount that is already being spent is more than enough.

Exclusion from health care and inequality of treatment

Medicaid Workfare: Poverty as a moral failure and the exclusion from health care

Recent policies have created another battleground for vulnerable citizens at the crossroads of the labor market and the health care system. Medical care for those who depend on it has repeatedly come under severe pressure from policies that have been inspired by a deeply rooted conviction in American political culture that poverty has its origin in moral failure, rather than in circumstances that can be extremely difficult to overcome. Stephen Pimpare describes in his 2008 book *A People's History of Poverty in America* how in the 1800s poorhouses in cities such as Chicago and New York so-called work tests were introduced: in order to demonstrate their 'deservingness,' people had to carry rocks from one side of the yard to another and then carry them back again. These practices continued an even older European tradition in which poverty was associated with immoral, even criminal behavior demanding severe methods of correction.

An early example of such institutions is the late 16th century Amsterdam *Spinhuis* for young women who were found begging or roaming the streets without a respectable home or families to protect them. According to the authorities they had to be disciplined to become productive by spinning wool or making nets. Young men who were living similarly at the edge of society were destined to be re-educated in the *Rasphuis*; an institution that could be entered through a gate with the motto '*Wild beasts must be tamed*', where their days would be filled with shaving wood. Such rather unpleasant episodes in the history of the protestant work ethic inspired Michel Foucault's early work on the origin of disciplinary institutions such as the asylum for those who were found unable to behave in an orderly way (1965) and the prison (1978) for those who were seen as criminals (cf. Wacquant 2009).

In a more indirect but not necessarily less destructive way this tradition resurfaced in political rhetoric of the Reagan-era about 'welfare queens' who were sitting around the house collecting checks. The title of the large 1995 New York 'workfare' program instigated by Mayor Rudy Giuliani – *The Work Experience Program* – emphasized once more that those who were dependent on social benefits had to get accustomed to work. However, according to Pimpare, arguments in favor of work requirements for those who receive social benefits have mostly been based on lack of knowledge about the populations that have been forced into such programs. If we confront the suspicions that inspired these policies with evidence from the 2015 *National Health Interview Survey* it becomes clear that these programs try, indeed, to solve problems that don't exist; at least not to any degree that would justify these expensive large oppressive programs. On the contrary, these programs are creating additional problems and unnecessary hardship for many vulnerable people who try to survive in a harsh society. The data show that practically all healthy Medicaid beneficiaries were already working. To be more precise: the 48% of adults covered by the Medicaid expansion who were not working were permanently in poor health or disabled, having serious physical or mental limitations caused by conditions like cancer, stroke, heart disease, cognitive or mental health disorders, arthritis, pregnancy, or diabetes. To demand that they do the physically demanding work that is typical for low-wage jobs makes no sense. The large majority of the other 52% were already working. Only 13% of the total category of adults covered by Medicaid's expansion were able-bodied and not working; the large majority of these people, however, were in school, seeking work or unable to work because they had to care for family members.

The misguided expectation has been that, as a result of 'stern but righteous' policies, large numbers of able-bodied lazy people would move into steady jobs once they had learned to appreciate the virtue and joy of working. This expectation neglects the structural realities that workers at the lower end of the labor market face, where short term contracts prevail, jobs don't come with benefits or collective bargaining rights and the paychecks do not lift their families out of poverty. Often these workers even need support such as child care or transportation subsidies to be able to continue working.

In cases where medical care is interrupted because people are excluded from Medicaid (cf. Estes & DiCarlo 2019), they may go very quickly from able-bodied to disabled, increasing the risk of collateral damage for all recipients, including putting their families at risk of homelessness and hunger. The costs of a bureaucratic apparatus forcing a small unemployed minority of Medicaid recipients into a labor market that will not lift them out of poverty are impressive in terms of human suffering and financial costs. The punitive approach may satisfy some misguided feelings of social justice but is bound to increase the problems it aims to solve.

Another pressing problem at the lower end of the labor market that is undermining the health status of the workers and may even prevent them from seeing a doctor is work and schedule precarity. This has become a more general feature of labor markets as employers since the neoliberal turn have gradually transferred more of the risks and uncertainties of doing business onto workers and their households. Work has become especially precarious in the US where many workers have experienced an erosion of job quality; not only reductions in the real value of their wages, loss or reduction of benefits such as retirement plans and health insurance, but also an increase in job insecurity. Almost 60% of the US labor force is paid by the hour; so, fluctuations in hours automatically translate into unreliable earnings. The large majority of these hourly workers in the US, who are active, for instance, in the retail and food service sectors, are confronted with unstable and unpredictable work schedules with variable work hours, short advance notice of weekly schedules, and frequent last-minute changes to shift timing.

Schneider & Harknett (2020) from the *Berkeley Shift Project* have studied the effects of this type of shift work which differs from the more traditional forms of shift work with, for instance, regular changes from daytime to night work. Having to work with unstable and unpredictable work sche-dules increases not only household economic insecurity, it also leads to more tensions between the demands of work and the needs of family life such as caring for children, family meals or school drop-offs and pickups. This can be quite disruptive for family life and may lead to all kinds of behavioral problems in children. Moreover, the adults face increased psy-chological distress and diminished sleep quality with detrimental effects on their health that can easily lead to a downward spiral.

Schedule precarity disproportionately affects low-income workers of color and female workers who are overrepresented in the service sector. As so often, the negative health consequences of unstable and unpredictable schedules contribute to the health inequalities by race, class, and gender. The 2019 *Sche-dules That Work Act* requires that workers receive additional pay when they are put 'on-call' without any guarantee that work will be available; when they are sent home early on slow days or receive schedule changes with less than two weeks' notice. It remains doubtful, however, whether 'additional pay' will really help these disadvantaged workers who are still stuck with precarious employment and the negative effects of unpredictable work schedules. More-over, the rapidly growing gig economy appears to be one of the latest blessings of the free market, where 'independent' workers are hired for short-term commitments so that corporations can avoid paying for health care insurance or pensions. Again, societal risks are transferred to the most vulnerable on the markets (cf. Freeman & Gonos 2009).

Another example from a potentially much longer list are recent threats by the US government to cut off people receiving the extended benefit from the Supplemental Nutrition Assistance Program. The editors of the *Journal of the American Medical Association* (JAMA) have responded with indignation: 'As physicians, with the authority to spend almost unlimited dollars on health care—much of which is not helpful—our inability to get patients the food they need is absurd' (Covinsky and Katz 2020, p. 606). The richest country in the world threatens its most vulnerable citizens with taking away the food that they need; because they do not deserve it or might sell it for a profit?

Racial discrimination in US health care institutions

Restricted access to health care can become a nightmare for those who need it desperately. But the story of inequality in health care does not end when patients have crossed the threshold of a hospital. After gaining access, inequalities are not over; problems of access are just the early stages in a chain of events in which health care institutions reproduce and even amplify pre-existing inequalities (Arber et al. 2004).

Researchers from the *Institute of Medicine* have undertaken a large scale project to study the extent of inequalities in the types and quality of health services received by US racial and ethnic minorities in comparison to non-minorities. Their report *Unequal Treatment: Confronting Racial and Ethnic Disparities in Health Care* (Smedley, Stith & Nelson 2003) documents important differences in the ways in which racial minorities are being treated in comparison to white people, irrespective of the type of health care facility. Even when insurance status, income, education, age, and severity of conditions were comparable, African-Americans and minorities in general were less likely to receive medical care according to standardized protocols or even routine medical procedures, such as appropriate cardiac medications, bypass surgery, kidney dialysis or transplants. But they were more likely to receive less-desirable procedures, such as lower limb amputations for diabetes and other conditions. Lutfey and Freese (2005) came to similar conclusions for patients with low socioeconomic status.

In trying to answer the question why such serious inequalities occur, the researchers conclude that 'multiple factors' are responsible but that racism or 'unconscious bias' by health care professionals plays a prominent role. They point to the fact that negative beliefs about race are deeply ingrained in US culture, even deeper than those who reject racism may be aware of. Some of the origins of such 'unconscious bias' have been explored by a content analysis of the books, newspapers, and other materials that numerous college educated US adults are likely to have read. In these respected texts the word 'black' was most frequently paired with, in order of frequency, 'poor', 'violent', 'religious', 'lazy', 'cheerful', and 'dangerous'. 'White' was most frequently paired with 'wealthy', 'progressive', 'conventional', 'stubborn', 'successful', and 'educated' (Verhaeghen, Aikman & Van Gulick, 2011). Against this background it should come as no surprise that negative stereotypes about, for instance black persons, play a disturbing role in the behavior even of those who are committed to principles of racial equality and sympathize with people who have experienced injustice. The report from the *Institute of Medicine* confirms, indeed, that health professionals generally care deeply about their poor and minority patients, but that the problem of unequal care may nonetheless be rooted in racism and that very little progress has been made over the years. Even though, in 2008, the *American Medical Association* apologized to the black community and black physicians for racist practices of the past, more profound reforms remain necessary.

From the side of the minorities there is also a problem of mistrust. Historical events such as the Tuskegee Syphilis Study play a role in the collective memory of African Americans, and their lack of confidence grows at every moment they sense racism in health care as an institution: in hospitals, health clinics or insurance plans. It appears that most people trust their own physician, no matter what race they are. But that doesn't mean they trust the larger institution. Apparently, more minority health care providers are needed, especially since they are more likely to serve in minority and medically underserved communities. Also, more interpreters should be available in clinics and hospitals to overcome language barriers that may affect the quality of care. As an African American nurse in the *Institute of Medicine* study (2012) has put it:

> I don't think necessarily you have to be an African American to provide good care to African Americans, but if you're not, you really need to be aware of the culture and some of the issues in that culture, and really look at how you feel about dealing with people from that culture.

There appears to be growing awareness about the need to increase recruitment of underrepresented minority students in medical schools which might help to improve this situation (Hill et al. 2020; Hill, Gross & Boatright 2020). Language barriers are, however, not the only problems that must be overcome: advice to 'visit the website', experiments with telemedicine, and other digital service often collide with the reality of a lack of access to the necessary technology, the absence of home monitoring tools, or insufficient digital skills. Developing such skills should become a priority as they are increasingly necessary for a wide range of tasks, such as education, housing, social services, job applications, or food delivery in communities with pandemic outbreaks. Although telemedicine might help patients, on the condition that it is set up and maintained with great care, it can also increase health inequity. Such more specific inequalities are a continuation and a reproduction of broader inequalities in society that are contributing to worse health and life expectancies for members of minority groups in comparison to better situated citizens. It is, indeed, much better not to have to live in situations that increase the chances of becoming sick. This would benefit both disadvantaged citizens and society at large.

Ageism in health care

An ageist culture is, basically, disrespectful to all older persons, whether wealthy or poor. However, ageism will typically strike when older people find themselves in situations of vulnerability and helplessness (see Ch.4). So, to have an ageist culture in institutions where people are per definition vulnerable, such as in health care, will be harmful to all older people who happen to get there. In health care there is often a reluctance to work with older people. Caring for them is usually seen as having low prestige because there would not be much to achieve in terms of a cure of chronic diseases and even less in prospects of returning to a productive life. But to conclude that the lives of older people are basically residual and caring for them practically pointless remains inhumane. We can only hope that Levenson's (1981) statement that medical students' attitudes reflect 'prejudice against older persons surpassed only by their racial prejudice' (p. 161) is gradually losing its ground.

This remains doubtful. Research on the attitudes of beginning medical students towards older people shows that ageism is part of a broader culture that pervades and darkens attitudes towards later life (Reuben et al. 1995; Wilson, Kurrle & Wilson, 2018). Over the last decades there have been a large number of reports about the treatment of older people in the health care sector, by scientists as well as journalists and – in spite of the admirable work of many of those who work in difficult circumstances – the results are shocking: stealing money from older people, physical or sexual assaults, and a general denigrating attitude (Scrutton 1990). Among the growing population of older adults, elder abuse is prevalent with more than one in ten reporting neglect or at least one form of emotional, physical, financial, or sexual mistreatment in the past year (Sirey et al. 2015). Shortage of funds and personnel are helping to raise stress and reduce the time and attention available for older patients.

Beyond ageist attitudes and practices by health care professionals there are some more structural mechanisms at work. There are some indications that the organizational settings and systems in which care is delivered to older patients contribute to a dissatisfaction of medical professionals that may surface in ageist attitudes (Samra et al. 2015). Other examples include an overemphasis on rigid procedures and technology-driven tests with little tolerance for the sometimes complicated and time-consuming process of geriatric care, combined with insufficient numbers of geriatrics trained providers (Wyman, Shiovitz-Ezra & Bengel 2018). Moreover, upper age limits on funding for diagnostic tests and screening for several types of cancer or vascular disease are common practice, despite the high prevalence of such diseases among older adults. And, finally, older patients are typically excluded from the development and testing of new forms of treatment. According to the research of Witham and McMurdo (2007) persons who are older than 65 years are systematically underrepresented in clinical drug trials for cancer and coronary artery disease, in spite of medical data that incidence for both conditions increases with age. The same trend has been observed in research on intervention for strokes and on stroke rehabilitation: in both cases, there is evidence of widespread age bias, as the mean age of participants in clinical trials reported in the stroke literature turned out to be a decade younger than the average age of stroke patients (Hadbavna & O'Neill 2013). In the context of evidence based medicine this means that if there is no evidence – because of lacking research – which supports the use of new treatment for older people, they are not likely to receive this. The consequence may be that they will profit much less from the possible benefits of medical innovation.

Myopic diagnoses: individual health choices in a pathogenic society

We have been hearing a lot about the importance of adult lifestyle in relation to health and life expectancies, with an emphasis on negative aspects such as smoking, excessive drinking or drug abuse and on positive aspects such as exercise and healthy nutrition. There is, indeed, a wealth of evidence that, especially, detrimental health behavior of adults plays an important role in the genesis of chronic diseases. Such advice makes sense but we need a broader perspective on the upstream forces because health behavior does not originate as a purely spontaneous or autonomous individual process without being influenced by social contexts. The discussion of research on *The Long Arm of Childhood* and *Fetal Origins of Adult Disease* (see Ch.3) will show, for instance, that societal conditions already impact maternal and fetal health with important consequences for heart conditions and mortality in later life. This does not imply that childhood conditions would directly determine adult heart disease: the influence of the *Long Arm of Childhood* appears also to be mediated by adult lifestyle and societal circumstances along the life course.

After these considerations it may seem strange that Brian Barry in his *Why Social Justice Matters* (2005) debunks 'life style' as a red herring. A problem with the issue of lifestyle is, however, that it is too often misused to shift the responsibility for bad health, even if it affects large populations, to the individuals who would be to blame for their own problems absolving public policy of all responsibilities. Systematic differences in health expectancies between groups with a different socioeconomic status strongly suggest, however, that these outcomes are not merely a matter of individual decision. According to Critser's study *Fat Land. How Americans became the Fattest People in the World* (2003) significant numbers of the middle and upper class have been experiencing huge weight gains, but the largest concentration of the obese, regardless of race, ethnicity and gender, can still be found in the poorest sections of the American nation. Such evidence suggests that obesity is a more general development in society but, again, with most devastating consequences for the citizens who are already the most vulnerable. In view of research on the long-term effects of early obesity (cf. Ferraro & Kelley-Moore 2003) it is quite worrying that many schools have heavily reduced physical education and that the poverty of their resources have apparently necessitated them to allow the sale of fast food, including supersized soft drinks and ice cream within their walls. Many of these products contain extreme concentrations of sugar and bad fats, contributing to hitherto unknown numbers of Type 2 Diabetes in children.

Changing trends in alcohol consumption or drug abuse leading to the opioid crisis with its many deaths can hardly be explained by spontaneous health behavior. In case of the opioid crisis it makes more sense to look at the impact of social abandonment in the wake of the financial crisis. This period of austerity, with the biggest public services cuts in the most deprived areas, has led to rises in child poverty, homelessness, food poverty, despair deaths and a general deterioration in mental health (Taylor-Robinson, Lai, Whitehead & Barr 2019; Loopstra et al. 2015, 2016a, 2016b). In England, for instance, increasing inequalities across a range of causes of death have been observed during these years along with rising child poverty that caused an unprecedented rise in infant mortality (Kontopantelis et al. 2018; Steel et al. 2018; Taylor-Robinson et al. 2019a). It is hardly convincing to explain such developments by pointing to irresponsible individuals who have suddenly decided in large numbers to change their life style. Telling someone who has started to drink heavily because he has lost his job and has been cast out into the street, that he should stop drinking, without any help in improving the underlying situation does not promise to be an effective approach. There is, however, ample evidence showing that public investments improve health outcomes, and that disinvestment has the opposite effect (Barr, Bambra & Whitehead 2014; Loopstra, McKee et al. 2016).

Can good or bad health be explained by good or bad health choices?

According to Perry (2002) childhood neglect transforms the expression of genetic potential and, generally, epigenetics research on the actualization of genetic predispositions affirms the importance of gene–environment interactions over the life course (Gluckman and Hanson 2006). In their study *Mismatch: Why Our World No Longer Fits Our Bodies* (2005) Gluckman and

Hanson argue that surviving under-nutrition (such as low birth weight) does not prevent robust adult health unless one assumes sedentary life and high-fat diet, which may then lead to harmful health consequences. Obesity appears to be caused partly by predispositions that may be formed in early childhood but its full development into a disease depends also on what is happening later along the life course. Although gestation and early child-hood deserve special attention as important systems are locked in during these crucial developmental processes, apart from dramatic situations or genetic defects, negative predispositions can often be prevented from turn-ing into disease if the environment becomes and remains more favorable and supportive. Negative and positive potentials are built up in early life and continue to have influence on the organism, but their actualization largely depends on their continuing interactions with environmental contexts. In adverse circumstances negative predispositions can lead to serious health problems, but in more favorable contexts they may remain latently in the background. So, a healthy life style does play a role, but not in isolation from environmental conditions.

In a highly unequal society, location matters. A poor neighborhood will most probably have poor educational possibilities and the opposite will be true for a rich area. Choices such as beginning to work as soon as possible or postponing this to attend college will also be heavily influenced by the available material and cultural resources. In contrast to the many theories about the choices that parents and children have to make regarding educa-tional opportunities it must be feared that many young people are sorted at a very young age for stratified educational tracks by their family back-grounds and the opportunity structure of the area where they live.

As university graduates embark on an inspiring career, their chances grow that they will live relatively long and healthy lives. But does this mean that their choices have been determined by such prospects of longevity? When the university graduates find good jobs they are most probably not excited because they see their chances increase to live long and healthily but because the job looks promising, interesting and it pays well. Because the whole context of those who work in well paying jobs is likely to bring many other advantages such as relatively clean air, healthy food, a good house, medical insurance, regular working hours, holidays and respect from others, they will probably live longer and remain healthier than those who dropped out of high school and began to do underpaid heavy physical work at a young age. Uncontextualized 'choices' for a certain life style are abstract constructs that not only risk ignoring the range of options that are available in given situations but also the intentions of the persons concerned.

Most people would agree that being in good health is very important for them. However, this does not mean that health figures predominantly in the choices they make. This may change when they are forced to pay more attention to the health consequences of what they do because they have a sensitive condition; looking back on the life course from the vulnerabilities of older persons may lead to a perspective in which health choices appear to be more important than they actually were at the time. Is maintaining good health the main consideration when we think about the major choices in life or even leisure activities? Many people love to take risks and pay a lot of money to enjoy them: they travel extensively during their holidays although it might be safer to stay at home; some like to climb mountains, others like to race down a mountain by ski or on a bike, to jump out of a plane or into the deep with a long rubber band around their ankles. It appears that activities are appealing not because they are unhealthy but because they are attractive and rewarding to us. All these activities are not typically those of disadvantaged people which indicates already that they have more limited choices. Meanwhile, we can have a cautious eye on the health risks we take with them: how many drinks can we have in one day? What are the risks of climbing this hill? In this more limited sense we might still speak about health choices.

Moreover, these balancing acts are usually about leisure time: a time when we have more room to do as we please. These are choices about unhealthy snacking and drinking while watching a movie, dining with friends or leisure activities and holidays. And they are important but to define health risks in terms of individual choices narrows the perspective on what needs to be done to make responsible health behavior possible, such as monitoring the quality of healthy food and making sure it can be bought nearby at a reasonable price. Beyond leisure time, health choices enter a territory that can much less be controlled individually. When it's about the kind of work, the sort of house or the area people live in, we cannot simply assume that there has been a choice between several attractive options. Of course, a wealthy person will be able to move out of a bad area – if he were to live there to begin with – but such options are limited for more disadvantaged citizens.

Young workers in low pay jobs may nevertheless feel strong and healthy for many years but in midlife they may begin to feel less vigorous as they get stuck in neighborhoods with much pollution, noise, unemployment and bad public facilities. Meanwhile, many of their age peers who were fortunate enough to get adequate material and cultural support, entered good jobs and were able to move into better neighborhoods will remain much longer in good health. Such influences of neighborhoods and communities on social life and health cannot be reduced to the choices of their individual residents. In his book *The End Game* (2015) Abramson demonstrates the importance of neighborhood and community support in contrast to the tendency to see the lives of older people as determined by their ages and health complaints:

> Those in more affluent areas have access to a greater variety of services, and these tend to be of a higher quality ... Seniors living in the more

affluent neighborhood were likewise better supported by all manner of auxiliary services, from meal programs to volunteer visitors to adult education.

(2015: 138)

Even residents who are not interested in improving the qualities of their neighborhoods will profit from others who do pay attention to environmental concerns or quality of community care. Advantaged people are likely to be protected from risks and burdens that more deprived others are not protected from: they have better houses that are better maintained and built on safer spots; they drive safer cars, have better health care, enjoy more respect from others, have more bargaining power and more influential friends. Neighborhoods are very different in aspects that are important for people of all ages but especially for older citizens. They would probably benefit from safe and comfortable public transportation, community activities, mutual support, grocery stores, visiting programs or quality health care nearby.

To reconstruct health outcomes as the results of individually chosen lifestyles is abstract and misleading. This conclusion is supported by Robert Sampson's study of neighborhoods in *Great American City* (2012). In contrast to views that we act solely as individual agents who choose our fate independently from our surroundings, or are helplessly at the mercy of global forces beyond our control, he shows the vital importance of communities and neighborhoods. Instead of proclaiming individual resilience as the way to solve social problems it might make more sense to increase community resilience (e.g. Chandra et al. 2010). Such 'social life worlds', as Habermas (1987) would call them, that depend on communicative action of their participants without being primarily guided by the state or market forces, have a strong influence on a remarkably wide variety of social phenomena, including crime, health, civic engagement, home foreclosures, teen births, altruism, leadership networks, and immigration. In a similar vein Abramson (2015), in his study of evolving inequality among older people, emphasizes the importance of social network inequalities. Social networks matter and being connected is better than being isolated, but networks that look similar on the outside may give very different results and function very differently. The often observed shrinkage of networks with age does not merely homogenize or level down the differences between older people, but also highlights differences in the vulnerabilities or strengths of their networks. What is important is not only how many people you consider to be your friends or who you know, but what facilities are nearby and what kind of resources the people from your network will be able to provide. Do they have time to help without losing pay? Do they have a car, digital skills, or are they able to hire extra help, to assist in dealing with bureaucratic institutions or medical authorities? Such network qualities stratify the options that are available to seniors, accumulating advantage and disadvantage without actions of the persons concerned.

When academic culture meets cultures of survival

It is easy to misunderstand the health behavior of poor people because their situations are usually very different from the situations that researchers, politicians or health professionals tend to live in. Powers & Faden (2006), astonishingly, found in their research among HIV positive poor women that they were not worried about getting AIDS because they did not expect to live that long. Daily problems such as violence, homelessness, or drug overdoses had drained the capacity to envision a life for themselves. Such findings shed another light on seemingly irrational, self-destructive behavior that may actually be less irrational and more realistic in view of limited options, hopelessness and early death (Boardman et al. 2001; Galea and Vlahov 2002; Gold et al. 2002).

Similar problems will be relevant for efforts to reduce smoking, which still contributes to nearly half of the male mortality in the lowest social class in England, Wales, Poland and North America (Jha et al. 2006). Research by Leventhal et al. (2019) has shown that cumulative socioeconomic disadvantage not only accounts for much of the prevalence of smoking among US adults of 25 years and older; but that these disadvantages increased between 2008 and 2017. Besides the problem of initiation in this highly addictive habit by a culture where smoking is advertised as cool and sexy – with more advertising for tobacco and alcohol in neighborhoods with relatively bad socioeconomic conditions (Adler & Newman 2002) – smoking cessation can be a rather abstract goal for disadvantaged people. For them, it provides probably some stress relief and smoking may be seen as a problem that is largely exaggerated by others who are not confronted on a daily basis with unemployment, hunger and bad housing. Programs that have been successful in helping to stop smoking have focused on these contextual issues in addition to education about the risks of smoking, especially during pregnancy (Emmons 2000)

In a rather improvising sketch of the consumption culture of survival, based on different forms of research, the following traits stand out. First, there seems to be a deeply rooted conviction that opportunities to eat as much as you like are scarce. So, when fast food chains offer cheap all-you-can-eat menus this can easily lead to eating more than would be healthy. Second, some choices of what to eat have become an anachronism: they were more adequate in the past, when hard physical work was much more common and calories were more easily burned. Third, major parts of the population – not just poor people – suffer from a continuation of patterns of passive leisure although it is no longer a well deserved rest after a long day of physical activity. Such a sedentary life style often leads to long-term health damage. Fourth, it appears that obesity is often interpreted in terms of 'being big' or physically impressive and strong – a residue of an outdated culture of physical prowess – instead of being a sign of unhealthiness. Fifth, the ways in which health advice is received betray rebellion and mistrust in experts who may be seen as typically disagreeing amongst each other and keen on controlling or even taking away that little freedom that lays in consumption. As an older man once told me: 'These days you are not allowed any more to eat big steaks, or even meat; you are forbidden to drink or smoke; in short to have fun like we have always done ... If I can't eat, smoke or drink as I like, what's left to live for?' Sixth, as poor people have other problems to worry about than the more advantaged, they may just enjoy being irresponsible in the sense of giving themselves completely to eating, drinking, smoking or whatever they enjoy. This may extend into daily life in the form of stress relieving consumption of comfort goods: a moment of freedom for yourself. Finally, In her 2001 book *Nickel and Dimed: About (Not) Getting on in America* Barbara Ehrenreich gives several examples of the importance of comfort goods such as smoking, and concludes that smoking, heavy alcohol consumption, and eating for comfort are most likely responses to anxiety and stress. So, unhealthy behaviors are not per se irrational; they are also ways to cope with bad situations that leave little opportunities to choose well. It may well be a sign of an intellectual, information based life style, to assume that such behavior will change by improving information about its possible negative effects without changing the situations in which problematic choices become appealing.

Health inequalities are indicators of the long term effects of unequal opportunities to participate in a society; reducing them to individual choices, access to institutions or information neglects the ways in which strategies of interacting and negotiating are formed by culture. Such cultural resources vary between groups and are influenced by shared experiences with school, bosses, bureaucracies, doctors or police in an unequal society: culture is 'forged in prior experiences that are organized by inequality' (Abramson 2015, p.142). Culture functions as an interface between, on the one hand, experiences of inequality along the life course and, on the other hand, strategies and styles in the present. If health interventions are conceived from the perspective of academics who are keen on being on top of the latest scientifically based information they will tend to reach only those groups in society that will gladly accept this from experts. There is a danger that those who need this least will benefit most, while those who need it most will benefit least so that the basic inequality may even be reproduced by interventions that intend to change this.

Covid-19 and the neglect of pre-existing social conditions

The Covid-19 pandemic has not generally been perceived as originating from individual choices, although these have become a major issue as the pandemic developed, but as caused by an infectious disease that would hit especially older people. This corroborates a popular pattern of explaining major problems: if they are not caused by individual choices they must be caused by nature; an explanation that typically serves to occlude constitutive social factors. Beyond the mutations of a vicious virus and responsible individual behavior the pandemic has, however, especially gained momentum because of a long term lack of protection of disadvantaged groups. The unequal mortality rates from Covid-19 have made the pre-existing conditions of social inequality more visible (cf. Christakis 2020).

The *Gerontological Society of America COVID-19 Task Force* has outlined many questions that need to be explored in the coming years (Resnick & Zimmerman 2021). A major question is certainly this one: why has Covid-19 hit ethnic minorities so much harder than others? (cf. Hamler et al. 2022; Bui, Peng, Mutchler & Burr 2021). One of the answers that has been given is that they are more likely to be exposed to the virus because they disproportionally work in 'essential' jobs that are poorly paid and come with few welfare protections: in cleaning or care; as supermarket staff, truckers or security guards. Jobs that include regular and close contact with the public, increasing their risk of infection. Even when their colleagues and family members were dying they were expected – and often were proud – to continue their work because the well being and even survival of many others depended on this. Essential workers are also more likely to use ill-maintained public transportation, live in deprived neighborhoods of cities, and in crowded multigenerational homes, increasing their exposure to any virus. Many disadvantaged persons live with an essential worker and have a higher likelihood of exposure even when they can shelter at home, where women disproportionally feel or are held responsible for providing care to family members with Covid-19 with all the risks of overburdening or becoming infected.

When people from ethnic minorities catch the virus they are more likely to die from it than white people because of pre-existing conditions such as obesity, diabetes and heart disease that are more common among ethnic minorities as a result of accumulated health insults since early life. Moreover, they often have more limited access to health care, so that they receive medical attention in a more advanced stage of their illness. Those with limited digital skills or English proficiency, and especially limited health literacy, also are more likely to have worse health outcomes as they are not adequately informed about the dangers of contamination. Finally, undocumented migrants and their relatives have been reluctant to go to testing centers as they were afraid of the authorities. They may even be 'essential workers', a label which reflects society's needs but does not mean that society will honor or reward those workers after the pandemic is over; nor, more importantly, improve their socioeconomic position and protection in the future.

'Working from home' has become a much used phrase to typify the Covid-19 reality of the workplace. Many popular characterizations of the changes in society by politicians, scientists and journalists presuppose privileged positions and tend to influence the policies proposed to bring solutions but that actually reproduce inequalities. Working from home is a privilege that many people don't have and even when someone has this opportunity the home situation can be hugely unequal, from a nice, spacious house with a garden to a small overcrowded apartment that will drive you up the wall. The results have been more domestic violence and child abuse, mental health crises and suicides. In many disadvantaged communities computers are still scarce and Wi-Fi unreliable, and what if you do have a well functioning computer but also three children who need to study from home?

Before the outbreak of the pandemic many older people had already been confronted with difficulties acquiring healthy food due to insufficient financial resources. As the economy shut down and stay at home orders went into place, such food insecurity became an even bigger problem, also for younger adults who lost their jobs and incomes. Older adults were particularly vulnerable, given that they had to navigate new ways of procuring food while they sheltered in place to avoid exposure to the virus. But the pandemic has become a catastrophe for the residents in nursing homes and assisted living that will probably never be fully documented.[3] The *Long Term Care Community Coalition* has criticized 'the nursing home industry, through its multi-million dollar lobbying firms and associated academics' for refusing to take responsibility for resident safety and care in the face of a growing death toll.[4] Their report documents how too many nursing homes had a significant history of lax infection controls, lacked safe staffing going into the pandemic, and failed, even during the pandemic, to implement basic infection control practices.

The disproportionally high number of Covid-19 deaths in nursing homes is the result of much more than the decline in immune systems and increasing health conditions of those who reside in nursing homes. Indifference and ageism led to living arrangements that create opportunities for the virus to spread. According to a comparative study by Neil Gandal and colleagues (2020) from Tel Aviv University European countries and US states with fewer care homes also had fewer Covid-19 deaths, all else being equal. Generally, long term care is underfunded, understaffed and inadequately regulated: 'the ugly stepchild of health policy' (Werner, Hoffman & Coe 2020). The residents of care homes may have been most at risk but they still remained at the back of the queue when it came to things like testing or supplying personal protective equipment. Consequently, workers in care homes were about twice as likely to die of Covid-19 as their colleagues in hospitals. All this shows, again, the urgency of reforming care for older citizens. This will not be easy when even accountability for bad practices is evaded: as a bizarre answer to the catastrophic events more than half of the US states have granted legal immunity to nursing homes.

Hospitals were overwhelmed with patients and painfully confronted with the failure of governments to stockpile the necessary personal protective equipment. Although nobody knew *when which* specific virus might lead to a pandemic, it has been expected for years that a pandemic was inevitable or at least highly probable. Yet the health care system wasn't adequately prepared. This has caused immense suffering and death, especially amongst older people. According to popular ageist assertions these would be 'old people who were about to die anyway' but there were many victims like the mother and grandmother of the doctor at a clinic who was interviewed by CNN about the initial health care chaos and told the interviewer, by the way, that he had lost both of them within one week. They drove themselves to the hospital and didn't come out alive.

Hospitals are not free from structural inequalities 'outside'; on the contrary, they are part of these and actively reproducing them. Some experiences of the Dutch intensive care doctor Jan Bakker who was working in New York through the Covid-19 crisis illustrate this.[5] He speaks with indignation about the American healthcare system and the inequality it highlights. 'What this crisis has made clear is that the US healthcare system is pretty much the worst system we know in the developed world. It is best if you have money and want to get every possible treatment until your last breath. But if you're broke, you're screwed!' Dr. Bakker works at the Langone hospital, which is affiliated with New York University and is known as a rich hospital for well-insured New Yorkers. At the Langone doctors, nurses and other healthcare workers were scrambling when the number of occupied ICU beds suddenly increased from 24 to 200. But the situation was reasonably under control and there was more than enough protective gear. Bakker, however, also works shifts at the Bellevue Public City Hospital, just a few blocks from Langone, where the situation was completely different. Here, healthcare workers feared for their lives due to a lack of protective gear which they had to improvise by using garbage bags. Their patients often had untreated health issues; some of them would only inject insulin twice a week because they could not afford the daily dose. Bakker also noticed an astonishing lack of cooperation among the hospitals. In the public hospital he proposed contacting the top institutions in the city, to arrange for patients to be distributed among various hospitals to relieve pressure. This is regular practice in the Netherlands where in crises patients may even be brought to intensive care in Germany or Belgium and vice versa. 'There was a long silence, and then they chuckled. Yes, nice idea, we are not going to put any energy into that, because nothing will come of it. We're struggling enough, they said, to make sure they don't hijack our nurses. They offer more salary than we do.'

As health inequalities are to an important degree the consequences of social inequalities similar health inequalities will also be found in EU countries and their health care systems will also contribute to these outcomes. But these problems appear to be much more extreme in the US. The ideology of a free market in health care has led to distributional inequality and entrepreneurial strategies in for profit hospitals that are extremely problematic in terms of social justice or health justice. Richard Horton, the editor-in-chief of the leading medical journal *The Lancet* published in 2021 *The COVID-19 Catastrophe* struggling with the question: how did the UK and the US, two of the richest, most powerful and most scientifically advanced countries in the world get it so wrong, and cause such ongoing pain for their citizens? Answers cannot evade the erratic political leadership that was hawking 'Taking Back Control' and 'Making America Great Again' while, at the same time, combining indifference towards the suffering of citizens with messages that everything would be under control. Trump's politicizing of the very existence of, and personal protection from, the dangerous new virus is another case in point.

But we need to look behind the headlines of breaking news that tend to reduce historical developments to daily events. As a consequence of the neoliberal turn the supportive life course that had gradually been built up in the past has been crumbling except for the sectors that generate large profits. The result has been an impressive loss of public health workers, especially public health nurses who were entrenched in the community, went door to door, talking to people who would trust them. Decades of disinvestment have left the public health system and social care in jeopardy, with a fatal blow during the decade of austerity that was supposed to solve the financial crisis in many developed countries. The inevitable result has been a further weakening of population health and a poor protection of many communities against a dangerous virus.

Another fundamental problem has been the dominance of biomedical perspectives in approaching the pandemic (cf. Estes & DiCarlo 2019). The cause of the Covid-19 crisis was identified as an infectious disease; accordingly, interventions focused on cutting lines of viral transmission in order to control the spread of the pathogen. The attention for pre-existing conditions was limited to medical factors instead of broadening the concept of pre-existing conditions to constitutive social inequalities. These structural origins of pre-existing medical conditions are lost in medical files although they are plausibly connected to patterns of inequality that are deeply embedded in society. Disadvantaged social contexts facilitate the spread of non-communicable diseases such as obesity, heart disease or diabetes that interact with infectious diseases. Meanwhile, average life expectancies in the US further came down by about 18 months in 2020, marking the largest annual decline since the Second World War, according to data from the CDC's National Center for Health Statistics, with Covid-19 deaths accounting for nearly 75% of the decline (Arias et al. 2021). The average number should not lead to a neglect of the fact that the drop in life expectancies has been much worse for Hispanics and Black Americans. No matter how effective a treatment or protective a vaccine, without effective intervention in these constitutive social contexts there will be no adequate answer to future pandemics.

Is individual bad health the main cause of socioeconomic inequality or is it the other way around?

Now that we have discussed a broad range of issues related to social inequalities and health inequalities over the life course, we can try to answer this important question. Inequalities of income and wealth, education, segregation and discriminatory processes, such as misogyny, racial discrimination and ageism, appear to generate and reproduce health inequalities. However, bad health can also have major consequences for occupation, income and wealth. This has been called the problem of a bidirectional connection between socioeconomic status and health; although, of course, educational status as an index of socioeconomic status is mostly not affected if somebody becomes ill.

Besides the usual gathering of 'risk factors' and other data, there have also been some discussions about the probable causes behind these developments (e.g. Wilkinson & Pickett 2015; Coburn 2015; Pickett & Wilkinson 2015). Kröger, Pakpahan and Hoffmann (2015) have given a transdisciplinary review of the literature of the last 20 years assessing the relative importance of the *health selection* hypothesis versus the *social causation* hypothesis. The first hypothesis states that differences in health lead to differences in social position: those who are in good health are able to achieve favorable positions in society while those in poor health have worse chances and will only achieve low-status positions. By contrast, the social causation hypothesis states that the general circumstances of those in higher socioeconomic positions are more beneficial to their health than the circumstances of those in lower socioeconomic positions. The social gradient in health would therefore be the result of 'differences in resources, support, knowledge, behavior or other factors that are socially stratified' (p. 951).

Especially in studies of older workers health selection and social causation compete with each other in explaining inequalities. An obvious explanation for the link between health selection and the labor market is the influence of health on productivity or on absence through sickness, which will lead employers to favor workers who are healthy and dismiss those who are least healthy. In that way health inequalities may drive people out of employment (Crystal 2006). Especially on the battlefield of midlife a chronic or prolonged disease may introduce a long period of misery for older workers and their families. Having to pay for health care after loss of a job, or because one does not have the right health insurance, can have disastrous consequences. In the absence of universal health care, health problems are a major reason for bankruptcy in the US. In that way health will have an important impact on socioeconomic status. However, this is not some abstract causal necessity that works for all time and all places, it is clearly the result of political choices and much less likely to happen in Europe or Japan (Himmelstein et al. 2005), provided they stop following the US as the ideal example of a rich society that has gradually been shedding responsibility for the well being of its population.

The research outcomes that have been discussed above raise the question whether the distribution of good and bad health on the labor market has not already to an important degree been structured by broader pathogenic circumstances. Here we can think of the influence of poverty on early life which can have long term consequences for adult health and mortality as will be discussed in the section on the 'Long arm of childhood inequality' (Ch.3). Moreover, the actualization of certain predispositions that are built up very early in life depends on continuing interactions with societal contexts. In adverse circumstances negative predispositions can lead to serious, even early health problems, but in more favorable contexts they are more likely to remain latently in the background. Moreover, unemployment as a result of de-industrialization or outsourcing and the political choice to shift the burden of such transitions to the former workers and their families are hardly caused by bad health of the workers but will nevertheless hit them hard. Generally, unemployment is strongly associated with worse health and higher mortality (Bartley & Plewis 2002). Also, the stressful burden of discrimination or status related denigration along the life course are not caused by bad health but they do have negative effects on health in adulthood and later life.

The conclusion has too often been that health inequalities are part of American life, so deeply entangled with other social problems that it remains difficult, even for experts, to say which factors are cause and which are effect. The confusing result is often characterized as a gigantic chicken-and-egg puzzle. In evolutionary perspective this puzzle is easily solved: the egg was there long before the appearance of what we now call a chicken. We need to go back in time and follow the origin of the problems upstream.

Based on the empirical evidence it appears that the social causation hypothesis carries more weight: socioeconomic factors have already an important influence on early childhood, education and health. These factors will continue to have major implications for chances of finding good work and income which will increase chances of becoming or remaining healthy (Kawachi, Adler & Dow 2010). Health selection should be understood as a part of social selection processes, not as their refutation. Policies for more equitable income redistribution, equal opportunities for a good education, employment, responsible lifestyles, mutual respect or adequate disability and retirement benefits are crucially important to improve public health and to stop the hopeless task of trying to mop up water while the fire hydrants are blasting.

This does not mean that health care becomes less important; only that it would no longer be overburdened with the consequences of problems it cannot solve. All along the life course, from gestation to very old age, people may get sick and this will have consequences for their lives. They will need treatment but also a protection against problematic health effects of their daily situations. To approach this massive problem in terms of health choices of autonomous adults is to neglect that 'many individuals live, learn, work, and play in disadvantaged contexts where it is nearly impossible to pursue healthy choices' (Williams and Wyatt 2015: 556).

The public burden of the health care system: mopping up while the fire hydrants are blasting

The health care system has been placed in the impossible position of being faced with a structural overload of health problems that could largely be prevented by addressing causes outside the clinic so that medical professionals could concentrate on treating the many health complaints that will remain. A metaphor that captures the absurdity of this situation is that of a downstream care system that is overly busy with pulling large numbers of half drowned people out of the water, while forgetting to catch the villains upstream who are throwing them in. Working upstream means in this context not only medical prevention but also support, if necessary, during infancy, education, working life and retirement. The upstream/downstream metaphor is useful to clarify some of the positioning of the health care system but its generalizing image of the upstream contamination is too undifferentiated. This neglects that the clinical health care model works much better for the most advantaged who do not feel the burden of, for instance, insufficient income, bad housing or insecure jobs which tend to lead to disproportionately high rates of morbidity and mortality. Different streams with different forms and degrees of social pathogens are flowing in and out the health care system.

The upstream–downstream syndrome has received a vivid illustration from the lead poisoning scandal in Flint, Michigan. In 2015, a local pediatrician recognized the relationship between an increase in her patients' blood lead levels and the city's recent change in water supply. The ensuing public health crisis was both tragic and bizarre. Large numbers of children were found to have blood lead levels that put them at neurotoxic risk and an entire community became dependent on bottled water. Four years later, the *US Preventive Services Task Force* (USPSTF) released its updated recommendation statement on screening children for elevated lead levels in the blood. Although it acknowledged the harm of elevated lead levels and confirmed the accuracy of lead screening tests, it found no evidence for *treating* screen-detected lead poisoning. On this basis, the USPSTF concluded that the evidence was insufficient to assess whether screening for lead levels in children would make any sense (Silverstein, Hsu & Bell 2019).

This bewildering process and the logic behind it demonstrate that a system that is closed from the environment will short-circuit when forces from the environment enter the system anyway. What can be learned is that public health problems do not necessarily have effective individual clinical solutions. There is an astonishing disconnect between the prevention of public health crises, including screening regional water supply and installing a safe system on the one hand, and a clinical, individual oriented approach to prevention and treatment on the other hand. Another example of such disconnect is individual-level screening for depression, for which, in contrast to lead poisoning there is solid evidence. The value of depression screening depends, however, on the availability of high-quality mental health services and even when these resources are sufficiently available individual treatment may not be as effective as community-based initiatives to prevent or reduce community violence.

The Flint tragedy has been another episode in extended discussions about the importance of the 'social determinants of health' perspective (cf. Estes & DiCarlo 2019) that has been struggling against more traditional clinical models and is only gradually receiving the recognition it deserves. It focuses on the social and economic circumstances in which people live and work, trying to answer the question how such circumstances upstream influence health and quality of life, resulting downstream in needs for clinical help (Braveman, Egerter & Williams 2011). There has been slow but – helped by the Covid-19 pandemic – increasing acknowledgment that social determinants explain more of the variance in health outcomes and inequalities than do narrower traditional constructs of access to and quality of medical care. Seen from a clinical perspective prevention includes screening for malignancy, such as mammography, and chronic disease management, such as treating hypertension. The upstream perspective may seem unnecessary and even contrary to the medical ethos to help anyone with a health problem irrespective of how it occurred and who may be responsible, and the influence of the upstream perspective on the clinical diagnosis or treatment of the individual patient may even be negligible. But this is all beside the point.

Many health problems arise because of 'insulting' situations in which people have been trapped for many years. Therefore, it becomes crucially important to reassess the interaction between clinical and public health approaches. This does not imply mutually exclusive either–or arguments: when individuals are actually sick they deserve treatment that is both instrumentally effective and respectfully addressing their needs. In contrast to the present reality, clinical care should be seen as complementary to policies that address social determinants. Social determinants are, moreover, not only relevant for creating public health problems, they are also influencing profit oriented strategies in the health care system such as encouraging the expansion of the clinic by importing public health concepts into clinical care, changing intervention targets from populations to individuals. This misses the point of prevention upstream.

Addressing social determinants requires government officials and community leaders to think innovatively and cooperatively about the everyday realities that affect citizens' health, from air pollution to toxic waste and the designs of neighborhoods or transportation systems. It needs the engagement of different disciplines but also of organizations that represent the interests of the people concerned, such as labor unions or school parents' associations to assess and improve conditions that prevent citizens from participating in their communities with equal opportunities. Health care organizations need to broaden their perspective to improve initiatives on education, housing, employment, and other important health-related social issues that are located outside the clinic but produce the victims that are eventually brought in for treatment. The health care system needs also to have more professional attention for nonmedical pressures that patients may face downstream, after leaving the clinic; ranging from an urgently needed air conditioner for a poor older patient with asthma to helping post-operative patients with grocery shopping or cooking.

Policies aiming at decreasing the major inequalities in health and life expectancies require adequate fiscal policies to obtain the necessary public resources to target upstream sources of health problems. This would benefit the whole population but especially large Medicaid populations, which tend to be relatively young and socioeconomically disadvantaged. There is no reason to assume that the majority of these populations would not become more productive with improving health which would at the same time reduce health care costs (LaVeist, Gaskin & Richard 2009). But most importantly, all citizens should have equal opportunities to be as healthy as possible in any given society. Medical care should not be used as a bandage over the health-damaging effects of underlying unjust living conditions; even if people are completely cured from preventable disease, this cure does not compensate for the suffering of becoming and being sick.

The opposition from those who cling to the monopoly of the clinical perspective is awkward and counterproductive because the social determinants of health perspective clearly show that the health care system is chronically over-burdened with problems that it cannot solve in the clinic. If every night a large number of young people are brought in with stab or gunshot wounds it makes sense to treat them well, but also to try to do something about the sources of violence without giving in to the myth that the American people need to engage in an arms race to defend their homes or to have a good time in the city. If the clinic is overrun by patients during a pandemic it makes sense to change something in the way people are relating to each other outside the clinic and to stop the cultural programming that every individual is only responsible for himself. Persistent social inequalities are legitimated and covered up by ideologies of individual responsibility that obscure and confuse efforts to improve situations. A health care system that assumes that the problems are only coming in from the outside to be solved inside has fallen to the illusion of standing outside society. The examples that have been given above of racial discrimination and ageism illustrate that the socio-pathogenic forces do not only exist outside the clinic but permeate its practices. As the health care system reproduces itself, it tends to reproduce these problems, creating burdens for itself that it cannot handle. As long as this circle is not broken the health care system represents a small part of the solution but a much larger part of the problem.

Notes

1 https://www.prb.org/todays-research-aging-healthy-aging-longer-life-spans/ (accessed July 12, 2022)
2 In Ho's (2022) comparative analysis these countries are Australia, Austria, Belgium, Canada, Denmark, Finland, France, Germany, Italy, Japan, the Netherlands, Norway, Portugal, Spain, Sweden, Switzerland, and the United Kingdom. Barbieri (2022) has added Iceland, Ireland and Luxembourg with similar results.
3 https://www.wbur.org/cognoscenti/2021/01/19/biden-covid-pandemic-national-mourning-ceremony-margaret-morganroth-gullette
4 https://nursinghome411.org/ltccc-alert-osha-covid-violations/ (November 2, 2020)
5 https://nltimes.nl/2020/04/28/dutch-icu-doc-exasperated-new-york-youre-broke-youre-screwed

Chapter 3

Main forms and temporal dynamics of social inequality

Overview

Having made plausible that health inequalities reflect social inequalities, the focus in this chapter will be on their different forms and dynamics. The discussion intends to go beyond important limitations of dominant discourses on social inequality over the life course: (a) the tendency to gather data about possible causalities between factors without identifying plausible structural patterns; (b) the one-sided focus on socioeconomic factors while neglecting racial, gender or ageist discrimination; and (c) a one-sided focus on identity politics while neglecting socioeconomic factors. The main forms of social inequality are income and wealth, education, gender and racial discrimination – leaving ageism to be discussed in Chapter 4 – and, finally, spatial and geographical segregation. This systematic analysis of different forms of social inequality is followed by a discussion of their temporal interaction over the life course. The basic dynamic of this temporal interaction can be summarized as 'The rich get richer, the poor get poorer'. From the discussed research it can be concluded that initial advantages have a tendency to accumulate over time; initial disadvantages, however, have an even stronger tendency to accumulate. This temporal dynamic will be explored further by focusing on the long term consequences of advantaged versus disadvantaged circumstances in early childhood. Looking back on three chapters in which the health and social inequalities of an exemplary wealthy nation have been investigated a troubling perspective emerges. The life chances of a growing part of the population are diminishing to such a degree that the habitats of disadvantaged citizens are being threatened or even destroyed; not intentionally but as a silent systemic process.

Life, health and other expectancies: different conceptualizations but similar results in terms of social inequalities

For a long time life expectancies were one of the most used indicators of a population's health status or even well being, but now more differentiated

DOI: 10.4324/9781003392590-4

measurements have been developed. It is not only relevant to know how long citizens can be expected to live, it is also important to know how healthy their lives will probably be as they grow older. Adequate information about both expectancies is important in many ways: to organize retirement systems, to prepare for future healthcare costs and assistance needs, as well as to plan pension systems and anticipate developments regarding social participation and social inclusion of older people. In combination with life expectancies, measurements of health expectancies can also give important information about social inequality. There has already been quite extensive research on 'health expectancy': the number of years a specific population can be expected to live in good health. The concept of 'health', however, can be interpreted in several ways: as living without disabilities, living without chronic disease or, in terms of subjective health, as rating one's own health on a scale ranging from 'excellent' to 'poor'.

Some measures that have been developed are 'disability adjusted life expectancy', 'disability-free life expectancy', 'healthy active life expectancy', or 'health adjusted life expectancy'. To reduce the heterogeneity of measurements of health expectancies there have been some proposals for standardization. The WHO has proposed a conceptual framework: the *International Classification of Functioning, Disability and Health*. However, measurements in this domain of research have remained heterogeneous.

In spite of the heterogeneity of indicators and methods used to measure health expectancy, Pongiglione and colleagues (2015), who conducted a systematic review of studies analyzing inequalities in health expectancy among older people, conclude that there has been strong homogeneity of the results in terms of inequalities. Regardless of how health expectancy was measured, the significance of an educational gradient affecting positively both life expectancy and health expectancy has generally been confirmed, except for discriminated minorities; as well as the fact that belonging to higher socioeconomic classes tends to lead to longer and healthier lives.

Of course, not all members of a disadvantaged group will be disadvantaged to the same degree. Although some black people are highly educated, in high professional positions or wealthy, and it has even been possible for a black person to become President of the US, that does not imply that this group would not be generally disadvantaged. There is ample evidence that black people as a group have suffered and still suffer from less wealth, lower educational attainment, and lower incomes. They are overrepresented in low-wage entry-level jobs and underrepresented in positions of high occupational rank or political power compared with white people.[1]

I will not use the term 'health disparities' that has often been used in the US to refer to similar phenomena because this term has become broad, ambiguous and unclear as a result of many different definitions (Braveman, Egerter & Williams 2011). Moreover, this term has often been used to refer to health differences between racial or ethnic groups that would assumedly be rooted in biological or cultural differences rather than underlying structural disadvantage. Above all, I want to emphasize the constitutive connection between health inequalities and social inequalities.

Regarding the analysis of these social inequalities I would like to go beyond three important and fruitful approaches that tend to overemphasize, however, a specific methodological approach or theoretical perspective. These approaches should be honored for their contributions to the understanding of social inequalities but we need to search beyond them to find a more comprehensive approach. The *first* of these is the conceptualization of health inequalities or 'health disparities' in terms of 'risks' and 'exposures' as is customary in much epidemiological research which tends to add up singular causal or semi-causal relations, clouding the perspective on structural pressures and dynamics that are behind isolated empirical finds. The *second* approach is to conduct research on social inequality in a life course perspective without including processes of discrimination. Unfortunately, this has even been the case in research on cumulative (dis)advantage (CDA; see p.115ff) as has been acknowledged by Dannefer, Gilbert and Han (2020, p. 109): 'the discourse that has been elaborated around CDA has all but entirely ignored the matter of race relations'. An exception has been Daniel Rigney's *The Matthew Effect: How Advantage Begets Further Advantage* (2010). This is in spite of a decades long discussion since *Black Marxism* (Robinson 1983) and numerous media reports on poverty and discrimination. Fortunately, there have been some initiatives to resume studying the constitutive interaction of race and class (respect and resources), such as the *National Race and Capitalism Project* at the University of Chicago, the discussion between Michael Dawson (2016) and Nancy Fraser (2016) in *Critical Historical Studies* or the debate about Racial Capitalism (Ralph & Singhal 2019).

One reason for this major omission has been the use of limited indicators of 'socioeconomic status' the most important of which have been educational attainment, income, accumulated wealth, and residence in geographic areas with particular social or economic conditions. The flipside of the neglect of racial or gender discrimination can be found in a *third* group of approaches that focus on diversity, difference, deviant or 'atopian' identities. Although these approaches have enlarged the possibilities of understanding complex combinations of cultural (dis)advantage, the attention to identity tends to neglect the importance of structural pressures in the distribution of material resources (see Ch.7).

To get a better understanding of the dominant patterns of social inequality we need to pay more attention to the interaction of structural and cultural dynamics. Structural patterns of inequality are to an important degree maintained through cultural strategies of discrimination, denigration and marginalization that are employed by those in power to legitimate their superior position. These strategies typically target embodied characteristics such as skin color, gender, disability or age in an attempt to ground the inequality between the supposedly superior and inferior in natural characteristics. I will discuss such 'naturalization' in the next chapter in relation to ageism and aging but the basic processes remain the same for many forms of discrimination. Although historically and genetically we are all migrants, some of the many differences between people are selected by dominant groups and turned into markers of inequality. This can also be speaking a dialect, coming from a certain region or practicing a certain religion. Moreover, a society that values individual wealth and success above shared wealth and well being, will tend to produce processes of denigration and status related stress for anyone who did not 'make it'. Analyzing the complex of social inequalities as well as changing these require attention to resources *and* respect (see Ch.7). Therefore, I have included racial and gender discrimination in the following account of the main sources of social inequality. Although ageism certainly belongs in this list, I will discuss this more elaborately in Chapter 4. Besides making some specific points I will give also a more general overview for readers who are not familiar with these subjects.

The main sources of social inequality

A The fault line of income and wealth

To the degree that social rights of citizens have to be bought as marketed services, shortages of income and wealth, especially if they are prolonged, will have a major negative impact along the life course. This makes it understandable that America's poor, regardless of educational level, geographical location, gender, race or ethnicity are much worse off than Americans with sufficient income or wealth. Health inequalities form along several societal fault lines, but most analysts agree that, especially in the US, the deepest and most persistent divide stems from income and wealth (Daly et al. 2002; Herd, Goesling & House 2007; Wilkinson & Pickett 2006). In the above discussions there have already been many examples of the significance of this relationship. It remains difficult, however, to separate income and wealth from education because most citizens are dependent on jobs for their income and, usually, the income they get from these jobs depends on their educational level. Moreover, the quality of the education children receive depends in the US also on the income and wealth of the family. Clearly, dimensions of social inequality can be distinguished but cannot be separated; far from that, they are often strongly correlated, mutually enforcing each other in vicious or beneficial circles (see below). When, for instance, poverty goes together with low education, being a member of a discriminated minority, and living in a socially impoverished neighborhood.

Crystal, Shea and Reyes (2017) have investigated how income inequality has evolved in the US in successive cohorts since the early 1980s. They have tried to include all sources of income using annuitized assets to include wealth in their estimates. Figure 3.1 shows how income inequality in a

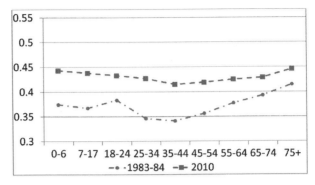

Figure 3.1 Gini coefficient by age, 1983–1984 and 2010.
Source: from Crystal, Shea and Reyes 2017.

broad sense has grown since the beginning of the 1980s for all age groups. The lower line represents the Gini coefficient of inequality[2] that existed in 1983–1984 for each age group from 0–6 years to 75 and older and shows how inequality got lower at working ages to climb substantially for those who have reached old age.

The upper line shows how income inequality was considerably higher in 2010 for all age groups, beginning with a much higher level of household inequality for young children and ending also much higher for those older than 75 years. The dip in inequality during prime working years was less prominent in 2010 than in 1983–1984, reflecting sharp increases in inequality within the working-age population. Moreover, according to Crystal and colleagues between 1983 and 2010 the upper income quintile became increasingly male (from 50% to 56%) and increasingly college-educated (from 44% to 76%), with a dramatic decline (from 16% to 1%) for those with only elementary education. College education appears to have become a minimal requirement for entering the top income quintile, but does not guarantee any upward social mobility: in the lowest income quintile the proportion of those with college education quadrupled to 28%.

The research article by Crystal and colleagues also presents evidence of increasing inequalities since the neoliberal turn; specifically between five income groups (quintiles) of citizens over the age of 65 years. Although the incomes of the top quintile remain hard to pin down exactly – with the consequence that inequality is probably underestimated – it is clear that for the wealthy elite Social Security plays only a moderate role. As the amount of Social Security is closely connected with earned income, high-income individuals received more than twice the amount from this source as the lowest quintile. Nevertheless, in 2010 Social Security accounted only for 18% of the total income of the highest quintile, while 10% came from pensions, 40% from annuitized assets and 21% still from wages and salaries.

So, the moderating effects of Social Security were more than outweighed by income from investments, pensions and other resources. While the ideal is that income for older people should come from three sources: Social Security, pensions and assets, many of those in the highest income quintile still had salaries, so that their material position was like a comfortable chair well supported by four legs. In contrast, those in the lowest income quintile only received Social Security. The chair of the lowest two income quintiles of people older than 65 years was precariously balancing on one leg, with small additional income from wages and assets.

What about the implications for health inequalities? Researchers from Stanford University, Massachusetts Institute of Technology, Harvard University and other institutions have combined their resources in the *Health Inequality Project* and conducted a large-scale investigation of the association between income and life expectancy in the US (Chetty, Stepner & Abraham et al. 2016). They used new data from 1.4 billion anonymous earnings and mortality records to construct more precise estimates of the relationship between income and life expectancy at the national level than has been feasible before. Their results indicate that the richest American men live 15 years longer than the poorest men, while the richest American women live 10 years longer than the poorest women. Moreover, they found that income based inequality in life expectancy at the national level increased between 2001 and 2014. Individuals in the top 5% of income distribution gained around 3 years of life expectancy. In contrast, the lifespans of Americans in the bottom 5% of the income distribution did not increase between 2001 and 2014. The researchers from the *Health Inequality Project* conclude that these findings are broadly consistent with the conclusions of prior studies that used smaller samples, although the magnitudes of the gaps are larger than suggested by prior work.

B Education-based inequalities

Many studies measure socioeconomic status by educational level in terms of the number of years that have been spent in education or whether something like a college or Bachelor degree has been obtained. The main advantage of this research strategy is that most individuals complete their educational path in early adulthood so that this indicator remains relatively stable along the life course and everyone can be classified accordingly. Moreover, as it precedes most of adult life, it can easily be treated as a causal factor that might explain the chance of anything happening later in the life course.

There are several ways through which educational attainment is linked with health. First, education can lead to improved health by increasing health knowledge and healthy activities and practices such as regular exercise, eating healthy food and avoiding the abuse of alcohol and drugs.

Second, education plays a crucial role in employment opportunities which determine for the majority of people their access to economic resources; especially in avoiding unemployment with all its bad health effects and in finding jobs with good health-related benefits and compensation. But also in avoiding unhealthy or risky working situations: persons with lower levels of schooling are several times more likely than the well-educated to experience work disability by their 50s, further contributing to late-life inequalities (Crystal & Shea 2003). Third, more education appears to increase the chances that the members of one's network are socially advantaged, enhancing access to employment, housing, and other opportunities and resources that can in their turn influence health (Braveman, Egerter & Williams 2011).

In the earlier discussed overview of scientific research about inequalities in health expectancy among older populations by Pongiglione and colleagues (2015), a large majority of studies confirmed the advantage of being highly educated in terms of both life expectancies and health expectancies. In studies that used multiple indicators for socioeconomic status, education was also found to be the most strongly predictive measure for both expectancies (Crimmins & Saito, 2001). In the US, studies of the period 1960–1980 found increasing differences in life expectancy between men who had enjoyed high education versus men with the lowest level of education. Subsequent studies of the period 1980–2000 found a further widening of these educational differentials in mortality for both men and women. Those who already tended to live longer enjoyed a further increase in life expectancy while life expectancies stagnated or decreased among the lowest education group (Jemal et al. 2008; Meara et al. 2008).

Avendano and colleagues (2010) examined mortality rates for different socioeconomic classes (based on educational level) in the US and in a number of European countries, including Denmark, England, and France. They found that among those with a low level of education (equivalent to 11 years or less), the mortality among men and women in the US, both black and white, was higher than in Western European countries. The high mortality and low life expectancy rates of the US population are mainly, though not exclusively, caused by the early deaths of its low educated citizens.

In spite of extensive research, an important part of educational inequalities remains still invisible. Because of the focus on educational attainment, the *quality* of education has rarely become a subject of research. Not only are educational categories only roughly comparable from country to country, but measuring educational attainment by the number of years that were spent in education neglects important differences in the quality of education and even degrees. Insofar as educational status is meant to explain social inequality, it can be tricky because it is also the result of social inequality in the sense of a stratified system of social reproduction. In the US schooling system, the quality of schools depends largely on the residential affluence or poverty. As Mirowsky and Ross argue in their book *Education, Social Status, and Health* (2003) the chance to obtain a prestigious PhD or just to complete the minimal number of years in elementary education depends not only on the educational status of the parents but especially, in countries like the US, on the necessary material resources to give their children a good education. However, the role of educational quality as a gateway to employment opportunities, prestige, social networks, and other advantages accompanying a degree from an elite institution, is still rarely considered in health studies. When such preconditions are neglected, the reference to educational status may also suggest that individual efforts are decisive for outcomes, which affirms an influential but biased view on social inequality as it assumes a level playing field or equal access to educational opportunities.

In the US, prestigious institutions for higher education have several strategies to exclude outsiders and monopolize access to ensure that children of alumni are treated with preference. These strategies of exclusion are combined with strategies to define the standards of excellence, turning exclusion into a sign of institutional superiority. As places become more limited, the market value goes up and disadvantaged students who are encouraged by society to chase their dreams are not supported but abandoned. Raj Chetty and colleagues (2017) conducted extensive research on the wealth distribution of American college students and found that students from the top 1% of households are 77 times more likely to be admitted to and attend an Ivy League school than students from families who make less than $30,000 a year. Although some prestigious institutions share this discomforting diagnosis and offer free or reduced tuition to high-achieving kids from needy families, this still gives few opportunities to the many ambitious talented students whose parents cannot afford the heavy sums that are involved. In 2022 the total national student loan debt had grown to $1.76 trillion. In theory, college education is the great equalizer; in practice it is still a great stratifier.

C Gender inequalities: beyond the gender paradox

Too often health and life expectancies are limited to differences between men and women. A popular example to illustrate the relevance of health expectancies besides life expectancies is the so-called *gender paradox* in health and mortality: the finding that women live longer than men, but tend to have worse health than males. Women have a higher prevalence of nonfatal but disabling diseases such as arthritis and osteoporosis than men who have a greater chance of fatal diseases such as heart disease or stroke. There is much research that confirms the gender paradox but this tends to reduce the differences between women and men to biological differences, occluding the fact that much depends on the socioeconomic and cultural contexts in which they live (Moss 2002; Stafford et al. 2005). Socioeconomically disadvantaged women may well die long before wealthy men begin to develop chronic disease.

Another example of the use of life expectancies to gloss over constitutive inequalities is the presentation of the *gender gap* in longevity between men and women as an unproblematic straightforward biological condition. This neglects important factors for both sexes. Part of these gender differences in life expectancy are caused by detrimental life styles of disadvantaged men, such as smoking, drinking, violent or risky behavior, as documented in the Promundo Report about *Masculine Norms and Men's Health* (Ragonese, Shand & Barker 2019). It is hardly adequate to explain such life styles by pointing to biological drivers when these life styles are not to the same degree adopted by men who live in better circumstances. Broader intersectional accounts of masculinity that incorporate ethnicity and class are presented by Lohan (2007) and in Raewyn Connel's book *Masculinities* (1995), as well as in Demetriou's (2001) article on hegemonic masculinity in the labor market, the family and the state.

The gender gap must also be seen in the context of a much broader gender inequality. Its injustice becomes more noticeable when confronted with the phenomenon that Amartya Sen (1992, 2003) has criticized as the 'missing women' phenomenon in India, China and other countries. Given the evidence that women tend to live longer than men it is deeply worrying that a large number of women are simply 'not there' – as Sen puts it – compared to what might be expected. For a very long time the mortality rates in these countries for women of all age groups have been higher than for men, much like this used to be in Western countries until the 20th century. Only recently has the life expectancy of women in India overtaken that of men, but still not to the degree that might be expected. Moreover, medical technology has led to another recent development that works against the opportunities of women: the selective abortion of female fetuses. This denial of the right to live may be the most extreme version of a much more general negative attitude towards women.

The gender gap in life expectancies and, especially, healthy life expectancies cannot be taken for granted; it still leaves the question open whether these expectancies are not lower than they should be. That women tend to live longer than men is no reason to assume that they are already so much better off that it would be futile to explore this any further, as Norman Daniels has proposed (see Ch.7). It is clear that women are still disadvantaged in terms of care load, career perspectives, equal pay for the same work, and respect. Therefore, even if they live longer, they are more often confronted with insufficient material resources because, for instance, they have less opportunities to save or build up an adequate pension. On average, older women received about $9,900 less annually in retirement income in 2016 than older men due to lower lifetime earnings, time taken off for caregiving, occupational segregation into lower wage work, and other issues. Older women of color fare even worse.[3] Less pay because of gender discrimination, part-time work or a 'family care penalty' (Estes & Wallace 2005) from interrupted careers are common causes of their poverty in old age. Consequently, they run more risk of being confronted in old age not only with poverty but also with ageism, on top of misogyny, as ageism tends to strike out especially when people are in vulnerable situations.

Crimmins and colleagues (2011) conclude that women in the US had decades of stagnation in life expectancy, leaving them at the bottom of the group of wealthy countries. This stagnation has been concentrated among those with low education; however, female US citizens of all educational levels had lower life expectancies than the average score for European women in the comparable educational levels (Olshansky et al. 2012). Although many women in the US are wealthy and some hold top positions in enterprises or political institutions, they are still disadvantaged as a group. According to data from the US Census Bureau they are more likely than men to be poor, more likely to earn less than men at a given educational level, and to be underrepresented in top positions.

Over the last decades gender issues have slowly expanded from male–female differences to include LGBTQIA+ identities. The US has seen significant milestones on the way to more equity for sexual and gender minorities, from the 1973 removal of homosexuality as a mental illness in the DSM to the 2015 US-wide legalization of same-sex marriage. While these events mark notable progress, considerably more work needs to be done to document and overcome the inequalities that confront them. Following the groundbreaking work of Kimberlé Crenshaw (2019) intersectionality approaches have enriched the understanding how different contextual factors interact with different identities. However, the attention for diversity, difference and identity should not lead to a neglect of socio-economic inequalities (see Ch.7). Life course research on sexual and gender minorities is relatively scarce; their disadvantages and cumulative risks are even more rarely addressed. The available evidence shows, however, that older members of these minorities are disproportionately affected by poverty and health problems due to discrimination and other disadvantages in opportunities along the life course.[4]

D Racial discrimination

Another source of social inequality that runs the risk of being explained away by naturalization (see Ch.7) or by an overemphasis on cultural diversity is race/ethnicity. In the US race has been a central axis of inequality since Europeans invaded the newfound continent and began to repress and annihilate its original inhabitants. Since then, race has remained a crucial factor in the structuring of opportunities. Studies of racial inequalities in health expectancies are, unfortunately, almost exclusively set in the US where they are mainly focused on differences between black and white citizens. These health inequalities have a long and highly divisive history of repression and exploitation of black people in the US, continuing after the official abolition of slavery and into the present.

As Conley (2002) and Darity (2008) have documented, the liberated slaves were promised that they would be compensated for their long time exploitation by granting them 'forty acres and a mule' so that they could finally begin to gather some resources and be included in the American Dream. Another example of idle promises was the 1866 *Southern Homestead Act* which was to open up public land to settlement and farming by African-Americans and white persons alike. The racially biased implementation of these programs by individual state governments and violence from white farmers brought, however, little improvement for black families. Unfortunately, this pattern of advertised equal opportunities and continuing racial inequality has been repeated throughout most of the history of the *Social Security Act* of 1935.

Although Social Security has brought an important reduction of old-age poverty it has too long served to reproduce and sustain patterns of racial discrimination and exclusion. The official ideology of equal opportunities has led to little interrogation of the racially biased implementation of this act. Katznelson's book *When Affirmative Action Was White: An Untold History of Racial Inequality in Twentieth-century America*, published in 2005 and Poole's 2006 book *The Segregated Origins of Social Security: African Americans and the Welfare State* have broken this silence by documenting extensively how access to the benefits of Social Security has from its very beginning been framed by race-related politics. Most black workers were excluded from eligibility, as the program aimed to support only workers of large companies or industries excluding, quite intentionally, the forms of work that were most commonly available for black American laborers: agricultural and domestic work. Moreover, since racist state governments were charged with implementing the Social Security Act, the benefits black workers received were substantially less than what white workers would receive: much of the officially advertised benefits never reached black citizens. According to Katznelson the same exclusionary strategies were employed in the ways in which the GI Bill after the Second World War was implemented, giving a clear advantage to white veterans.

Although there has been some progress, black families in the US still face an impressive lag in the intergenerational accumulation of family wealth: according to a Pew report by Shapiro, Meschede and Osoro (2013) black families possess 5% of the wealth of white families. Black families, especially those who achieve middle income status are not able to pass their economic advantages onto their children in the same way as white parents. Only 31% of black children born to middle-income parents make more than their parents' family income, compared to 68% of white children. Almost half (45%) of black children from middle income families end up falling to the bottom of the income distribution, compared to only 16% of white children.[5]

Racially biased institutional and structural forces still tend to exclude black citizens from equal opportunities in access to mortgage loans, high quality education, or from receiving equal respect as a citizen. The racial color-blindness of 'All Lives Matter' is a continuing attempt to convince the public that the problem of racism has long been solved, and that equal opportunity as a societal goal has been essentially realized. Given this ideology of equal opportunity, the conclusion must be that those who do not succeed have only themselves to blame. As long as race continues to be introduced into the study of the life course as an individual characteristic, the structural and institutional constitution of racial inequality remain invisible (Dannefer, Gilbert & Han 2020).

In the light of the vast research on the constitutive importance of education for health it is worrying that education does not bring the health advantages for blacks that it does for whites: higher levels of education do not lead as much to higher life expectancies. This indicates that discrimination has stronger effects than education (Shuey & Wilson 2008). Highly educated blacks in the US have a higher chance of dying at a relatively young age than the highly educated of any other developed country. These data, however, may also tell us something about the quality of education. Despite decades of legal action against racial segregation, racial residential segregation persists and, with it, educational segregation. This condemns most black children to schools of poor quality reducing their chances of obtaining good jobs with adequate income as adults, so that they will also be unable to give their children better opportunities. Black students who get to college are less likely than others to complete their courses; black men, especially, have an poor chance of making it to graduation. In 2016 only 29% of black adults above the age of 25 had an associate degree or higher, compared with 44% of white adults. Because black families have less familial wealth, their children's student loans are nearly triple the amount of those of white graduates.

Higher mortality rates among the black population have reduced overall levels of life expectancy, explaining part of the gap between the US and other countries. Many African Americans live in poor housing and degraded environments, being confronted with lack of access to healthy food and relatively high levels of environmental toxins including lead poisoning which may result in early brain damage. There has been little attention for the diversity within racial and ethnic minorities but where data are available, similar patterns of inequality emerge for American Indians, Native Hawaiians, Asian populations and US-born Latinx with low socioeconomic status. Especially the suicide rates of young male adults (aged 18–24 years) among American Indians and Alaska Natives have been alarmingly high; they have been more than twice as likely to commit suicide as young adults compared to other racial and ethnic minorities (Espey 2014).

Levine and colleagues (2001) have given an overview of black–white inequalities in mortality and life expectancy in the US between 1933 and 1999. Compared with whites, black individuals had earlier onset of multiple illnesses, greater severity and more rapid progression of diseases, higher levels of comorbidity and impairment throughout the life course, and increased mortality rates. The authors estimate that during that period black–white differences in mortality accounted for the premature deaths of 260 African Americans every day. According to more recent research, blacks still have much higher mortality rates than whites in the US. Ethnic inequalities in health appear to increase with age: they become visible in early childhood, tend to disappear in early adulthood, to reappear again in early midlife, continuing to widen into old age unless they lead to death in midlife. A common finding is that whites, as compared to any other ethnicity, enjoy more years in good health, but that the gap between blacks and whites grows smaller at higher ages (Pongiglione, De Stavola & Ploubidis 2015). This is partly because of selective mortality (Ch.2) as the most disadvantaged will tend to die earlier; partly because of a so-called race crossover effect in longevity as blacks and Latinx from a certain advanced age on experience lower mortality throughout the remaining life span.

The destructive health effects of racial discrimination demonstrate the importance of equal opportunity to receive a decent amount of material and immaterial resources, and, moreover, respect. Those who are not usually exposed to discrimination have difficulty in even imagining how discrimination can be an experience that pervades daily life, from the labor market to access to bank loans, housing, purchasing a car, or hailing a taxi (Pager & Shepherd 2008). Lewis, Cogburn & Williams (2015) have extensively documented the negative health effects that flow downstream from this source of socially constituted stress. They showed that self-reported measures of discrimination had negative effects on hypertension, all cause mortality, incident asthma, incident breast cancer, and mental health. Moreover, there were harmful effects on several early indicators of clinical disease such as inflammation, carotid intima-media thickness, visceral fat, obesity, coronary artery calcification, shorter telomeres, and cortisol dysregulation; and, finally, on health behaviors such as poor sleep quantity and quality, cigarette smoking, and substance use. Not only the actual experience or exposure to discrimination but also its perceived threat turns out to be related to increased cardiovascular response, symptoms of poor mental health, and hypertension. Perceived discrimination has also been associated with lower levels of health care seeking and adherence behaviors that have a negative effect on health.

The daily experience of racism as a form of prolonged and effortful coping with social injustice demands a high physical price. Living in a racist environment increases stress hormones and harms the health of all black people, even for those who do not directly experience racism, as they have to listen to the stories and share the experiences of those close to them. Even the search for answers to the long lingering question what might cause the major differences in low birth weight and premature birth between black and white babies, which lead to inequalities in infant mortality, child development, and adult chronic disease, points in the direction of racism stress and racial residential segregation (Dominguez et al. 2008; Hearst, Oakes & Johnson 2008; Lu & Halfon 2003; Wadhwa et al. 2001).

The inequality in life expectancies between black and white males went down from 6.6 to 4.3 years between 2000 and 2017. The main reasons appear to be substantially fewer deaths from homicide and improvement in the treatment of the HIV epidemic which caused many early deaths for black men. Moreover, two developments are worth mentioning. First, differences in income and wealth among the black population have grown and more affluent blacks have been doing much better than those with lower incomes. A second, maybe more remarkable development is that more affluent blacks are living longer while the prospects for disadvantaged whites, especially young and midlife adults have sagged.

Remarkably, racial bias can also backfire on white people. An example is the opioid addiction and overdose-related deaths that have affected whites at much higher rates than blacks. Death from opioid overdoses has especially taken its toll on disadvantaged white persons. Mortality rates for whites caused by drugs has more than quadrupled from 1999 to 2017, and according to the CDC more than 75% of those killed by opioids in 2017 as well as 2018 were white.[6] As drug epidemics used to hit especially non-white Americans, policies were developed to restrict prescribing opioids to black people. White people, on the contrary, were much more likely to obtain an opioid prescription with tragic consequences.

However, although the black–white health gap has steadily narrowed over the last century, black men still live around four-and-a-half years shorter than white males. Many of them are still poor, like many members of other ethnic minorities. When the health of black and white people are compared at equivalent levels of income and education, racial inequalities are reduced but remain evident at all levels of socioeconomic status (Williams et al. 2010). Black males continue to fare worse than black women and white Americans of both sexes in life expectancy, infant health outcomes, age- and cause-specific morbidity and mortality, insurance coverage, and access to adequate health care (Bond & Herman 2016).

Racial segregation: the long shadow of Jim Crow

The eruption of protests after the killing of George Floyd have drawn a level of attention to race relations unseen since the 1960s. Now that videos from witnesses are documenting police actions, it has become clear that a part of the police force enjoy denigrating black men and, if they think this is necessary, emptying their guns on them. The fact that unarmed citizens killed by American police forces are disproportionately black calls for a thorough evaluation and change of the police and the criminal justice system, to become more respectful and considerate in their actions. But these are not the only reforms needed to realize Martin Luther King's dream of civil rights for all, including social rights. A major problem appears to be the degree to which the concentrated poverty in largely segregated black communities blocks their members from opportunity.

As millions of African-Americans during the early and mid 20th century moved to the big cities in the north, a mixture of law and prejudice forced them to live in neighborhoods that became almost exclusively black. As a result of such redlining, in 1970 American cities were almost completely segregated. Forty years later, at the time of the 2010 census, this number was reduced to 70%, an improvement that is hardly worth cheering. The ways in which urban deindustrialization and mass incarceration hit black men have pressurized and destabilized black families. In his 2014 book *Stuck in Place: Urban Neighborhoods and the End of Progress Toward Racial Equality* Patrick Sharkey investigates the effects of growing up in poor neighborhoods with at least 20% of families having incomes below the poverty line. Children who grow up in poverty tend to do badly by various measures. But children who do so in communities where over 20% of the population is poor do very badly indeed. Whatever their race, in these situations children face increased risks of dropping out of school, getting pregnant while still teenagers, being incarcerated, experiencing poverty in adulthood and dying early. And for black children in America, as for Native American children, poor neighborhoods have been the norm. According to Sharkey, only 6% of white children born between 1985 and 2000 spent part of their childhood in neighborhoods with a poverty rate of 20% or more. For black children the figure was 66%; growing up in such neighborhoods has been normal even for middle-class black families. Their schools are usually not so good because they lack all kinds of resources. Moreover, as research by Francis Pearman (2019, 2020) has shown, even when the school is good, poor neighborhoods have a negative impact, not only on students' math scores, but also on Prekindergarten activities.

The situation that confronts Sharkey in 2014 is not much better, with 26% of black children living in neighborhoods where the poverty rate is even higher than 30%, compared to only 4% of white children. The chances for black families to live in substandard housing are 70% higher than they are for the rest of the population, and black children are nearly three times as likely to have high levels of lead in their blood. Compared with white children they live in situations with heavy exposure to fine particulate matter; they are almost one and a half times as likely to have asthma and five times likelier to die from it (White, Haas & Williams 2012). In their *Roadmap to Reducing Child Poverty*, a committee from the National Academies of Sciences, Engineering, and Medicine (2019) concludes that child poverty costs the nation between $800 billion and $1.1 trillion annually in terms of lost adult productivity, increased health expenditures, and increased costs of crime.

Young children and students of color are at risk of being caught in the infamous 'school to prison pipeline', created by school disturbance laws, zero tolerance policies and practices, and an increase of police presence in schools. As Libby Nelson and Dara Lind from the *Justice Policy Institute* observe, out-of-school suspensions have more than doubled since the 1970s, with black students three times more likely to be suspended or expelled than white students.[7] Students who are disciplined by schools are also more likely to end up in the juvenile justice system; for many young blacks the chance of going to prison is greater than of getting a job.

Besides sorting children for different educational and occupational tracks, the most disadvantaged are placed in situations where criminal careers can easily seem attractive or even the only way to survive. Instead of offering high quality education or vocational training and support to vulnerable families, incredible amounts of capital are spent on punitive systems. Sometimes state policies seem to aim at keeping ex convicts in criminal trajectories by continuing to punish them, for instance, by life time exclusions of ex convicts of a drug offence from welfare benefits. Trying to control criminality through an enormous and enormously expensive system - impressively portrayed by Brian Berry (2005) as *Black Gulag* - has turned out to be both immoral and counterproductive (Wacquant, 2009; cf. Estes & DiCarlo 2019 on 'Prison Industrial Complex'). What the US lacks in education, care and support for those who need this, it tries to make up by investing hugely in punitive approaches: there are more drug offenders in jail in the US than in all Western Europe on all offences. In total it has the highest incarceration rate in the world; nearly five times the OECD average. Although the US represents about 4.5% of the world's population, it houses around 20% of the world's prisoners. According to research from the PEW Center, Black Americans made up a third of the sentenced prison population in 2018; nearly triple their representation in the US adult population as a whole.[8] The figures are particularly stark among some age groups: in the 35–39 age bracket about 1 in 20 black men were in state or federal prison in 2018. They also make up a disproportionate number of fatal police shootings. There have been some ups and downs: the imprisonment rate rose by 23% from 1995 to its peak in 2007 and 2008 (506 sentenced prisoners per 100,000 residents in both years). It then fell back below the 1996 level (which was 427 sentenced prisoners per 100,000 residents) in 2019.[9] In international comparison, however, these numbers still seem like messages from another world: per 100,000 population the incarceration rates in Japan, Germany and France are, respectively, 38.4, 76.6 and 105. Usually, poverty and crime have the same social background: discrimination, disintegrated families, unemployment or bad work conditions. Locking up those who commit crimes will not diminish crime as long as neighborhoods are created where crime is learned as a way of life because there are no or too few other options. The astronomical costs of the penal system would, at least partly, be better spent on improving supportive institutions along the life course.

E Socially distancing: spatial and geographical segregation

'If you want to get an idea of the gap between the world's sickest and healthiest people, don't fly to a faraway land. Just look around the United States'

Ichiro Kawachi

A common ingredient in the constitution of social inequality is segregation, both in terms of role and space. According to Charles Tilly (1999) segregation is fundamental for social inequality in the form of opportunity hoarding. Many basic problems of social inequality, such as exposure to violence, poor public services, segregated schooling, and the persistence of stereotyping can be traced back to intentional policies of segregation. By trying to preserve the status quo for the advantaged and contain tensions and unrest, these policies have not only reproduced problematic situations but have often created bigger problems over time.

There have always been health differences between regions stemming from environmental qualities such as a harsh or friendly climate, or geographical location in relation to resources for commerce or productivity. However, the changes that have been taking place following the neoliberal turn have put certain regions that used to do reasonably well with their industrial activities into deep misery by neglecting to compensate and support the population, especially the older workers and their families, by letting them share in the profits that were increasingly made in other regions. Since the neoliberal turn some regions have benefited from the new economy whereas others have suffered serious declines. Studying health inequalities at the national level yields an incomplete picture because there are substantial regional and local differences. Generally, metropolitan areas saw life expectancy gains as a result of the concentration of people with college degrees and high incomes. Life expectancy also increased in Pacific regions, home to new globalized tech giants such as Meta/Facebook, Apple, Amazon, Google/Alphabet, Microsoft, Netflix or Disney, and in states with strong economies such as Texas, or New York. The reverse, however, occurred in areas where traditional industry collapsed, such as the industrial Midwest or Appalachia.

The last two decades have seen a growing number of studies about the role of geographical factors in the constitution of health inequalities in the US (Ezzati et al. 2008). Wilmoth and colleagues (2010) found that, in contrast to the populations of other developed countries, geographic inequalities in mortality in the US increased over the last two decades of the 20th century for both men and women. According to their findings this process has not even benefited the most advantaged. They conclude that

> any proposed explanation of the divergence in levels and trends of life expectancy observed among high-income countries in recent decades needs to acknowledge that even the most advantaged areas of the United States (at the state or county level) have been falling behind in international comparisons.
>
> (Wilmoth et al. 2010, p. 360)

Researchers from the earlier mentioned *Health Inequality Project* have analyzed differences in life expectancy across commuting zones: geographical aggregations of counties that are similar to metro areas but also cover rural areas. Differences in life expectancy across zones did not appear to depend on the quantity and quality of medical care, the fraction insured or measures of preventive care. They were highly correlated with health behaviors like rates of smoking, obesity, and exercise. However, these health behaviors turned out to be significantly influenced by social contexts: low-income individuals tend to live the longest in affluent cities with highly educated populations and high levels of government expenditures, such as New York and San Francisco. Cities with such characteristics also experienced the largest gains in life expectancy among the poor from 2000 to 2010. An important part of the gap in life expectancy between rich and poor people across counties is driven by the life expectancies among the poorest citizens. The results showed that life expectancy of low income people was five years higher in cities such as New York, Miami and Los Angeles compared with the worst scoring cities: Tulsa, Indianapolis and Las Vegas. For low-income people, life expectancy was highest in states as California, New York, and Vermont. It was lowest in Nevada. According to Daniels, Kennedy and Kawachi (2000) the US states with the most unequal income distribution (less taxes) also spend less on public education, have larger uninsured populations and less spending on social safety nets with major consequences over the life course.

In 2017 Dwyer-Lindgren and colleagues published the results of a nation wide research project on inequalities in life expectancy among the different US counties since the neoliberal turn, from 1980 to 2014. During these years the inequality in life expectancy between these counties increased to an alarming level: in 2014 there was a difference of more than 20 years between the counties with the lowest and highest life expectancy. But if we look beyond the average scores from relatively large populations, at smaller communities, the differences are even more impressive.

The CDC has initiated a major project to investigate differences between life expectancies at birth in small communities, with only a few thousand inhabitants, all over the US: the so-called *U.S. Small-area Life Expectancy Estimates Project*.[10] Based on census data it provides a rich source to explore some of the stunning differences between wealthy and poor communities of the same country. At one extreme we find Stilwell, Oklahoma where most people are native Americans: part of the Cherokee Nation that was forcibly relocated to the territory in 1830. More than half of the children in Stilwell are living in poverty and newborns can expect to live to the age of 56 which is only a few years above the life expectancy of the poorest country on the planet. The citizens of Stilwell have a median household income of $25,000, less than half the national average. At the other extreme we find Fearrington, North Carolina, where practically all inhabitants are white. None of the children live in poverty and their life expectancy at birth approaches a century (97.5 years) while median household income is $81,900. This difference in life expectancy of over 40 years between two American communities demonstrates the extremely unequal distribution of opportunities to participate in society for citizens of the same country.

Such inequalities are not the result of bad luck or a mere coincidence. Disadvantaged geographical location has often been the result of direct oppression. Although they deserved respect as the original inhabitants of the lands that only recently became the US, the Cherokee people have been forced to settle down in places with the worst conditions. In urban areas more indirect structural mechanisms such as housing markets force disadvantaged people into underserviced areas and bad neighborhoods because they cannot afford to live in better environments. In cities, zoning rules tend to keep the costs of housing high by restricting supply, making it very hard for less advantaged families to move to better neighborhoods. Zip codes have not only become a useful tool for marketing purposes but also for a quick assessment of investment risks or the height of insurance premiums, with major consequences for the distribution of opportunities. As a consequence of this systemic segregation wealthy people have ample options to choose where they want to live and, as economic inequality increases, wealthy families drive up the price of homes near good schools, further concentrating poverty. As a sad result, census tracts a few miles apart can show huge differences in life expectancies.

The temporal interaction of inequalities over the life course: the accumulation of advantage and disadvantage

In the preceding section I have discussed the most important structural and cultural forces behind social inequality: income/wealth, education, racial/

gender discrimination and segregation. This raises the question which of these forces might be the most important and how they interact with each other over time, strengthening or weakening their effects. From many research reports education emerges as a more powerful predictor of socio-economic life chances than income or wealth. The situation may, however, be more complicated. In a neoliberal society where high quality education and many forms of care or support are marketed as services, income and wealth will remain crucially important. In the US income or wealth of the parents, in combination with the differences in resources of schools in poor and affluent locations, will be a big influence on the educational chances of their children. Not surprisingly, children from wealthy families are much more likely to complete college. So, income or wealth might be the decisive factors behind education and, therefore, the most important factor behind social inequality. This still assumes that good education is a gateway to good jobs and higher income but this is not generally the case for Black, Latinx or Asian Americans. Moreover, historically, the chance to become wealthy has been strongly dependent on race. So, might racial discrimination be the strongest determinant of social inequality?

Apparently, there are no ultimate causes of social inequality or linear relations between an ultimate cause and its effects. Income/wealth, education, gender, race, segregation and ageism are all relevant dimensions in the constitution of social inequality but interact in complicated ways: they may strengthen, neutralize or mitigate each other. This picture of 'co-determining' factors, interacting in changing configurations becomes even more complicated in a temporally extended life course perspective.

Over the last decades there have been several research paradigms that have focused on temporally extended patterns of social inequality; especially on the long term effects of socioeconomic adversity or disrespect. In Chapter 2 I have already discussed research on the effects of prolonged stress from occupational hierarchies and racial discrimination in the form of rising levels of allostatic load or a shortening of telomeres; both having a negative impact on health in later adulthood and life expectancies. Besides questions about the effects of prolonged disadvantage there is a question as to what extent initial situations may limit chances of upward mobility. Not only do people inherit material resources from their parents, such as savings or a house, they also inherit immaterial resources related to the parents' educational level; they inherit the neighborhood in which they grow up, with major differences in opportunities to attend a good school, find good work and receive high quality health care. Moreover, they inherit a skin color with potentially far reaching consequences as long as skin colors are targeted by discriminatory practices.

Such inherited advantages and disadvantages are not the result of individual choices, efforts or other merit by those who receive them, but they still exert a major influence on opportunities over the life course. Initial advantages and disadvantages tend to initiate processes of accumulation over the life course with the disadvantages tending to cluster more strongly together, reinforcing each other. This is what disadvantage does: it blocks or limits alternative options, especially those that might improve the situation. In a society such as the US, with little public support over the life course, those who begin their lives as members of a materially disadvantaged and discriminated minority will tend to remain disadvantaged with the risk of slipping down even further as they get older. Those, however, who begin their lives in advantaged positions will tend to keep these advantages obtaining even more favorable positions as their careers unfold. Such processes are examples of the cumulative (dis)advantages that become visible in the internal dynamics of cohorts. These mechanisms become especially striking in aging because inequalities tend to accumulate over the life course. Although there will be those who succeed in breaking away from their initial disadvantaged situations, longitudinal life course research shows how severe inequalities in opportunities tend to be reproduced through subsequent cohorts and become more pronounced as people become older or are denied the chances to become older.

Cumulative advantage and disadvantage

This phenomenon of increasing intra-cohort inequality has been explored by several researchers such as Stephen Crystal et al. (2017), Dale Dannefer (2003, 2020), Ken Ferraro et al. (2009) and Angela O'Rand (2002). This body of research on what may be called *Cumulative (Dis)Advantage* has gained considerable importance over the last three decades in its focus on the differences and inequalities *within* birth cohorts, correcting the still dominant emphasis on differences *between* seemingly homogeneous birth cohorts.

The investigation of the long-term effects of initial (dis)advantages has been guided by several theories. One of the most cited sources of this general research perspective has been the work of Robert Merton (1968) on scientific careers. The analysis of cumulative processes of advantage and disadvantage has, however, been much more developed in the work of the Swedish-American economist and sociologist Gunnar Myrdal (Dannefer, Gilbert & Han 2020). In his famous work on racial problems in the US *An American Dilemma* (1944) Myrdal already highlighted the crucial importance of cumulative (dis)advantage in understanding problems of race and articulated its systemic origins. Moreover, Myrdal already criticized the functionalist legitimation of these processes as beneficial to 'the system' that would later resurface in Merton's approach.

But Merton's article on scientific careers can still serve to introduce the basic point of this approach. He observed that small initial differences could result over time in major differences in outcome. A small initial difference in the reputation of teachers or an institute may lead to an early major grant in a specific discipline with opportunities to attain an avant-garde position which leads to more grants and still more publications, resulting in increasing inequalities between scientific careers that are largely independent of personal merit. Merton acknowledged the possible injustice of this mechanism but concluded that it would be beneficial for the larger system. He called this mechanism the *Matthew Principle*, referring to a quotation from the Gospel of Matthew: 'For unto every one that hath shall be given and he shall have abundance; but from him that hath not, shall be taken away even that what he hath' (13:12). To be clear, this 'Matthew Effect', as it has been called often, should not be taken as a Christian principle of justice. A little later in the text Matthew records the words of Jesus

> Truly I tell you, it is difficult for a rich man to enter the kingdom of heaven. Again I tell you, it is easier for a camel to pass through the eye of a needle than for a rich man to enter the kingdom of God.
>
> (19: 24)

But the first citation has proved to be a powerful metaphor for processes of social inequality in which the rich get richer and the poor get poorer (Dannefer, 1987; Rigney 2010).

One example to clarify the basic mechanism of the Matthew Effect over the life course is wealth accumulation. Take two persons who are both determined to save money to be able to face future financial challenges. Person A, who is not so poor that he cannot save at all, places $ 1,000 into an account in which the annual profits are reinvested, at an average rate of 4%. Person B, who is more affluent than A succeeds in investing $ 100,000 at the same rate. After a year A will have added $ 40 to his savings whereas B will have gained $4,000. After ten years A will have a total of $ 1,480 while B has seen his investment grow to $148,000 and if he succeeds in getting a higher annual return, let's say 7%, on his investment through bonds, shares, an investment fund or other ways that usually are beyond A's horizon, B will practically have doubled his initial investment and possess $196,715 after ten years. In fact, both the savings of A and B have grown but the initial difference ($99,000) has now grown to $195,235.

In absolute terms, both A and B have gained in wealth (leaving factors such as inflation aside), but in relative terms the difference in wealth between A and B has almost doubled and it is hard to see how A can ever catch up with B or, more importantly, ever attain a critical mass of economic security. At some moment A will probably need to cut into his savings to handle an emergency or because the fridge has ceased to function. The initial difference has grown considerably over time and in this sense A's disadvantage compared with B has accumulated. There is ample evidence to suggest that similar processes have long been representative for black–white inequality in the US. Because historically whites had more wealth than blacks, white children more often had the privilege to begin with an advantage in initial wealth and from there the inequality within their birth cohorts increased even further (Oliver & Shapiro 1995; Winship et al. 2022).

Cumulative disadvantage can have different forms. Teenage pregnancy, for instance, can easily lead to dropping out of high school, job insecurity, prolonged unemployment and financial insecurity, increasing the likelihood of marital conflict and possibly physical abuse leading to divorce, social isolation and becoming chronically ill. Without adequate support or intervention a single negative life event that might be absorbed in a situation of sufficient resources and adequate support can trigger a further range of negative effects that extend along the life course. Teenagers from advantaged backgrounds are much more likely to be supported in early stages of such unfortunate chains of events.

Some analyses of the growth of inequality in society emphasize processes of cumulative (dis)advantage that are generated in social interaction. According to Gould (2002) social hierarchies emerge from behavior that is led by four basic assumptions. The first assumption is that there are important differences between people in terms of their quality; secondly, that one's welfare is enhanced by associating with individuals who are assumed to be of higher quality. However, (third) such differences in quality are not fully observable, so that (fourth) that quality can only be inferred by observing the amount of attention a particular individual receives from others. The social processes that follow from these assumptions imply that the person who is initially assessed as getting more social attention than others, gets even more attention and comes to be seen as a special person with eminent qualities.

Present day social media offer a vivid illustration of these processes: there is an assumption that persons who are very active on social media in posting, blogging and vlogging are worth following because many others are already following them. The social attention that has been gathered by an individual generates more attention and still more attention from others. The compounding attention increases the perceived quality of sharing in this display of attention and therefore the welfare gains from associating with that person. Eventually it may be assumed that this person has something important to say about any subject that can be raised or that their commercial support of certain products can be trusted and deserves following.

Another example of research in this domain is Rosen's (1981) economic analysis of the careers of superstars. Rosen explored market mechanisms to answer the question why small differences in noticing talent can lead to situations in which, for instance, the top 10% of surgeons may get 300% more pay than less known colleagues, or top-10 pop stars earn thousands times more than unknown bands. As in Merton's approach there is an emphasis on an initial advantage in social attention or reputation that continues to generate more advantages over time.

Finally, the classical source of a critical analysis of processes of accumulation of (dis)advantage is Marx's critique of capitalism. His analysis in *The Capital* (1867/1967) aimed to show that the accumulation of riches for those who possess the social production forces fed on the exploitation and accumulation of misery of the workers: the immiseration (*Verelendung*) of the 'proletariat'. Their only possessions were their children (*proles*) – also a kind of old age insurance – and their bodily labor force. But Marx assumed that there would be an inevitable systemic inversion of the relations between the advantaged and the disadvantaged. This was grounded in his basic theorem that labor would be the only source of economic value so that, in the end, capitalism would break down because of its relentless exploitation of its only source of richness: the worker. This expectation has not been fulfilled and insofar as protest against inequalities could be tamed by a combination of repression and social rights, capitalism has succeeded in advancing the living standards of large populations but not without immiserating other large populations.

In contemporary capitalism theory Thomas Piketty (2014) appears to come close to Marx's view that severe inequalities belong to the nature of capitalism. In other words, the slow expansion of a supportive life course until the neoliberal turn would be an anomaly in the history of capitalism. Joseph Stiglitz (2015) is more optimistic about the potential of capitalism to improve the living conditions of the population. For him the growth model of postwar years is an example of what capitalism could and should be, with regular periods of rapid growth and more widely shared prosperity during which those at the bottom see their incomes grow faster than those at the top.

The long arm of childhood inequality

Although there is much attention for the effects of adult choices on health and the idea that chronic disease comes from bad health decisions of adults, the maturation of life course research has made it possible to establish plausible connections over long periods of time. To include childhood conditions in surveys of population health has been exceptional for a long time but this has been changing during the last decades. There is growing evidence that initial conditions: gestation, quality of fetal nutrition, maternal health, maternal nutrition around the time of conception or toxin exposure during gestation can have major consequences for health in later life. Besides concern about the destitute situations in which many children suffer as they grow up, there is rising concern about the long term effects of disadvantaged childhood on later life. Beyond establishing connections between early life conditions and later health problems, even birthweight or health of grand-parents and the possible consequences for their offspring have come into focus. Life course perspectives are eminently suited to undertake studies on inter-generational (dis)continuity of favorable or unfavorable health patterns, including socio-economic, biological, behavioral and psychosocial conditions. Scientists such as Davey Smith (2003) and others have begun to explore the inter-generational genesis of unequally distributed health conditions (Davey Smith, Harding & Rosato 2000; Davey Smith, Whitley, Gissler & Hemminki 2000; Shaikh et al. 2019). These studies also contribute to understanding how improving the situation of children can help to break repetitive cycles of poverty and disadvantage.

Since the late 1980s there has been much research on *The Fetal Origins of Adult Disease*: a research paradigm that was initiated by studies that showed how certain groups of adults with cardiovascular disease had been dis-proportionately low birth weight babies (Barker et al., 1989). According to this deepening and expanding research, poor growth in utero can lead to a predisposition for a variety of chronic disorders; not only cardiovascular disease but also type 2 diabetes, osteoporosis and hypertension. Growth in utero is an example of what authors from life course epidemiology have called a critical developmental period (Ben-Shlomo & Kuh 2002). Typical of a critical period is that certain environmental conditions can easily lead to lifelong effects as unfavorable developments during such periods are wholly or partially irreversible. During intrauterine life and early childhood immune, neurologic, respiratory and endocrine systems are being pro-grammed and locked in so that negative influences can have a large impact on health in later life, including effects on reasoning abilities. Examples include permanent damage to brain development and cognitive capacities as a result of malnutrition or lead exposure in early life (Verina, Rohde & Guilarte 2007).

Being born with low birth weight or being exposed to other childhood deprivation is not something that happens at random. Such bad starts in life tend to be distributed according to patterns of social inequality. According to research on a national sample of high risk infants in the US, 35% of toddlers from families with low income appeared to be exposed to detrimental conditions such as: being born with poor health and less than 1500 g birth weight; having an unemployed, depressed high school drop-out teenage mother who is pressed down by stressful life events and inadequate social support; father absence; too many people living in a small place, and negative parenting values. In contrast, only 5% of the toddlers from middle class families suffered similar levels of risk (Liaw & Brooks-Gunn, 1994).

Further research on *The Long Arm of Childhood* (Hayward & Gorman 2004) has shown that the period that is likely to be constitutive for health predispositions in later life is not limited to the fetal period but extends into infancy and childhood. This has been supported by biological, especially epigenetics research[11] on childhood origins of health and disease (Gluckman & Hanson 2006). Research on later life consequences, in particular dementia, of vascular risks in early adulthood has prompted the editors of *JAMA Neurology* to emphasize that the understanding and effective prevention of dementia will require going beyond the dominant amyloid hypothesis with its focus on elderly patients as the best targets for preventive interventions, to include not only adolescence but also early-childhood and perinatal factors (Lane & Barnes et al. 2019; Seshadri 2019).

In Chapter 2 I have already discussed the worrisome effects of prolonged stress from, for instance, occupational hierarchy or racial discrimination on adult health. Prolonged stress is, however, not only a problem for adults. A study of a group of 466 European American and 100 African American boys and girls from a broad range of socioeconomic levels who were followed from age 5 to 10 years showed that children from families with a low socioeconomic status had a significantly higher risk of being burdened by stressful circumstances (Deater-Deckard et al. 1998). Examples included single parenthood, high child–adult ratio, teenage pregnancy, unplanned pregnancy, maternal social isolation, low parental involvement of father, marital conflict, violence, harsh discipline, physical harm, lack of positive parenting, peer rejection, and unstable peer groups. The researchers conclude that one-third to almost one-half of the problems in middle childhood, such as hostile and aggressive physical behavior toward others, impulsivity and hyperactivity, and noncompliance with adult and peer limit setting, can be predicted from risk factors present at the age of five years. Generally, the lower the household income, the greater the risks that children are raised by an overburdened teenage mother; that they are growing up amidst family turmoil and conflict; go through maternal partner changes; that they are separated from their family, and exposed to violence.

Children are the poorest age group in the US, with poverty rates that are much higher than among adults. According to the 2017 report of the US Census Bureau on *Income and Poverty in the United States*[12] children under the age of 18 years were among the prime victims of the 2008 recession as the child poverty rate climbed to 22%. In 2017 it declined to 17.5% which is still higher than the poverty rates for adults ages 18–64 (11.2%) and adults ages 65 and over (9.2%). Although children formed only a little over a fifth of the US population, they represented in 2017 a third of all citizens in poverty. But the consequences can be severe: poor children are more likely to experience lead poisoning (Rabito, Shorter & White 2003); they are less likely to be immunized; they are more likely to be obese – with higher risks for later heart attacks and diabetes – and to have a higher chance of having asthma and reduced lung capacity. Finally, they have a higher chance to die in childhood (Yu et al. 2022). As can be expected, there were important differences between white children and children from minorities; while a third of black children lived in poverty, only a tenth of white children suffered from these conditions. Besides children's suffering from such miserable conditions which are in no way caused by their own actions, their health, economic security, and quality of education are likely to have far-reaching effects, some of which are manifested decades later. It would have been better to prevent these problems, both on humanitarian grounds and in terms of a growing burden on society.

But are adults who were born in such disadvantaged situations doomed to remain within the boundaries that were set for them when they were born? Should policies to address pathogenic developments forget about the cohorts who have already been born and concentrate on improving the situations of newborns? Denying this should not evoke ideas of the heroic individual who can transcend the limitations of the past if he only tries hard enough. Disadvantaged childhoods may have lasting negative health effects but circumstances along the life course may mitigate such effects or make them worse.

In exploring the, possibly, life long damage that is inflicted on young children there is an important difference between the *latency* approach and the *pathways* approach (Keating & Hertzman 1999). The latency approach argues that psychosocial and socioeconomic conditions early in life have strong impact on later life, independent of intervening experience. The pathways approach focuses on cumulative effects of life events and the reinforcing or mitigating effect of differing psychosocial and socioeconomic circumstances throughout the life course. According to this view early childhood experiences are just one form of life events with, possibly, long-term effects while later experiences and life events, including interventions, have a co-constitutive effect on later results. Generally, life course evidence supports the pathways approach: there is, in other words, not one single 'critical period'; there is much research demonstrating how childhood effects are mediated by adult circumstances (e.g. Kelley & Huang 2017).

Chioun Lee and Carol Ryff (2019) have explored how early-life adversities such as socioeconomic disadvantage, family instability, and abuse may result in elevated risk of mortality in midlife and old age. There are, however, no direct links: so-called life-course mediators such as material, psychological, and social resources, healthy lifestyle and substance abuse play a role in determining the situation in later life. In a study covering a 20-year period (1995–2015) early life socioeconomic status and abuse turned out to be most salient. Although childhood abuse was found among families with different socioeconomic status the highest risk of death was for men and women where a background of low socioeconomic status was combined with frequent abuse. But for women frequent abuse increased the risk of mortality even if they grew up in families with a middle or even high socioeconomic status. Of the life course mediators, material resources played the most significant role, albeit more strongly for men than for women. Lee and Ryff concluded that traumatic experiences during the critical period of early life may compromise later-life health more for women than for men.

So, growing up in situations of poor resources (low socioeconomic status) may have health undermining effects although these may be mitigated or compensated by later experiences. But, as shown above, these processes do not work in the same way for men and women. A second example of the different effect of low socioeconomic status in childhood on men versus women is given by Lee, Tsenkova, Boylan & Ryff (2018). They investigated the effect of socioeconomically disadvantaged childhood on adult health practices such as leisure time physical activity and diet. Both practices are key factors in the development of metabolic syndrome and are open to change by policies. Both men and women of these backgrounds developed a tendency not to participate in leisure-time physical activity, the domain most consistently linked with health benefits; even when their socio-economic status had improved in adulthood. For *men*, lack of leisure-time physical activity and unhealthy food consumption largely explained the association between early-life disadvantage and metabolic syndrome. For *women*, leisure-time physical activity partially accounted for the association; for them there appeared to be a stronger effect of a socioeconomically disadvantaged childhood. These findings also underscore the need to develop gender-specific interventions in adulthood.

Locking in children's social opportunities...

That important bodily systems may be permanently damaged during gestation and childhood is in itself bad enough but, unfortunately, not the whole story: social opportunities also tend to be locked in at a very young age. A research project from the *Rochester Longitudinal Study* followed 1st grade to 12th grade children from 145 families with different socioeconomic and racial backgrounds (Gutman, Sameroff & Cole 2003). Children from families with a minority background and low socioeconomic status were confronted more often than their more advantaged age peers with such problems as father absence, stressful life events, poor parenting beliefs, maternal anxiety, poor maternal mental health, and low levels of positive maternal child interaction. As a result these children generally had lower achievement test scores, more grade retentions and course failures, and fewer completed years of schooling than their more advantaged peers. Beginning from disadvantaged backgrounds children tended to fall still further behind as they passed through school. Although there have been speculations, for instance by Gottfredson (2004) that intelligence might be the 'fundamental cause' of social class inequalities in health, the *Rochester Longitudinal Study* shows that early scores of high intelligence were usually sustained or improved for advantaged children but, unfortunately, had no protective effects for children who grew up in difficult circumstances.

Childhood socioeconomic conditions, the type of community the family lived in, family living arrangements, and mother's work status have been shown to have major consequences for adolescent development, educational attainment, occupational achievement, and adult poverty or wealth, as well as for later life outcomes, such as longevity, disability, functional limitations, and mental health (Case, Fertig & Paxson 2005; Elo 2009; Last et al. 2018). Life long enduring harmful effects of early childhood inequality for income, somatic and psychic health and life expectancy have also been demonstrated by several British studies of cohorts born in the 1930s and 1940s (Evans, Wolfe & Adler 2012). Children who grow up in advantaged socioeconomic conditions tend to complete more education, have higher earnings, accumulate more wealth and live longer in good health. Early disadvantages in these domains tend to set in motion a series of cascading socioeconomic and life events that are likely to shorten life, while those who were born into advantaged circumstances retain some of those advantages throughout a relatively long life.

...and perspectives to unlock them

As we are gradually getting a clearer picture of the dynamics of social inequality along the life course, the opportunities to change some of these mechanisms in a more favorable direction are also emerging. Initial disadvantages may be harmful enough but much depends on whether disadvantaged children are kept within trajectories which keep them separate from those who were born in more advantaged situations; moreover, whether they are supported in early childhood *and* later along the life course. Bad starts in life do not have to be fully determining: low birthweight babies, for instance, are only at risk for non-insulin dependent diabetes if they continue to get more calories than they need (Hales & Barker 2001; Bateson, Barker & Clutton-Brock 2004). Depending on their severity the scars of childhood adversity may continue to have a negative impact, however, with adequate support, people are not necessarily caught in their pasts. Early childhood interventions appear to be especially effective if they take a more comprehensive approach to alleviate the multiple social risks in children's lives rather than targeting singular effects from deprivation. Moreover, early supportive programs such as *Head Start* need to be followed up so that earlier gains are not lost (Dannefer, Kelley-Moore & Huang 2016). Conditions in adulthood can erase, mitigate or amplify negative as well as positive influences.

To enlarge our understanding of how social inequalities are reproduced since childhood and how such processes can be changed in a positive direction, beside health related studies on the 'Long Arm of Childhood' we need also to look at studies like '*The Long Shadow: Family Background, Disadvantaged Urban Youth, and the Transition to Adulthood*' by Alexander, Entwistle & Olson (2014) on growing up in disadvantaged urban neighborhoods. This particular study is about Baltimore which, like so many East Coast and Midwest cities after the implosion of manufacturing jobs since the neoliberal turn, has been confronted with a rapid onset of poverty and high unemployment in combination with public poverty to alleviate economic distress. In that troublesome context the West Baltimore study highlights the significance of early-life opportunities available to low-income populations. It followed children who grew up in West Baltimore over 25 years, focusing on the question of how opportunities available to them as early as first grade shaped their socioeconomic status as adults, and affected their long-term wellbeing. The results show that children who lived in more cohesive neighborhoods, had stronger families, and attended better schools, tended to fare much better in life.

Early support of vulnerable families may save their children, their parents and society much misery. Although parents remain responsible for taking care of their children as best as they can, reducing structural problems to their individual responsibility, calling for punitive responses to childhood abuse may sound great as a testimony of a firm moral stance, however it evades public responsibilities that will not only lead to much higher costs along the life course, but also to an impressive loss of individual wellbeing and future productivity. Chances of living a reasonably long and healthy life or living for many years in bad health and to die relatively early, depend not only on early childhood, but also on circumstances in adulthood. Demonstrating the continuing influence of childhood circumstances on adulthood should not lead to the assumption that, once maturity has been reached, social contexts do not matter that much.

Life course perspectives on intervention, however, typically neglect adulthood (cf. Halfon & Hochstein, 2002). They contain programs for intervention during childhood, adolescence and old age, focusing subsequently on family needs, peer groups and social networks. 'Normal' adults are targeted by a commercial advice industry which spreads its seductive messages, ranging from health behaviors to life style and investment opportunities with consumers in mind who can afford their products. Most adults would benefit more from policies that protect their income, safety and self respect in working situations; not unlike what trade unions have been trying to do for their members in many other high-income countries.

It would be a shame if advances in this domain of public health were blown by policies which assume that the uncontextualized 'individual' will flourish whatever the circumstances, if he only makes the right choices and remains determined to succeed. The collapse of manufacturing; the downward mobility of blue-collar workers, or urban decline can hardly be explained by irresponsible behavior of the victims (Burton & Whitfield

2006). Likewise, the choices of African Americans or Native Americans cannot explain why and how processes of discrimination originated, why they continue, or why institutions fail to intervene so that disadvantages continue to cumulate with long-term effects. An impressive account of such accumulation of problems with limited options for individual choices resulting in almost inevitable misery is given by Timothy Black in his 2009 book *When a Heart Turns Rock Solid: The Lives of Three Puerto Rican Brothers On and Off the Streets*. It tells the story of a Puerto Rican family confronted with challenges, such as failing education policies, failing protection of work situations, a War on Drugs, and a booming incarceration industry.

In adulthood, occupationally and environmentally based hazards, industrial accidents, occupational stress, and limited access to health services continue to lead to major health inequalities (Wilkinson 1996; Marmot & Wilkinson 1999). People who are working in unskilled occupations are twice as likely to suffer from disabilities, compared to those working in higher skilled occupations (Ginn & Arber 1993). The impact of societal forces may be disproportionally strong in early life, but they can also be overwhelming in adulthood. As soon as society comes into heavy weather, be it through an economic crisis or a pandemic, the overload of pressure on those who are already vulnerable will highlight structures of social inequality that were not as visible before. As those who are in advantaged positions are better protected, the negative consequences of anything calamitous will hit the most vulnerable. They bear the disproportionate brunt of climate change, natural disasters, mass unemployment, economic crises, or pandemics.

A troubling perspective: the destruction of human habitats…

As we have seen in discussing the many factors that are constitutive of social inequality, citizens in deprived socioeconomic circumstances have a much bigger chance of living in unhealthy and burdening environments that are rich in exposure to toxins, hazardous wastes or ambient pollutants *and* noise, crowding or congestion *and* broken families *and* substandard housing *and* poor neighborhood conditions, including higher traffic volume or abandoned lots, *and* poor municipal services regarding transportation, clean water or sanitation *and* fewer suitable places to engage in physical exercise *and* less opportunities to purchase healthy foods, along with more hazardous working conditions. Moreover, as Matthew Desmond describes in his *Evicted: Poverty and Profit in the American City* (2016) poor families not only have to struggle to keep a roof over their heads or to have access to health care, but they are also confronted with a lack of recognition as a dignified person. The effects of macro societal structures interact with daily labeling as a person of negligible importance.

The physiological consequences of chronic stress, together with feelings of powerlessness and alienation from society, combined with poor social support from similarly marginalized people weigh heavy on daily life and on future chances for improvement. For those who are growing up in such circumstances the chances of getting a good education and a decent job are not very favorable, resulting in high risks of chronic disease in midlife, a relatively short life expectancy combined with a relatively long period of health problems and disabilities. Poor citizens are contained and pushed into neglected, badly maintained and impoverished areas. This may all seem to be happening because of bad luck, bad coincidence or because of bad choices of those concerned, but it is the consequence of an unequal society led by power elites who are primarily interested in continuing this inequality, by accumulating and concentrating societal wealth even more.

Health inequalities and broader social inequalities have not been brought into the Western world by the neoliberal turn of capitalism. But it has deepened them by breaking down a modestly supportive life course, pushing growing parts of the population into a socioeconomic uncertainty that is propagated as exciting entrepreneurialism. Before, even unskilled workers used to have stable contracts with their employers, being backed up by labor unions to negotiate their working conditions. The contemporary situation is one in which the majority of US citizens are exposed to macro developments beyond their control; social protection has not kept up with these changing conditions although wealth has grown to proportions that could only be dreamt of at the beginning of the neoliberal turn of capitalism.

The destruction of secure human habitats where people can live well has become a global concern with regard to such developments as climate change. But even within high-income countries there are structural processes that are putting human habitats under increasing pressure. Its inhabitants may be formally protected as citizens but their habitats are being destroyed with shocking indifference; not unlike the destruction of habitats of, for instance, Amazon tribes or endangered species. This is not primarily a process of bloody murdering, but rather a silent systemic process of malign neglect: nothing personal, just business…

…and the need to address this – emerging questions of social justice

In this chapter we have seen ample evidence that processes of cumulative (dis)advantage are the main drivers of increasing inequalities over the life course, resulting in the perverse longevity gap of shorter but more miserable lives or, if disadvantaged citizens live long enough, poverty and insecurity in old age. Is it possible to prevent these processes from happening? According to DiPrete and Eirich (2006) increasing inequality inevitably takes place within any population over time: it would be 'a general mechanism across any temporal process … in which a favorable relative position becomes a resource that produces relative further gains' (p. 271); a view that has also been articulated by Dannefer (2020). If, indeed, mechanisms of cumulative (dis)advantage take place within any population over time and will be repeated in every birth cohort so that intra-cohort differences as well as inequalities will increase as the cohort members get older, it would be realistic to acknowledge that and stop holding the disadvantaged responsible for these mechanisms. Moreover, it will be necessary to support those citizens who see their disadvantages accumulate without being able to break out of vicious circles. In spite of the systemic accumulation of disadvantages an organization of the life course that supports citizens in difficult situations might prevent problems from begetting more problems. It has been demonstrated over the last four decades that political agendas can be implemented quite effectively, albeit in the wrong direction. There may continue to be growing differences between citizens over the life course but they don't have to become grave inequalities.

The dominant political and economic elites, however, appear to have abandoned the population: they profitably manipulate situations of insecurity and crisis leaving the majority of citizens without proper social rights. In their alarming book *Deaths of Despair and the Future of Capitalism* Anne Case and Angus Deaton write: 'The Sheriff of Nottingham has taken up residence in Washington DC, and the good cops have left town. Robin Hood is nowhere to be seen' (p. 261). Although they may have aimed at Trump, he is mainly a personification of much broader trends in US society and even the US is 'only' the most prominent example of a developmental model that has been embraced by international elites for its high rewards, whilst failing the large majority of the population. It is as yet unclear whether these trends will be mitigated or reversed in the near future. They are certainly not inevitable. A large minority of the US population, including an important minority of its political elite, is open to facing these problems and actually tries to change some of them for the better. But the continuing concentration of wealth cannot be separated from a concentrated power that will be determined to defend and increase its advantages.

Notes

1 See McKinsey & Company (2021) 'Race in the workplace: The Black experience in the US private sector'. https://www.mckinsey.com/featured-insights/diversity-and-inclusion/race-in-the-workplace-the-black-experience-in-the-us-private-sector

2 Income (including annuitized value of wealth) inequality was measured using a series of Gini coefficients indicating inequality in scores between 0, indicating complete equality, and 1, a situation where one person owns everything.

3 National Institute on Retirement Security. 'Still Shortchanged: An Update on Women's Retirement Preparedness': https://www.nirsonline.org/reports/stillshortchanged/

4 https://williamsinstitute.law.ucla.edu/visualization/lgbt-stats/?topic=LGBT#density

5 https://www.brookings.edu/wp-content/uploads/2016/06/02_economic_mobi lity_sawhill.pdf
6 https://www.kff.org/other/state-indicator/opioid-overdose-deaths-by-raceethni city/?dataView=1&currentTimeframe=0&selectedDistributions=white-non-hispanic–black-non-hispanic–hispanic&sortModel=%7B%22colId%22:%22Location %22,%22sort%22:%22asc%22%7D
7 http://www.justicepolicy.org/news/8775
8 https://www.pewresearch.org/fact-tank/2020/05/06/share-of-black-white-hispanic-americans-in-prison-2018-vs-2006/
9 *Prisoners in 2019* Bureau of Justice Statistics https://www.bjs.gov/index.cfm?ty=tp&tid=11
10 https://www.cdc.gov/nchs/nvss/usaleep/usaleep.html
11 Epigenetics is the study of heritable changes in gene expression (active versus inactive genes) that do not involve changes to the underlying DNA sequence — a change in phenotype without a change in genotype — which in turn affects how cells read the genes.
12 http://bit.ly/2NTJ8wS

Chapter 4

Ageism as a form of social inequality

Overview

This chapter discusses ageism as a form of social inequality, followed by a questioning of some dominant interpretations of age and aging. The specific meaning of ageism will be explored, in contrast to racism or sexism, and placed in a historical context. An important field of tension exists between, on the one hand, older people who are growing in number while many of them retain their vitality and continue to play a creative, productive or caring role in society. And on the other hand, new forms of ageism that tend to obstruct or systematically misrepresent their participation in society, for instance in the media, on specific internet sites and on Facebook. Next is a discussion of the relationship between ageism and other forms of social inequality as distinguished in Chapter 3. The typical neoliberal reframing of aging will be debated: ongoing participation as an individual entrepreneur who remains in control of his own life as a successful, productive or active senior citizen. Part of this reframing has been the transformation of pensions into more precarious forms such as entrepreneurial investment strategies with less than satisfactory or even disastrous outcomes. I will discuss some critical approaches to ageism based on scientific research, together with activists who have become vocal in their protest against different forms of ageism. In the last section there will be a critique of that popular habit to generalize in a negative way about people above a certain age; as if 'age' works like a clock inside people, determining their capacities and needs, in complete neglect of all differences between them. To clarify the issues that are at stake in this chapter it is important to distinguish different uses and meanings of the expression 'aging'.

Introduction

One of the propositions of this book has been that social inequality needs to be seen in a life course perspective. Although much depends on adult agency in the form of completing education, choice of partners,

DOI: 10.4324/9781003392590-5

commitment to work and career it has become clear that adult agency can be supported or frustrated by cultural and structural forces. Those who are blessed to be born in a wealthy and loving family; who don't have to go through the shocking childhood experience that they are discriminated against because they have the skin color of the ones they love; who have the opportunity to enjoy an excellent education opening the path to interesting and well paid work, may not even notice those structural and cultural forces because they work for them, not against them. Those, however, who are born into a poor broken family in a bad neighborhood; who go to a school with too few resources and too many social problems will have much more difficulty finding entry into higher education or good and rewarding work. The research that has been presented in the earlier chapters of this book indicates that for them, the chances to reach 'old age' in good health are not very favorable. Once people have become 'old' in a formal, age related sense such inequalities tend to be overlooked. 'Old age' tends to be seen as a uniform natural process where genetics rule, or it is seen as a phase when life styles show their consequences. Aging studies that limit their research to those who have already become 'old' miss an opportunity to understand how major inequalities among those older people have come about.

Previously accumulated inequalities will probably continue to evolve as people get older but this does not mean that the transition into old age can be seen as a neutral process. On the one hand, it is a transition to a more protected situation: being entitled to Medicare and Social Security will be a major relief for many citizens, not least for those who have been deprived, yet live long enough to qualify for them. On the other hand, once people are seen as 'old' they are potentially exposed to ageism, which may already hit them well before reaching retirement age. The exclusion of older people from 'adult normality' is often accompanied by subtle but also by rude forms of degradation, denigration or contempt. The fact that older people cannot clearly be demarcated and don't act as a social group does not mean that there is no ageism. Age related policies and attitudes will potentially affect everyone who falls into this age category, although the damage it does depends very much on their material and immaterial resources.

It is astonishing how little attention ageism has received in political philosophy or theories of social justice. References to ageism are really scarce and discussions even more so. Iris Marion Young, for instance, does criticize in her book *Justice and the Politics of Difference* (1990: 135) the Foucaultian 'normalizing gaze' of modern science which medicalizes old age and perceives older people merely as old bodies. The broader debate about identity politics or 'politics of difference', however, appears to be absorbed by problems of race, ethnicity, or gender identities. Even in theories about social justice and aging, respectively the life course (discussed in Ch.6), there is little sign that there might be something like ageism as a problem of disrespect with major consequences. In the *Generational Equity* pamphlets (Ch.6) ageism is even legitimated in the name of equity or equality between 'generations'. The one-sided emphasis on material resources in relation to the dreaded 'bottomless pit of health care costs' (see Ch.7) contrasts remarkably with the emphasis on respect and identity that we see in public discussions of ageism among senior citizens

What is ageism?

The term was coined in 1969 by the psychiatrist Robert Butler who was shocked by the dismissive and contemptuous attitude toward older people and their diseases by many of his teachers at medical school. Butler defined 'ageism' as 'a process of systematic stereotyping of and discrimination against people because they are old, just as racism and sexism accomplish this for skin color and gender' (Butler 1980, p. 9). Wilkinson and Ferraro (2002) have expanded the meaning of 'ageism' into a constellation of elements, to prejudicial *attitudes* towards older people, old age, and the aging process, to discriminatory *practices* against older people, and to *institutional* practices and policies that perpetuate stereotypes about elderly people.

An important element that these different forms of discrimination have in common is the underlying ideology that the perceived inferiority of the discriminated is justified by their inferior nature. This naturalization (see Ch.7) of inferiority is a classical but nasty form in which prejudice is justified or legitimized. Such 'natural facts' are often not only accepted by those who assume to benefit at least temporarily from this form of discrimination but even by those who suffer from it, although it diminishes their ability to form, revise and pursue more meaningful ways of living.

Ageism is a form of cultural oppression in which false beliefs regarding the worth of typified older people are transmitted and displayed in denigrating attitudes and harmful actions. In many cases it is fed by a broader tendency to identify the perceived *instrumental* value of groups with their *intrinsic* value as persons or citizens. Even in Kant's famous formulation of the categorical imperative we find already this ambivalence: 'Act in such a way that you treat humanity, whether in your own person or in the person of any other, never merely as a means to an end, but always at the same time as an end' (1785/1993, p. 36). 'Never merely', so in principle, *also* as a means to an end.

This distinction between intrinsic and instrumental value helps to articulate some differences between discriminatory processes that were seen as identical by Butler: racism and sexism on the one hand and ageism on the other (Wagland 2004; Bytheway 1995). Although racism is characterized by a strong depreciation or even denial of the intrinsic value, the moral worth and human dignity of other races, this does not imply that they are seen as people without any instrumental value: many slave-owners have gathered fortunes thanks to the work of enslaved persons. Patriarchal sexism does not doubt the instrumental value of women: they are seen as very valuable, especially to give birth to sons, and they are regarded as a formidable working force. But although they may be loved by the sexist in some peculiar way, they are not really taken seriously as autonomous persons. They are seen as dependent on guidance from men which diminishes their intrinsic value as human beings. The inferior nature of the discriminated implies that their intrinsic value as human being is inferior to those who are actively discriminating.

Ageism is different from racism and sexism because it targets all people as they get older: it affects the older woman as well as the old sexist patriarch who may be ridiculed by his offspring because he lost his prowess. He may, however, still retain much of his status; this difference in impact of ageism will be discussed later. Here, we are dealing with the difference between racism and sexism on the one hand and ageism on the other hand. Whereas racism and sexism would be legitimated by the idea of an innate natural inferiority, ageism assumes a natural process of decline from 'normal adulthood' which would owe its intrinsic value to its instrumental value, into an 'old age' that would have become intrinsically inferior because it has lost this instrumental value.

Do people have a choice in this? They can try to evade ageism in trying to hide wrinkles, grey hair and other signs that they may fall in that ambivalent category. However, ageism does not depend on whether people regard themselves as 'old': others are defining them as such. At a certain moment, depending on circumstances, people experience that they are seen by others as 'old'. The German philosopher Ernst Bloch (1885–1977), who lived a long and intellectually productive life, recalls in his major work *The Principle of Hope* (1995) how he suddenly and shockingly realized that he had become old in the eyes of others when a young woman stood up and offered him her seat on a bus. Never before had he thought of himself as being 'old'. This may be typical for the experience of getting older: people don't (like to) think of themselves as being old and even try to convince others that they are still young. This already tells a lot about how unattractive it has become to be seen as old. Although many people live much longer than they expected, they don't identify with becoming older. As long as they can, they tend to identify with being a 'normal adult' and regard 'aging well' as staying young; which seems contradictory and underlines the absence of a meaningful conception of growing older (Baars 2012). As soon as they undeniably need help the age-defying narratives of the third age make place for the decline narratives of the fourth age (Laceulle 2018). The consequences of being labeled as 'old' may be exclusion from contact; not to be taken seriously; to be taken advantage of; being seen as deaf, forgetful or even dementing.

Because of the disqualifying characteristics that are associated with 'being old', older people are reluctant to define themselves as members of such a group. This membership is not chosen and would rather be avoided, which reveals its origin in power and domination.

Even when people have accepted that they have become old as a matter of fact, this doesn't mean that they want to be identified with the ways in which older people are highlighted and framed by the media between the extremes of dementia and the spectacular vitality of old superheroes. Anyway, they usually have stronger ties to younger people, for instance in their family, than to other older people. Throughout their history they were not old but young: they recollect being very small, at school, dating, beginning to work, having children and so on. Older people do share a history with their cohort but not as 'old people', rather as their opposite.

A question that may be raised is whether the concept of ageism should be limited to discriminatory processes affecting only older people or should it also include, for instance, young adolescents as was recently proposed by the *Global Report on Ageism* (WHO 2021). Both age categories are often seen as marginal, a threat to social order and established morality because they typically divert from 'normal' adulthood. They tend to be seen as burdensome because they are seen as vulnerable, dependent or in need of control 'for their own good'. There is, however, an important difference between these age categories because the young will grow out of discrimination, whereas older people are trapped in it. The negative effects of ageism – I will continue to use this as referring to the discrimination of older people – may even become stronger as they become more vulnerable.

Some of the dynamics of such a process have been explained in a classical article by Kuypers and Bengtson (1973) about the social-breakdown syndrome of 'normal' aging. They argue that an individual's sense of self, his ability to mediate between self and society, and his orientation to personal mastery are heavily influenced by the ways they are labeled over the life course. Because of the loss of respected qualities (such as being productive or being a parent) and a lack of positive perspectives for a possibly very long phase of 'old age', the dependence on external, but increasingly negative labeling leads to a loss of coping abilities and the development of an internalized sense of incompetence. It does not help that many older people have had negative attitudes towards older people while they were young or 'normal' adults. They may find out with a shock that they are now the subject of the same negative prejudice they have held for a very long time. Ageism works like a boomerang: when you project it into the future it will come back to strike you (Levy 2022).

Ageism in historical context

Unfortunately, negative cultural stereotypes about older people have deep historical roots. Although many appear to think that we have lost a respect for older people that was taken for granted in the past, such historical generalizations collide with the facts. In terms of Peter Laslett's (1988) historical study we can call this a version of the 'world-we have-lost' syndrome. In his broad historical study of aging David Troyansky (2015) has shown how diverse the situation of older people has been: in some cultures they encountered growing respect as they got older, but in other cultures they were confronted with negative prejudice and disdain. Other historical studies, such as the work of Pat Thane (2005) show this same pattern of ambivalence: respect for older people did exist but the reverse is also true. In *Aging and the Art of Living* (2012) I have discussed how the ancient Greek philosophers, who are often praised for their veneration of old wise men shared this ambivalence as they wrestled with respect for tradition versus critical argumentation. In his book *Geronticide: Killing the Elderly* (2001) Mike Brogden even argues that different forms of geronticide have been around for a very long time and that they are still a threat to older people. So, we have ample reason to doubt that there has ever been a golden age in Western culture where 'old age' was highly respected without ambivalence or contradiction (Parkin 2003).

Extensive research on age stereotypes has shown, however, that these have increased in negativity over the last 200 years (Levy 2009). This conclusion has been based on two content analysis studies of materials that were widely read by the public. The first of these examined the development of age stereotypes over time by analyzing the *Corpus of Historical American English*, a database of over 400 million words drawn from books, magazines, newspapers, and academic journals that were published between 1810 and 2009. The conclusion was that age stereotypes tended to be positive during the first 80 years of these two centuries and that they became increasingly negative later (Ng et al. 2015). The second study was based on *Google Books Ngram Viewer*, determining the frequency of words drawn from over five-million digitized books that were published in English from 1800 to 2000. Here again, analysis of the usage of terms and adjectives describing 'the elderly' revealed that there was a shift from more positive to less positive or negative terms (Mason, Kuntz & McGill 2015). The term 'geezers' was rarely used since its first appearance in 1900 before it became popular among contemporary ageists.

The results of these studies are backed up by earlier historical work demonstrating that older persons tended to be integrated into daily life and honored in colonial America, whereas they have become increasingly segregated and disparaged in more recent times. One indication of a loss of positive age stereotypes is the elimination of privileged seating arrangements in meeting halls for older members of the community (Achenbaum 1995; Chudacoff 1989; Cole 1992). This did not always mean undivided respect for all older people: much veneration of old age was actually a veneration of wealth and poor older people were not necessarily respected (Dannefer 2022).

Multiple paradoxes in the tenacity of ageism

Until recently, the last two centuries have seen major improvements in terms of health and life expectancies in the developed countries. Oeppen and Vaupel (2000) calculated – before the more recent declines – that there has been an 20–25% increase in best practice life expectancies for each period since the early 19th century. One would expect that this would lead to a more positive view of aging and older people (Levy (2017). *First*, on average, the health of older people has been steadily improving. Over the last century there has been a widely documented decrease in the rates of disability, hip fractures, dementia, visual problems, arthritis, emphysema, and heart disease, as well as declines in cholesterol level, and blood pressure. Improved health might also have served as a refutation of negative age stereotypes, which are predominantly based on the assumption that bad health is inherent in aging (Levy 2003). *Second*, as a growing percentage of the population becomes old and continues – in spite of ageist obstructions – to participate in society, one would expect an increase in contact between 'the young' and 'the old' which might break down negative stereotypes. This is usually the case when there is more contact between groups that have prejudice towards one another. Unfortunately, according to Hagestad and Uhlenberg (2005) there has been an increase in the 'spatial, group, institutional, and cultural separation of persons who are in different phases of the life course' (p. 345). It appears that there is a societal perception that it is beneficial to separate older from younger persons (Chudacoff 1989). *Third*, several other previously stigmatized groups have increasingly been regarded more positively. A survey covering the past 100 years concluded that a 'Humanitarian Revolution' has occurred, in which negative stereotypes about disempowered groups have become more positive because of a decline in the 'dehumanizing and demonization of minority groups' that 'transformed Western culture' (Pinker 2012, pp. 168, 392). Indeed, from 1933 to 2001, the percentage of students that described African Americans as 'ignorant' fell from 38% to 3.5% (Madon et al. 2001). Other groups also appear to suffer less from exclusion such as publicly self-identified gay and lesbian people who have seen the legalization of same-sex marriage and the removal of homosexuality from the American Psychiatric Association's *Diagnostic and Statistical Manual of Mental Disorders* that used to legitimize prejudice against them. If we can accept this rosy picture at all, this 'Humanitarian Revolution' has not yet embraced older people (Levy 2017).

As age stereotypes appear to become more negative this invites the question what the reasons might be behind this development. Probably a combination of different factors, such as a positive premium during the continuing process of modernization on what is (supposed to be) new, combined with commercial pressure of a growing youth culture since the 1960s (Baars 2006, 2012a). Another important element is the 'bottomless pit of health care costs' syndrome that has also become popular in different theories on social justice and aging, ranging from the *Generational Equity* advocates and Callahan to Daniels (see Ch.7). Research among college students across 26 countries, including many of the Western world, on views of aging within their cultures showed that there were relatively strong negative views about aging and about 'the old' as drainers of scarce resources (Löckenhoff et al. 2009). Moreover, the multi-billion-dollar anti-aging industry also contributed to a negative view of aging as they thrive on portraying aging as a process of inevitable and rapid decline unless you are willing to buy the products that will save you from such a horrible fate. The paradoxical result of this commercial enterprise has been to draw increasingly young people, even teenagers, into a battle against decline that they are threatened with losing if they fail to use the creams that will prevent the young skin from developing the feared deep wrinkles of old age. As a result of this commercially manipulated anti-aging culture young people are portrayed as 'getting older' at an increasingly younger age. The flipside of this 'paradox of the increasingly younger older person' (Baars 2012) is that in an other market segment older persons are portrayed as staying young and dynamic. These markets target especially the well off and their advertised life style of luxury leisure can easily lead to mixed feelings among those who have to struggle daily to make ends meet. Ageism clearly interacts with social inequality; it does not hit all older persons equally hard (see below).

It is of course possible to deny the relevance of ageism; just like this has been done with sexism or racism and to retreat to an 'age blindness' that is covering up discriminatory practices. Many have argued that ageism does not exist outside the minds of 'some radical egalitarians' who 'see discrimination everywhere', as Richard Posner has put it (1995, p. 204). But it does exist and it can have serious consequences. It influences the ways in which younger persons perceive older individuals and relate to them. Moreover, it influences their expectations about future life and they will be confronted with these expectations when they suddenly realize that they are getting older. Becca Levy has warned the reader in several articles of the negative health consequences of cherishing negative age-stereotypes. Although we need to be cautious about accepting simple unidirectional influences from stereotypes to health, Levy and her colleagues have found that those with more positive age stereotypes tend to experience better cognitive functioning, reduced risk of disability and cardiovascular events, less accumulation of Alzheimer's disease biomarkers, lower stress response, and increased longevity (Levy et al. 2016; Levy et al. 2009; Levy 2003; Levy et al. 2002).

The acceleration of obsolescence in the digital and academic world

Since the rapid development of digital technology we have seen an acceleration of the tempo in which crucial professional competence has become outdated. This has especially hit the Baby Boomers; even the highly educated among them. In a situation of economic growth, these relatively large cohorts established an unprecedented youth culture characterized by widespread high education, well organized and articulated protests against the establishment, experimenting with sex, drugs and Rock&Roll. There was a major cultural difference between these cohorts and those who were born before the war. A common prejudice among young Boomers was never to trust anyone above 30.

This fixation on one's age and, especially, the importance of being young, or at least being regarded as young, has sneaked up from behind to bite the aging Boomer. Those who assumed that they would be 'forever young' became confronted with younger cohorts that were much smaller in numbers but favored by rapid technological developments that they could more easily digest than their parents. At the same time the Boomers had to come to terms with an approaching 'old age' that had never been part of their self-image, they were confronted with wiz kids living in a digital world, communicating through evolving social media, leading to continuing challenges for older people to catch up.

In *Disrupted: My Misadventure in the Startup Bubble* (2016) Dan Lyons tells the story of his working experiences with a Silicon Valley start-up. Being laid off as a 51 year-old *Newsweek* reporter, because 'they could hire five kids right out of college' for his salary he takes a lower-paying job at HubSpot. Lyons arrives for work in the traditional uniform of a midlife achiever – 'gray hair, unstylishly cut; horn-rimmed glasses, button down shirt' – to find himself surrounded by brogrammers in flip-flops who nickname him Grandpa Buzz. He meets his boss Zack who could have been his son and who has only been there for a month. Lyons' stories about some of the bizarre sides of the Silicon Valley culture also lay bare its stark ageism. The idea that nobody above 30 can be trusted returns, not only because they would be square and old fashioned, but especially because they are too hopelessly retarded to contribute anything of value to the world in terms of marketable innovations. Such as the calling of HubSpot to make the world a better place by selling spam email. Many who still want to find some clarity in age-related distinctions may say that '50 is the new 30' but in the subcultures of technological innovation 30 may be the new 50 or any other age of antique irrelevance. In the same process, historical consciousness shrinks to weeks or months, at most to generations of soft ware.

In a way, this may all not seem very remarkable. The tendency to idealize anything that is new belongs to the core of modernity as an ongoing process and throughout history it has probably been normal for young people to think that everyone who is a bit older is an outdated fool. However, the consequences of these rapid technological developments might be that the life course will be reorganized in a short productive part that will be dominated by the race to become rich in a few years, followed by a very long consumptive life for those who can afford this. But where does that leave those who cannot gather a fortune that will sustain them for the rest of their lives?

In an article by Margaret Morganroth Gullette on ageism in the academy called 'The Monument and the Wrecking Crew' (2018) she described how new forms of ageism are also transforming the academic world. Academia has long been seen as a place where experience and merit count but institutional ageism has been growing slowly but steadily over the last decades. She refers to data from the *American Association of University Professors* which show that tenured faculty are gradually phased out to be replaced by ill paid, unprotected young associates who have high hopes to work at the university during a long productive life and to become a grey, experienced and well respected professor. But they rightly fear being laid off when they are in their 40s and have become relatively expensive compared to the many young PhDs who are eager to take their places. This is, as Morganroth Gullette points out, not just nostalgia for old institutions that were 'best before' 1980. It is a loss for the whole society when even young people are taught to fear that they will soon be too old for opportunities to advance within academia. It is a symptom of a society that is loosing its respect for learning that requires experience and longevity to mature. As Gullette states: 'young people have to be able to look up to elders in order to look forward to their own ascent up the ladder of years'. When so many relatively young people are afraid to become older this is also a moral problem.

To many people this may be surprising because the labor market has been one of the first domains where anti-ageism legislation has been developed. The US has been one of the first to specifically address age-discrimination in the labor market with its 1967 *Age Discrimination in Employment Act*. There are important differences in the ways in which countries have structured their legislation against age discrimination in general (O'Cinneide 2003). But these laws have mostly not been able to stop the neoliberal flexible marketization of domains that used to be relatively protected from the market like the academic world. This kind of legislation for the labor market typically leaves a grey area for 'legitimate employment policy' or 'reasonable justification' of age discrimination (Friedman 2003). This means that older workers rise and fall with the tide on the labor market: when there is a scarcity of workers or of specific qualifications they are encouraged to work but they are laid off when the tide turns. The *Age Discrimination in Employment Act* does not protect older workers with flexible contracts so that many 'encore careers' remain precarious. The recently favored policies of raising retirement age and lowering pension benefits are superficially legitimized by the ideology that older workers would be able to find an adequate income on the labor market if they were only willing to work (see below). These policies rob older citizens of their income protection and feed the anxiety about becoming older.

How are older adults represented in the media and on the internet?

Researchers from the FrameWorks Institute in Washington have published an extensive review of the ways in which older adults are represented in the US media and in the magazines, newsletters, issue briefs, reports, which are published on the websites of 50 of the most important organizations working on issues of aging and older adults (O'Neil & Haydon 2015). There are many organizations active on the internet with advice, inspiration and discussion of the best ways to handle problems that may arise when people get older. Some advocacy organizations play a critical role demonstrating how governmental policies on aging, such as federal spending cuts on health care and programs for low income Americans, are actually creating problems for older people. According to the Frameworks research such a critical perspective could not be found in the media: 'Importantly, the *Government As Problem* narrative is not present in the media' (O'Neil & Haydon 2015, p. 19).

The media[1] play an important public role as a gatekeeper, selecting and amplifying the messages that enter into public conversations about aging. By consistently telling certain stories and excluding others, media discourse creates and reinforces public understanding over time. Experts describe this as a 'drip, drip effect', as these stories steadily carve channels in the public's imagination that shape the way in which people think about a particular issue.

Generally, older adults, and particularly older women, are grossly underrepresented as 'normal' adults: when they are featured in the media as older persons, they are presented as examples of two opposed perspectives on aging. Either as frail, diseased, demented representatives of the aging-as-decline perspective, who need expensive long term care; or as active, healthy, wholly independent representatives of the defying-aging perspective: vibrant and independent seniors (Laceulle & Baars 2014). Whereas the media tend to feature idealized representations of aging, advocacy organizations more often present problem-oriented stories. A popular one remains the *Demographic Crisis* narrative warning of impending catastrophe due to a Silver Tsunami that will disrupt society as we know it. Although countries such as Japan or Germany have already been living for years with a population in which around 25% of its citizens have been 65 years or older, a rise to nearly 20% by 2030 is constructed as a catastrophe for the US.

The most popular narrative in the media and on the internet is the *Vibrant Senior* narrative who excels in motivation, willpower, and individual agency. The media and advocacy constructions of this narrative are similar in many respects. Both focus on how older adults must *decide* to remain active: they are personally responsible for how well they age. Often these stories turn around epiphany moments in which older adults suddenly realize that their fate is in their own hands, and that they must change their lives and become active if they are to enjoy their older years. The leading idea is that becoming active means to train for amazing physical fitness which would lead to a radiant vitality, brightness, cheerful extroversion and life affirming optimism.

This guarantees media interest for the oldest person to swim the Channel or cross a desert. There is much fascination for stories about idiosyncratic individuals like Min Bahadur Sherchan who succeeded in 2009 in reaching the summit of mount Everest at the age of 76, to be surpassed in 2103 by the 80 year-old Japanese climber Yuichiro Miura, while the 85 year-old Sherchan attempted in 2017 to climb Everest again to regain the title but died of cardiac arrest during the effort. The problem with the *Vibrant Senior* narrative is a neglect of inspiring everyday examples of older people who live their lives with others without being fired up by what they, as representative of their age category are challenged to perform. Instead, the media attention goes out to high performing older individuals, presenting their excruciating training schedules as idealized ways of aging that promise to overcome disease and depression. The traditional admonition that hard work can accomplish anything is transformed into pseudo-prophylaxes to avoid the most strongly feared aspects of aging such as dementia. Another narrative that is closely related to the *Vibrant Senior* is the *Independent Senior* narrative which represents 'successful aging' by staying 'in control'.

In Chapter 2 of my book *Aging and the Art of Living* I have discussed similar programs of 'activating' care for older adults to transform 'being' into 'being busy'. After excluding older people from participating in society in meaningful ways the stage is set for the functionalist surrogates of 'old age'. In a historical perspective David Eckert (1986) has pointed to the transforming of the protestant work ethic into a 'busy ethic'; similarly, Stephen Katz (2000) speaks about molding people into 'busy bodies'. One of the most striking aspects of these programs is the overemphasis on functionality at the detriment of meaning.

The researchers from the FrameWorks Institute observe that caregiving responsibilities are typically not part of the activist agenda for older people. Besides the tendency to portray them as isolated individualists this is probably inspired by another popular but seriously biased idea about older adults. In spite of the fact that numerous older people take care of their partners, relatives or friends, the main message remains that they don't take care of others, but need to be cared for, by overburdened professionals and 'normal' adults. This amounts to a disrespectful negligence of, especially, the numerous older women who, as a result of a silent gender contract, carry most of the load of informal care. Because most of them have been doing this for decades, older women face the 'family care penalty' as Estes and Wallace (2005) put it: long term unpaid caregiving by women may well be rewarded by poor resources in later life, increasing dependence on precarious public budgets.

Generally, the media frame the problems associated with an aging population as private concerns featuring stories that narrowly focus on the trials and tribulations of individuals, paying relatively little attention to the contexts, environments, and systems in which individuals are embedded. Idealized constructions such as 'successful aging' are presented as the result of optimal individual lifestyle and consumption choices such as choosing to eat well, exercising regularly, and being disciplined in financial matters. When the reality falls short of such idealizations the verdict must be that these poor individuals have themselves to blame because they have made the wrong decisions.

The *FrameWorks* report confirms earlier research (Lindland et al. 2015; Rozanova 2010) demonstrating that public policies, social infrastructure (support, housing, public transportation) are largely absent from public discussions of aging: individuals are exclusively responsible for how they age. In that way, both media and advocacy organizations reinforce the public's highly individualistic understandings of the aging process. This is in line with Shanto Iyengar's (1991) analysis of the way in which television in the US frames political issues: when all individuals are responsible for their own fates, no one is responsible for anyone else. This basic drip-drip message has impoverished political discourse in the US and beyond.

Ageism on Facebook

'Facebook leads to a better understanding of the lives and perspectives of others'

Mark Zuckerberg (2012)

A domain of the internet where ageism has particularly flourished is Facebook. Becca Levy and colleagues have conducted a content analysis of each publicly accessible Facebook group that, according to its own description, explicitly concentrated on older individuals (Levy et al. 2014). After analyzing the site descriptions of 84 groups, with a total of 25,489 members, it turned out that all but one of these groups focused on negative age stereotypes. The mean age category of the group creators was 20–29 and all were younger than 60 years. From the site descriptions, 74% excoriated older individuals, 27% infantilized them, and 37% advocated banning them from public activities, such as driving and shopping. From the shadows of anonymity it appears to be easy to let out the most outrageous statements inviting others from the same in-group to go even further in depersonalizing and dehumanizing older persons. Regarding shopping one post reads: 'Either age-check them at the door or implement a volunteer euthanasia program. I'd happily volunteer to top one of them'. Another: '...any OAP [Old Age Pensioner] that pass (sic) the age of 69 should immediately face a fire (sic) squad they are a burden on society' (in Levy 2009, p. 173 ff.). The main arguments that could be found in the Facebook descriptions that were categorized as 'excoriating' were that the young would be disadvantaged by the debilitation of the old.

It may be true that age stereotypes are internalized from childhood onwards, as Levy (2009) has stated but, as we will see (Ch.6) in the publications of the ongoing *Generational Equity* advocacy, these prejudices are not only transmitted in private domains; they are also actively propagated in the public domain. Levy tends to see the horribly violent Facebook posts as 'exaggerated imagery in the negative age stereotypes' (Levy et al. 2014, p. 175), following Allport's definition of a stereotype as 'An exaggerated belief associated with a category' (Allport 1958, p. 191). Many outrageous Facebook posts can, however, hardly be seen as exaggerations of tendencies or aspects that can actually be found in older persons but are outright dehumanizing statements.

Still, even these extreme outbursts of ageism are often not taken seriously. Just like we have seen in Pinker's (2012) eulogy of the 'Humanitarian Revolution' the discrimination against older persons remains unnoticed in Facebook's policies:

> Facebook does not tolerate hate speech. Please grant each other mutual respect when you communicate here. While we encourage the discussion of ideas, institutions, events and practices, it is a serious violation of our terms to single out individuals based on race, ethnicity, national origin, religion, sex, gender, sexual orientation, disability or disease.
>
> (Facebook 2012)

Again, age is absent from the list of discrimination targets.

The frustration of the freedom to move around that has been felt by numerous young people during the Covid-19 outbreaks, has led to a stronger antagonism between 'young' and 'old' people. On top of having no productive or other positive meaning for society older people are now seen as becoming a burden in the everyday lives of young people, instead of remaining an invisible burden in their nursing homes. The Covid-19 pandemic has added an extra wave of ageist messages exemplified by the '#BoomerRemover' Twitter hashtag, which was widely shared in social media at the beginning of the pandemic. An important trend in these communications was to downplay the importance of the pandemic because it hit especially older people who 'were about to die anyway' – a common ageist comment – whereas young people who are 'still able to enjoy life' were hit extremely hard by the lockdowns. An analysis of 82,629 tweets relating to older people and the pandemic identified over 1,300 death jokes that made light of the pandemic since it mainly affected older adults (Xiang et al. 2021).

According to early research by Soto-Perez-de-Celis (2020), social media content appeared to be especially influenced by culture. Posts in Spanish and on the Chinese social media platform *Weibo* contained mostly messages highlighting the problems of health care and the contributions of older adults to society. Such differences in ageist content in social media mirror the experiences of older individuals across societies. According to Palmore (2004) more than 80% of older adults in the US have felt discriminated because of their age, while this figure is 18% in Mexico, and only 4% in Spain (INEGI 2017; Ministerio de Sanidad 2013).

Social inequality: How ageism hits hard or is hardly felt

Discrimination of older people has multiple sources. For many older people ageism comes on top of other forms of discrimination that were already 'familiar' to them, targeting class, race, ethnicity, sexual orientation or gender. Ageism may hit women much earlier in life than men because of a cultural programming that they must satisfy particular standards of youthful beauty. The volume *Contemporary Perspectives on Ageism* (Ayalon & Tesch-Römer 2018) shows that intersectionality approaches can help to clarify the ways in which different dimensions configure into changing pictures. However, in this rich collection of ageism studies, as in most other publications on ageism (e.g. Wagland 2004) socioeconomic aspects (income, wealth, education) have largely been neglected. The empirical data that have been gathered in previous chapters, indicate that socioeconomic status plays a more important role in creating disadvantage for older people than has generally been acknowledged in intersectionality perspectives on aging and ageism. Theories of cumulative (dis)advantage (e.g. Crystal 2006; Rigney 2010; Di Prete 2006) however, have neglected other than socioeconomic forms of social inequality, such as racial discrimination (Dannefer, Gilbert & Han 2020).

As said before, society reveals its true face in the ways it treats the most vulnerable. A society that tends to surrender its institutions to the market and puts the gains of a small economic elite above the wellbeing of its citizens will also tend to push out those who cannot or can no longer support themselves. They are marginalized and in extreme cases they will be thrown out into a wasteland that is inhabited by those who are not even part of a reserve army of workers. The same basic mechanisms threaten disadvantaged older people. Having already reduced the chances of many disadvantaged citizens to survive into old age, the opportunities to live a decent life as they get older continue to be distributed very unequally. The fact that poverty rates among the older population are lower than for the 'active' population may, besides indicating selective mortality, also say something about the general state of the population. For too many older people their socioeconomic situation remains one of insufficient resources and chronic uncertainty because arrangements for 'old age' remain precarious and may be reduced drastically when the political climate becomes even harsher.

To the degree that citizens are reduced to their economic relevance older citizens are destined to be either a burden or to be reduced to a consumptive role. The essence of humanity seems to be the *homo economicus* who has to prove his material value and usefulness. As the productive contribution of older people to society – in a limited marketed sense – declines, so does their intrinsic worth as a person. Consequently, they risk being pushed into isolation, boredom and loneliness. None of this disrespect or exclusion can be explained by their age.

If society is seen as a constellation of self-regulating markets it comes as no surprise when the public domain, which is supposed to support those parts of society that are neglected by the markets, is in a constant danger of collapse. In such a situation, supporting those older people who don't have enough resources to live through an 'old age' of uncertain length will not be high on the agenda. Even the discussions about social justice and 'old age' or about social justice between 'the young and the old' have mainly been discussions of the costs of all those older people, especially about the 'bottomless pit' of health care costs (see Ch.7). Ageist stereotypes of 'old age' are often constructed as opposites to an idealized productive and dynamic 'normal adulthood' that is hardly representative of the average worker. Older people learn to neglect the cynical fun-house mirrors that surround them in which they are supposed to see themselves as static, declining, unproductive, parasitic, selfish, and irrelevant; except, of course, for the burden they would impose on the society of 'normal', healthy adults.

Although developed countries generally provide assistance to older people regarding income and health care this does not mean that profound inequalities become less problematic as people get older. Above all, the chances to reach old age in good health are unequally distributed. As we have seen, many disadvantaged citizens die before they enter the relative protection of 'old age' and if they do, they may be scarred by the cumulative effects of negative societal conditions, from their early childhood through education, the labor market and health care into later life. Ageism comes on top of this history when they get older; it is per definition a general phenomenon that may hit anyone who has become too old to be a 'normal' adult in the eyes of the ageist, but it does not hit every older person in the same way. Ageism accentuates and deepens the inequalities that have already accumulated over the life course as a result of income/ wealth, education, ethnicity or gender.

This form of discrimination presses down on the identity and self-respect that are necessary to affirm and support somebody's existence in old age. If these supporting structures are resilient enough, the denigrating impact of ageism will not be as strong as when somebody has already for decades suffered from socioeconomic inequality and discrimination. Older people with sufficient resources are able to protect themselves, to a certain extent, from ageist denigration while those who already suffer from accumulated insults must bear the full brunt of ageist practices. Those who lack sufficient resources and depend on public services or charity are much more vulnerable to suffering ageist remarks or poor treatment. Citizens who have enjoyed a long history of being wealthy and well respected are more likely to have a strong sense of self respect but also the material resources to be greeted and treated with respect as a welcome customer of a limousine service, in a restaurant, hotel or resort. Advantaged situations and contexts can offer much protection, whereas the opposite may make older persons more vulnerable to ageist attitudes or practices.

Caroline Dunn has these observations from the UK that are also strikingly relevant for other developed countries: 'increasingly things such as autonomy, dignity, respect, and the provision of basic social and medical services, which should be taken as a right in a civilized society, appear to be becoming the prerogative of those with money'. They have 'the choice of living in specially designed retirement apartments, for instance, where any degree of dependency can be catered for with dignity and designer décor', whereas 'the elderly poor are increasingly condemned to a life of being grateful for seemingly reluctantly given charity' (Dunn 2012, p. 56; cf. Smedley, Stith & Nelson 2003 for the US). Health inequalities are deepening when disadvantaged older patients feel as if they are swept aside by ageist attitudes or get lost in the complexity of a bureaucratic, fragmented health care system whereas those who are highly educated and wealthy can assert themselves and are likely to receive whatever medical intervention, treatment or daily assistance they need. As a result, as we have seen before, the US does well for those who have already reached high ages; the most advantaged have the best chance of being served well in all respects.

A society that celebrates the ideology of individual responsibility for one's fate is unlikely to provide more than minimal assistance for those who would otherwise die in miserable circumstances. The basic message appears to be 'Get Old at Your Own Expense'. This means that those who have accumulated enough material resources have a good chance of doing well in old age. The more unfortunate will have to continue their daily struggle to survive; a struggle that may become more difficult as their needs for care and assistance grow. Withholding support where it is clearly needed may, however, be quite irrational in terms of good financial management as adequate help with transport, communication, custodial care at home (assistance with cooking, cleaning, shopping, bathing), and preventive services such as a home safety assessment will help to keep frail older persons safe so that they can continue to live their lives without having to place them in much more expensive care facilities.

To assess aging and ageism adequately it is important to understand the interaction between ageism, on the one hand, and the disadvantages or advantages that tend to accumulate as people age along the life course on the other hand. The processes that are involved in this interaction are crucially relevant to answer the question why there are within age groups such impressive differences in health and life expectancies. Rich developed countries use two consecutive forms of exclusion along the life course. First, the most disadvantaged categories of people are pushed to the margins of society and, secondly, later in the life course all people run the risk of being marginalized as soon as they are regarded as 'old'. The result is that those who have suffered lifelong socioeconomic and cultural insults enter an 'old age' that will become increasingly precarious. Those, however, who are well off will also experience ageism but their material and immaterial resources will enable them to avoid or endure these insults without the existential threat that comes with complete dependency on the help of others.

Although they have more resources to escape or neutralize ageist practices, wealthy older persons may also suffer maltreatment. This can easily happen in the anonymity of the public domain when they are in the way of somebody who is in a hurry or when they need help. Ageism can be treacherous as it will hit unexpectedly; especially when people stand out in their vulnerability and would expect help. Before that moment they may have been fine and, maybe, didn't experience that they were looked upon negatively because of their age. But when older persons cannot take care of themselves – even when it is for a short period of time – or when they are perceived as too slow or in the way; when they don't understand something or have difficulties remembering, the sting of ageism may be felt.

The entrepreneurial framing of aging

In the context of the modern institutionalization of the life course (see Ch.1) age-related policies have become a way to regulate and formally define the temporal boundaries of basic processes such as education, work, and retirement. This multifaceted process was partly motivated by the wish to protect and educate children, to create better working conditions and to protect vulnerable older workers. However, the main force behind the institutionalization of the life course and the later assault on its protective qualities since the neoliberal turn, has been to optimize the productive value of citizens. This instrumentalist perspective on the value of people leads to a depreciation of their moral worth or dignity as soon as their market related productivity is actually or merely assumed to be diminishing. As birth rates went down after the Baby Boom but life expectancies continued to go up, it began to dawn on politicians that the age-related composition of the populations of the developed countries would increasingly become out of step with the expectations that accompanied the improvement of the life course infrastructure during the 1950s and 1960s. Following the neoliberal turn, the US government has mainly favored the wealthy segment of the older population by a profit driven health care system and policies that support existing inequalities. Instead of supporting those who were falling behind, taking selective mortality seriously, governments have more generally assumed an ambivalent position: taking pride in the rising life expectancies of their populations but at the same time trying to diminish public expenditures that are necessary to make these life expectancies less unequally distributed and to support those older people who are becoming increasingly dependent on public resources. The general message has been that each individual participates in society at her own risk: the traditional qualities of citizenship are transformed into entrepreneurial strategies.

An important result of the neoliberal policies has been a thorough reframing of 'aging' in the context of a broader impoverishment of the infrastructure of the life course. To obtain what governments might prefer as acceptable levels of public expenditure, progress had to be made on two fronts: first, keeping older people healthy for a longer time so that they will not overburden the health care system; and, secondly, to try to keep them working for a longer time to increase productivity. The ensuing policies are seen as strengthening each other: healthy aging would help older people to remain productive and their occupational engagement would bring them important health benefits. The biased assumption of these new aging policies was that the aging population would consist mainly of highly educated workers with a good health status. This assumption has had negative consequences for those who have been disadvantaged in these respects. Proposals to raise retirement age for the whole population as a way to compensate or support Social Security and Medicare funds have major distributional consequences and are not fair to those with relatively low life expectancies (Grenier, Phillipson & Settersten 2021).

The policy driven redefinitions of aging that were initiated in the 1980s and developed in the 1990s might seem to be a more elaborate rerun of a basic debate between proponents of disengagement and activity theories in the 1960s (cf. Estes & DiCarlo 2019 and the extensive discussion in my *Aging and the Art of Living*). The more recent approaches, however, have been much more strongly driven by political pressure to enlarge the productive contribution of the older population and reduce the public burden of health care costs and pensions. These policy driven approaches to aging have redefined aging in entrepreneurial terms as 'successful', 'productive' and 'active'. For vital older people these approaches often had an emancipatory appeal as they challenged negative generalizations about aging and older people as unfit to work.

To counter such denigrating stereotyping there remains a need for emancipatory approaches, including pointing out that many activities of older people are actually vitally important for society in a broad sense. Even when they are retired older people contribute in many ways to society, for instance, in voluntary work and charity or by taking care of partners, (grand)children, sick relatives and friends. If these informal activities would have to be done by professionals this would involve gigantic sums. Such a utilitarian recognition of the active older population can be illuminating but the basic problem is a pervasive ageism: a lack of respect for their basic dignity; especially when they are frail and dependent on others.

The emancipatory impact of the new paradigms redefining aging has been highly ambivalent. On the one hand, their proponents emphasize the individuals' potential for maintaining physical, social, and mental wellbeing throughout the life course by continuing engagement in productive activities, and participating in social, economic, cultural, spiritual, and civic affairs (Rowe & Kahn 1998; WHO 2002). On the other hand, the one-sided implementation with a focus on individual health or productivity disregards the social inequalities of populations that tend to increase as people get older, with disturbing health consequences. Moreover, this focus neglects the broader implications of human aging in terms of dignity, vulnerability and finitude (Baars 2012, 2017). Although prolonged occupational activity may be beneficial for many people, for many others it will at some inevitable moment do more harm than good.

The positive characteristics of idealized adulthood surface when governments are trying to reinterpret aging in a positive way, which usually means that aging must be seen as an extension of entrepreneurial activities: older people need to be successful, productive and active. In the following I will briefly discuss the two main paradigms that have dominated the entrepreneurial framing of aging.

1. *Successful aging.* This paradigm has been initiated by Rowe and Kahn (1998; cf. The Gerontologist 2015) and aims to differentiate between *pathological* processes that occur in old age; *normal* aspects of aging (such as a modest decline in cognitive and motor speed), and exceptional or *successful* aging which would be characterized by avoiding disease and disability, maintaining high mental and physical functioning, and remaining socially engaged. Although the 'successful aging' paradigm may have given an important impulse to research into the origin and prevention of pathologies that are frequently seen among older people, it remains doubtful whether it leads to a more positive inclusion of aging in society. It reflects a society in which 'good' has become equated with 'successful', and it is not clear how such a career-oriented concept can be adequate to represent heterogeneous forms of aging which, moreover, imply increasing vulnerability and eventually, decline (Baars 2012, 2017a; Walker 1999). This contradiction in terms has serious consequences for chronically diseased persons who represent the inevitable counterparts of the 'successful agers' and must endure that 'being a failure' is added to their suffering: a toxic by-effect of meritocracy (see Ch.7). The distinction between successful and unsuccessful agers constructs a 'successful' old age as a continuation of a vital adulthood that knows no illness and deterioration (Calasanti 2015). As many older people will simply not be able to be, or even to present themselves as 'successful' the 'deficit and decline' model of aging returns, but now it specifically targets those who are in the 'fourth age' as opposed to the group

of older people who are still more or less 'normal adults' who are living in a 'third age' as Laslett (1991) has called this. This separation allows relatively young older adults to preserve their status as 'normal' adults, denying that they are 'really' old by comparing themselves favorably to those who live in frailty, dependence and suffering. This reproduces and reinforces ageist tendencies to define older people in terms of decline, alienation and exclusion from society (Gilleard & Higgs 2011; Higgs & Gilleard 2014). Moreover, as we have seen before, for instance, in discussing the research by Makaroun and colleagues in Chapter 2, the chances to become disabled – hence to enter the 'fourth age' – were three times higher for the poorest 20% of the US population compared to age peers from the wealthiest 20%. And, as we have seen in the section on health and life expectancies, many die before even getting beyond midlife.

The main objections against the 'successful aging' approach come from this neglect of social inequality and the tendency to make people responsible for their own health, without regard for the differences in social context and situation. The responsibility for the failure to 'age successfully,' which includes a large portion of the population of older adults, is put squarely on the individual. Rowe and Kahn, the main proponents of successful aging, have even claimed that aging is 'largely under the control of the individual' (1998, p. 37; Liang & Luo 2012). In the success-oriented culture of winners and losers, from which this paradigm originated, those who are confronted with chronic disease or disability run the risk of being deprived of the necessary care and dignity unless they have the private means to cover the costs. Appealing to success in aging can hardly be separated from the notion that the situation in which people find themselves is the result of personal achievement or failure: older people are framed as being individually responsible for their physical and financial wellbeing. This fits well in the entrepreneurial reorganization of the life course with its transfer of risks to the individual: if you do not decide to control your aging process you have only yourself to blame: societally produced risks are transformed into personal challenges.

2. 'Productive' and 'active' aging programs. Other policy driven approaches that have redefined aging have targeted not primarily the health status of older people but their contribution to the labor market. During the first three decades after the Second World War the large majority of workers still retired at a formal retirement age; usually around the age of 65 years. In 1983 the age of eligibility for full Social Security benefits was raised from 65 to 67, with higher benefits, up to 130% for those who would continue to work and with penalties for premature withdrawals (Shuey & O'Rand 2004; Quadagno 1996). Nevertheless, the crisis of the early 1980s with a collapse of sectors that used to be major economic pillars, such as the production of steel, textiles and coal, resulted in many older workers retiring early from the labor markets of most developed countries. Between 1978 and 1988, in just ten years, the labor force participation rates of men aged 60–64 years fell in the US from 60.8 to 53.8; in the UK from 75.8 to 55.1 and in the Netherlands from 59.9 to an extreme low of 14.6 (Kohli 1991). Some countries decided to facilitate well funded early retirement schemes, usually with the argument that this would give younger workers a chance, although this was hardly the case and youth unemployment in the EU remained high until the mid 1990s (Baars, Knipscheer & Breebaart, 1993; Blanchard 2006). These early retirement schemes did not last very long; gradually all countries followed a less supportive line and adapted early neoliberal policies in which the problems of a changing society were shifted to the individual workers and their families.

As the economy began to grow in the 1990s older workers came into high demand so policies were developed to integrate them in the workforce. 'Productive aging' programs have predominantly been advocated in the US while 'active aging' has been the dominant approach in the European Union, supported by the WHO (2002). Both programs have started with broad visions. The 1995 *White House Conference on Aging* inspired a broad agenda of 'productive aging' in which older people, praised as repositories of wisdom and experience but in need of purposeful and meaningful roles and activities in life, would continue to make contributions benefiting themselves, their families, and their communities. The implementation of 'productive aging' programs has, however, focused strongly on prolonged labor market contributions.

The other approach, called *Active Ageing* was the contribution of the World Health Organization to the 2002 Second United Nations World Assembly on Ageing in Madrid. It celebrated 'the critical gains in public health and standards of living that have allowed people to live longer in almost all parts of the world' and defined 'active ageing' as 'the process of optimizing opportunities for health, participation and security in order to enhance quality of life as people age' (WHO 2002: 12).

This broad vision was initially adopted by the EU but, like its predecessor 'productive aging', its implementation has been more limited. Much to the regret of some of its initiators, it was subsequently narrowed down as employment became the EU Commission's main focus (Walker 2009). In 2009, its *Ageing Report* emphasized a productivist approach to aging maintaining that increasing retirement age, limiting access to early retirement schemes, and maintaining stronger links between pension contributions and pension benefits, would provide much needed incentives for older workers to remain in the labor market (European Commission 2009; Foster & Walker 2015). In spite of the broader initial perspective of the 'active aging' program, those who were active in their communities but not in paid employment were not acknowledged and supported as 'aging actively', and the valuable contributions they did make to society were once more ignored, reducing this discourse to its precursor 'productive aging' (Boudiny 2013).

On the one hand, the entrepreneurial aging programs appeared to combat ageism on the labor market emphasizing that the mere fact that workers are 'older' should in no way lead to their devaluation (O'Reilly & Caro 1995). On the contrary, their experience and wisdom should be respected. On the other hand, their inclusion in society followed the narrow path of gainful labor with an emphasis on individual responsibility, possibly legitimating a further reduction of income support for those older citizens who do not succeed in staying healthy or who are unable to (find) work.

Older workers and retirees have become an increasingly diverse population over the last decades. Some will continue to work in the same job beyond retirement age, others will retire early, and still others will re-enter the labor market in other jobs or remain unemployed long before pension age. Not only do workers migrate on a global scale, but retirees also move to other states such as Florida or even to other countries, like the North European pensionados who live in Spain or Portugal (Uhlenberg and Mueller 2003; Vincent 1995, 2006).

However, the opportunities to evade structural and cultural pressures are not equally distributed; on the contrary income inequalities among the older population have been growing (Crystal, Shea & Reyes 2017). Taylor (2010) concludes in his overview of cross-national trends in work and retirement that decades of research tempers optimism that older workers have real choices over the circumstances in which they work or retire and that many gradual retirement schemes actually promote early retirement instead of facilitating a more gradual withdrawal from the labor market. Those who postponed their retirement voluntarily turn out to be mainly well-educated, highly compensated workers, but for the majority early retirement meant a lower pension. The labor market tends to favor those older workers who have already the best jobs; they have greater chances of living long enough to enter 'old age' in good health and they have more opportunities to continue work that is more interesting and less burdening than lower paying jobs.

Many of those who had minimal incomes and not been able to gather enough resources to retire have been forced to continue working; not because they enjoyed it but out of sheer necessity. The jobs that are available to them are usually physically demanding and not very interesting. If older people have difficulties standing all working day and have to supplement their incomes by greeting customers or bagging groceries this comes at great physical costs (Burdorf, 2006; Rossignol et al. 2005). In such cases, sound bites such as 'encore careers' or 'mentoring younger workers through experience and wisdom' may rapidly lose their attraction. For the less fortunate this means that the battlegrounds of midlife have been prolonged into old age (Phillipson 2018).

Proposals to raise retirement age for the whole population as a way to reduce the pressure on public funds have generally not been fair to older people with low incomes.[2] Moreover, these disadvantaged older people tend to have already relatively low life expectancies so that policies of increasing retirement age can have highly problematic consequences. Because of selective mortality the scope of these problems tends to be underestimated. The main objection against the 'productive/active aging' policy frameworks, especially against their implementation under the pressure of powerful political interests is, again, a neglect of social inequality. The entrepreneurial aging programs need critical monitoring as governments tend to use them for their agendas to reduce budgets to support older citizens.

'Restructuring' pensions

Generally, retirement security has gradually but significantly improved in developed countries since the 19th century. That is, until the beginning of the 1980s, when neoliberal policies began to change regulations around retirement and pensions. There has been a constant rhetoric that retirement can no longer be 'afforded', as some corporate and political leaders have maintained, creating pressure to increase retirement age and reduce pension benefits (Phillipson 2002). Since 1981 US workers have been put under pressure to invest heavily in 401(k)-type programs, even though such plans were originally designed to supplement rather than provide the basic resources for retirement. This retirement model was strongly supported by the Reagan administration and ideologically supported by Milton Friedman's Chicago School.

In his book *Social Insecurity: 401(k)s and the Retirement Crisis* (2015) James Russell analyzed this disastrous financial policy, promoted by neoliberals and aggressively peddled by Wall Street. For most people retirement seems to be an abstract thing in a distant future and they don't think about it much until the moment arrives when they may think about nothing else for some time because they have just found out that their future income will be shockingly low. This was even true for an expert like Russell: it appeared difficult to foresee what his retirement income would look like, which may be typical for a scheme in which you only know what you have to pay; not what you are going to receive. When he saw what had happened to his own retirement income Russell had an unpleasant close encounter with the consequences of the turn from more secure defined-benefit plans (pensions) to riskier defined-contribution plans (401(k)s). A traditional pension would have granted him 70%–100% of his final salary as income, but despite a frugal lifestyle, he had only 45%–50% of his income, between his 401(k) and projected Social Security. According to Russell tens of millions of Americans have discovered that they would have been better off with traditional pensions.

The propagated neoliberal narrative is that the modern worker should see herself as an entrepreneur who invests in her own retirement fund and, therefore, has to bear the risks of her own investment strategies. However, the publicized do-it-yourself retirement systems in which individuals with modest incomes are expected to invest their savings in order to reap the same rewards as high-end money managers is not working; at least not for those who depend on it. Tempted by promising booms on the volatile financial markets workers have been investing in markets without adequate knowledge of risks and costs and without the financial stamina that governments or big investors have to winter bad times and make long term gains. More individualized retirement savings such as investment funds are much less secure and less protected from financial hazards in the markets, as many small investors found out in 2008, as they watched 25% of their funds evaporate overnight. But this is not the only problem: according to Russell many 401(k) plans have gutted retirement security by charging exorbitant hidden fees. He protests that these plans have resulted in a substantial transfer of wealth from moderately earning workers to Wall Street financiers and have mainly benefited the financial services industry.

These schemes may have worked well for the most advantaged: in 2013, nearly 90% of the families in the top income quintile had considerable retirement account savings, while most families in the bottom half of the income distribution had no retirement account savings at all (Morrissey 2016). This means that few workers from the bottom half of the income distribution – half of the working population – will be able to accumulate enough wealth to ensure financial security later in life. Many of the large lower middle class will be poor or nearly poor in retirement. Russell fears that a severe retirement crisis is looming because many Americans have become the victims of a swindle perpetrated by think tanks and the financial services industry.

Similar neoliberal retirement plans have been adopted in other countries such as the UK. In his 2004 book *Banking On Death* Robin Blackburn has criticized the malfunctioning of private retirement provision, arguing that pension funds have been depleted by wasteful promotion and used as gambling chips by ruthless and overpaid top executives. In other European countries like France, The Netherlands or the Scandinavian countries pensions have also been reduced but the more extreme neoliberal plans have been fought more or less successfully. But also in these countries, pensions have come under severe pressure and have become more precarious (Macnicol 2015). Sometimes ages for eligibility have been rising which may present no problem for those who have good jobs and like to postpone their retirement, however for those who have to retire early or remain unemployed the chances of gathering an adequate pension are seriously reduced. In many cases indexing formulas to keep the level of pensions intact in relation to the costs of living or the rise of salaries on the labor market have been lowered or completely skipped. Moreover, in many segments of the labor market individual workers have been forced into contractual positions where they are actually employed but become formally individual entrepreneurs who have to manage their own professional risks and pension prospects (Freeman & Gonos 2009). Although there are many who prosper in such a market because their expertise is in high demand, the incomes of most entrepreneurial workers in the lower middle class are insufficient to save or to pay into pension funds. And then, we are only discussing diminishing perspectives for citizens, who continue to enjoy at least some protection while even legal immigrants often get severely insufficient pensions or none at all.

Last but not least, in the absence of adequate funds for home care and other forms of support, many women see no other way than to postpone their careers because somebody has to take care of dependent relatives. Women are still not compensated for their caregiving work and usually they receive less pay for the same work that men do; the consequences are interrupted work histories for women and growing gender gap in wages and salaries with further negative effects along the life course (Phillipson 2013).

Protesting ageism

A respectful integration of older people in society is still a desideratum of social justice. This requires efforts to raise awareness among the general public about their own ageist bias and the ways in which ageist thoughts, ideas and practices have actually become part of the daily functioning of governments, labor markets, hospitals, nursing homes or the media and how this all impacts the lives of senior citizens. Although some people are able to retain self respect even in situations of public humiliation, this does not justify ageism or make it less important or less hurtful (see Ch.7). Fortunately, emancipatory anti-ageist movements have been steadily growing over the last decades inspired by authors who have already been mentioned such as Becca Levy or Margaret Gullette, but also by Ashton Applewhite (2016), Laura Carstensen (2009) and Margaret Cruikshank (2009). As life expectancies have been rising over the last decades, be it very unequally and with major hiccups, many more people than ever before will live through 'old age'; all the more reason to acknowledge this as a valuable part of the adult life course.

Stereotypes about 'the young' and 'the old' that have even permeated egalitarian theories of social justice and aging, from the *Generational Equity* pamphlets to the more considerate work of Callahan, Daniels and McKerlie (see Ch.6), reproduce the mutual segregation of age groups that has become common practice in the developed world. To suppose that Daniels' or McKerlie's 'elderly' are living through a homogeneous life stage neglects and twists the differentiated reality of all those people who merely share with each other that they are regarded as too old to be a normal adult, although there are more differences between them than in any other age category. There appears to be a assumption among 'normal' adults that the lives of 'the old' are miserable and pointless: a gloomy and useless residue of life in spite of all money that is thrown at it. This is not only a patronizing caricature, it also clouds the future of the ageists as they will be faced with their own ingrained prejudices when they have become old.

Seen from these perspectives it would be a surprise that most older people, even if they suffer from bodily discomfort, appear to be happier than most young adults; a phenomenon that has been called the 'positivity paradox' (Carstensen 2009; Levy 2017; Lacey, Smith & Ubel 2006). Or, rather, they are likely to experience the same range of happiness or unhappiness as others. According to the principle of 'equal opportunity for happiness' that has been constructed by the egalitarian theorist of social justice Richard Arneson, this would mean that any support of older citizens beyond what 'normal' adults would get will be withdrawn: as they are happy, there would be no reason to support them (Anderson 1999). Such harsh egalitarianism denies the reality that many older people are no longer able to work so their happiness depends also on the support they receive.

Denigrating stereotypes neglect the many ways in which older people not only contribute to society in regular jobs but also in the form of voluntary work, charity, community services and as crucial members of families. The evolutionary perspective of 'disposable soma' (Kirkwood 1999) might lead us to believe that adults have lost their reproductive value for the species as soon as their children can take care of themselves but this seriously reduces the meaning of (grand)parenthood and of elderhood in general (Aronson 2019). Retired senior citizens should be treated with the respect that a country like the US has for veterans: people don't ask whether they have actually been in life threatening combat but have a generalized respect for their status as veterans. Senior citizens also, should be seen in a generalizing perspective of appreciation as veterans of the front lines of society without assuming that their poor pensions or miserable situations are a just reflection of their poor contribution to society. They are entitled to capabilities that support and enable them to participate in society as equal citizens (see Ch.7).

This is not only a matter of adequate resources but also of mutual respect. A society in which senior citizens would receive sufficient material resources without including them in society or where distribution policies are accompanied by ageist contempt for their parasitic existence – a tendency that has become visible in the pamphlets of the *Generational Equity* advocates – stands in flagrant contradiction to any equality or equity. In contrast to the dominant discourse on social justice and aging the reality of ageism reminds us that equality is more than the distribution of material goods; it is also a matter of mutual respect.

Achieving this may require emancipatory movements that protest against ageist stereotypes and practices demanding equal citizenship for older people. As soon as they retire, older people tend to fall from sight of busy citizens, so bringing the issues that are relevant in their specific situations to the attention of the public may require loud voices, large numbers, and drama. To be able to bridge the distance of neglect and indifference it may be necessary to disturb daily routines and demand attention. This can be as differentiated as the experiences of ageism or the precarious situations of older people. In cases of serious neglect of the lives of older people in disasters such as the Chicago Heat Wave (see Ch.7) the responsible authorities need to be held publicly accountable without giving in to their ageist stereotypes that the victims were 'about to die anyway'. But it may also be necessary to protest against miserable pensions or 'youthist' images of beauty by showing beautiful images of people who have experienced the joys and sufferings of life. This does not mean that being regarded as beautiful is important to act as an equal citizen nor would this imply that older people need to be admired instead of younger people; the point is to protest against the deprecation of older people because of their deviation from a commercially distorted version of beauty.

This leads to the further question whether genuine respect or appreciation can be enforced by legal means. Of course it remains important that experiences of ageism in different societal domains lead to legal protection from insult, humiliation, degradation, or age discrimination. However, recognition of the autonomy and dignity of those who are defined by others as 'old' would require a supportive and inspiring culture of aging: a shared *art* of living that supports different individual *lifestyles* and serves as a source of inspiration for growing older (Baars 2012).

A short note on existential fears as a source of ageism

To give such a culture a chance it is crucial to face shared existential issues that are not the subject of this book but obviously emerge in a distorted form in such phenomena as ageism. Ageist attitudes and practices have everything to do with how we approach and live finite life; questions that confront every person. Aging as a process that is inherent in life confronts us with questions about the meaning of life, its highs and lows, its vulnerabilities, the inevitable dependence on others, and the meaning of death. Culture has a major influence on the ways in which these questions are posed, or avoided, and the answers that are suggested.

In some respects ageism involves similar identity political struggles that confront movements for peace, environment, or race and gender equality. In other respects, however, ageism poses specific challenges because it confronts us all with the fear of being vulnerable and finite in a culture of control. Especially frail older people are a living reminder of the mortal condition that young people, overly busy adults and *Vibrant Seniors* prefer not to think about. Vulnerability and death are easily repressed in a culture that takes pride in exercising control through technology and, consequently, has difficulty in accepting that we are still finite beings who have to die. In a culture that promises that you can be or buy anything you want, if you really want it, any functional decline will inevitably be seen as an unwelcome limitation of active life and be pushed to shadowy margins.

For those who have put their faith in technology it would be especially sobering and bitter to get old before the anti-aging industry has delivered on its promises to reverse biological decline and even abolish death; an enterprise that might in itself be interpreted as a symptom of the fear of becoming old and having to die. This fear makes it difficult to accept aging as a process that may also bring fulfillment and deep satisfaction with one's life. When this fear is not addressed it will remain hard to grant old age a place of respect. We need to allow older frail people to live among us; fostering respect for them and bolstering self-esteem. This requires encountering and reconciling – instead of commercially feeding – fears of getting 'old' and trying to calmly accept our inevitable deaths.

One of the problems standing in the way of establishing a culture in which there is place for the vulnerabilities *and* the increasing complexities and experiential richness of aging appears to be this fearful one-sided association of older people with decline and death. Rising life expectancies imply that death is no longer a familiar experience in all age groups, as it used to be throughout history, now that death is mainly taking place in late life. But the uncertainty remains, because fundamentally death accompanies life at all ages. A neoliberal culture which embraces unrestrained markets will have problems to accept limitations. However, the finitude of natural resources, the vulnerability of the earth as an ecosystem that can sustain human societies and its violent response to our transgressions are writings on the wall that we have to learn to respect finite life. One of the basic problems to see growing older as a meaningful phase of life appears to be this inability to face and appreciate what it means to live a finite life and to identify with those who remind us of this inevitable condition (Baars 2012, 2017a).

Is 'age' a reliable indicator of adult aging?

An important ageist assumption about human aging is that aging, in this case identified as processes of decline, develops in synchrony with somebody's age. Crossing or even approaching the threshold from 'normal adulthood' into 'old age' the age of a person would not only begin to explain much of her behavior but also give a reliable prognosis of her cognitive and physical competence. The aging person is seen as being slowly engulfed by the waves of decline. According to Starr (2017) 'age' has become a risk factor for all kinds of health problems making 'old age' an undifferentiated pool of diseases with no other identified cause than 'age'. Given the increasing diversity between older persons and the sheer length of 'old age', ranging from mid 60 to 110 and more years, such trust in age as an inborn regulator is clearly absurd. Governments and large scale organizations have also discovered 'age' as a tool to manage their populations (Katz 1996). To oppose these developments it should be pointed out that human aging is driven by manifold processes, including the effects of social inequality. All of these processes can be studied retrospectively and measured in metric time but this does not mean that aging develops in synchrony with a basic clock that is innate to human beings.

These issues are inherently related to our understanding of 'time'. Modern science has broken with traditional narratives about the essential connections that exist between time and its objects of measurement. An essential part of this modern understanding is to disconnect 'time' from the multitude of processes and actions taking place on earth so that these can be measured in an objective chronometric perspective. The rigidity of the movements in the solar system and our inability to influence them have made it possible to found metric time and to enable objective chronometric measurement. The repetitive movements in the solar system that have been foundational for scientific measurements of time are dictated, not by any rhythms of living nature, but by the gravitational movements of enormous bodies of dead weight. Insofar as these movements are not regular enough for present standards of precision, they are corrected by the rhythms of other dead materials: extremely frequent and stable atomic oscillations. To underline the distance from an inherent connection between time/age and a basic *Logos* (Greek for 'cosmic order') of human aging as suggested by the term 'chronological' I will use the terms 'metric time' and '(chrono)metric age'.

In *Aging and the Art of Living* (2012) I have explained more extensively how Western societies have seen a bureaucratic reorganization of the life course over the 19th and 20th centuries, in which chronometric *age* began to play a crucial role in defining childhood, adulthood, and old age (Kohli 1986). One of the results of this chronometric ordering of human life, beginning with prenatal care and continuing through childhood with its age-related structuring of schools and curricula, has been a growing awareness of one's own and other people's metric age (Chudacoff 1989). In Europe the registration of newborns already had a long history at the local level of parishes; it became obligatory for all citizens of the countries that were occupied by Napoleon, mainly for reasons of taxation and conscription. This awareness of age as a measurable characteristic of all individuals has made it possible to use it as an explanatory variable. That this could lead to a straightforward set of simple formulas in which scientific precision and practical use would be united was stated with much self-assurance by Jim Birren, one of the leading gerontologists of the 20th century:

> Chronological age is one of the most useful single items of information about an individual if not the most useful. From this knowledge alone,

an amazingly large number of general statements or predictions can be
made about his anatomy, physiology, psychology, and social behavior.
(1959, p. 8)

As we shall see, the author of these lines later expressed serious reservations
about such claims, but many institutions and organizations that finance
research on aging and ask for straightforward data about 'older people', 'the
elderly', or 'seniors' are still under their spell.

Nevertheless, the impressive collection of data that has been gathered
about aging and aging populations over the last decades defies the statement
that 'age' (as time since birth) is a reliable indicator of aging: the differences
between them tend to undermine the averages. Developmental regularities,
for instance, may be relatively strong in embryological phases, although
even there contextual influences will have their impact as we have seen in
the research on *Fetal Origins of Adult Disease*. After early childhood these
regularities, however, begin to decline rapidly. Comparative research on
aging identical twins has demonstrated that genes account for approximately
30% of developmental outcomes in old age; the remaining 70% is a playing
field of contexts and personal agency (Gurland, Page & Plassman 2004). At
a macro-level biodemographic research informs us that average life expectancies in affluent societies have almost doubled over the last 150 years
(Oeppen & Vaupel 2002). After the initial decline in infant mortality there
has been a further boost: most of the additional years that were added to life
since the last decades of the 20th century were realized at older ages (Vaupel
2010). Such average scores about national populations still hide important
internal differences, which can be expected, as an average score means that
half of the measured population scores above average, the other half below
average.

Major differences within national populations are, *first*, those between
birth cohorts. It has been widely documented that there are important differences between birth cohorts because they grow up and older in different
circumstances. For instance, whereas it was assumed for a long time that
intelligence would begin to decline steadily at a more or less fixed age,
researchers such as Paul Baltes and Warner Schaie already in the 1970s
found important differences between people of the same age, depending on
their birth cohort. Since 1956 the *Seattle Longitudinal Study* has documented
the ways in which cohort differences affect IQ-scores of people of the same
age, for instance 75-years olds, who were born in different years and,
therefore, experienced different forms of education (Schaie 2013). Consequently, an explanation of certain characteristics of aging persons as caused
by their ages has to keep its explanation clear of cohort effects. The episte-
mological situation becomes even more complicated with the introduction
of period effects: developments or events that influence all age groups, not
only those in the 'formative years' of their youth. Examples of such

formative period effects are the effects of a popular culture of smoking or junk food or the effects of pandemics and lockdowns on sedentary activities.

With the acceleration of social and cultural change in late modern societies it becomes increasingly difficult to disentangle cohort and period effects. For example, if a high proportion of people between the ages of 60 and 65 are found to be obese, it will be hard to determine whether this is caused by age, cohort, or period effects such as a wide availability of cheap junk food. This conundrum of causalities has been called the APC (Age Period, Cohort)-conundrum in life course analysis. Several authors have tried to separate these different effects statistically (Robinson & Jackson 2001) but skepticism prevails and, according to specialists such as Glenn, these attempts have been futile, leading to 'much pseudo-rigorous research and almost certainly to many incorrect conclusions' (Glenn 2004, p. 475; cf. however, Yang & Land 2013). A major problem is that these effects are not additive but interrelated: age, period and cohort effects interact with the dependent variables researchers on aging are interested in.

Second, as their members get older *intra*cohort differentiation increases as cohorts are torn apart by accumulating inequalities in resources and respect with serious consequences for the ways in which they age, resulting in major differences in morbidity and mortality. Such effects have been demonstrated and discussed in the chapters so far.

These observations should suffice to question the view that people's age in itself represents an adequate assessment of aging persons. Generalizations about people of a certain calendar age actually presuppose a causal concept of age: because time would have worked in them for a certain number of years, certain inevitable effects should be reckoned with. Moreover, the effects are assumed to develop steadily and universally according to the rhythm of the clock. However, such a causal concept of age can never generate knowledge that could explain the differences that exist between human beings of the same age. Nor could it help to uncover the many processes that contribute to social inequalities but remain hidden behind generalizing concepts that are based on average scores. While it is true that all causal relations are also temporal relations, or relations working 'in time', it would be wrong to identify causality with time or to reduce the process of aging to 'causal effects' of time. The same Jim Birren whose high expectations for the predictive power of chronometric age were quoted above, later articulated a similar view:

> By itself, the collection of large amounts of data showing relationships with chronological age does not help, because chronological age is not the cause of anything. Chronological age is only an index, and unrelated sets of data show correlations with chronological age that have no intrinsic or causal relationship with each other.
>
> (Birren 1999, p. 460)

Because aging involves many different processes at different levels, these processes must be understood in terms of their specific temporal dynamics but 'at the same time' as interacting with other dynamics: aging processes evolve or take place in time, but not according to the rhythm of chronometric time. Although all processes can be measured in chronometric time, their specific properties and effects are not caused by time. To assume that this is the case leads away from an understanding of aging, although it may produce neat distributions of average characteristics of persons of any given age.

What about intrinsic clocks of aging?

One of the questions that will arise from this critical interrogation of chronometric representations of aging is whether human aging might not follow regular changes of its own, that could be seen as a basic natural clock with its own formative rhythms over the human life course that might be counted or expressed in a different time scale that would adequately assess aging processes (Baars & Visser 2007; Baars 2012b; Baars 2017b). If chronometric age is so inadequate in explaining the dynamics of human aging, would it not be better to base our assessment of the age of a person on clocks that are intrinsic to human aging? This interesting question has been explored by several authors (Schroots & Birren 1988; Hershey 2010; Hershey & Wang 1980; Richardson & Rosen 1979; Yates 1988, 2007).

If such an intrinsic clock could be found it would make it possible to assess functional ages that would indicate precisely the relative state or phase of the human organism on a scale that ranges from birth to death. It would make it possible – at least in a biological or, more generally, a functional perspective – to establish clear indicators of 'normal' functioning for different stages or functional ages. These differently marked ages could then be located on a continuum from birth to death. This would have to go beyond biomarkers such as the aspartate racemization in the teeth, which is used in forensics to assess the age (as time since birth) of a body for which there is no further information available (Yekkala et al. 2006). Such biomarkers do not represent 'age' as the functional state of the whole organism, as we still don't understand why one person who appears to be around 60 years old shows some serious functional decline in vital organs, while another who appears to be around 80 years old is much more healthy. These biomarkers are just alternative measurement estimates of time since birth.

There have been some sophisticated attempts to conceptualize intrinsic clocks of aging, drawing upon different theories from the natural sciences such as *Quantum Mechanics* (Yates 2007). But usually, the *Second Law of Thermodynamics* has been called upon to develop an intrinsic age in terms of the entropy production of a given system over time (Hayflick 2007a, 2007b). The main problem with this approach is that open systems such as human organisms, that rely on interaction and exchange with pluriform contexts, do not fit well in the models of intrinsic dynamics or intrinsic times that presuppose that the system in question is sealed off from the environment (Uffink 2007). Surprisingly, the human genome is relatively simple compared to that of the water fly or the loblolly pine with its seven times larger genome. The complexity of the human genome stems, however, from the interactions of the genes with each other and with the environment. While some degree of intrinsic openness may be a characteristic of all organisms, this becomes much more complex in the case of humans given their long term formative dependence (cf. Dannefer 2022). Moreover, the idea of a human organism interacting as an integrated whole with different contexts is much too simple. The reproduction of the human organism over time involves complex internal interrelations of cells, tissues and organs that are also relatively independent from each other.

Consequently, the intrinsic age of the human organism dissolves into a multitude of intrinsic ages: lung capacity, maximum heart rate, hearing sensitivity – as many as there are organs and other identifiable subsystems in the body. The complicated processes of functional decline in cells, tissues, organs, or different parts of the brain may each have specific dynamic properties, but these dynamic properties include an openness to the environments inside and outside the human body, extending from personal lifestyles to ecological or social contexts in a broad sense. Emerging social scientific research on environmental effects in genetic studies of aging (Reynolds et al. 2019) as well as research from ecological developmental biology on the social organization of genetic expression (epigenetics) demonstrate how complex these interactive processes are (Gilbert & Epel 2009). These interactive processes defy a general objective *Logos* of aging and must be discovered in their specificity, and in the course of this discovery metric time can only serve to measure specific durations.

Occasionally, usually in connection with female fertility and menopause, the idea arises of a biological clock that would regulate aging processes. So far, however, biological clocks have only been clearly identified for circadian rhythms, although there have been attempts to apply the model of a biological clock to the human life span (Yates 2007). These attempts have been unsuccessful, precisely because of the intrinsic openness of the human organism. This is the main reason why the changing rhythms that we see in living nature, as a result of the dynamic interaction of living organisms with inner and outer contexts, could not be used as a basis for chronometric time. The earth or the moon are not known to engage, like living nature, in active explorations of their environments, or to explore the options they might have to improve or to survive challenging situations. Life is part of the solar system, but even if we agree that living systems are also physical systems, this does not mean that all the theories that are needed to understand human life can be derived from the laws of physics (Baars & Visser 2007). The regularities and averages that may be found do not have the status of the classical laws of physics but remain open to change at different levels.

The relative openness of living organisms and the formative influence of specific contexts are also demonstrated in the differences in longevity that we see in experiments with fruit flies, nematodes, mice, rats, or monkeys. Processes of functional degeneration and regeneration over time are manipulated in laboratory contexts to investigate how far they can be slowed down so that these experimental populations reach higher ages, and in particular, how the results might apply to humans. Insofar as these experiments result in prolonging the life spans of these animals, they illustrate once more the intrinsic malleability of these processes (Kirkwood 2005). Of course, such intrinsic openness is only possible within the limits of the species – fruit flies that live much longer remain fruit flies – but the whole point of these experiments is that we do not know what these limits are.

Madame Calment had the longest life on record – 122 years and 164 days – but that doesn't mean that nobody will be able to live longer; like any other record, longevity records have only empirical status, not a normative one. As life is finite there will be a terminal phase of life but this can be extremely short or quite long and such a phase does not begin at a specific age. Eventually, functional decline will become inevitable in later life but this is not determined by age and many problems that older people are confronted with can be prevented or mitigated by improving the daily situations in which they live. For society this openness promises high returns on investments to improve the supportive qualities of social contexts, but also a warning about the vulnerability of major parts of the population under market oriented policies that are merely targeting customers who will be able to pay for their services of support and care.

Ageism and the ambiguities of 'aging'

'Age' seems to enable us to categorize adults according to the amount of time they have lived. This may have practical advantages but, if we want to understand and explain aging, many questions arise. In addition to the difficulties that surround 'age' as an indicator of 'aging', there is also the confusing usage of the latter term which doesn't help in debunking ageism.

'Aging' can refer to a shared but *personal experience* of *living a finite life* which can be distinguished from being *measured and categorized* from the outside. This social-existential discourse plays a central role in my book *Aging and the Art of Living* (2012; cf. Baars 2017a, 2020, 2021). As long as a society is populated by human beings such personal experiences will remain important to share. Secondly, the term 'aging' is used to refer to the process of *getting older* or reaching a higher chronometric age. This is the way in which 'aging' is often used in everyday life. Such chronometric assessments of 'aging' play a central role in concepts such as life expectancies, mortality rates, or birth cohorts. They are crucial for analyzing macro-processes such as population aging and in critical analyses as presented in this book, but they only have *empirical* meaning, not a *normative* one so they are open to change. Thirdly, 'aging' can refer to the interplay of degeneration and regeneration of biological or, in a broader sense, functional perspective. Examples are expressions such as 'aging cells', 'aging tissue' or an 'aging heart'. A reason to distinguish this meaning of 'aging' from the chrono-metric approach is that all hearts do not 'age' at the same rate, which can be established by comparing the functional qualities of hearts of persons with the same metric ages. One way to distinguish a functional approach to aging from the use of chronometric age is to insist that there is no aging when there is no functional decline although the organism or human being has become older in a chronometric sense (Gavrilov & Gavrilova 2006).

Anyway, the conclusion must be that chronometric age cannot be an adequate indicator of aging processes. It remains extremely precarious to make reliable age-related assessments of adults; usually the differences within populations are more impressive than the averages, especially for those who have been labeled as 'older people'. Ageist tendencies have emerged from the many reports that have been written since the neoliberal turn by orga-nizations such as the OECD about the burden that aging populations represent, especially, for the rich countries. Although there have recently been more hesitant approaches, the grand ambition of many overviews of aging populations over the last four decades – ranging from those produced by supra-national institutions such as the IMF, the World Bank to national governments – has been to establish how societies would be bankrupted if they continued the present level of income support and care for their older citizens. The focus has one-sidedly been on people above the age of 65 years not being able to work or even look after themselves, being demented and needing long term care. Such 'unconscious' bias of ageism in reports from prestigious transnational organizations is extremely worrying because it sets the tone for policies on aging.

Moreover, these analyses typically neglect the social inequality that lies behind the problems they aim to solve. The pressure to reduce public expenditures on older citizens will disproportionally hit the most vulnerable among them. Many problems that face older people have nothing to do with their age: 'age' as a basic category of the analysis of aging population conveniently leaves out social inequality as the manifold source of the basic problems. To clarify these issues the emphasis should, for instance, be less on 'age' and more on the effects of *durations* in favorable or unfavorable situa-tions; especially the long term effects of living in disadvantaged situations (insufficient income, toxic environments, bad housing etc.) deserve more attention (cf. Schaie, in Baars & Visser 2007 about 'event time').

As has been repeatedly emphasized here, aging populations do pose major challenges but it is urgent that problems are not made worse by the ways in which they are approached (cf. Marmot's alternative scenarios in Ch.7). The dominant tendency to increase social inequalities among the populations of

Western countries will continue to generate and enlarge differences between people of the same ages, which implies that 'age' will become even less reliable as an indicator of aging processes. This does, however, not necessarily imply that ageist discrimination will disappear: it may even become more popular in the form of disrespect for those who didn't make 'it' although they had decades of 'equal opportunities' to succeed on the free market.

Looking back on social inequality – looking ahead to social justice

The developments that have been discussed in the previous chapters pose urgent questions of social justice. Social inequality, in its broad sense, and consequences such as selective mortality or the perverse longevity gap are not just problems that can be solved by the individuals who are confronted with them. The neoliberal message that social justice is only a matter of uncontextualized 'individuals', who are solely responsible for taking care of themselves and their families, has not only proven insufficient but also destructive. We are confronted with a society which forces individuals together in groups with very unequal initial opportunities. And these inequalities are tearing societies apart. The irresponsible deterioration of public policies is covered up by the manipulative use of slogans from moralistic traditions that have been emptied of sincere engagement with society, such as 'the hard working individual', 'family values', or 'patriotism', without much concern for the structural undermining of individual autonomy, the quality of working conditions in a broad sense, and the wellbeing of families or the population.

For an adequate diagnosis of social inequality it remains important to grasp the macro structures and processes that make 'society' what it is. In the previous chapters I have gathered evidence about some of the ways in which social inequality in its different forms develops and is reproduced over the life course. A major concern of the next chapter is that a critical perspective on society and its inequalities has been fading away since the neoliberal turn of the early 1980; just when it was needed most urgently. In Chapter 6 I will discuss how life course inequalities have been addressed over the last decades by prominent theorists of social equality and what their proposals for a more just organization of the life course have been. In the final chapter I will draw comments and criticisms together and try to sketch an alternative perspective.

Notes

1   The media sample included articles taken from national newspapers, national television broadcasts, and news-oriented blogs including *The New York Times, Los Angeles Times, The Washington Post, San Jose Mercury News, Detroit Free Press, The*

Denver Post, Minneapolis StarTribune, The Dallas Morning News, New York Post, The Arizona Republic, U-T San Diego, The Cincinnati Enquirer, The Columbus Dispatch, The Tampa Tribune, Las Vegas Review-Journal and broadcasts from Fox News Network, CNN, and MSNBC. Moreover, The Internet activities of 50 advocacy organizations were included and blogs such as Drudge Report, TheBlaze, The Huffington Post, and The Daily Beast.

2   See, for instance, the Program on Retirement Policy from the Urban Institute, Washington D.C. https://www.urban.org/policy-centers/cross-center-initiatives/p rogram-retirement-policy/testing-ways-improve-retirement

Chapter 5

Social inequality

From central concern to its marginalization

Overview

This chapter begins with a short characterization of the main differences between libertarian and egalitarian approaches to social justice. In the wake of the Civil Rights movements, the student protests and the feminist movements there was a strong urge during the 1970s to develop critical egalitarian perspectives to be able to question a patriarchal and racially biased life course. During this period some groundbreaking work was done by John Rawls with his *A Theory of Justice* (1971) and Amartya Sen who presented his *Capability Approach* in 1977 with his *Tanner Lectures* from where he has continued to develop this approach. The declining interest in social inequalities that we see in post-Rawlsian egalitarian theories since the early 1980s is part of a transatlantic defensive shift in social theory which coincides with the rise of neoliberal policies. Although there have been important exceptions, the prominent publications from otherwise very heterogeneous social theorists of the 1980s, such as Giddens, Habermas, Foucault, MacIntyre, Sandel, or the post-modernists moved away from a growing societal inequality towards individualistic and communitarian concerns and meta-theoretical linguistic issues. The growing tension between deepening inequality over the life course and its theoretical oblivion has led to new interdisciplinary research paradigms such as Critical Gerontology and life course studies.

Libertarians versus egalitarians

> We have a statue of liberty, not a statue of equality…
>
> Krauthammer

To give a background to the different approaches to social justice we can begin with the observation that for many thinkers about social justice social inequality presents no problems. The so-called 'libertarians' remain preoccupied with the protection of individual freedom and are opposed to public responsibilities as they view the activities of the state as a main threat

DOI: 10.4324/9781003392590-6

to individual freedom. They may have their own specific problems with the neoliberal turn their country has been taking since the early 1980s, but I will leave these aside. Beyond the many differences between libertarian theories I will briefly portray the general libertarian position because this is important to understand the development of egalitarian thought on the life course since the triumph of neoliberal policies in the US.

Striving for less inequality has its libertarian opponents who are especially critical of the ideal of equality that they tend to ridicule in reducing this ideal to 'sameness'. Libertarian thinkers like von Hayek (1960) or John Lucas (1965) emphasize that striving for equality would be futile because humans are not equal and will remain so:

> We can secure Equality in certain respects between members of certain classes for certain purposes and under certain conditions; but never, and necessarily never, equality in all respects between all men for all purposes and under all conditions. The egalitarian is doomed to a life not only of grumbling and everlasting envy, but of endless and inevitable disappointment.
>
> (Lucas 1965, p. 306)

Another criticism that is raised against egalitarians is that they want to equalize all talents (Nozick, 1974), taking goods away from the deserving (Bauer 1981). This would result in a general 'leveling down' because free riders, lazy people, and limitless spenders would always be bailed out. Yet another problematic tendency would be to undermine personal responsibility by guaranteeing income independent of people's choices (Mead 1986). Generally, the libertarian evaluation of egalitarian ambitions to eliminate social inequality between people is that everybody will be worse off in the end.

According to a libertarian such as Nozick (1974) whose work was already referred to because of his influence on Thatcher (see Ch.1) there should be no interference with independent individuals: they can do as they please as long as they don't harm others. Nobody would owe anybody anything, except for refraining from harming each other and keeping voluntary promises and contracts. Every individual has a right to gain more property than others by gift, trade or hard work. As libertarians are especially concerned about governmental interference in the lives of citizens, in their view governments have very limited rights and responsibilities beyond securing property rights. Nozick even maintains that taxes are illegitimate.

Libertarianism may have had its strong points in defending individual freedom and autonomy. Continuing to defend uncontextualized individual freedom brings, however, not so much a fruitful perspective on the problems that have been documented above as it is a part of these problems. For egalitarians the problems with the uncontextualized idealization of individual responsibility begin – or should begin – in confrontation with situations where the assumption of individual responsibility remains an empty construct and an easy excuse to evade public responsibility. When we learn from research, for instance on the *Long Arm of Childhood*, that the conditions of gestation and early childhood exercise already a major influence on later life it is hard to maintain that all citizens have the same opportunities to assume responsibility for their lives. To improve the prospects of all citizens to become responsible agents much needs to be done to improve the situations in which they grow up, are educated or have to work (see Ch.7). To shift the responsibility to 'the family' makes sense only when there is a family and this family has the adequate resources to assume responsibility (Fishkin 1983).

The goal of egalitarianism is not to make everybody 'the same'. The basic problem of egalitarianism is not that there are differences between people or 'all men' as Lucas put it. All people are different from others, not only in their bodily characteristics such as finger prints, iris or DNA but also in their personal biographies. Egalitarian critique begins when particular differences such as skin color or gender are transformed into markers of distinction – exclusion or privilege – obstructing or frustrating the bearers of such markers or stigmata in their participation in society. Even the implementation of social equality in the form of equal rights and duties of citizenship does not solve problems of social inequality. There are many ways in which precisely articulated equal rights can function in ways that include some citizens and exclude others. Every citizen may have the same legal rights but if some people can afford expensive lawyers while others can't afford even to begin to defend their case, we must conclude that rights that seem equal and were intended to function that way, lead in the practice of daily life to social inequality. Another example would be to assume that all citizens have an equal share of political influence because every one of them has only one vote, neglecting the many ways in which big corporations or rich people can effectively influence political decisions (see Ch.7).

Although thinking about equality has a long tradition, it received a major impulse from egalitarian movements such as the struggles for independence of former colonies after the Second World War, the Civil Rights movements in the US, and the international student protests of the 1960s. The political theories that guided the last protests delivered rather frontal attacks on a society that was perceived as inherently oppressive and deeply alienating. Such a 'total' rejection of the present society, demonstrated by 'dropping out' and being 'uncommitted', was forcefully articulated in popular books such as Herbert Marcuse's *One Dimensional Man* (1964).

Later thinkers such as John Rawls, Amartya Sen and Jürgen Habermas, however, confronted themselves with the problem of trying to articulate *criteria* of critique that would make it also possible to distinguish potentials for emancipation and social justice in that same society they were also determined to criticize for its oppression. Habermas, for instance, tried to build his critique of society on a quasi-transcendental theory of communicative action while John Rawls relied on a constitutive discourse in an 'original situation' (cf. their discussion in *The Journal of Philosophy* 1995).[1]

I will begin my critical analysis of egalitarian thought on issues related to social inequality over the life course with a brief discussion of the work of John Rawls and Amartya Sen. Both theorists developed their approaches during the 1960s and 1970s. John Rawls published his magnum opus *A Theory of Justice* in 1971. Sen began to articulate his Capability Approach with the famous *Tanner Lectures* of 1977, but his work on inequality had begun earlier, with several articles and influential books such as *Collective Choice and Social Welfare* (1970) and *On Economic Inequality* (1973). Some introduction to the theories of Rawls and Sen is necessary to understand the approaches that emerged after the neoliberal turn, such as luck egalitarianism and the work of Norman Daniels, probably the best known theorist of social justice and aging.

John Rawls: a theory of social justice

The Harvard philosopher John Rawls is arguably the most influential Anglo-Saxon theorist of social justice of the 20th century. Right at the beginning of his major work *A Theory of Justice* (1971) Rawls states that the primary subject of justice is the basic structure of society, because 'its effects are so profound and present from the start' (7). This basic structure of society would be the way in which the main political and social institutions of society fit together into a system of social cooperation as these institutions distribute fundamental rights and duties and determine the distribution of advantages that result from social cooperation. 'The most fundamental idea in this conception of justice', so Rawls (2001, p.5) tells us, 'is the idea of society as a fair system of social cooperation over time'.

What he means by 'the basic structure of society' is not very well elaborated but the problem that concerns him above all is the way in which for many citizens the initial chances in life, for better but especially for worse, are to an important degree determined by the political system as well as by economic and social circumstances. The profound effect of the basic structure of society on the life course is that people are born into different positions and, in fact, into what Rawls calls 'deep inequalities': 'Not only are they pervasive, but they affect men's initial chances in life; yet they cannot possibly be justified by an appeal to the notions of merit or desert. It is these inequalities, presumably inevitable in the basic structure of any society, to which the principles of social justice must in the first instance apply' (1971, p. 7).

In developing his theory of justice Rawls tries to avoid an opposition between the aggregated interests of all citizens (utilitarianism) on the one hand and the interests of the individual (libertarianism) on the other hand.

According to him utilitarianism does not fully respect the rights of individuals or 'the distinction between persons' (Rawls 1970, p. 27) because in utilitarianism the interests of an individual are sacrificed if that leads to gains for many more people. But he also maintains, in contrast to libertarianism, that we owe each other a just society. In thinking about how we could conceive of a just society he finds himself confronted with what Habermas (1987) has called the problem of modernity: how can society on a moral basis be possible after the collapse of pre-modern naturalistic models of harmony? If all people are morally equal, so that each person must be respected as an autonomous source of value exercising her own potential for freedom and rationality, how can a shared moral basis of society be possible? How is such a society possible when there is this irreducible plurality of conceptions about what would be good without being able to refer to an authority or institution, respected by all, as a shared foundation to decide what is good or false, right or wrong? Both thinkers want to develop perspectives that lead beyond contemporary 'solutions' such as a fundamentalist state, a technologically sophisticated totalitarian regime or a media supported dictatorship. To address this problem Habermas tries to prepare a common ground in developing a theory of communicative action and practical discourse, while Rawls tries to find a similar shared foundation in the heuristic construct of an 'original' discussion of free, equal and independent persons about what they would see as a just society.

Rawls' approach stands in an old tradition of Western thought about society, according to which the basic principles of a 'human' society – in contrast to a raw 'natural' state – emerge from a 'Social Contract', in which free and equal participants agree on principles of justice. Social philosophers who wanted to lay a rational foundation for a just society in order to emancipate their societies from traditional legitimations of oppression such as Johannes Althusius (1557–1638), Thomas Hobbes (1588–1679), John Locke (1632–1704) and Jean-Jacques Rousseau (1717–1778) have elaborated such models of negotiation between equals which still resonate in contemporary debates about 'intergenerational contracts'. Rawls' original contribution to this approach is the development of the social contract as a heuristic device that is designed to show how the principles of justice animating a constitutional democracy might be derived in an 'original position'. In this hypothetical situation free and equal citizens are challenged to think about the basic structure of a just society. The contractors in the original position are blinded by a 'veil of ignorance' (Rawls 1971: 17, 136) about their own position or life plan in that society so that they would not be able to know whether or how they might profit from the arrangements they are constructing together. The participants are forced to think about the basic structure of a just society, without being able to favor or represent their particular interests because they do not know what these might be. The original position is meant to articulate conditions under which an

agreement about the principles that could govern a system of fair cooperation can be reached: a method for working out principles for fair political
agreement.

The contractors agree that they will, even in that just society, disagree
about basic conceptions of the human good. The citizens of the projected
just society will have to be responsible for pursuing their own conception of
a good life within the limits of fair social cooperation. They are assumed to be
rational in the sense of being able to pursue, reflect and revise their particular
view of what is valuable in human life; in other words: they would have the
capacity for an articulate conception of the good. In his 2001 *Justice as Fairness.
A Restatement* Rawls clarifies further that this underlines their *freedom*: they are
free in the sense that they regard both themselves and each other as having a
conception of the good. This includes being entitled to make claims on institutions to enable them to advance their particular conception of the good,
insofar as they don't collide with justice. What individuals make of their
opportunities and resources, what kind of lives they lead is their own business,
not in any way the political responsibility of society.

Moreover, Rawls assumes that even though they have particular, not
unreasonable but possibly conflicting conceptions of ways of life and the
human good, the contractors seek consensual fair terms of cooperation. In
other words, the contractors are supposed to be not only *rational* but also
reasonable: having a pragmatic orientation of being committed to cooperate
with others on fair terms, seeking common ground with others. This
underlines their *equality*: they are regarded as equal in the sense that they are
capable of engaging in social cooperation over a complete life as an equal
among equal citizens. This would include a willingness to cooperate with those
who are not reasonable according to one's own standards, but still open
enough to respond to objections or changing circumstances. Reasonable citizens are able to follow fair terms of cooperation, even when this is not in their
own direct interests, provided that others are also willing to do that; in other
words: they have a sense of *justice*. 'The most fundamental idea in this conception of justice', so Rawls (2001) tells us, 'is the idea of society as a fair system
of social cooperation over time' (p 5). The participants of this system are considered free and equal, each with his or her own life to live, but also living
together. Such a system of cooperation aims to realize appropriate conceptions
of freedom and equality simultaneously.

The point of justice as fairness is to distribute advantages and burdens in such
a way that a fair system of cooperation among free and equal citizens is pre-
served. The 'basic structure' of society includes positions with different powers
and economic advantages that are mediated by a legal, political, and economic
framework of institutions. If citizens have no reasonable complaint about their
access to these various positions or to their connected rights, liberties, and
opportunities for economic advantage then that structure can be considered
just. Based on the rationally anticipated outcome of the discussions in the

original position, Rawls claims that a just society would be possible under the following conditions:

a   All persons are treated, both by others and political institutions, as *free* in their perspective of the good and as *equal* with regard to their rights. Being 'free' means, for instance, that each persons' plans of life are respected insofar as they don't collide with others' plans or with justice. Being 'equal' refers to the citizens' 'basic rights and liberties' such as the right to vote and the freedom of speech and association: rights that are inherent in the status of citizens in a democracy and must therefore be equal for all citizens.

b   Society maintains a non-oppressive form of cooperation that allows each person to participate with equal opportunities giving her the right to a fair share of the fruits of that cooperation. Regarding 'opportunities' Rawls makes an important distinction between formal and fair equality of opportunity (cf. also Rawls 1999). The last principle implies that every individual with the same talent and motivation should have the same prospect of success in competing for advantaged positions. The influence of families, their class positions or prejudices regarding race or gender would have to be completely neutralized (see Ch.7). There will inevitably be social and economic inequalities but in such a way that they are optimal for the least-advantaged members of society; this complex condition that Rawls refers to as the 'difference principle' will need some more discussion below.

c   There needs to be an acknowledgement of the irreducible pluralism of conceptions of the good, combined with a shared perspective regarding the distribution of primary social goods, so that every person would be enabled to realize her conception of the good in freedom. The major social institutions distribute certain primary goods: 'liberties and resources that every rational man is presumed to want' (1971, p. 62). In spite of their different conceptions of the good life or different capacities everybody will need these primary goods: the basic rights and liberties mentioned above; opportunities and powers; income and wealth; and the social bases of self-respect (pp. 62, 92). Self-respect, finally, 'a sense of one's worth' is seen by Rawls as 'perhaps the most important primary good' especially its social bases, because 'our self-respect normally depends upon the respect of others' (Rawls 1971: 62, 440, 178). Just like in Kant's moral law 'Act in such a way that you treat humanity, whether in your own person or in the person of any other, never merely as a means to an end, but always at the same time as an end' (1785/1993, p. 36) this basic human dignity is not the sort of respect persons must earn or of which they must show themselves worthy. In the Rawlsian system, individuals receive shares of primary goods without needing to show themselves worthy or deserving of it.

d   This underlines the ways in which the autonomy of citizens depends on their being recognized by social institutions giving them a sense of self-worth and the confidence to carry out their life plans. One of Rawls' main concerns was how people would be able to realize their own conception of what is valuable in life, in the absence of a shared conception of the good. He insisted that this requires not only a certain moral freedom but also the resources to make this process possible. This is what Rawls intended with his theory of primary goods: whoever demands respect for a life plan that is self chosen must also acknowledge that others should have the opportunity to pursue such a path. For Rawls social (in)equalities in the distribution of formal freedoms and in the distribution of material resources are precisely what social justice is about.

e   All persons should see it as their moral duty to support societal institutions that incorporate such a shared concept of justice.

How to approach social inequality?

Rawls is especially concerned to give an answer to inequalities that arise from unequal starting positions in life; such inequalities appear to be inevitable in any society and cannot possibly be justified by appealing to notions of individual merit. To assume that these structural inequalities arise from individual voluntary choice, for which individuals may be held responsible, neglects that people are born with different talents and are raised under unequal circumstances. So, the natural distribution of talents and skills – which he calls a 'natural lottery' – is mediated by a social lottery. As we shall see in the later discussions of *Luck egalitarianism*, Rawls' theories about natural and social lotteries have led to a widespread popularity of the concept of 'luck' in later discussions about social justice.

Rawls acknowledges that the social lottery, deciding under what circumstances people are born, is crucially important:

> Even the willingness to make an effort, to try, and so to be deserving in the ordinary sense is itself dependent upon happy family and social circumstances. ... The better endowed are more likely, other things equal, to strive conscientiously, and there seems to be no way to discount for their greater good fortune.
>
> (1971 p. 74; 312)

Rawls' basic idea is that the position from which citizens begin to participate in society is the result of 'their social fortune or their luck in the natural lottery'. 'The natural distribution is neither just nor unjust; nor is it unjust that persons are born into society at some particular position. These are simply natural facts.' 'What is just or unjust is the way that institutions deal with these facts ... society must give more attention to those with fewer native assets and to those born into the less favorable social positions' (1971: 75, 102, 100).

Rawls' rejection of individual responsibility or merit as causes of social inequality is also motivated by the practical impossibility to gain the information that would be needed to make reliable judgments at the level of public institutions. Individual responsibility cannot conceivably be measured by any institutions we could devise. This does not mean that merit cannot play a role within specific contexts where people work together such as a company or a school. Within such contexts performances can be assessed and criteria like merit can motivate participants to perform optimally to further their common goals. Different rewards flow to different positions while talents and ambitions play their role in the allocation of persons to positions. But at the level of society individual responsibility or merit cannot serve as a fundamental value of justice.

Beyond a one-sided libertarian emphasis on freedom and an egalitarian plea for complete equality Rawls argues for a combination of, on the one hand, *equal civil liberties* and, on the other hand, *social rights* including a distribution of primary goods that should not be strictly equal but as equal as possible. In Rawls' thought experiment the social contractors will not conclude that income and wealth should be equally distributed, because this would harm their common interests. Material inequalities would be justified to a certain extent because they function as incentives for the citizens to develop their talents and skills, taking entrepreneurial risks and improving productivity. This competition would increase GDP and when the societal pie grows bigger, everybody can and should get a larger slice. Institutions should be arranged in such a way that the position of the worst off in terms of their income and wealth would be as favorable as possible; this is Rawls' famous and extensively discussed difference principle (cf. Williams 1995). In the context of an implementation of the difference principle in the form of tax and transfer policies that redistribute resources, Rawls gives an example of the maximal minimum that the worst off would deserve. This would be located at a statistical point where the amount of taxes that are used to support the worst off begin to interfere so strongly with economic efficiency that the prospects of the least advantaged begin to decline (Rawls 1971, p. 286).

Rawls accepts that the natural and social lotteries form no basis for allowable inequalities but sees no other solutions than to accept the inevitability of some degree of social inequality and to mitigate the negative effects for the worst off. The natural talents of a society are seen as a common asset that should be shared with the worst off but the aim of the difference principle is not a level playing field. Rawls underlines the importance of *acceptable* social and economic inequalities. To mitigate their disadvantaged position the worst off should retain optimal shares of the societal pie that would also secure the social basis of their self respect. This would counteract feelings of being unfairly cut out and lead to a better social cohesion:

> undeserved inequalities call for redress; and since inequalities of birth and natural endowment are undeserved, these inequalities are to be somehow compensated for. Thus the principle holds that in order to treat all persons equally, to provide genuine equality of opportunity, society must give more attention to those with fewer assets and to those born into the less favorable positions. The idea is to redress the bias of contingencies in the direction of more equality. In pursuit of this principle greater resources might be spent on the education of the less rather than the more intelligent, at least over a certain time of life, say the earlier years of school.
>
> (Rawls 1971, p. 100ff.)

Rawls underlines the crucial role of institutions to secure the just background conditions against which the actions of individuals and associations take place. Unless the basic structure of society is appropriately regulated and adjusted, even 'an initial just social process will eventually cease to be just, however free and fair particular transactions may look when viewed by themselves ... the overall result of separate and independent transactions is away from, and not towards background justice' (Rawls 1978, p. 53).

One of his major concerns is that unmitigated social inequality would disturb the liberties and political rights that should be equally awarded to all citizens. At several points in his work Rawls has criticized that in the US economic wealth is misused for political dominance. In his *Political Liberalism* (1993) he has protested against the ruling of the Supreme Court in *Buckley vs. Valeo* that it would be unconstitutional to limit the personal expenditures of citizens on their own political campaigns. According to Rawls such a verdict against limiting the influence of economic power increases the political power of rich people while their freedom of speech would not be unfairly limited if restrictions were to apply. Also in his debate with Habermas, Rawls has pointed out that the present system in the US 'woefully fails in public financing for political elections, leading to a grave imbalance in fair political liberties' (Rawls 1995, p. 159).

Justice between generations

In his theory of justice Rawls also discusses what he calls 'the problem of justice between generations' that would 'subject any ethical theory to severe if not impossible tests' (1971, p. 284). The concept of 'generation' (see Ch.6) that he uses seems to be derived from the relation between fathers and sons (288) but it is also used to indicate 'the stage of civilization' of a society (285). The problem of justice between generations is approached from the theory of the social contract: in the hypothetical original situation there would be representatives from all generations having to decide the best way to organize relations between generations without knowing in which generation they will live. Historically the generations are seen as advancing in prosperity and the contractors must decide about a just savings principle that would determine what should be given to the next generation.

The historical development is driven forwards and upwards because 'men have a natural duty to uphold and to further just institutions' (293). The moral aim of history is not the endless accumulation of wealth but 'the full realization of institutions and the fair value of liberty' (290). Each generation makes a contribution to later generations and receives from its predecessors but 'in the course of history no generation gives to the preceding generation, the benefits of whose savings it has received' (290). There is no reciprocity between them. According to Rawls this situation is unalterable: 'it is a natural fact that generations are spread out in time and actual exchanges between them take place only in one direction' (291).

In the light of the body of research on intergenerational reciprocity (see Ch.6) this is a strange claim. In contrast to his otherwise subtle theory Rawls' theory of history and its generations makes a rather primitive impression. History is approached in terms of stages – a type of theory that also dominates Daniels' theory of aging – and the main 'arguments' for this approach are uncontextualized natural phenomena such as 'natural facts' or 'natural duties'. With these comments I have already made the transition to a critique of Rawls' theory.

Some critical comments

(1) The Difference Principle

The practical implications of the difference principle, that the worst off should maximally benefit from the riches that are gathered by the more successful, depends very much on its interpretation and implementation. For instance, Cohen (1991) has presented a rather strict version that would allow very few incentive based inequalities, but Daniels tolerates more inequality because he fears that generous transfers would diminish the productivity that is needed to support the worst-off (Daniels 2003, 2008, p. 98; see Ch.7). However, he still claims that the difference principle would be more beneficial than trickle down policies and 'produce less health inequality than any other principles that allow inequalities' as it 'requires maximal flow to help the worst-off groups' and flatten the social gradients 'as much as possible' (Daniels 2006, pp. 93, 97). According to Powers and Faden (2006, p. 55), however, the expectation that the difference principle in combination with the principle of 'Fair Equality of Opportunity' would even result in a decent minimum for the worst off is unwarranted. Indeed, the help or support that the worst off should get according to the difference principle is not connected to a political discourse about *sufficiency* as an implication of equal citizenship (see Ch.7). Another basic problem with Rawls' difference principle is that social inequality is seen, on the one hand, as a fundamental problem but on the other hand as an incentive for competition and economic growth. There is too little differentiation of the basic processes involved.

(2) Naturalization and normalization

As we have seen, primary goods are introduced as answers to the *needs* of free and equal citizens.

> These are things that it is rational to want whatever else one wants. Thus given human nature, wanting them is being part of being rational … The preference for primary goods is derived, then, from only the most general assumptions about rationality and the conditions of human life.
>
> (Rawls 1971, p. 253)

In Rawls' later work *Justice as Fairness: A Restatement* (2001) the account of primary goods still ultimately depends on the nature of persons: on 'various general facts about human needs and abilities, their normal phases and requirements of nurture, relations of interdependence and much else' (2001, p. 58). One wonders whether these facts, for instance, about 'normal phases' are indeed so self-evident (see also Ch.7 about naturalization).

With such emphasis on natural needs it comes as a surprise that health and its distribution are neglected in Rawls' theory of justice. Although Rawls devoted some attention to health *care*, for instance in his book *The Law of Peoples* (1999), he refrained from discussing health. In contrast to the primary goods that were discussed before, which he sometimes calls *social* primary goods, health and vigor, intelligence and imagination are also seen as primary goods but they would be essentially *natural* goods. Although he admits that 'their possession is influenced by the basic structure, they are not so directly under its control' (1971, p. 62). This may be true but to stop at this point evades the 'deep inequalities' he set out to improve with his theory of justice.

(3) 'Being normal' as a precondition for equality

Although Rawls has developed a sophisticated account of justice, some of the limitations of his approach are typical of the broad tradition of justice as a social contract between independent equals. The 17th century social contract theorist John Locke characterized them already as 'Men being, by nature, all free, equal and independent, no one can be put out of his Estate,

and subjected to the Political Power of another, without his own consent'
(1690/1970: 348). The assumption that the social contractors would be
equal in their male, healthy and vigorous independence from each other has
created problems for the social contract tradition of justice because, for
instance, dependency has been difficult to integrate in its constructs (Nussbaum 2007).

Rawls is quite straightforward regarding what he assumes that citizens
should be:

> all citizens are fully cooperating members of society over the course of
> a complete life. This means that everyone has sufficient intellectual
> powers to play a normal part in society, and no one suffers from unu-
> sual needs that are especially difficult to fulfill, for example, unusual and
> costly medical requirements.
>
> (Rawls 1980, p. 546)

In his 1985 essay 'Justice as Fairness: Political not Metaphysical' he writes:

> Since we start within the tradition of democratic thought, we also
> think of citizens as free and equal persons … we assume that persons as
> citizens have all the capacities that enable them to be normal and fully
> cooperating members of society. This does not imply that no one ever
> suffers from illness or accident; such misfortunes are to be expected in
> the ordinary course of human life; and provision for these con-
> tingencies must be made. But for our purposes here (determining what
> persons as citizens might be, J.B.) I leave aside permanent physical dis-
> abilities or mental disorders so severe as to prevent persons from being
> normal and fully cooperating members of society in the usual sense.
>
> (1985, p. 234)

But what is 'being a normal and fully cooperating member of society in the
usual sense'? To exclude persons with physical disabilities from the full status
of citizens because they would fail to be 'normal' or 'fully cooperating'
reproduces the lack of esteem they often encounter in society and conflicts
with Rawls' insistence that the social bases of self-respect may be the most
important primary good. His tendency to regard a certain type of persons or
citizens as 'normal' and 'natural' neglects not only the heterogeneity of
persons but also that dependency is inevitable in human lives. The assumption that 'all citizens are fully cooperating members of society over the
course of a complete life' represents a drastic reduction of the very idea of a
complete life.

This leads, for instance, to a neglect of the fundamental importance of
dependency in human lives as a 'normal' phenomenon at all ages which,
therefore, plays a major role in human society. Such reductionist

understanding of citizenship and society has led to criticism from different perspectives. Communitarians such as Sandel (1982) have protested that for Rawls the task of a theory of social justice is reduced to articulating terms of fair competition and rules of mutual advantage that are acceptable by a community of 'normal' rational persons who are mutually disinterested and live freely chosen relations between equals. This reductionist view of society fails to acknowledge that persons are also interested in each others' well-being and that they live in, and have been formed by, communities and relationships they have not freely chosen. This general criticism of Rawls' implicit idea of mutually disinterested citizens also resonates in the critical comments of, for instance, Annette Baier, for whom the implementation of Rawls' theories 'may *unfit* people to be anything other than what its justifying theories suppose them to be, ones who have no interests in each others' interests' (1994, p. 23). Or in the verdict of Powers and Faden (2006) that Rawls' work is incapable of understanding or helping people to live lives that are characterized by dependency and interdependency, vulnerability and the potential for exploitation.

The Capability Approach: equality of what?

With his Capability Approach Nobel laureate Amartya Sen proposes an approach to justice that is quite different from Rawls' social contract theory. Like Rawls' theory, Sen's Capability Approach is complex and differentiated, but unlike the work of Rawls it has been applied in many practical contexts of policy development and evaluation. The main characteristics of the Capability Approach can be explained as follows:

a   Since his 1977 *Tanner Lectures* Sen has emphasized that he is primarily concerned with what people are actually able to be and to do. This leads to a distinction between what people would *value* or like to be or to do, versus what they are *able* to do. Sen calls the valued ways of doing and being *functionings*. Examples are: being nourished, being healthy, being educated, being free, being able to take care of others, to travel or to work. These valued ways of being and doing are distinguished from the feasible *opportunities* to realize and enjoy the functionings one desires; what Sen calls *capabilities*: the opportunity to achieve valuable combinations of human doings and beings.

b   In this difference between what people would like to be and do versus their feasible opportunities to actually realize such desired states, they are confronted with their (un)freedom. If citizens are free to go to a hospital but lack transportation or cannot afford the treatment they need, they are confronted with a merely formal freedom. Actually, they lack the capabilities to do that. What people are in reality capable of depends on all kinds of factors in their situations. Besides personal differences such as physical or mental abilities there are also important differences in non-personal resources such as public health care, societal cohesion, helpfulness of the community or environmental diversities (climatic, disease, local crime).

c   Situations that deserve assistance from a perspective of justice can be caused by personal incapacities such as the inability to walk or being blind. But many practical hurdles of disabled people are also caused or aggravated by their circumstances. A blind person or somebody who cannot walk will need more and other resources to achieve an equal or, given their condition, an acceptable level of capability as people who are considered to be 'normal'. Giving the person who cannot walk a wheelchair does not solve his problems to move around freely, when public spaces are designed with 'normal' people in mind. The adaptation of public space to the needs of a blind person or a person in a wheelchair cannot be achieved by giving them more money but requires adequate public spaces and facilities.

d   These different analytical levels lead in Sen's economically oriented theory of justice to a distinction of different conversion factors that refer to ways in which resources can be converted into feasible opportunities. The personal conversion factor in this case refers to an inability to walk that may be improved by supplying the person with a mobility scooter. Environmental conversion factors refer, for instance, to insufficient sidewalks to move around in such a scooter because the design of a city presupposes that driving such a scooter would not be 'normal'. Social conversion factors can help or sabotage the productive use of a certain resource such as a wheelchair, for instance when other people are treating persons in a wheelchair respectfully or disrespectfully. Another concept is that of Capability Sets, drawing attention to the fact that capabilities are not unrelated to each other and may actually presuppose or exclude each other when, for instance, a mother is capable of taking care of her parents and her children and is also capable to work to support her family but she cannot shoulder all of these tasks within the available time. This may occur when she has to travel too far to work or to her parents or when a child or another family member needs more attention than would be 'normal'.

e   Having capabilities should not imply that the person has to put them into practice: if a person has the capabilities to go to a hospital this does not mean that she is obligated to do this. Sen even gives the example of somebody who decides in freedom not to eat, like Gandhi did in his struggle with the British Raj. He was as hungry as any other person would be, but Gandhi chose not to eat as a sign of his freedom. Freedom has intrinsic importance for the quality of people's lives: 'choosing may itself be a valuable part of living, and a life of genuine choice with serious options may be seen to be – for that reason –

richer' (Sen 1995, p. 41). According to Martha Nussbaum, the other main representative of the Capability Approach its goal is 'the capability to function well if one so chooses' (1988, p. 160; cf. Sen 1993, p. 36).

f   So, although resources are certainly necessary, the moral emphasis is not on an equal distribution of resources but on enabling people to lead the life they want to lead. Sen and Nussbaum explicitly refer to an Aristotelian inspired moral and political philosophy emphasizing that the goal of political activity should be the capability of human beings to flourish (Ruger 2004, 2012).

g   The Aristotelian influence is also present in another characteristic emphasis of the Capability Approach: human beings are social beings, from the very beginning to the end of their lives. Nussbaum expresses the difference of the Capability Approach from the social contract tradition and, especially, Rawls' theory as follows: The person leaves the state of nature (if, indeed, there remains any use for this fiction) not because it is more mutually advantageous to make a deal with others, but because she cannot imagine living well without shared ends and a shared life. Living with and toward others, with benevolence and justice, is part of the shared public conception of the person that all affirm for political purposes

(Nussbaum 2006, p. 158)

Instead of assuming that human beings are independent, human autonomy is thought of as relational and interdependent throughout the life course (see Ch.7). Human beings will not survive and develop their potential to be autonomous without extensive care and education. They remain dependent on others and others will depend on them.

This social and relational 'nature' of human beings does neither imply that they are the same nor should social justice aim at treating them the same: 'We differ in age, sex, physical and mental health, bodily prowess, intellectual abilities, climatic circumstances, epidemiological vulnerability, social surroundings, and in many other respects' (Sen 1992, p. 28). 'Human diversity is no secondary complication to be ignored, or to be introduced later on; it is a fundamental aspect of our interest in equality' (Sen 1992, p. xi). This concern for differences between citizens and their situations has led to Sen's most pointed critique of Rawls: an equal distribution of primary goods does not lead to equality but deepens inequality. Because citizens and their situations are so different it does not make sense to treat them all the same. It is a bit like giving everybody a ten percent income raise: this does not reduce but increase income differences.

Representatives of the Capability Approach differ regarding the need to make a list of what should be regarded as basic capabilities. Martha Nussbaum, for instance, has attempted to make a list of central capabilities that would be necessary for a life that is 'not so impoverished that it is not worthy of the dignity of a human being' (Nussbaum 2000, p. 72). Sen has refused to make such a list; he explains that respect for the freedom and diversity of human beings and their situations implies that for each situation the people concerned should select, sequence, prioritize, trade off capabilities as they see fit. He explicitly warns against the determination of central human capabilities by theorists from other social contexts without any public debate by the people who are directly concerned (Sen 2005). Capabilities are not commodities (Sen 1985); it would make no sense to apply a pure theory or some mechanical standard such as income. What counts is whether persons in specific situations are able to lead the kind of life they want; or as he puts it, the kind of life they have reason to value: 'it is the people directly involved who must have the opportunity to participate in deciding what should be chosen, not local elites (political or religious) or cultural experts (domestic or foreign)' (Sen 1999, p. 31 ff.). Sen has repeatedly underlined that he regards this openness to continued public reasoning of the people concerned not as a weakness but as a strength of his theory (Sen 1999).

For Sen, social justice is ultimately about what people are enabled to be and to do: what their capabilities are. This fundamental focus on outcomes or indicators that are more directly relevant for citizens is also characteristic for the different indexes that Sen has designed for United Nations monitors such as the *Human Development Index* (Anand & Sen 1994). As indicators such as Gross National Product (GDP) do not have intrinsic value, these should not be seen as adequate estimates of living standards. Moreover, the availability of many public goods, such as transport, infrastructure, electricity or means of communication cannot be captured by private incomes. Therefore, besides indicators such as GDP, the *Human Development Report* since the early 1990s includes also adult literacy rate, gross enrollment ration for primary, secondary and tertiary education or life expectancy at birth. This early index has evolved into several other indexes such as the *Inequality-adjusted Human Development Index*, the *Gender Development Index* or the *Gender Inequality Index*.

Sen about Rawls

Sen's respect for the diversity of people and the openness of his theory for the specificity of situations leads to a theoretical modesty. This explains his criticism of general theories of equality and, especially, Rawls' theory. Sen criticizes what he thinks is a dominant motive in theories of justice: the pretention to construct a perfect theory of justice and a perfectly just state of affairs, for all times and all places. In this perspective Rawls' theory is a brilliant example of a more general but unfortunate tendency. This pretention to present the perfect theory is typical of what Sen calls a 'transcendental' approach (Sen 2010). In contrast, he calls his own theory 'comparative' as it evaluates different approaches and tries to identify the best alternative among them. Sen has a much more pragmatic approach: not having a perfect theory does not mean that we cannot evaluate situations or proposals. After all, many suggestions to improve society are not very controversial: good and affordable housing, clean water, good nutrition, time to work, care and relax, holidays and parental leave, social protection, vaccinations, health care ...

In his later work Rawls has sometimes made remarks that suggest his approval of some of Sen's theories. He writes, for instance, in *Justice as Fairness* (2001) 'it should be stressed that the account of primary goods does take into account, and does not abstract from, basic capabilities: namely, the capabilities of free and equal persons (in virtue of their two moral powers)' (p. 169). And in *Political Liberalism* (1993) he affirms that any index of primary goods 'will consider basic capabilities, and its aim will be to restore citizens to their proper role as normal members of society' (p. 186).

Some critical remarks

In the years since Sen's first publication on the capability approach there have been many questions, criticisms and responses about subjects ranging from conceptual and policy issues to methodological concerns about operationalization, measurement and aggregation of capabilities. Moreover, the capability approach has been widely used in different fields of study such as education, health, development, disability or gender. However, as Gopinath (2018) concludes in his overview there have been few applications of this approach in aging studies (cf. however, Nussbaum & Levmore 2017; Stephens & Breheny 2018).

When the goal of the capability approach is stated as enabling people to function in ways 'they have reason to value' many questions arise when there is, indeed, no shared conception of the good, as Rawls would say. What if people want functionings that others find offensive or overly expensive? Does a call for equality of outcomes mean that the capabilities of a person have to be brought to the level of anyone who has superior capabilities? Would this justify continuous medical interventions because somebody has reasons to value being as beautiful as technologically possible? As discussed above, this problem prompted Nussbaum to make a list of basic capabilities. One reason that the Indian economist-philosopher Sen did not bother putting maximum limits on capabilities was his constitutive interest in improving situations of poverty in developing countries. But in his later work there he has underlined that people should have *sufficient* sets of capabilities instead of equal capabilities or open ends (cf. Nielsen & Axelsen 2017). I will return to this issue in Chapter 7.

A strong point of the capability approach is its emphasis on the importance of feasible and valued opportunities. Instead of just assuming or proclaiming that everybody has equal opportunities and must therefore be held responsible for their situation Sen would ask: has it really been possible to choose from viable alternatives or has it rather been a choice between the bad and the worst? However, the fundamental presupposition of the potentially autonomous adult who exercises his freedom by choosing functionings from a range of capabilities has also a problematic side. Cohen (1993) has rightly commented that for those who are not the typical autonomously choosing adult, such as children, very ill people or mentally disabled people, the moral emphasis should be on *being* well-nourished or sheltered etcetera; not on having the choice if one so wishes. In all situations in which persons are not able to voice their preference it is vital to go beyond offering feasible opportunities and to secure functionings. In childhood and in situations of extreme dependency on others, such as in grave medical conditions it can be completely unrealistic to offer opportunities one could chose from. To be fair, Sen has acknowledged that such problems would indeed arise in emergencies but this does not acknowledge that such situations are inevitable along the life course and in that sense normal.

Finally, it must be said that the functionalist terminology to describe preferred ways of living as 'functionings' is unfortunate as this terminology reduces ways of living to economic or bio-medical functionings (Powers & Faden, 2006). It obscures the personal dimensions and socially shared meanings of ways of living. Older people are already too often exposed to functionalist approaches (Baars 2012, pp. 63–65; Gilleard & Higgs 2014). Such reductionist functionalism is undoubtedly not intended by Sen or Nussbaum, but as words have consequences this remains a problem, especially because this concerns a basic concept of the capability approach.

The marginalization of social inequality in social theory of the 1980s and 1990s

With the change of dominant political realities in the late 1970s, thinking about social justice and inequality also began to change. Rawls' *A Theory of Justice* (1971) had become a catalyst for further discussions, just like the influential libertarian Robert Nozick had stated at the beginning of the 1980s: 'Political philosophers now must either work within Rawls' theory or explain why not' (1981, p. 183). In the decades that followed, Rawls' theory served as a theoretical platform from which new theories of social justice were launched; in forms of critical negation or elaboration. As we have seen, Rawls was deeply concerned about what he called pervasive 'deep inequalities' (1971, p. 7) that affect initial chances in life and cannot possibly be justified by an appeal to the notions of merit or desert. Moreover, he worried that unmitigated social inequality would disturb the liberties and political rights that should be equally awarded to all citizens.

Unfortunately Rawls' approach to social inequality was hardly developed any further by his egalitarian successors; inequality as originating, for instance, in early life – a central theme in the work of Rawls – was pushed to the periphery by a dominant emphasis on adult individual responsibility (see Ch.6).

This neglect of social inequality fits a broader trend. In European as well as American social theory we see a similar retreat from interest in social inequality. It made sense to rethink the Marxist discourse which dominated approaches to social inequality in the late 1960s and early 1970s. However, as the neoliberal turn of capitalism gained momentum social inequality disappeared from the agenda to make place for communitarian concerns and abstract procedural and linguistic issues.

Communitarians versus Liberals

One of the new influential paradigms in social theory of the early 1980s was 'communitarianism', prominently articulated in books such as MacIntyre's *After Virtue* (1981) and Sandel's *Liberalism and the Limits of Justice* (1982). The communitarians criticized 'liberalism', especially Rawls' concepts of society and justice as abstract procedural constructs that neglect the essence of communities. Sandel criticized Rawls for avoiding a substantive conception of the good by asserting the primacy of procedural justice; this would amount to a denial of shared conceptions of the good, reflecting a society that is nothing more than 'a plurality of persons, each with his own aims, interests and conceptions of the good' (Sandel 1982, p. 181ff.). Sandel (2005) argued that the liberal 'politics of rights' should be abandoned for a 'politics of the common good' in order to revive communal life and public morality. Such a communitarian emphasis on a 'common good' was also seen as a healthy counterweight against individualizing 'rights talk', as Glendon (1991) has put it. Amitai Etzioni, who has been called the 'guru' of the communitarian movement, later proposed to combine a concern for universal human rights with particularistic conceptions of the good, which may in some cases override individual rights. So, the values of particular communities could to a certain extent override universal human rights: whereas torture or ethnic cleansing would never be justifiable, denial of free expression or even the violation of women's rights could be defended in accordance with the values of more traditional communities (2006, pp. 73–78).

MacIntyre framed his diagnosis in terms of a defensive anti-modernist stage theory:

> What matters at this stage is the construction of local forms of community within which civility and the intellectual and moral life can be sustained through the new dark ages which are already upon us'… 'In a society where there is no longer a shared conception of the

community's good as specified by the good for man, there can no longer either be a very substantial concept of what it is to contribute more or less to the achievement of that good.

(MacIntyre 1981, pp. 126, 232)

This historical conflict between modernity and community would even affect 'qualities of character, reflectiveness and friendship that depend on the possibility of constitutive projects and attachments'. These would have to be grounded in 'a deeper commonality ... a commonality of shared self-understanding as well as enlarged affections' (Sandel 1982, p. 183). The communitarians protest against Rawls' neglect of shared values; as if values were only the result of subjective choice and people were only connected to each other by rationally chosen or contractual relationships. Denying any shared conception of the good would result in a moral deficit. In aging studies a similar communicative and communitarian perspective has been defended by Rick Moody in his *Ethics in an Aging Society* (1996) as he defended the priority of particular interpretations of 'solidarity to the common good' (239) above 'claims by the elderly' (235).

There are several important aspects to this communitarian critique. There is indeed a strong hermeneutical deficit in social contract theories that begin with individual contractors who are abstracted from any historical context in order to design together a just society for all times and all places. Societies are indeed more than a collection of individuals who are kept together by markets or abstract procedural constructs, but societies are also more than a collection of communities distinguishing themselves from other communities in their particular understanding of the common good. Moreover, the shared values of a community can be difficult to identify because they are usually contested as long as there is some freedom of discussion. There are also democratic advantages in granting rights to individuals and not only to communities, as community rights may also be controlled by a small elite excluding deviants from being recognized as members of the community.

Moreover, individual rights such as freedom of speech or freedom of association are not individualistic rights: they give individuals also the freedom to unite and protect or strengthen communities. Unchosen community values and unchosen commitments cannot be idealized and put above critical questioning. As Iris M. Young noted in her article on 'The Ideal of Community and the Politics of Difference' (1990) communities are not per se idyllic environments; they can also be sources of prejudice, patriarchy, ageism or gender phobia. In this context Habermas (1987) has insisted that life worlds remain different from systemic worlds but still need to be open to critical discourse. It is good to remember that the idea of 'the common good' has a long history, beginning with Aristotle, of legitimating social and political inequalities and suppressing minorities. Nevertheless, proposals regarding the 'common good' deserve to be debated, not discarded. Finally, if communities want to remain more or less intact in a neoliberal society they also need to address broader, societal processes of increasing inequality that will eventually tear them apart or set different communities up against each other.

The eclipse of society and social inequality from social theory...

Although social inequality had become an increasing practical concern in most developed countries as their governments were beginning to follow neoliberal politics, dominant social theorists of the early 1980s were turning away from a critical analysis of societal macro developments. Throughout the 1980s and 1990s there was an increasing tendency to insist that societal inequality had become something of the past. There have been important exceptions such as the work of Bourdieu (1984; orig. 1979) or the different approaches of feminist writers who were laying the foundation for a broad discourse of gender identities and intersectionality (see Ch.3 and Ch.4). The dominant trend, however, was away from social inequality, especially of material resources.

In Foucault's work, for instance, we find a movement away from his earlier studies of institutional strategies to keep poor or deviant people in line, such as the asylum or the prison (Foucault 1965, 1978), towards studies of the 'care of oneself' in his *History of Sexuality* (1990; orig. 1976, 1984). We can see a similar movement in the work of Anthony Giddens. In the context of his analysis of late modernity Giddens developed his thesis about the dusk of 'emancipatory politics' with its primary imperatives of justice, equality and participation: 'concerned above all with liberating individuals and groups from constraints which adversely affect their life chances' (Giddens 1991, p. 210). In his view, this emancipatory politics with its focus on life *chances* had to be left behind for *life politics* which would primarily be concerned with life *styles*: 'Life politics concerns political issues which flow from processes of self-actualization in post-traditional contexts, where globalizing influences intrude deeply into the reflexive project of the self, and conversely where processes of self-realization influence global strategies' (Giddens 1991, p. 214). In his *Theory of Communicative Action* (1987a; orig. 1981) Habermas distanced himself from Critical Theory (especially from the work of Horkheimer and Adorno) and broke away from his earlier project of a critical interrogation of the different interests that would be constitutive for the production of knowledge which had laid the ground for his concept of a critical social science led by an emancipatory interest. The result of his reorientation was that problems of social inequality in terms of material reproduction and, especially *unequal life chances* with their many different causes, were neglected in favor of conflicts arising in the domain of cultural reproduction: 'The issue is not primarily one of compensations that the welfare state can provide, but of defending and restoring endangered ways of life. In short, the new conflicts are not ignited by distribution problems but questions having to do with the grammar of forms of life' (Habermas 1987a, p. 392). In this linguistic emphasis on the grammar of forms of life – albeit interpreted quite differently, based on a theory of speech acts – Habermas resembled the post-modernists he criticized so vehemently in his *Philosophical Discourse of Modernity* (1987b). Moreover, his emphasis on communicative action in life worlds brought him close to the defensive position of the communitarians. It should be added to his defense that he continued to intervene for a broad audience with critical comments and analyses on actual political developments.

The retreat from critical analyses of society was much stronger in the heterogeneous configurations of post-modernism that gained intellectual momentum with the publication of Jean-François Lyotard's *The Postmodern Condition* (1984, orig. 1979). Its leading authors, such as Jean-François Lyotard, Jacques Derrida or Andre Glucksmann were active Marxists before they became disillusioned post-modernists. The fundamental opposition which negatively united their otherwise rather heterogeneous work was directed against the Hegelian idea that history harbors a meaningful direction or end which can be rationally and systematically understood; an idea which had been turned into a historically grounded political program by Marx. The developments in the late 1970s convinced them that their expectations had been built on sand and this experience led to a thorough questioning of knowledge and language. Critical intentions were overwhelmed by uncertainty whether language could even grasp reality. Instead of dialectics, thinking in terms of differences took center stage. Lyotard's *Differend: Phrases in Dispute* (1988; orig. 1983) contemplated the heterogeneity of discourses while Derrida's much earlier work *Of Grammatology* (1988; orig. 1967) suddenly gained popularity pondering *Différance* as an unending process of searching for meaning without finding solid ground. The dominant mood has been one of questioning the possibilities to articulate any critique or even the possibilities to grasp realities that confront us. Such questioning forms an integral part of all scholarly work but should not lead to paralyzing constructive social critique, especially when society is moving in a direction that is so obviously problematic.

It must be said that many of the postmodern authors, especially Derrida, inspired a broad movement of 'deconstruction' in the humanities and the arts and were important for a further articulation of feminist and gender studies in the broader context of identity politics. But the basic interest in exploring and acknowledging 'differences' rarely led to criticizing *unac-*ceptable inequalities. This general post-modern mood was also supported by authors such as Ulrich Beck whose original publication in 1986 of *Risk Society* (1992) coincided with the Chernobyl disaster, which explosively highlighted the message that in this new society everybody would be equally at risk, making old social class distinctions more or less irrelevant. Finally, Fukuyama seemed to have delivered the final blow with his 1992

The End of History in which the historical search for a better society ended with the collapse of the Soviet Union.

...and the rise of Critical Gerontology and life course studies

Meanwhile, the neoliberal retrenchment of the welfare state, beginning in the US and the UK but steadily spreading across other developed countries, led to critical studies about the many problems this created for numerous citizens. Among these critical studies an important role has been played by longitudinal life course studies about education, work careers or social inequality demonstrating the impact of policies over time. Within these studies longitudinal research on aging in a broad sense – not only about 'old age' – is of special interest because such studies show how structural and cultural processes such as discussed in Chapter 3 select citizens for unequal trajectories. These selection processes determine the chances to have, for instance, a long and inspiring career or to suffer early unemployment; a long and healthy life or an early death after many years of chronic disease. Long term effects of social inequality resonate into later life which puts aging studies in an eminent heuristic position to identify structures and processes having long term implications for citizens.

Moreover, the ways in which older people who are dependent on public support are treated by a society shed light on its priorities and humane qualities or lack of these. For a long time critical reflections about the ways in which older people were viewed and treated have been rare. Simone de Beauvoir's *Coming of Age* (1972) has stood out for a long time. Another early contribution came from medical anthropologist Margaret Clark (1973) who pointed out that the most prominent social function of older people in the US would be: getting sick. Looking back in 2009 Margaret Cruikshank argued that this role had grown in importance since Clark's publication because of the increasingly large role corporate health care was playing in the US, also in shaping public policy on aging. 'In America, where useful-ness is defined as productivity, many who are old do not appear to them-selves or others as useful because their paid work has ended. In a market economy, however, they produce something of great monetary value: ill-ness. The business of the old is to be sick' (p. 38).

With her pioneering work Carroll Estes laid the foundation for a scien-tifically reflected answer to neoliberal life course policies with the estab-lishment of the *Institute for Health & Aging* (1979) at UCSF and her influential work *The Aging Enterprise* (1979). She pointed very early to an important constitutive interest behind life course policies: the profit driven bio-medicalization of aging. According to this perspective, advanced by many powerful agents and enterprises, aging is basically a biological process of decline; consequentially, its problems can only be treated in medical contexts creating a costly and highly profitable 'aging enterprise' (cf. Estes &

DiCarlo 2019). Because aging is basically seen as a prolonged process of terminal decline, governments, health insurance companies and individuals would need to realize that the aging population will require enormous amounts of money to invest in new medical technologies and expensive pills. The bio-medicalization of aging leads especially to ignoring the needs of older people for material resources, respect and social connectedness.

Gradually the term 'Critical Gerontology' emerged as the nominal umbrella for different critical approaches to aging under the neoliberal regime. Although any scientific work should be critical, the need to disturb the silence of the main stream about the conditions in which people grow up and grow older has justified the use of the adjective. In the UK Alan Walker was one of the contributors to the first issue of Ageing & Society with his article 'Towards a Political Economy of Old Age' (1981) while Chris Phillipson published in 1982 his Capitalism and the Construction of Old Age. Both continued a tradition of social criticism represented by authors such as Peter Townsend and went on to publish critical analyses of policies targeting older people. In 1987 they explicitly made 'The Case for a Critical Gerontology'. In Canada Marshall and Tindale (1978) had already published their 'Notes for a Radical Gerontology', while Rick Moody presented his version of Critical Gerontology from a humanities inspired background in 1988. My first contribution to this international discussion was to show how aging processes as well as ways of studying and organizing aging processes were constituted by constellations of power at different levels of society, such as political and economic elites deciding about public budgets for pensions and health care; selective funding of research agendas by governmental and corporate actors; developing markets for profit oriented forms of care; pharmaceutical repression of outspoken residents of nursing homes; favoring profitable biomedical approaches to aging, etcetera (Baars 1991).

Especially during the 1980s and 1990s research agendas about aging were pushed in specific directions by governments setting up large projects that researchers could participate in, while at the same time reducing budgets for independent research. The result was a strong growth of studies about 'the elderly', with large inventories of their numbers and problems leading to unprecedented needs for care. The subjects that were opened for research were predominantly biomedical or strategic explorations of ways to organize care 'cheaper and better'. The results were enormous amounts of data without much theoretical analysis or interpretation; the identification of 'the elderly' with 'needs for care' and a restriction of aging studies to psycho-medical problems of 'the elderly' and their care arrangements. The political consequences of these developments have been a silencing of critical questions about public responsibilities for the structural generation of major problems of older persons that had little or nothing to do with their ages.

For many years Critical Gerontology was pushed to the periphery. Over the last two decades this paradigm has gained in strength by expanding life course research and including and articulating a diversity of critical perspectives on how older people are structurally and culturally positioned and treated in a broad variety of settings. Many representatives of Critical Gerontology were gathered in the 2006 volume *Aging, Globalization and Inequality: The New Critical Gerontology* (Baars, Dannefer, Phillipson & Walker 2006).

Over the last two decades the diversity and inequality of aging persons have increasingly been understood from different constitutive contexts, including the organization of the life course. Examples include *Ageing, Meaning and Social Structure. Connecting Critical and Humanistic Gerontology* (Baars, Dohmen, Grenier & Phillipson 2012); *Precarity and Ageing. Understanding Insecurity and Risk in Later Life* (Grenier, Phillipson & Settersten, 2021); *Aging A-Z. Concepts toward Emancipatory Gerontology* (Estes & DiCarlo 2019) and Dannefer's 2022 *Age and the Reach of Sociological Imagination. Power, Ideology and the Life Course.*

While egalitarians were struggling to gain access to dominant media and academic platforms, the *libertarians* were largely in tune with the political powers that had gained dominance since the early 1980s. For libertarians growing societal inequalities presented no moral problem because these would be a matter of individual responsibility; for them, threats to individual freedom from the state were an ongoing source of concern. In spite of major American programs such as the *New Deal* and the construction of a more supportive life course during the 1950s and 1960s, Cold War McCarthyism has succeeded in planting fear in the hearts of many Americans of a totalitarian form of socialism that was lurking behind any proposal to reduce social inequality or organize universal health care. This 'un-American' ghost of socialism, it was feared, would take over the country, threatening all that remained of their individual freedom, increasing taxes that would disappear into a bottomless pit, while pampering those responsible for their own problems. According to Daniel Bell's early criticism, Rawls' *Theory of Justice* was 'the most comprehensive effort in modern philosophy to justify a socialist ethic' (1972, p. 29) and in his book with the telling title *The Politics of Procrustes* Antony Flew attacked Rawls' work as a book for 'those belonging to the clerisy of power … tailor-made for those for whom egalitarianism and central power are but two sides of the same coin' (1980, p. 215).

Mounting questions about egalitarian responses

Perhaps this is what could be expected from libertarians. However, since the beginning of the neoliberal turn of capitalism with its program to 'pick the winners' and to 'stop backing the losers', there has been too little egalitarian counterweight. Instead, its most prominent authors looked away, giving free rein to the divisive neoliberal policies that were set to support big corporations instead of populations. It is, indeed, hard to see how the populations of the US and other developed countries – apart from the most wealthy 10% – have benefited from the neoliberal model, although it is still presented as an attractive ideal or inevitability by important parts of the dominant elites. Therefore, it remains necessary to document the consequences of this model with empirical research but also to articulate moral reflection, critique, and explorations of other ways forward. Typically, such activities should be the ambition of reflective forms of social theory and, especially, of theories of social justice. This leads to the question: how did American egalitarian theorists of social justice, especially those who have been writing about aging or more generally about the life course, respond to such issues as social policies, long term social inequalities or the persistent idealization of individual responsibility and self regulatory markets? How did they evaluate these in terms of social justice or human rights? This will be discussed in the next chapter.

Note

1 Elsewhere I have extensively discussed Critical Theory as developed by authors such as Adorno, Horkheimer and Habermas (Baars 1987; cf. Clingan 2012 for a discussion of these texts in the context of the Dutch reception of Critical Theory). Here, I will only marginally refer to the debate between Habermas and Rawls; not only because an extensive discussion would take too much space but also because Critical Theory or Habermas' questions in his debate with Rawls have not played any role in the post-Rawlsian theories that I will discuss in the next chapter.

Chapter 6

Theories of social justice and equality over the life course

Overview

How did American theorists of egalitarian social justice respond to the deepening social inequalities over the last four decades? To answer this question the chapter focuses on five of the most prominent egalitarian perspectives on social justice over the life course. To prepare this critical account a Rawlsian principle is introduced, that is shared by these different perspectives: that equality has to be over 'complete lives'. The only exception is the priority view from McKerlie that will be discussed in the last section of this chapter. The first approach advocates Generational Equity: demanding equality of public burdens between 'the old' and the young, working 'generation'. Because most of the arguments in this rather diffuse and one-sided polemic focus on a supposed opposition of 'generations' this concept is examined more closely. The second approach is a more reflected version of the polemic position of the Generational Equity advocates such as the Fair Innings Argument articulated by Daniel Callahan. The next section discusses the approach of the arguably most prominent contemporary paradigm of social justice and political philosophy in the US, called Luck Egalitarianism, inspired by the work of Ronald Dworkin. After this analysis the focus shifts to the publications of Norman Daniels, one of the most prominent theorists of social justice and public health over the life course and the author of an influential book on *Justice Between the Young and the Old*. The luck egalitarians and Daniels continue in different ways Rawls' work on social justice but without his interest in 'deep inequalities'. Finally I attend to the prioritarian work of McKerlie. His work *Justice between the Young and the Old* can be seen as the opposite of the advocates for Generational Equity, as McKerlie argues that helping 'the elderly' must have priority over utilitarian concerns of justice.

Complete lives egalitarianism: equality of 'whole lives'

'Call no man happy before he dies....'

Aristotle

DOI: 10.4324/9781003392590-7

We have already witnessed Rawls' interest in social inequality and we may wonder what role aging or the life course have played in his theory. With his concept of 'complete lives' Rawls had an important influence on egalitarian theorists who began to think about life course perspectives. This concept remained underdeveloped in his theory but does play a major role in his theory of primary goods: 'the index of primary goods is an index of expectations of these goods over the course of a complete life' (2001, p. 172). According to McKerlie (2012) this perspective on the life course as a whole has become customary in egalitarian theories of justice that were more or less inspired by the work of John Rawls. This leads to what McKerlie calls *Complete Life Egalitarianism*: the 'normative principle that different people's share of resources, or welfare, should be equal when we consider the amounts of those things that they receive over the complete course of their lives' (McKerlie 1989, p. 476).

The reason that this temporal dimension of distributional equality has become important is a recognition of the fact that governments of developed countries have gradually assumed some responsibility for the productive development and wellbeing of their populations over the life course. Child care, education, work, health care, income protection in situations of disease or disability and pensions have been organized, more or less explicitly in the context of the institutionalized life course (see Ch.1). And as public goods are distributed to make this possible the question arises how such temporally extended distributions can be justified. When the state imposes taxes to invest, for instance, in education or pensions, it needs a life course perspective to legitimize its mandatory interventions taking, for instance, from the working population and giving to children and pensioners.

For egalitarianism this is also a fundamental theoretical question: as soon as it has been acknowledged that it would make no sense, for different reasons, to equalize resources of all citizens at every moment in time the question arises how to distribute resources 'equally' over the life course. As soon as the temporal dimension of the life course is added to issues of equal distribution many new questions arise. Thomas Nagel has been one of the first to take up Rawls' life course perspective: 'egalitarianism would be especially concerned with aspects of an individual's life taken as a whole' (1979, p. 117). In his later work *Equality and Partiality* he basically repeats Rawls' statement: 'the subject of an egalitarian principle is not the distribution of particular rewards to individuals at some time, but the prospective quality of their lives as a whole, from birth to death' (1991, p. 69). In this context Nagel has elaborated the idea of compensation: in matters of distribution we should first compare the complete lives of the persons concerned and if some actual harm was compensated in the past or will be compensated in the future, there is no need for interpersonal distribution because in such cases there would be no inequality between complete lives.

Larry Temkin agrees: 'an egalitarian should be concerned about A's being worse off than B to the extent, and only to the extent, that A's life, taken as a *complete whole*, is worse off than B's, taken as a *complete whole*' (1993, p. 233).

In a way, this makes sense. From birth to death people can be expected to go through times where things are going very well and times when life is less well. Not all fluctuations need to be evened out by public resources and if somebody who had become unemployed finds a good job his problems may soon be forgotten. It is not clear, however, how we can measure and decide whether 'A's life, taken as a *complete whole*, is worse off than B's, taken as a *complete whole*'. Moreover, as long as someone is alive, it is impossible to oversee her 'complete life'; future compensation, especially, will be hard to ascertain. Even calculated life expectancies are no more than, exactly, expectancies that are based on extrapolations of averages from the past.

In the theories that will be discussed in the next sections we can find three basic approaches. The first is to put a maximum age on a complete life, so that people who are older than, for instance, 75 years would no longer be entitled to public support. This is the position that is taken by those who criticize the entitlements of older people in the *General Equity Debate* and the *Fair Innings Argument*. The second approach is to give every citizen at an early stage of the life course an equal amount of money and leave it to them to distribute the resources over their 'whole' future lives. This is the approach that is advocated by Dworkin and other *Luck Egalitarians*. The third approach is to divide the life course in stages such as youth, adulthood and old age and distribute resources according to the needs that would be typical of these stages. This is the approach that is taken by Norman Daniels with his *Prudential Life Span Account*. McKerlie's theory of 'Justice between the Young and the Old' does not figure in this list as he has distanced himself from *Complete Lives Egalitarianism*.

The legitimation of ageism

Complete Life Egalitarianism deserves some critical attention because it has been used to justify ageist policies (Wagland 2004). This tendency is typical for a culture in which ageism has too long been taken for granted and not taken seriously as a form of discrimination. Geoffrey Cupit (1998), for instance, has claimed that the standard argument against discrimination – unequal treatment – does not hold in the case of ageism. Ageism would be different from discrimination on the basis of gender or race because

> We all get a turn at being young, and most of us can expect a turn at being old. Ignoring for the moment that some die young, it seems that discrimination in favor of, or against, members of a particular age-group need not undermine efforts to produce a more equal distribution of

resources or outcomes, at least when considered over complete life-times ... once we take the view that it is benefits over a lifetime which are to be equalized, the equalizing of benefits argument against age discrimination is undermined.

(Cupit 1998, p. 703ff.; cf. Singer 2020)

According to Cupit, policies that discriminate on the basis of age – such as 'devoting minimal health resources to those over seventy-five' (707) – are in everyone's interest and treat everyone the same. If benefits and burdens are equally distributed according to age everybody will eventually be treated the same. The basic idea is that we are taking turns as we are getting older: in the first stages of childhood and vital adulthood society provides ample opportunities and support, whereas these get reduced to a minimal level when people are entering old age. 'Considered over complete lifetimes' there would be no problem of inequality.

The problem with this approach is that this 'equality' over a complete lifetime is, on the one hand, weighed in terms of a maximum amount of resources that citizens would be entitled to receive from public funds, neglecting broader contexts of inequality in the distribution of resources and opportunities. On the other hand, the publicly supported infrastructure of the life course tends to be dominated by the idea that the life course consists of three stages of life in which the first phase is meant as a mere preparation for the second phase which is supposed to be the apex of human life: to be productive, in an narrower economic sense but also in the sense of raising children, the productive workers of the future. This idealization leads to a denigration of the last phase of life: old age would only have a residual meaning, deserving only minimal resources because these resources would have to be taken away from people in the first two stages. Because those who have become old were once young and profited from this model, it would be justified to neglect them in 'old age'. If everybody would go through a happy youth, a fulfilling working life and a sad and difficult old age, there would be no moral problem: old people should be satisfied to remember that they have been happy as children and young adults. The past would compensate for their present and future misery. As we shall see, there is a strong conviction in many egalitarian theories that investing in health care for older people tends to be a bottomless pit because their productive lifetime has expired and they are about to die anyway. To put it crudely: even if all old people were to be treated badly there would still be equality because in that case we are just taking turns in being treated miserably in old age.

Stage theory is a poor theory of aging. The idea that human lives go through a happy youth, followed by a fulfilling adulthood and a difficult old age assumes that life is dominated by a natural rhythm of rising, shining and fading away. Life is finite but it is a poor understanding of aging to assume that functional decline would run in synchrony with older people's age regardless of personal or contextual influences. Not all people have the same chance of getting old and their living conditions in old age and further health and life expectancies are very different. Moreover, the idealization of a happy youth and a gratifying working life stand in flagrant contradiction to the experienced reality of a large part of the population. Many disadvantaged people don't even reach 'old age', whereas most of the wealthy live for many years after having reached this more or less formally protected phase and their wealth can hardly be seen as a compensation for having been 'worse off' in earlier life. The underlying logic is a simple *naturalization* of aging (see below): everybody would go through the same natural sequence of a happy youth, hard working adulthood and pitiful old age, unless they die early of purely natural causes. Older people should be satisfied with looking back on a happy past and silently accept that old age comes with problems. Besides its strong ageist implications, the problem in terms of social inequality is that those who depend on public support will be hit hard by policies that are based on this perspective. While the wealthy will be able to finance their later life without any problem, the proposed reductions in material resources and health care for older people will in practice mainly hit disadvantaged people. According to Kant's famous categorical imperative human beings should be treated as ends in themselves and never only as means. In Cupit's vision old people are not only treated as means: they are treated as means that have become useless. We will encounter similar thoughts in the next sections.

Between ageism and social justice: 'Generational Equity'

One of the key ingredients of arguments in favor of the neoliberal turn was the diagnosis that the 'bottomless pit' of welfare expenditure had undermined the prosperity of the US, causing it to fall back behind other countries such as Germany and Japan. The effects of Reagan's political rhetoric about 'welfare queens' who were sitting around the house collecting checks did, however, not stop at the policy of getting people of working age off welfare. All forms of welfare were affected, including Social Security and Medicare for the older part of the population. Especially the changing demographics as a result of the aging population of the US have been exploited in public debate, using apocalyptic narratives demanding drastic policy changes to avoid that young people might be squeezed out by old people who would live in comfort and wealth, because of their entitlements to public funds.

The changes in social, especially welfare policies that took place from the early 1980s on, were accompanied by a debate that explicitly called for more 'justice': the *Generational Equity Debate* (Williamson, Watts-Roy & Kingston 1999). The main proponents of 'Generational Equity' have, however, been too preoccupied with opposing seemingly familiar but actually artificial and vague constructs such as homogenous 'generations' to each other to present reflections or ideas about what 'equity' might be in this situation. In this 'debate' there is much about 'generations' and very little about 'equity'. To put the problems in perspective it should be noted that the population of the US comprises a relatively low percentage of older people. According to 2016 World Bank data the number of people aged 65 years and older as a percentage of the total population was 15.03% for the US. For Switzerland this was 18.23%, for Germany 21.27% and for Japan even 26.56%.[1] Quite in contrast to these relatively modest numbers, the US has been the platform of an extremely ageist movement, with public debates about the older population as a collection of selfish parasites and greedy geezers.

Samuel Preston (1984) was among those who initiated the debate by ringing the alarm bell about the future of the nation. The interests of the country's children were jeopardized by the older generation who would shortsightedly and selfishly cling to their entitlements without any consideration for people of other age categories who depend on the same public finances but without having the same solid entitlements. Those who shared his fears united themselves in *Americans for Generational Equity*. Their diagnosis of the problems of the aging society was that the older 'generation' would be better off than previous generations of old people, better off than the young, and better off than the next generations of old people could ever hope to be. Nevertheless, they didn't want to give up their privileged positions. On the contrary, with their large numbers they would organize a powerful 'gray lobby', vote in favor of 'gray interests' at the costs of children who could not vote and were thus doomed to lose this political battle.

The *Americans for Generational Equity* were supported in their indignation about the 'selfish grey vote' by the luck egalitarian Philippe van Parijs, who published in 1999 an influential article about 'The Disenfranchisement of the Elderly, and Other Attempts to Secure Intergenerational Justice'. In this article Van Parijs discussed several ways in which the voting power of older people could be blocked or strongly reduced. The article again enjoyed some acclaim in the ageist aftermath of the 2016 *Brexit* vote, when many *Remainers* were convinced that the disastrous outcome for the young was caused by the votes of older people who didn't care about the long-term consequences of their vote, forgetting other factors such as the role of education or the fact that 64% of the 18–24 year olds didn't vote. They could easily have changed the outcome of the referendum.

The ageist assumption that older people tend to vote egoistically for their short term interests has not been supported by empirical research on this subject (Vincent, Patterson & Wale 2002). According to Hudson & Gonyea (2012) members of the Baby Boom cohort are as politically diverse as other cohorts. Older people are the most diverse age category and usually they don't identify with being old. In spite of much concern about powerful lobbies of older voters there are no indications that these represent a major political force. On the contrary, older voters tend to transcend their immediate interests including the possible future of younger family members, such as grandchildren, in their political considerations. Moreover, the indignation of the *Americans for Generational Equity* appeared to be rather selective and rhetorical as there was hardly any effort from their side to eradicate child poverty or improve situations of vulnerable younger people who had become increasingly under threat from neoliberal policies (Walker & Walker 1997).

The tone of the attacks on older people has been far from subtle. The British journalist Henry Fairlie portrayed older people as selfish *Greedy Geezers* and Philip Longman emphasized that the main duty and prospect of young people in the US was to pay for those unknown 'elderly' who had lived an easy life and had decided amongst each other that 'the young' should keep them comfortably alive. Those who were already old or were about to enter this life phase, would have enjoyed such rich lives that they hardly deserved to get anything more from public resources. Supporting older citizens at current levels would therefore be unjust. These views were supposed to be strengthened by *Generational Accounting* of the public resources that were brought in and taken out by subsequent generations (Kotlikoff 1992). Such calculations have, however, been conducted in the UK and these data show that the contributions and benefits of subsequent generations over the past century have been more or less equal (Walker 2018).

Nevertheless, major international institutions such as the OECD, the World Bank, the IMF and even the CIA have also been spreading bleak diagnoses since the early 1980s and have continued to intervene with their often uninspiring and divisive future scenarios. The OECD published in 1988 two reports: *Reforming Public Pensions* and *Ageing Populations: The Social Policy Implications* with overviews of demographic developments such as declining birth rates and increasing longevity and economic outlooks on declining productivity and growth. In these reports the ideological choices have remained hidden in seemingly self-evident extrapolations of age-related figures of labor market participation and health care costs (Baars 1990). These ideologies have become more manifest as the bitter fruits of the policies targeting public expenditure have become more obvious. Fortunately, *Social Security* has remained popular among the population and relatively spared from neoliberal onslaught.

This may be one of the reasons why easy sounding *Generational Equity* slogans have resurfaced time and again. Indignation about the costs of population aging has remained a popular genre, appealing to elementary survival mechanisms by using threatening terms such as 'tsunami', 'catastrophe' or other natural disasters. In 1987 Philip Longman joined the first wave of publications with his *Born to Pay: The New Politics of Aging in America*, continuing his alarmist crusade in 2004 with *The Empty Cradle: How Falling Birthrates Threaten World Prosperity and What To Do About It* and other publications trying to ward off the 'Gray Tsunami' that would be sweeping the planet. In 1999 Peterson published *Gray Dawn: How the Coming Age Wave Will Transform America – and the World*, while Wallace (1999) sounded the alarm about an *Agequake: Riding the Demographic Roll-ercoaster Shaking Business, Finance and Our World*. Kotlikoff and Burns (2005) warned the American public about *The Coming Generational Storm*.

To give a more serious account of 'Generational Equity' would imply that the interests of different 'generations' – provided such a concept could bring us any further in these issues – would have to be weighed in the context of a society that can only continue to exist thanks to the contribu-tions of subsequent 'generations'. Indeed, Baby Boom cohorts are larger in size than later cohorts, which may pose specific problems which do not appear to be unmanageable as other developed countries such as Japan or Germany have much higher percentages of older people among their popula-tions without visible signs of collapse. There has been little interest to learn from countries with a higher percentage of older people which have eagerly been portrayed as hopelessly doomed. The typical juicy expressions of the genre may be easy reading but have little to do with a proper analysis. The British author Paul Wallace (1999), for instance, writes about Germany that 'the lights are programmed to go out in the powerhouse', although we have seen little of that in the last two decades. About Japan he exclaims that its 'Rising Sun scenario seems as outdated as only past fashions in paranoia can be'.

Aging populations or 'the older generation' are excluded from a 'normal' society or, rather, included as its unbearable burden which would press down on the 'healthy, vital and productive' society. This threatened social entity is enlarged by Wallace (1999) to include 'Business, Finance, and our World'; for Peterson (1999) this is about 'America – and the World' and Longman (2004) fears for 'World Prosperity'. Fishman's book title *A Shock of Gray: The Aging of the World's Population and How it Pits Young Against Old, Child Against Parent, Worker Against Boss, Company Against Rival, and Nation Against Nation* (2012) adds another bizarre impression of aging populations as the root of all evil.

The specific targets of these pamphlets are 'the elderly' – more denigrating references are also used – and, especially, their public entitlements. On the way, the lives of older people are reduced to useless, costly residues of lives that may have been productive but have lost their value. However, the scarce interest in improving, for instance, child poverty or other dire situations of young disadvantaged citizens gives the impression that the *Generational Equity* offensive is mainly a crusade against public responsibility and public spending. The proposed reductions of public funds for 'the old' but also for 'the young' will hit especially the disadvantaged of all ages, whereas the more advantaged will be able to buy housing, education, or health care on the market.

These political narratives have continued to be trumpeted as if they were the most recent uncovering of a hidden conspiracy. Meanwhile, these alarmist publications have also been contradicted. Examples are Phil Mullan's 2002 *The Imaginary Time Bomb: Why an Ageing Population is Not a Social Problem*, and Lincoln Caplan's 2014 'The Boomer Fallacy: Why Greedy Geezers Aren't Destroying our Financial Future'. Actually, from the beginning of the neoliberal turn against social policies there have been answers to these divisive constructions; answers of concern, critique and reflection. Bob Binstock (1983) criticized the sudden scapegoating of the aged, so shortly after a period in which their rights had finally begun to be respected. Minkler (1986) rightly pointed out that the proponents of *Generational Equity* worked with false assumptions: as if all older people were affluent or financially secure and as if only older people had a stake in public expenditure on health and social security. Robertson (1990, 1997) criticized the irresponsibly divisive constructions of apocalyptic demography exploiting even widespread fears of Alzheimer and neglecting the vital interdependence between persons of different ages. According to Quadagno (1988) there was failing evidence for a conflict between generations because social support for Social Security remained strong. Moody (1996) put the *Generational Equity* debate in a broader perspective noting that behind the 'generational warfare' (p. 235), there was a genuine concern that the public responsibility for Social Security, pensions, health care or national debt would be postponed into the future. Instead of accumulating the common debt of future generations, it would be better to face the future with sustainable institutions in the context of a society that solves or improves its problematic aspects here and now.

The ambivalent narrative of a costly aging population, aiming – in the spirit of Estes' *Aging Enterprise* – at creating and expanding profitable markets has indeed been highly successful insofar as the US holds the world record in health care expenditure per capita, even though large parts of the population are not adequately covered and life expectancies remain relatively low. In the following pages we will frequently encounter the alarmist message of a 'bottomless pit' of overly expensive but supposedly futile advanced medical technologies to extend the lives of older patients. These narratives aim at reducing public expenditures on health care without improving public health, which will hit especially those who cannot afford to take part in the profit driven health care system of the US. Meanwhile, older people who are privileged to be covered by expensive health insurance remain a highly appreciated clientele.

Aging populations continue to be presented as a threat to Western economies mounting pressure on the most vulnerable. In spite of all evidence about the vital importance of a more protected and secure life course for people of all ages and in spite of the obvious need for aging populations to become more integrated instead of divided according to ages, setting age groups as 'generations' against each other has remained disconcertingly popular in public debates.

Generations – a look at confusing terminology

As the concept of a 'generation' is basic to the discourse of those who plead for 'Generational Equity' it may be useful to give some attention to this concept. Especially, because in opposing generations to each other, inequalities *within* these generations are neglected. The concept was theoretically developed in neo-Kantianism which explored the question whether knowledge would be influenced and shaped by factors which Kant would have considered as being external to 'pure reason'. Might not historical circumstances profoundly influence world views, theories or convictions? These questions were hotly debated in the 19th century by thinkers such as Wilhelm Dilthey (1833–1911), Ernst Troeltsch (1865–1923) and Georg Simmel (1858–1918). These discussions encouraged the sociologist Karl Mannheim (1893–1947) in the first half of the 20th century to develop his 'Sociology of Knowledge': a program to investigate the social backgrounds of different forms of knowledge. A first step in that direction was his early essay on the 'Problem of Generations' (1928/1952). Generations used to be seen as composed of different people but basically remaining the same in their ways of life as they replace each other through the life cycle. Mannheim's interest was roused by indications that new generations did not just follow traditions that were only changing very slowly but made the impression of actively exploring new ways of living and thinking, for instance because they grew up with newspapers or the radio extending their horizon beyond the perspectives of their parents and grandparents.

Based on the extensive research that has taken place over the last century there is no reason to doubt the influence of wars, major catastrophes or crises on the ways in which people grow up and learn to see the world. Technologies also play their part: newspapers, cars, telephone, radio, air planes, television, computers, the internet or smartphones. Meanwhile, the rate of technological change has also undermined the differences between generations. The idea that formative periods change slowly so that one generation grows up with candlelight and the next with electricity has been overtaken by the acceleration of change. As social and technological changes follow each other more rapidly it becomes difficult to identify a major formative period that impregnates, so to speak, a whole generation so that it becomes clearly different from other generations. Important innovations such as electricity, cars, airplanes or the internet tend to exert their formative influence on people of all ages, not only on youngsters growing up. The 'generation' that grew up without computers also gets used to them and to smart phones or robots. There may still be differences between people who grow up with smart phones and those who got used to them as they were older but such differences tend to depend, for instance, on education or occupation. Although the idea of different generations presupposes some amount of change in basic technologies, cultural developments or historical situations, it makes more sense in a relatively static society. Nevertheless, the idea that society is populated by different generations has remained vivid, not only in public but also in scientific discourse where the Great Generation, Baby Boomers, Echo Boomers, Millennials, Generation X, Y and Z are readily distinguished.

The concept 'generation' may be used to distinguish parents and their children as two subsequent generations. However, as people become parents at very different ages there may be a difference of 20, 30 or more years between the oldest and youngest child from the same father. Such age differences undermine the idea of a homogeneous generation even further. To grasp such differences, the concept of 'birth cohorts' has been developed, grouping people together who were born in the same year or in the same period of, usually, five years. By analogy, we can distinguish 'labor market cohorts' or 'retirement cohorts' by forming groups of people who are entering the labor market or retirement in the same year although they have quite different ages. Like generations, cohorts have to be situated and interpreted in time and place, including their internal differences. The lack of differentiation that is inherent in the concept of a 'generation' and some other difficulties have led David Kertzer (1983) to the diagnosis that 'generation' is a confusing concept that might still have some use but in a very restricted way (cf. also Alwin 2003; Alwin & McCammon 2007; Biggs & Lowenstein 2011).

The artificial 'generations' of Generational Equity

The advocates of 'Generational Equity' don't bother about such distinctions and work from a polemic standpoint that pretends to defend the supposed interests of 'the young' – including the working population – against 'the old': the rising tsunami of older people with their entitlements. This opposition between 'the young' and 'the old' has become taken for granted even in more considerate perspectives such as Daniels' 1988 *Am I my Parents' Keeper? An Essay on Justice Between the Young and the Old* (see below) or McKerlie's 2012 *Justice between the Young and the Old*. People with very unequal situations and different interests are thrown together in seemingly homogeneous 'generations'. From a viewpoint of social justice it is highly worrying to see how the problems and challenges of population aging are exploited to create or amplify divisions between citizens based on their age. Social inequalities on both sides of the age divide are neglected so that, unfortunately, the most disadvantaged of all ages will be the first to suffer from the radical therapies that are proposed. Therefore, some distinctions might be useful.

First, generalizations such as 'the old' or 'the older generation' or 'aging Boomers' are usually derived from an analysis of public expenditure on age categories. In this debate 'the old' or 'elderly' are those above the ages of entitlement to the public programs for senior citizens such as Social Security or Medicare.

Second, the assumption that expenditures on children and the elderly all come out of the same public money bag, so that they must fight for their share can be doubted. As Easterlin (1987) has already demonstrated, children are financially taken care of by market related income of their families whereas public pensions are financed from public resources. Bob Binstock (2010) has argued that poverty amongst children is caused by single motherhood and insufficient support such as affordable child care; not by overly generous pensions.

Third, in the context of families, where the concept of generation can have the clear meaning of those who share the same parents – while they can be members of different birth cohorts – the interchange and interdependence between generations is considerable (Arber & Attias-Donfut 2000; Kingson, Hirshorn, & Cornman 1986; Kohli 2002; Kohli 2004). Besides inheritance there are the *inter vivos* transfers from parents and grandparents to their offspring which often support young families. For retirees, who are easily portrayed as passive, it may be important for their self esteem that they are able to give; moreover, they can direct their gifts at special needs, which they can monitor more precisely than others. If retirees can count on a sufficient pension they don't have to worry about the future and can feel secure enough to give so that young parents can be more relaxed regarding the well being of their parents and may be able to count on them for grandparenting and financial support in times of need (Kohli 2006). Whereas instrumental support more often goes from younger to older family members, monetary transfers frequently go the other way and this process of interchange affirms mutual ties, strengthening the role of families in society. There is no mere opposition of interests which might explain why there is usually a robust support for public pensions among the general public; in the countries of the EU as well as in the US. A problematic implication of debates about entitlement 'crises' is declining confidence in the viability of these systems (Quadagno 1996). Research shows a strong support for Social Security but that apocalyptic discussions about the sustainability of these supportive systems undermine the confidence, especially of younger people, that it will be there 'for me when I get older' (cf. Altman & Kingson 2015).

Fourth, pensions are part of a wider context of interdependence between age groups (Kingson, Hirshorn & Cornman 1986; Bengtson & Achenbaum 1993; Williamson, McNamara & Howling 2003). This interchange represents a vital support for the civil society as many activities of older people, such as voluntary work or charity are crucial for the social cohesion of communities. Another example is given in a *Pew Research Center* report of 2013: 7.7 million children (10% of all children in the US) are living with their grandparents; 3 million of them are even primarily cared for by their grandparents (Livingston 2013). Such informal contributions of senior citizens tend to be neglected, much like the traditional neglect of work and care in the household. This has been counteracted by efforts to redefine these activities in ways that might be better noticed, for instance, by calculating what they would cost if performed professionally; with impressive results (Coleman 1995). Such calculations are informative but may also reduce the meanings of such important activities to a budgetary format; as if a society would be nothing more than market relations between individuals.

However, in these four points important questions that are relevant from a perspective of social justice and aging are still not posed. Until now it seems as if the assumption that, generally, retirees are affluent is still valid. But are all retirees really able to help their children financially? In such matters, measurements of averages, such as per capita income can be misleading as the incomes of many affluent people will elevate the incomes of those who live in less fortunate circumstances. The advocates of Generational Equity misleadingly suggest that all older people are wealthy compared to the 'younger generation' and, moreover, that they are wealthy because of overly generous benefits or entitlements such as Social Security or Medicare.

The Fair Innings Argument: equality of a 'natural life span'

Some authors have tried to give the *Generational Equity* approach an ethical foundation. Their major problem is one of distributive justice: the fear that the public funds of the aging society will be devastated when older persons are entitled to medical treatment that would prolong their lives, even when they have already lived 'long enough'. Granting such old people even more costly medical treatment would imply that younger people are robbed of the public funds that would also enable them to reach 'old age'. So, claims of 'the elderly' to receive publicly financed health care must be limited to protect the future of the 'younger generation'. This argument has been brought forward by several authors with different emphases and has led to extensive discussion (Bognar 2015; Bognar & Hirose 2014; Brock 1989; Kamm 1993; Nord 2005; Veatch 1988; Williams 1997)

In his book *The Value of Life: An Introduction to Medical Ethics* John Harris has called this approach the 'Fair Innings Argument' which

> requires that everyone be given an equal chance to have a fair innings, to reach the appropriate threshold but, having reached it, they have received their entitlement. The rest of their life is the sort of bonus which may be canceled when this is necessary to help others reach the threshold.
>
> (Harris 1985, p. 91)

Rivlin (2000) rightly asks what such a fair share of life actually means? Does it mean that 'life' can be overseen as a whole and then fairly divided between those who want as much from it as possible? He uses the example of a cake to clarify what a 'fair share' might mean: What is being shared? Who is it being shared between? Are people entitled to a share of it or, in certain situations, to somebody else's share? Could a person give his or her share to another person? However, life is not some 'thing' like a cake that we can divide or share at will. Do we know how small or large the cake will be or how long somebody will live after a medical intervention? Are we entitled to a certain, a 'fair' length of life? Who or what kind of processes do we hold responsible or important for being able to enjoy such a 'fair share' of life? Does the whole notion of 'fairness' not presuppose a context of cooperation between responsible actors – a fair society?

The idea of a fair share of life also raises the question of a maximum life span. This is usually assumed to be around 120 years as Madame Calment, the person on record to live longest, reached an age of a little over 122 years. This is, however, an empirical maximum, not a principal one: anyone who is going to live longer than Madame Calment will break the record. Establishing a maximum age for humans is extremely complicated as the human organism is open to the many contextual influences we have been discussing, including life extending interventions (see Ch.5 and Ch.7). But let's assume that 122 years is the maximum life span that everyone who values life will want to reach. Obviously, this is not what the advocates of the *Fair Innings* have in mind. So would such a long life be unfair to others? Should it only be permitted if you can convince the authorities from an imagined *Longevity Department* that you have the financial means to support such a long life? Should this be the prerogative of the very rich who can afford to attend expensive private clinics where advanced anti-aging technology may help you to live very long? Should an extremely long life be seen as 'unnatural' even when no anti-aging technology has been applied as appears to be the case in the life of Madame Calment?

It is typical of the work of Daniel Callahan, one of the founding directors of the Hastings Center to introduce the idea of a 'natural' lifespan and to see this as the way to strengthen the arguments that were used in the Generational Equity debate. He pretends that his version of *Complete Lives Egalitarianism* has a 'natural' foundation. In several publications, especially *Setting Limits: Medical Goals in an Aging Society* (1987; cf. also 1994; 2012), he has responded to Preston's call, discussed earlier, to change entitlement policies. In a retrospective article of 1994 he describes the main topic of *Setting Limits* as 'rethinking once again the place of aging in the lifecycle and that, in the future, scarcity of resources could force an *age* limit on medical entitlements for the elderly' (1994, p. 393).

We have to honor, according to Callahan, *'a natural life span'* in which life's possibilities have on the whole been achieved, and after which death may be understood as a sad but nonetheless acceptable event: 'a tolerable death' (1987: 66). However, over the last two centuries there have been impressive gains in life expectancies among the populations of Western countries. Have these gains been 'unnatural'? When people try to justify racial or gender discrimination there is often an attempt to elevate a specific form (theirs) to the level of the one and only 'natural' form. Such naturalization has usually been a sign of intolerance and pettiness: can this appeal to a 'natural life span' be taken seriously? All forms of health care and even simple medical interventions such as prescribing antibiotics are ways to influence or change 'natural' processes that would otherwise lead to more serious conditions or death. Therefore, it is farfetched to discuss activities as caring, curing a disease and life extension in terms of their '(un)naturalness'. The only natural characteristic of human life is that humans are born and that they die after a short or a longer period of time and sometimes even before they are born. It is very hard to see how an appeal to naturalness could help the *Fair Innings Argument*.

In spite of Callahan's rhetorical emphasis on a 'natural life span' his approach to aging is thoroughly medicalized and subsequently narrowed down to health care costs that should be diminished by creating an age related threshold in accessing publicly funded health care. The basic message of the *Fair Innings Argument* is that after a person has outlived her 'natural life span' there should be no publicly funded medical intervention to resist a 'natural' death. The death of such superannuated people may be regrettable but it is not a tragedy as when younger people die. Therefore, limiting the entitlements of 'the elderly' would be justified, especially when they compete with younger people for scarce resources. Daniels (2008, p. 180) has summarized Callahan's 'both unsound and invalid' argument as follows:

1   Life for the old is meaningful only if they serve the young;
2   They serve the young by being moral exemplars who surrender claims on lifesaving services in favor of the young;
3   The old can be compelled through age-rationing measures to carry out their obligation to the young.

After Callahan's rhetorical appeal to a 'natural life span' which would be identical to a 'whole life' or a 'long and full life' (1987, p. 40) the next attempt to defend the *Fair Innings Argument* is to introduce an existential reflection about aging: we humans should accept aging as a part of life, not just as another medical obstacle to be overcome. If we look at the human life cycle we must open ourselves to the idea that it is not a tragedy to die in 'old age'; no matter how much one would like to go on living. Callahan plays the chords of melancholy: 'while all death is a cause for sadness, a death in old age after a long and full life is, given the inevitability of death, the most acceptable kind of death' (1994, p. 396). There is, however, a sudden turn from melancholy about the fleeting presence of 'us humans' on this earth to the drastic reduction of support for older citizens that will hit especially the most disadvantaged. Conceiving the life course in terms of generations that come and go while mortal mankind can do nothing about it, prepares the ground for criticizing older people for still claiming their rights to healthcare although they are destined to die and have already become irrelevant for society, except for the fact that their entitlements and needs for care form a heavy burden on the 'younger generation'.

The finitude of life implies, however, that we do not know how long we will live but some of us will be living long and even very long lives, meaningful to themselves and others; lives that cannot be discarded as useless, residual or parasitic as soon as they have reached a certain age. Although it remains important to be able to let go of life when death is inevitably asserting itself, this moment cannot be prescribed by public policy. The finitude of life and its inevitable decline into death cannot be pinned down to a particular age. So, accepting finitude and limitations does not mean that we would be able to know in advance where our limits lie. What has been perceived as insurmountable limitations has throughout history been challenged and often we have benefitted from such creative efforts as our understanding of the realities in which we live was expanded and our practical options enlarged.

These experiential realities are shamelessly deformed and misused when utilitarian calculi announce that 'your time has come' because you have reached a certain age. I agree with Callahan that there is a tendency in contemporary Western culture to deny finitude (cf. Baars 2012, 2017a) but his existential reflections are instrumental for a harsh and unjust agenda that they must help to make acceptable. It appears that Callahan's references to human finitude and a 'natural life span' only serve to massage his audience into accepting his policy proposals. It remains hard to understand why his proposed limitations of health care would not amount to a denial of the value and dignity of older adults. Such an ageist tendency might also reflect the 'prejudice of an affluent, hyper-individualistic, technologically driven society' (Callahan 1994, p. 397); a criticism that Callahan likes to turn against contemporary society.

Callahan's naturalistic and solemn existential reflections turn rather abruptly into a strategy for a public policy that should stop endless crowds of older people who egoistically demand their share of the health care cake with the apocalyptic result that only a few crumbs will be left for younger people. He underlines especially the risks of emerging anti-aging technologies that will exhaust public resources, as the lives of already old people would be endlessly extended at the expense of younger people. Therefore, the research on life-extending medicine should be stopped. Not because life-extending medicine would be futile but because we will be ruined by its success: "It will be the efficacious, not wasteful, treatments that will cause us the most financial grief (Callahan 1994, p. 396).

Callahan moves from his macro perspective on the public funds of an aging society directly to micro situations of decision making, neglecting both structural issues and the specificity of personal situations. '*Age*' is going to bring the desired clarity: it would be the only clear criterion to decide whether or not to get 'life prolonging treatment'. If we were to leave such decisions to the patients, their families or doctors, the goal of cost control would never be achieved. He admits that any specific age limit will be arbitrary but only an arbitrary age limit would transcend individual differences and suit his policy purposes. In response to criticism of this fixation on age Callahan has responded that there is no alternative which can do the same: the only realistic way to contain the costs of an aging population is by setting age limits on entitlements. 'There is nothing unfair about using age as a category if the purpose of doing so is to achieve equity between generations' (Callahan 1987, p. 140). The old should give up claims to life extending treatments so that young persons would also have a chance to become old. The resources that are gained this way should be used to save the young; in that way we would realize Generational Equity.

In a little corner of his work Callahan makes some important caveats: 'age' would only be used as a categorical standard to cut off life-extending technologies *if and only if* some major health care reforms were to take place first: (1) universal health care for all, including the elderly; that would (2) help everyone to avoid an early, premature death; and (3) achieve a better balance between caring and curing, so that the overemphasis on cure would be corrected in favor of long-term care and home care (Callahan 1994, p. 393 ff.). However, it remains unclear what these caveats mean as Callahan has continued to defend in many publications his policy of 'setting limits' on health care for older people in a society where these conditions were not fulfilled.

In the context of the *Generational Equity* debate Callahan's program of 'setting limits' has encountered ample criticism by authors such as Bob Binstock or Rick Moody but his widely read publications have nevertheless been successful in encouraging discussions in the media about issues that were approached with more hesitant reflection before, such as: 'Alarming health care costs of Medicare beneficiaries in the last year of life'; 'Futile treatment and the high cost of dying'; 'Should elderly patients be admitted to the intensive care unit?'; 'Does patient age matter for decisions to withhold life-sustaining treatments from seriously ill, hospitalized adults?'; 'Should cardiopulmonary resuscitation of older patients be withheld without their consent?'. Health economists have also welcomed Callahan's proposals as an important way to handle what they perceived as problems that would be caused by population aging (cf. Williams 1997). Very little or nothing has been heard from Callahan to correct those who affirmed his harsh proposals. Building on Callahan's argument Shaw, for instance, defends ageism in an article in the *Journal of Medical Ethics* emphasizing that 'to prolong life for the very old is antisocial'. He concludes with a rather shocking rhetorical question: 'Why should clinicians discuss ageism if most practice it already?' (1994, p. 191).

'Old Age' as a redundant phase of life

Callahan's cost-driven emphasis on finitude and a 'natural life span' positions aging beyond a certain age as a residual or redundant phase of life. Whatever may lie ahead is not worth being protected by offering equal access to health care because "life's possibilities have on the whole been achieved" (1987: 66). Development and fulfillment of life's projects and dreams may still occur but should not any longer be supported by public means: life would be 'complete' in terms of life's projects. But why should life after 70, 75 or 80 years not be seen as a time for projects that are worth being completed? Should life even be seen as a series of projects? At this point we may remember Margaret Urban Walker's remarks about the limited idea of a 'typical male' linear career whereas many women do 'the sort of work that never "goes anywhere," in terms of social status, occupational importance, or increasing economic power' (Walker 1999, p. 105; see Baars 2012, Ch.1). The sort of work Walker refers to may, however, give a deeper satisfaction than many highly competitive careers, which could be one of the reasons many women continue to be involved in care even when the material rewards are not what might be expected. There is an abundance of research, for instance by Laura Carstensen (2009) and colleagues, documenting satisfaction and fulfillment beyond the ages that are proposed as the moment when older people should retire from life to make place for the young. Much ageism appears to come from fear of aging; a belief that life of older people is miserable. This view of aging neglects the ways in which life can not only be good for older people over 70 or 80, but it also denigrates what they can mean to others as partners, friends, supportive mentors, aunts, uncles or grandparents.

Callahan assumes that his harsh realism is justified by the growing costs that are the inevitable consequences of an aging society. Although population aging does present some major challenges in the coming decades, they look quite moderate for a wealthy country like the US compared to what many other countries such as Japan, Germany, South Korea or Singapore have already been facing for some time and they have far from collapsed. On the contrary, countries with more egalitarian policies that are relatively generous in supporting their citizens along the life course are among the most productive per capita (see Ch.7).

The overemphasis in the *Fair Innings Argument* on technological control over processes of bodily decline is reminiscent of the technocratic idea that the progress in life expectancies that has been made in the last century has primarily been the result of technologically advanced health care. There is an abundance of research to suggest that these developments are mainly the fruits of broader improvements of public sanitation, hygiene, care, housing, transportation, work conditions and income. We have seen in Chapter 2 how research by Michael Marmot and others has shown that the importance of health care should not be overrated. Advanced life saving medical technology certainly has its place, but to put this center stage is to divert the attention away from the other domains that contribute to public health (Sorenson, Drummond & Khan 2013).

Moreover, the expectations regarding the costs that might be saved following Callahan's proposals should not be too high. One of the most expensive forms of care is institutional long term care for people of all ages with physical or cognitive disabilities. These people will probably continue to need more personal care than expensive medical technology. To protect the health of healthy older people it will remain important to get adequate support regarding income, housing, transportation, care or facilitating contacts with others of different ages. The narrative of advanced life extending medical technology and its bottomless pit neglects that technologically advanced treatment is often not very suitable for chronic conditions and end-of-life care. Large longitudinal studies of aging such as *The Longitudinal McArthur Foundation Study of Aging in America* have shown that once people have reached the age of 65 years, their added years don't have a major impact on Medicare costs. Most costs are made in the last year of life – at any age – and older people often die within a shorter period of time than younger people (Rowe & Kahn 1998).

It is doubtful whether Callahan's harsh stance towards older people really brings the results that he promises in terms of protecting public resources for the 'younger generation'. His diagnosis even suggests that many young people may die prematurely because 'the elderly' lay an unreasonably high claim on public health care resources. These doubtful savings are bought at the social costs of damaging the public image of older people by portraying them implicitly as sad, futile and redundant persons who live at the expense of a younger 'generation'. In Callahan's perspective older people only seem to be relevant because they claim costly medical resources. His rhetorical appeal to the reader is to stop to see 'old age' as a condition that could be treated and improved by medical interventions because this would be unnatural or inauthentic in an existential sense but, especially, too costly.

Callahan's argumentation is far from convincing as he tries to support weak arguments with other weak arguments. His approach, however, has appealed to a larger audience because it supports and feeds on a widespread culture of ageism. It is shocking to hear a leading political figure such as Ben Carson, the US *Secretary of Housing and Urban Development* under the Trump Administration, uttering the following ageist words in a public speech of March 2017:

> The reason I became a pediatric neurosurgeon is because you can spend 10, 12, 15, 18 hours operating on a kid and if you're successful the return may be 50, 60, 70, 80 years of life. Whereas with an old geezer you spend all that time operating and they die in five years of something else. I like to get a big return on my investment (hahaha). I'm just kidding; I like old people (hahaha) but you see the point ....[2]

It might be good to begin to consider the moral dignity of the rest of our lives.

As Callahan does not tire to stress, there are tragic choices to be made but we must be firm because we do not live in a world where unpleasant choices are not needed. This is, however, no reason to take the present society for granted or even to idealize it. Callahan's writings are presented as a critical reflection but they are a rather harsh affirmation of existing health care policies in the US. An important ingredient of his uncritical neglect of societal contexts is the unqualified introduction of 'scarcity'. Because resources will always be finite scarcity must be seen in context. Another major flaw in the *Fair Innings Argument* is the failure to interrogate the neoliberal squeeze of public health or the strategies of principal players in health care such as Big Pharma, health insurance companies, governments or hospitals. It might also be possible to learn from other societies without assuming that the US has the best health care system because it is the most expensive one.

Finally, Callahan and other advocates of the *Fair Innings Argument* or *Generational Equity* avoid the reality of social inequalities. Their central conflict is supposed to take place between the younger and the older 'generation' but this turns out to be a conflict between disadvantaged and well off people of all ages. Callahan pretends to celebrate this age-based withdrawal from life as a form of altruism or wise resignation for the sake of a broader humanity or society but his proposals advocate a further dehumanization of society and will hit especially those who had all along diminished opportunities of growing old in good health. The dismal demography of aging populations neglects the fact that the most advantaged people who have also benefitted the most from the rising life expectancies are also better positioned to evade the consequences of the *Fair Innings* proposals than disadvantaged people. Without any improvement of the support that should be given by the major institutions along the life course, disadvantaged persons of all ages will continue to be hit by an agenda of setting limits to accessible health care.

'Of course', as Callahan writes in response to such criticism, his proposal would 'perpetuate a system in which the rich are able to buy health benefits not available to the poor' but 'we cannot achieve perfect equality in the world, much less in the health care system, without some harmful consequences' (1994, p. 394). His assumption appears to be that inequality should be perpetuated or aggravated because the harmful alternative would be 'perfect equality'. But who wants perfect equality? This is the standard worn out construct of libertarian theorists to ridicule any proposal for less inequality as a plea for perfect, almost dictatorial forms of equality where everybody would be forced to be the same, hence unfree and worse off. Moreover, Callahan's agenda is not free from 'harmful consequences': it will hit especially older people who are completely dependent on public resources for their health care. For them longevity would become even more of a risk and a burden. The main concern one can have about the *Fair Innings Argument* is not only that it articulates widely held prejudice against older people, but that it will hit especially those who are dependent on publicly supported health care.

Luck egalitarianism: an equal start for young adults

The consequences of the demolition of the supportive life course and other policies that have been inspired by the neoliberal turn pose serious questions of social justice. It can be expected that the libertarians are content with a state that reduces its activities and leaves most social problems to the individual responsibility of its citizens. A more critical approach may be expected from egalitarian thinkers and in this historical context it is interesting that we can observe since the beginning of the 1980s the rise of a widely influential post-Rawlsian paradigm of social justice which focuses on the question of how to change the organization of the life course in such a way that there will be more social equality. The leading author of this new egalitarian paradigm is Ronald Dworkin whose founding articles from 1981 inspired many others, resulting in a somewhat heterogeneous paradigm of egalitarian social justice with, nevertheless, some distinctive characteristics.

According to this new egalitarian approach individual responsibility had not been adequately addressed in Rawls' theory. His approach to justice pleading for a political system that would also be optimal for the worst off, was criticized for not asking whether these people might be personally responsible for ending up in their dire situations. Sen's Capability approach was also perceived as too vulnerable for attacks from libertarians that egalitarians would want the same outcomes for everybody regardless of their efforts. The new egalitarians acclaimed Dworkin's bold strategy to make individual responsibility of citizens for their social fate the founding stone of egalitarianism. Such an approach was expected to silence their libertarian opponents because the main principle libertarians have been eager to use to criticize egalitarian constructs would already be embraced by the new egalitarians. Eight years after Dworkin's founding publications, when the new paradigm was already in full academic swing, Jerry Cohen (1989 p. 933) praised Dworkin's historical achievement: 'Dworkin has, in effect, performed for egalitarianism the considerable service of incorporating within it the most powerful idea in the arsenal of the anti-egalitarian right: the idea of choice and responsibility'. Unfortunately, the empirically sound observation that social inequality might also or even mainly be caused by societal structures or discriminatory cultural traditions moves out of sight. As the project of a supportive life course, a shared and institutionalized responsibility for the wellbeing of the population, comes increasingly under attack, we see the rise of a defensive form of egalitarianism which embraces the reduction of society to individuals and markets.

In an influential article, Elizabeth Anderson (1999) has termed this perspective 'luck egalitarianism'. She presented a fundamental critique of ideas that were shared by an otherwise heterogeneous population of theorists such as Ronald Dworkin, Jerry Cohen, Richard Arneson, Eric Rakowski or John Roemer. This has led to complaints from these authors that they had been misunderstood and some have come up with alternative names for their common approach such as 'responsibility catering prioritarianism' (Arneson 2000). Ronald Dworkin (2003), the most prominent representative of this general approach has forcefully – although according to Scheffler (2003) hardly convincingly – rejected the characterization of his work as 'luck egalitarian'. In spite of such narcissism of small differences Anderson's criticism has gained much acclaim and the name 'luck egalitarianism' has widely been accepted to refer to this dominant contemporary paradigm of political philosophy (cf. Arneson 2012; Segall 2010).

As we have seen, Rawls had already introduced the role of 'luck' in *A Theory of Justice* (1971). According to Rawls the starting position of every person in society would depend, first, on a natural lottery of genetic predispositions, the outcome of which is arbitrary from a moral perspective. Second, it would depend on a social lottery: 'The extent to which natural capacities develop and reach fruition is affected by all kinds of social conditions and class attitudes' (Rawls 1971, p. 74). In a just society the citizens' share in the benefits and burdens of social cooperation should neither be decided by their social fortune nor by their luck in the natural lottery: 'Those who have been favored by nature … may gain from their good fortune only on terms that improve the situation of those who have lost out' (1971, p. 101), which is the point of the Difference Principle. However, Rawls accepts inequality: it is the inevitable product of the natural and social lotteries and, moreover, is necessary as an incentive of the talented to become more productive which would also be in the interest of the worst off. Those with less talents and skills may be worst off but he does not hold them personally responsible for their fate, so their situation should be as favorable as possible. This changes with the dawn of the new egalitarian approach.

In an overview article about *Luck Egalitarianism* Richard Arneson, one of its proponents, has briefly characterized this paradigm as follows:

It is morally bad – unjust and unfair – if some are worse off than others, and morally good – just and fair – if all are equally well off. The injustice and unfairness of inequality are, however, expunged if those who are worse off than others are so through their own fault or choice.

(2012, p. 154)

In the many publications that have been written by luck egalitarians over the last decades many distinctions and alternative constructs have been proposed, but the basic distinction remains the one between *option* luck and *brute* luck and both have, in principle, a good and bad version, although good brute luck remains largely undiscussed. Dworkin has classically defined these basic concepts: 'option luck is a matter of how deliberate and calculated gambles turn out – whether someone gains or loses through accepting an isolated risk he or she should have anticipated and might have declined.' Brute luck, however, would be 'a matter of how risks fall out that are not in that sense deliberate gambles' (2000, p. 73).

According to Dworkin's egalitarian theory of social justice, bad brute luck should be compensated, but the consequences of bad option luck should not be corrected: 'people should pay the price of the life they have decided to lead' (Dworkin 2000, p. 74). If people fare badly because of their own decisions they are on their own; they may be supported by charity, but they don't have a justified claim to be helped. Those who have accidents because they chose to take risks will ask in vain for support because they remain exclusively responsible for their 'bad option luck'. As we will see, this approach is extended by several authors to other forms of personal risk taking, such as smoking or even choosing dangerous professions such as being a firefighter. The typical example of bad brute luck, which does give a right to be compensated, is a natural disaster that can happen in external nature, such as fires or floods. But also within persons, in the form of genetic deficiencies such as disabilities or lack of talent which make people unfit to be productive and compete on the market without their being responsible for this fate.

Equality of welfare and equality of resources

An important difference between the major authors of the luck egalitarian paradigm is whether they are primarily concerned about equality of welfare or equality of resources. Representatives of welfare egalitarianism emphasize that the goal of social equality is not that everyone should have the same amount of resources but that there should be equality of welfare or wellbeing. Far from a concern about the wellbeing of populations, welfare egalitarians like Richard Arneson have argued that *personal tastes* must be respected and lead to entitlements for welfare, unless society wants to dictate how its citizens should live:

> If resource egalitarians accept the liberal requirement that theories of justice must be neutral among competing conceptions of the good, they cannot discriminate between involuntarily expensive tastes for mobility on the part of the handicapped and involuntarily expensive tastes for rare champagne on the part of gourmets.
>
> (1990b: 190ff.)

Expensive tastes are put on the same level as the needs of a paraplegic person who would have an involuntarily expensive taste for mobility.

Arneson (1990a) also pleads on behalf of so-called 'Needy Bohemians': people who suffer from a genetically determined 'decided and preference for leisure over money-making activity' (p. 1127). Being unable to overcome their genetic preference for leisure, these persons should receive the same compensation as those whose equally unchosen preferences lead them to enjoy productive employment. This peculiar concern affirms the anti-egalitarian prejudice that chronically unemployed people suffer from laziness and that egalitarians like hard working citizens to respect and support such idiosyncrasies whatever the costs.

Arneson insists that society should adapt to these individuals because they cannot be held responsible for their innate preferences and would even be unfairly treated if offered generous employment opportunities. Jerry Cohen (1989, p. 930ff.) has argued that equality requires that we compensate people for being temperamentally gloomy, or for being so irked by cheap activities that they can only enjoy expensive entertainment. While resource egalitarians see brute bad luck especially in the natural lottery of talents and (dis)abilities, welfare oriented egalitarians such as Arneson expand their exploration of brute luck to genetically determined personal taste and inclination. What one would be inclined to see as desires of rich spoiled brats is interpreted as a genetically determined complete dependency on the most exclusive wines or foods that should be placed on the same level of helplessness as bodily disability. These are the 'deep inequalities' that Arneson (1997) argues for; caused by inner 'circumstances' that are beyond the individual's control and thus not his responsibility.

According to Arneson (1997):

> the distinction between inequalities arising from choice and inequalities arising from unchosen circumstances turns out to be confused, because unchosen circumstances include each individual's talent endowment, and among one's talents are talents to make and implement good choices in formulating a conception of the good and devising a plan of life.
>
> (p. 80ff)

His genetic determinism precludes any acknowledgement of the role of socialization processes in changing and developing talents. Research on genetic predispositions is embraced in a rudimentary fashion, interpreting predisposition as determination. The social component of the processes in which genetic dispositions are actualized is completely neglected (see Ch.3 and Ch.4; Dannefer 2022 about epigenetics). Instead of beating the libertarians with their own arguments, the luck egalitarians have given them ample material to ridicule their own proposals; something that served the libertarians well in their efforts to justify a further destruction of the whole idea of a supportive life course or a welfare state that leads apparently to honoring such idiosyncratic demands.

Ronald Dworkin, the main representative of the resource oriented theorists of luck egalitarianism has, however, distanced himself from the welfare egalitarians. He emphasizes that tastes are personal choices and that we owe nothing to those who are worse off as a result of their own choices. He resists the idea of equality of wellbeing, because there is no clear way to measure, compare or decide whether different persons would enjoy the same level of wellbeing. For Dworkin, the main problem of this approach is that society would be highjacked by people with extravagant personal taste. From our experience in a status oriented consumer society we can easily imagine people who loudly voice their unhappiness because their luxury apartments are so unbearably uncomfortable and they even didn't have a refined dinner or some extremely expensive wine for a whole weekend, while those who are used to the reality of extreme scarcity or even starvation tend to accept their fate in silence. Taking personal 'happiness' as a criterion of distributive justice might lead to absurd consequences, such as a transfer of resources from happy poor people such as Dickens' *Tiny Tim* to the unhappy rich *Scrooges* of this world.

Dworkin's rejection of the claims of unsatisfied extravagants does not mean that he demonstrates much concern for those who get caught in hard situations if these are not caused by what he calls 'brute luck'. The moral rigidity of the luck egalitarians becomes more obvious in the work of Eric Rakowski, according to Elizabeth Anderson (1999) one of the authors on the harsh end of luck egalitarianism, but probably he is just more explicit about the implications of this paradigm. Rakowski takes the responsibility for option luck seriously: those who choose dangerous professions without choosing adequate insurance should not be entitled to publicly funded medical care, rehabilitation or compensation for their possible injuries. When they would have the bad luck to become disabled in the line of duty as policeman, firefighter or soldier, they will first of all be held responsible for taking a risky profession. They must face the possibly damaging consequences of their professions without any justified claim for help. The same moral logic would apply to those who are taking care of others. When women take care of family members out of moral obligations and bonds, this is seen as a free choice which would generate no claims of justice on others. Possible financial problems and other burdens are seen as consequences of a 'lifestyle', perhaps assumed out of a deep conviction but precisely for that reason not something to be pursued at the expense of those who don't share their 'zeal' or 'belief' that one owes duties of care to family members. Likewise, children do not have a claim to assistance from anyone but their parents:

> It is ... unjust to declare ... that because two people decide to have a child ... everyone is required to share their resources with the new arrival ... With what right can two people force all the rest, through deliberate behavior rather than bad brute luck, to settle for less than their fair shares after resources have been divided justly?
>
> (Rakowski 1991, p. 153)

According to Anderson (1999) Dworkin offers no better protection than Rakowski against, for instance, involuntary unemployment or predatory practices in the free market. There will be no help for dependent caretakers or those who become disabled as a result of the choices they made. Dworkin exclaims 'I show respect for others when I do not appropriate resources that are properly theirs – when I do not exceed my fair share at their expense' (Dworkin 2000, p. 280). The moral goal of this approach is to sanction that, apart from bad brute luck, people's lives are the result of their decisions: all individuals are equally responsible for the bitter or sweet fruits of their choices.

An equal start that comes too late

To prevent the libertarian critique on equality of *outcome* luck egalitarians move to their specific version of an equality of *opportunity* which emphasizes the importance of an equal start in life. Dworkin proposes a market oriented version of the traditional 'social contract' to ensure that everybody might have an equal starting position in life. This is envisaged as an auction where young adults of each 'generation' would gather to celebrate the inaugural moment when they have become fully responsible adults. At the beginning of this imaginary auction all participants are given the same amount of money so they would have equal bidding power. Dworkin acknowledges that such equality of material resources does not in itself give the young adults of that particular 'generation' equal chances to succeed in their future lives. Therefore, a next step in equalizing their opportunities is necessary: equalizing the unequal effects of their natural talents. Disadvantaged participants in the auction need to be compensated for the bad brute luck of handicaps, such as blindness and deafness, but also for talents with low market value. Remarkably, the main sources of social inequality are not sought in socioeconomic class, race or gender: the primary source of inequality would be inborn (lack of) qualities. In this respect Dworkin's auction can be seen as a partial answer to a concern of justice that had been voiced by Thomas Nagel:

When racial and sexual injustice have been reduced, we shall still be left with the great injustice of the smart and the dumb, who are so differently rewarded for comparable effort .... Perhaps someone will discover a way to reduce the socially produced inequalities (especially the economic ones) between the intelligent and the unintelligent, the talented and the untalented, or even the beautiful and the ugly.

(1979, p. 105)

For the resource egalitarian Dworkin, the value of a resource such as a talent is not determined by the amount of welfare it would give, but by the price it would get on a competitive market with equal information, bidding skills, talents and available cash. The price of specific disabilities is determined in an imaginary bidding process where the participants are blindfolded with a Rawlsian veil of ignorance about whether they would be, for instance, smart, stupid, blind, deaf or chronically ill. The outcome of this bidding process would reflect what people would be willing to pay to avoid such conditions. Those who are blessed with a 'normal' or surplus amount of inborn talents and abilities should give money to the less fortunate to equalize their starting positions. In that way, differences in opportunities that are generated by differences 'traceable to genetic luck' (Dworkin 2000, p. 91) would be equalized.

After this process of compensatory equalization in which inequalities in abilities or talents have been evened out through monetary transfers, the participants are not yet able to begin their adult lives in full equality. They still face an uncertain future where they may run into bad brute luck; not only in the form of natural disasters but also in the form of future disease or disability. Dworkin also has a marketed solution for this problem: with their equalized resources the young adults must decide against what kind of bad brute luck they want to be insured. Insurance plays an important role in Dworkin's thought because it is seen as a way to transform bad brute luck into option luck: no one can be held responsible when they get a chronic disease, but they can be held responsible for not buying available insurance against this risk. If it were possible to insure oneself against a particular form of brute bad luck and somebody gets hit by it without having bought the proper insurance, it would be unjust to expect help from others. The outcome of the auction would be that all participants have become equal in opportunities: they all have the same 'normal' talents and if not, they have been compensated by material goods so the handicapped will have equal opportunities to succeed in life. From that moment on, all young adults will be held fully responsible for anything that might occur to them, except for bad brute luck they could not have insured themselves against.

Dworkin's thought experiment is meant to present a model for policies addressing social inequalities: tax and transfer policies should copy the results of these imaginary markets so that unequally gifted citizens of a given society will get equal opportunities in the form of equal resources. Dworkin expects that the proposed hypothetical auction behind a veil of ignorance would make it possible to determine the amounts of premiums and payouts by averaging the decisions of the participants. The distributive justice of this whole thought experiment would legitimize a strict moral attitude toward personal responsibility: after the monetary equalization of everyone, citizens must bear the consequences of whatever will happen to them. Unless this is caused by uninsurable bad brute luck it will be seen as bad option luck: as consequences of their own choices. The luck and prosperity they will encounter will also be the fruit of their own choices: 'option luck'. If anyone who has not been insured ends up in a bad situation the only hope that remains is the hope for charity. The main point distinguishing the luck egalitarians from conservative libertarians is the idea that losses that have been caused by uncontrollable natural forces deserve to be compensated.

Some critical notes about Dworkin's equalizing auction

The goal of Dworkin's theory of distributive justice is a society where people's resources are the result of their choices by filtering out the impact of their circumstances (Dworkin 2000, p. 89). However, because his diagnosis of social inequality over the life course remains superficial, the proposed way to achieve social equality is not convincing. His proposal to equalize inequalities in material and personal resources by monetary transfers amongst the young adults raises more questions than it answers.

First, social inequality in pre-adult life is assumed to be caused by bad brute luck inside human beings in the form of inborn natural deficiencies or lack of talents. This amounts to a reduction of all socioeconomic and cultural processes that have a major formative influence from early childhood to adulthood, to a static genetic determination. It remains unclear how the suggested monetary compensation for the negative developmental influences of disadvantaged circumstances in the pre-adult phase of the life course could solve the many problems that may arise such as, for instance, chronic health problems. All societal responsibility for profound inequalities in pre-adult formative processes is reduced to monetary compensation.

Second, Dworkin's proposal aims to solve or reduce social inequality of pre-adult life which implies that the society in which the hypothetical auction is supposed to take place is still unequal. This means that the equalizing checks would help some but will mainly be an extra bonus for those who are already placed in advantaged positions. Even if they have to give money to the less gifted, this will probably be small change in comparison with their advantages such as a wealthy background, high education, good health status, and influential networks. Those who need support and encouragement are affirmed in their dependent situation: on the side of the most disadvantaged the anticipation of the monetary compensation can easily have the demotivating effect of avoiding more than basic education because the 'big check' will arrive anyway once they are adults. This is not a way to reduce social inequality but to reproduce and enlarge it.

Third, the young adults are assumed to have arrived at a moment in their lives when they can have a clean break with their past based on the weak argument that the particular cohort has reached adulthood. Furthermore, it is assumed that the (in)capacities that might be decisive for failure or success would 'normally' be fully developed at the beginning of adulthood. This developmental level would give a solid ground for the comparison, bidding and pricing of capacities, especially deficient ones. However, human talents cannot be expected to surface or crystallize in synchrony with a specific age. Moreover, the different socio-economic and cultural backgrounds will most probably continue to influence the young adults with important consequences for how they spend or invest their resources. The ability to choose well, resulting in good option luck is not linearly determined by capacities that are assessed at the auction. Poor judgment may be a matter of poor intelligence and seemingly simple to measure, but there are different ways, connected with different developmental assumptions, to assess such capacities, resulting in different competing forms of intelligence. The ability to solve mathematical problems is not the same as the ability to choose well in professional conflicts, family matters or between investment opportunities. Demonstrated poor judgment at the auction may not even reflect a lack of intelligence but rather the inexperience of a young adult or poor socialization in such matters as forming preferences, making choices, or executing plans. It is generally hard to assess how good people will be in the future at making choices, before they are actually making these choices amidst the full complexity of life. Moreover, it is questionable whether the price that would be established at the auction for a capacity that is seen as less than optimal has anything to do with the real costs or benefits of such conditions over the life course. It appears that the implicit standards to compare inborn characteristics are derived from assumptions about what would be necessary or favorable to succeed on markets. It remains unclear what they have to do with citizenship, assuming that a society is still more than the sum of its markets.

Fourth, as there is no clear yardstick to measure those who are supposed to be less gifted and in need of compensation we would have to trust that 'the market' is always right. Bidding at the auction will therefore tend to be centered around commonly known disabilities and incapacities that may, however, be twisted by general or cohort specific prejudice. Moreover, the market setting will encourage competitive market behavior: as the auction aims at compensating people for their perceived incapacities this may create an environment of competing diagnoses of diminished capacities. Not only blindness or deafness but advocating the costs of major and minor forms of physical and mental disabilities or incapacities may turn the auction into a chaos of diagnostic testimonials competing for a higher compensation.

Fifth, in order to receive compensation at the auction it will be necessary to demonstrate publicly one's specific incapacity. Although possibly well intended, this way of compensating people for their lack of talents or personal qualities so that they get an equal starting position, is morally problematic (Anderson 1999). The compensatory policy towards those who are labeled as in need of compensation has humiliating and demeaning consequences as it requires people to demonstrate in public beyond the protection of professional, for instance, medical confidentiality that they are disabled or lack certain capacities. With this egalitarian strategy of 'resources without respect' (see Ch.7) we are entering a morally precarious territory of prejudice that Wolff (1998) has criticized as a shameful revelation of individual incompetence. The luck egalitarian Jerry Cohen (1989) agrees that finding out people's relative levels of advantage may be intolerably intrusive. However, he suggests 'solving' this problem by defining it as an issue of freedom: the independent value of freedom should limit the degree to which welfarist policies should be implemented.

If the Dworkian auction were implemented in social policies this could easily result in a public denigration that hides behind a formal procedural equalization. The disadvantaged 'subnormal' citizen might receive messages like the following: 'As a result of our proceedings you have been categorized as a sub intelligent person of category III, combined with major deafness and limping. Because you cannot be expected to participate in society as a normal person you are entitled to a financial compensation (see enclosed check). Good option luck with your life.'

Interviews with older or disabled people generally show that they do not think their defect is so horrible; sufficient reason for the egalitarian Van Parijs to deny them special aid if they feel that way (1995, p. 57). Should young or old disabled citizens be obligated to feel miserable about their situation in order to get the support they need? According to research disabled citizens appreciate being helped if they need assistance but they are eager to claim their dignity as equals instead of being pitied as 'sub-normal' beings. Usually they don't complain about their condition but about being excluded from society as they need specific forms of enablement to be able to participate in society as equal citizens (see Ch.7).

The flipside of the pity for the less talented who should receive compensation from the more intelligent for the poor future that inevitably lies ahead, is a cult of 'natural geniuses' who should be liberated to enjoy their well deserved success after the less gifted have been bought off. The luck egalitarians appear to share in the 19th century romantic cult of the incarnated genius that has also enjoyed a renaissance in the bubbles of the financial world. In his anthropological study of London City Bankers Joost Luyendijk (2015) gives telling examples of this ideological cult. Bankers who get outrageous salaries and bonuses convince each other that they deserve these sums because they are exceptionally intelligent. This enables them to 'take care' of the financial needs of all these people they look down upon from their high buildings; those deplorables who are too stupid to understand the treacherous financial products they are developing for them. At the same time they demonstrate a blatant misunderstanding of their own position as an expendable part of a global financial industry; as they will find out when things go wrong and they are put out onto the street with a complimentary cardboard box in their hands.

Faced with these and other possible questions it must be doubted whether it makes sense to try to equalize material and personal resources at the beginning of adulthood instead of focusing on early life interventions, regular supportive follow ups, high quality education and protected work conditions to improve opportunities. Moreover, the influence of early formative circumstances cannot be expected to stop when children have become young adults. The continuing impact (be it not full determination) of unequal social conditions on gestation, early life, adulthood and even later life has been demonstrated quite convincingly in the empirical research that has been discussed in the second and third chapters of this book.

The social distribution of good and bad luck

It seems obvious that 'luck' plays an important role in our lives; as Nagel once observed, the area of life that is free of luck may shrink to an extensionless point. But that doesn't mean that bad luck, especially, hits people completely ad random. That is not even the case for 'brute luck': risks that are not a result of 'deliberate and calculated gambles' (Dworkin 2000, p. 73). In contrast to Dworkin I will, moreover, propose besides 'bad brute luck' (what he calls 'brute luck') also the relevance of 'good' brute luck.

The typical examples of bad brute luck in luck egalitarianism are natural disasters both outside and inside human bodies: floods, hurricanes and lightning as well as inborn disabilities or lack of marketable talents. Identifying all natural disasters as caused by contingent bad brute luck hides the structural dynamics that often play a prominent role in them. Apart from the influence of the socially structured production of toxins or fossil fuel emissions on climates resulting in more frequent and more intense natural disasters, there is a strong social gradient in the risk of being hit by them. Poor people are more likely to inhabit areas where disasters such as floods present a common danger. That they might be compensated for their bad brute luck is a small relief in view of the suffering and even loss of human lives that are usually the result of natural disasters. The more wealthy tend to live in safer conditions, in well constructed houses on higher grounds and they are much more unlikely to lose everything they own in a disaster.

The same logic works for the distribution of dangerous work, unsafe neighborhoods, unhealthy food, bad schools or insufficient health care. For an individual it is a matter of bad or good luck to be born in a poor or wealthy environment but in badly maintained, unsafe environments 'bad luck' is more likely to happen. The difference between opportunities for further development, health or personal safety is not a matter of sheer luck; unmitigated market forces or bad public policies are likely to play a prominent important role. The poorer the people, the more limited their opportunities to avoid 'bad luck' and to cope with its consequences.

The ways in which hurricane *Katrina* disproportionately affected communities of color have demonstrated once more the impact of white privilege, institutional racism, and structural inequalities that remain hidden behind the bad brute luck of natural disasters. Several scholars have examined the historical, institutional, and geographic causes for the disparate outcomes suffered by African Americans and other communities of color in the wake of this hurricane (e.g. Morse 2008). Their findings reveal how structural inequalities and lingering institutional discrimination shaped the inequality in experiencing the impact of the disaster. They help to explain why the world saw predominantly severely hit African Americans and poor people on their television screens. According to the researchers these inequalities were driven by a regional history of racism and socioeconomic inequalities that have been manifest from historical patterns of settlement, to the location of public works projects, and the contemporary lack of transportation resources.

The other type of bad brute luck in luck egalitarianism are natural disasters *inside* human bodies: inborn defects such as disabilities, chronic disease. 'We have been treating genetic structure as a matter of luck – the luck, good or bad, that people bring into the world with them' (Dworkin 2000, p. 347). However, according to epigenetics research outcomes of genetic predispositions are co-constituted by social factors. Bad social circumstances such as environmental pollution, lead poisoning, broken families, bad housing, unsafe neighborhoods, parents' drug abuse, or unhealthy nutrition have harmful health consequences from gestation to later life, leading to more inborn vulnerabilities and defects; more generally resulting in dramatically lower health expectancies for the worst off. In recent years there have been growing concerns that exposures to certain chemicals (so-called 'teratogens') during, or even before, pregnancy can result in high rates of miscarriages and children born with mental or physical disabilities and even cancer. Several epidemiological studies have contributed to the identification of a growing list of industrial chemicals as developmental neurotoxicants. In their extensive overview Grandjean and Landrigan (2014) postulate that many more neurotoxicants still remain undiscovered. Although such neurotoxicants may pose risks to people of all classes – this is the general message of Beck's influential book *Risk Society* (1992) – it is obvious that those who work directly with such substances in production, transportation or further processing run more severe risks than others. Increased risks of birth defects have extensively been documented for workers with a high occupational exposure to DDT but this is just one possible well known risk (Salazar-García 2004). Studies have also shown that mothers who live close to landfill sites that handle hazardous chemical wastes have a raised risk of congenital anomaly in babies. Wealthy people are not known to have a preference for living near such locations or being involved in directly working with developmental neurotoxicants, and empirical evidence gives us, indeed, reason to assume that social inequality may have something to do with the 'bad brute luck' of inborn disabilities or vulnerabilities (Dolk 1998). Favorable and unfavorable conditions are not randomly distributed or a matter of good or bad luck as luck egalitarians would like us to believe. Of course, the contingency of life cannot be fully avoided: somebody may fall down the stairs or suffer the consequences of a traffic accident without this being caused by socioeconomic adversity. The consequences of accidents can, however, be very unequal: somebody with a vulnerable economic position may lose his job or, eventually, even his home; whereas for another this might just be an unfortunate incident that may soon be forgotten.

To acquiesce those who fear that egalitarians want to change something in the present distribution of wealth the luck egalitarians emphasize that they don't want to take anything away from the deserving; they merely propose compensating undeserved bad brute luck. There is, however, a loud silence about the analytical distinction between good and bad brute luck. *Good brute luck* remains largely undiscussed, hiding structural mechanisms from view that are relevant to understanding social inequality. The emphasis on distinguishing deserved and undeserved poverty is not balanced by a similar interest in distinguishing deserved and undeserved richness even when the fruits can hardly be seen as the outcome of option luck. Luck egalitarianism fails to see how the accumulation of advantage is a structural mechanism that has also something to do with the market mechanisms that they idealize. A large quantity of coffee beans that someone has taken in stock for distribution among customers without any intention of 'deliberate gamble' may multiply in value when natural disasters destruct an important part of the global coffee harvest. Likewise, the value of more elevated properties will go up after extensive flooding in the area. Such market mechanisms work to the advantage of those who are already advantaged.

After the imaginary auction that would give all young adults an equal start in life they are not involved in shared forms of responsibility about their societal circumstances; whether in the form of institutions, communities or mutual care: they just care about themselves. According to Wolff (2010) luck egalitarianism has a strong relational deficit; there is little sense of what would be a good way to live together as equals and it is overly concerned with distribution of material goods, to organize once and for all Dworkin's 'envy free distribution'. Luck egalitarianism presupposes that individuals are completely independent from others, not in any way bound by mutual concerns or care that might interfere with the opportunities to gain an income or to pursue a career. The luck egalitarian approach is obviously inspired by some implicit vision of a better social world that it tries to construct, however it encourages selfish illusions of independence. In the end, the weight of social justice falls on those who are worst off: as long as they remain unable to prove beyond doubt that they have been the victims of bad brute luck they will not be supported.

Later life under Luck Egalitarianism

The young adults at Dworkin's hypothetical auction have to buy insurance against the possible harms they have reason to fear in the future. To be able to come to adequate choices they are supposed to have full knowledge of the risks of getting, for instance, a disease, together with the costs and benefits of health interventions, while remaining behind a veil of ignorance about their own genetic make up or future situation. This hypothetical allocation is also supposed to give a fair model for what society should provide for older persons, especially in terms of a fair allocation of their health care resources.

The typical auctioneer would be a 25-year-old with equalized resources and state-of-the-art knowledge of medicine. He may want to buy all possible kinds of insurance against every kind of risks, but the costs would of course be prohibitive. So, according to Dworkin, the inevitable alternative would be to select insurances that should *not* be bought: 'We can be confident, for example, about what medical insurance it would not be prudent for most people to buy, because some insurance would be a mistake no matter what happened in the future' (2000, p. 313). Being faced with an unknown future Dworkin has found at least one solid point of reference: 'old age' will be a residual affair after a productive life and hardly worth investing in. He assumes not only that a rational person would not buy life extending treatments if ill at advanced age but especially that he would decide against 'technology whose main results benefit people in relatively old age' (Dworkin 1993, p. 890; I will discuss this further in Ch.7).

Dworkin's *Complete Life Egalitarianism* with its equalization of budgets for a 'complete life' leaves little hope that there will be sufficient resources for later life. With the uncertainty of life's length and the depreciation of 'old age' that can be expected of young adults – especially when ageism is not in any way questioned – the chances that sufficient resources will be reserved for later life are not favorable, to put it mildly. It is not hard to imagine how the general attitude or approach that speaks from these practices would translate into pension policies. Somebody who just crossed the line into retirement might receive the following note: 'Congratulations with your blessed age which gives you the right to do nothing! You are probably already showing signs of bodily and cognitive decline or you will soon experience them. Therefore, to avoid inefficiency at the workplace it will be best for you not to be allowed to work for the rest of your life. You will be supported, in accordance with agreements made 40 years ago, until your complete life budget runs out.'

The possibilities for young adults to plan ahead for a complete life are largely overestimated. The general rule that situations confronting people in late life must be evaluated in terms of their decisions that were made 40 or 60 years ago is highly problematic. Even prudent people can end up in miserable situations. Should the young adults have known that the promising professions that they chose would become obsolete because of technological innovations they should have been able to predict? Should they have known that their company would outsource its production? What seemed to be a wise choice at the time, for instance, to trust a bank with one's savings, can easily go bad when the bank suddenly collapses or their highly praised investment opportunities turn out to be disastrous. Should these victims have known that their savings that were 'solidly invested' would become worthless or drastically reduced, although they prudently relied on expert advice from their widely respected bank?

In making individual choice and responsibility for their complete life the focal points of egalitarian concern, luck egalitarians presuppose that individual actors have a complete overview of the consequences of their choices over several decades. Besides the ageism that speaks from these constructions, they underestimate the accelerating rate of change in contemporary societies where the long-term consequences of actions that seem perfectly rational at the time are increasingly difficult to predict, even for experts. Apart from extreme cases, trying to distinguish those who deserve compensation from those who can be held fully responsible for their misfortune appears to be highly complicated and morally hazardous, especially in a life course perspective that stretches over several decades. Not all choices that turn out to be bad can simply be equated with irresponsible behavior in which there would be a direct causal link between choices and their consequences as suggested in the concept of 'bad option luck'.

The luck egalitarian embrace of the entrepreneurial life course

We can assume that the proponents of luck egalitarianism are motivated by concern about existing social inequalities. The equalizing auction and the resulting compensation that would be offered to victims of bad brute luck are indications that they try to advance an egalitarian agenda. However, their diagnosis of what one could presume to be their major problem – social inequality – remains superficial. By focusing on inborn assets, the cultural (race, gender) and structural (income, wealth, education, geographical segregation) sources of social inequalities affecting people's opportunities from early childhood on are completely ignored. These factors are dismissed with the claim that 'The insurance device that we have been studying aims to make people equal in their ex ante risk of bad luck' (Dworkin 2000, p. 346). The shared societal responsibility for inequalities during the formative years of pre-adult life is reduced to a monetary equalization of resources at the beginning of adulthood. This idea of equalized opportunities appears to be an abstract construct without much critical potential to assess whether opportunities over the life course actually live up to this slogan.

After the great equalization, social inequality would not be unjust because it would result from choices people have made: 'Some people will earn more than others through their choices for higher paying jobs or for more work and less leisure, or through investment gambles that prosper rather than disappoint' (Dworkin 2000, p. 346). This assessment suggests that the labor market is ruled by citizens who have equal opportunities to choose the kind of work they prefer to do as if jobs were not outsourced, qualifications not outdated by technological developments, or the protections and benefits of those who have jobs were not under pressure to be reduced.

Markets are seen as ideal platforms for social justice so it comes as no surprise that market risks are portrayed as relatively harmless; a kind of gambling with money that you do not really need. Dworkin actually uses the example of buying a lottery ticket to illustrate how individuals must be held responsible for the outcomes of their decisions (Dworkin 1981b, p. 294). But lottery gambling is not a necessity of life and if you lose you can't lose more than the price of the ticket. The structural force of market risks are cut to the size of the idea of option luck: 'a matter of how deliberate and calculated gambles turn out – whether someone gains or loses through accepting an isolated risk he or she should have anticipated and might have declined' (Dworkin 2000, p. 73).

The choices that people have to make over the life course are usually no 'deliberate and calculated gambles' or a matter of gaining or losing 'through accepting an isolated risk he or she should have anticipated and might have declined' (Dworkin 2000, p. 73). There are hardly 'isolated risks' when people have to choose between educational tracks or job opportunities: such decisions have far reaching consequences over the life course. It is astonishing that all these problems are reduced to the simplicity that, if things go wrong, it must be because someone has made irresponsible choices.

One of the major distinctions between relatively advantaged and disadvantaged people is this difference in the range of choices: well off people are able to move out of a neighborhood that has become violent to a region with better conditions for their health; they can afford the necessary medical interventions, the proper maintenance of their car or buying a new one, etc.

The choices of resourceful people can often change circumstances but for those with fewer resources a seemingly small setback can be overwhelming.

The principle of individual responsibility for choices gives a too narrow basis to explain or remedy social inequality. Crucial are the preconditions that enable people to choose and these are neither realized nor equalized with the proposed compensatory process at the beginning of adult life. As said before, this does not imply that responsibility would not be a consideration that affects what we owe each other, but its importance has to be weighed in relation to the options and alternatives that agents have. Depending on the situation, decisional freedom may be little more than the freedom to accept the only available option (a bad job or a bad house instead of none) or to have to choose between several bad ones. Because of the simple moralistic clarity of self responsibility the luck egalitarian suggestions may be appealing, but this approach evades the problems of an extremely unequal society, which remains a strange thing to do for any form of egalitarianism.

It seems as if the market of option luck should be a blessing for all prudent citizens as it would filter out those who are responsible for their own misfortune. But many forms of bad luck cannot be seen as consequences of irresponsible behavior or as purely natural catastrophes; Dworkin's proposed policies of social justice tend to support those who do well and add insult to injury to those who are incapable of breaking out of their disadvantaged positions. The verdict of luck egalitarianism is that over the life course everybody gets what they deserve: after the equalizing auction for young adults their lives would evolve in accordance with their choices. As Dworkin states repeatedly: people should pay the price for the life they have decided to lead and whatever comes from adult's choices is not contrary to social justice. If they end up in trouble they have only themselves to blame because if bad brute luck had hit them they would have been compensated. It is puzzling how those who claim to be egalitarians are so reluctant to offer protection against the downside risks of unregulated markets (Anderson 2008). The main problem of social inequality is identified in true libertarian spirit as one of bailing out irresponsible individuals at the expense of others. This egalitarian narrative risks reproducing prejudicial stereotypes that disadvantaged people are irresponsible individuals, and it supports the ideology of going tough on them as they only have themselves to blame.

Dworkin's theory of social justice results in a construct of society populated by individual adults who take and expect nothing from others, competing with each other on markets with assumedly equal opportunities, where bad luck is always be caused by bad choices. If people appear to have made wrong choices there is no claim of justice to help them. In response to criticism of the harshness of luck egalitarianism there have been some ad hoc revisions without, however, any change of the fundamentals (cf. Markovits 2008; Segall 2010).

What Cohen (1989 p. 933) called 'Dworkin's historical achievement', the incorporation within egalitarianism of 'the most powerful idea in the arsenal of the anti-egalitarian right, the idea of choice and responsibility' has become a Trojan horse. At a time when Reagan and Thatcher led the libertarian way towards a demolition of egalitarian inspired arrangements and institutions along the life course, luck egalitarianism presented an agenda in which market mechanisms were idealized as ways to achieve equal distributions, and citizens who became increasingly exposed to global market forces were presented as individually responsible for their 'option luck'. Right at the beginning of the neoliberal turn Dworkin demonstrated a keen but self-defeating sense for the rapidly changing political climate with its idolization of markets and the individual responsibility of entrepreneurial citizens for their lives.

The poor moralistic gain might just be that bad situations along the life course are legitimized as a result of bad individual choices. Luck egalitarianism runs the risk of becoming an ideology in favor of those who have had the wind in their backs along the life course. They are encouraged to think that they have succeeded in living the lives they decided to live, making them feel good about their own achievements. They would have chosen good jobs with prestige and excellent income, without noticing how they have been benefiting from the structures which support those who are already advantaged. The ideology of the 'self-made man' is once more dusted off: their own intelligence, strength and effort, sacrifice and determination helped them to see every problem as a challenge that only improved them. Those who fail have only themselves to blame: they didn't try hard enough or made the wrong decisions leading to bad option luck.

Norman Daniels: the equality of going thorough the same life stages

Since the mid 1980s, the prominent Harvard scholar Norman Daniels has been active in articulating a theory of justice for aging, specifically in relation to the distribution of resources over the life course, called the 'Prudential Lifespan Account'. On several occasions, looking back on how he began to think about justice and aging (cf. Daniels 2008) he stated that he was surprised how the discussion of ageism was dominated by an analogy with gender and race discrimination. This analogy is indeed typical of Butler's influential definition of ageism as 'a process of systematic stereotyping of and discrimination against people because they are old, just as racism and sexism accomplish this for skin color and gender' (1980, p. 9). Yet, according to Daniels there is a deep disanalogy, because aging is a process that everybody, irrespective of race or gender, will go through. His basic view is that, as members of a specific birth cohort, we pass through different age groups or age stages as we get older. These age groups or stages remain the same; the only change is that subsequent cohorts are passing through them. Meanwhile, each cohort must have confidence that they will be adequately provided for when they have reached 'old age'. Daniels proposes his 'Prudential Lifespan Account' as a way to think about fairness between age groups.

The argumentative structure of his theory follows to a certain extent Rawls' thought experiment in which social contractualists discuss in an original situation about what a just society might be, assuming they are pursuing their self interest but do not know what position they will hold in that prospective society. There are, however, also some important departures from Rawls's *A Theory of Justice* (1971).

As discussed above, Rawls neglected aging as he assumed that the contractors would be 'fully functioning adults over a complete life'. He underlined the importance of careers and, consequently, education to make sure that careers would be as much as possible open to talents. Daniels, however, emphasizes that over the course of a complete life people are confronted with different age stages that imply different age-related needs. The contractors should, therefore, design institutions that take care of these age-specific needs in the form of a balanced account of the differences between these stages of life. According to Daniels, Rawls neglected these differences; his preoccupation with careers would be inadequate for older people and even restrict their opportunities because, as people get older, health care concerns become more important than careers. Daniels appears to take up classical discussions about age- versus stage-specific needs that were initiated by Bernice Neugarten and others (Neugarten 1982; Neugarten & Havighurst 1976). Although these discussions aimed at differentiating age and stage, and rethinking what they might actually mean, Daniels proposes to integrate age and stage again.

In *A Theory of Justice* Rawls did not elaborate on health care as he assumed that income and wealth from careers would take care of this problem. But in his later work *Justice as Fairness* he explicitly underlines the importance of health care for his approach to the life course:

> the provision for medical care, as with primary goods generally, is to meet the needs and requirements of citizens as free and equal. Such care falls under the general means necessary to underwrite fair equality of opportunity and our capacity to take advantage of our basic rights and liberties and thus to be normal and fully cooperating members of society over a complete life.
>
> (2001: 174)

However, Daniels' early development of a theory of justice and health *care* did not imply that he confronted problems of *health* and social justice. In his 1985 book *Just Health Care* he even insists that "health is an inappropriate object, but health care, action which promotes health, is appropriate... a right claim to equal *health* is best constructed as a demand for quality of access or entitlement to health *services'* (p. 6 ff.). This emphasis on health care and its costs is also characteristic for the approach to aging in the context of the *Prudential Lifespan Account* that we encounter in his 1988 *Am I my Parents' Keeper? An Essay on Justice Between the Young and the Old.*

This last book has played a central role in discussions about aging and social justice over the last decades. A major theoretical problem regarding the structure of this book is that it suffers from a mixture of two basic theoretical models. On the one hand we encounter the constitutive Rawlsian contractors who would discuss just institutional structures providing goods through all stages of life, behind the 'veil of ignorance' concerning their specific age-related position. But on the other hand, Daniels uses the model of the lonely prudential planner who has to distribute his resources and savings over future life stages. As Daniels confesses in a later review: 'Unfortunately, I continued to illustrate such "prudent" reasoning by reference to an individual designing an insurance policy, confusing readers about my departure from standard notions of prudence' (2009: 39). At this point, Dworkin's' pre-occupation with prudential insurance has probably influenced Daniels' thinking.

In the following I will not try to disentangle these two theoretical models but will focus on Daniels' approach to aging over the life course. Both of these models cling to the assumption that aging is basically a uniform natural process in which people subsequently go through 'age stages' or 'age groups' with their specific age-related needs. The only differences that matter would be those between the age stages, not within them.

Introducing the Prudential Lifespan Account

As said, Daniels builds his theory partly on the Rawlsian thought experiment in which citizens discuss about a just social contract behind a 'veil of ignorance' that would guarantee impartiality and *fairness* in the distribution of resources. They don't assume, however, as in Rawls' proposal, that they are ageless adults, fully functioning over a 'complete life'. They are aware that their position might be that of a newborn child, a productive adult or an old person. The contractors are supposed to be exemplary prudent persons who have knowledge of basic empirical facts such as needs for resources at different ages, age related diseases, costs of medical interventions and life expectancies (1988, p. 75).

A crucial assumption that guides the prudential deliberation is that there is an important difference between, on the one hand, distributive problems *between* persons and, on the other hand, problems regarding the allocation of resources *within* a persons' life. The first category of questions and problems are put outside Daniels' perspective:

> We have put interpersonal issues of justice outside the frame of our problem by assuming we already have solutions for them ... by assuming that other principles of distributive justice already govern interpersonal distribution. These principles of justice define the overall budget that prudent deliberators must allocate over the life span. We must now consider what form of prudential reasoning is appropriate within this frame.
>
> (Daniels 1988, 53)

So, the dominant model becomes that of the prudent individual planner. For intra-personal allocations the ultimate rational goal would be that for each person the own life goes as well as possible. What would be rational to do for anyone is what brings the greatest expected benefit over a complete life; something the influential theorist Derek Parfit (1984, pp. 4, 8) called the *Self-Interest Theory*. In accordance with the goals of *Complete Lives Egalitarianism* Daniels' *Prudential Lifespan Account* wants to achieve fairness for complete lives of individuals: life as a temporal whole should be as good as possible. A fair distribution between the young and the old is what would be chosen by a prudent individual who allocates resources to temporal stages of life 'in order to make his life as a whole better' (Daniels 1988, p. 46). However, even if there is no unfairness in terms of complete lives, it may be that the distribution over the different *phases* of life is not adequate. What is supposed to maximize the quality of a complete life is a prudential distribution of resources over different stages of life: a rational person should be equally concerned about *all* stages of life (Daniels 1996, p. 285). This is what Parfit (1984, p. 313) has called the *Requirement of Equal Concern*. Daniels emphasizes that life stages are inherently different from each other while affirming – in contrast to Callahan – the moral claims of 'old age' in discussions about social justice between 'the young and the old'. His approach is built on *a theory of aging* claiming that there are basic differences between stages of life that should be respected:

> Because we age, treating people of different ages differently does not mean that we are treating persons unequally. From the perspective of institutions that operate over a lifetime, unequal treatment of different age groups does not generate inequalities among persons. Indeed, unequal treatment at different stages of life may be exactly what we want from such institutions. The lifespan account of justice between age groups builds on this basic point.
>
> (Daniels 1988, 42)

According to this version of *Complete Lives Egalitarianism* justice would be concerned with the distribution of resources over *complete* lives of *separate* persons in such a way that every life stage gets what would be appropriate given its position in a natural life cycle. Birth cohorts may be different from each other but they are supposed to be equalized as they go through the different life stages. Therefore, justice between 'the young and the old' would not be disturbed by cohort differences: each age group merely represents a stage in an ongoing life cycle of generations. The *Prudential Lifespan Account* is supposed to lay the foundations for institutions that operate over the life course, distributing important goods such as health care and income. The slogan 'Prudence guides justice' (Daniels 1996, p. 281) underlines this programmatic intent.

This distinctive type of prudential justice that is based on inherently different life stages would also offer a solution to the Generational Equity debate:

> The lifespan account involves a fundamental shift of perspective. We must not look at the problem as one of justice between distinct groups in competition with each other, for example, between working adults who pay high premiums and the frail elderly who consume many services. Rather, we must see that each group *represents* a stage in our lives. We must view the prudent allocation of resources through the stages of life as our guide to justice between groups ... What we need to see is ourselves at other stages of our lives, benefiting from our own ... prudent savings.
>
> (Daniels 1988, p. 45)

The dominant intra-personal perspective on aging makes it possible to suggest that there would not be any real conflict between the young and the old, but merely intrapersonal problems of distribution between different temporal stages of a single life. Interpersonal conflicts of distributing resources would only be the superficial manifestation of an intra-personal problem of prudential planning that can be solved by Daniels' *Prudential Lifespan Account*. It would all depend on how resources are distributed over the life stages and what the individual has saved for old age.

Because of Daniels' assumption that these stages would correspond with age groups, planning over the life course seems to get a clear hold. Resources should be distributed in such a way that they protect and restore the '*age-relative normal opportunity range*' of a particular stage of life (Daniels 1988, p. 74; 1991, p. 239). Daniels points out that a prudential distribution that grants more to some stages of life than to others does not lead to inequalities between lives: it just distributes equal amounts of resources differently over different life stages, in accordance with their specific 'nature'. If institutions that distribute goods over our lifespan treat us differently at different ages, but treat each of us the same way over our whole lives, this does not lead to 'objectionable inequalities', such as arise from unequal treatment by race and gender (Daniels 2008, p. 39). This proposed distribution of income and health care resources over different age groups appears to be the implementation of the moral and natural essence of an age-based human lifecycle.

Social determinants of health, but not of aging

Two decades after *Am I my Parents' Keeper?* Daniels published his 2008 book *Just Health: Meeting Health Needs Fairly*. In this later work Daniels tries to solve the theoretical problems that were caused by the earlier mentioned mixture of two theoretical models (institutional structures versus individual prudential planning) in the construction of *Am I my Parents' Keeper?* To this end Daniels devotes much attention to 'accountability for reasonableness', a discursive model of justice that might give a better way to approach questions of justice (cf. Daniels 1996; Daniels & Sabin 2002). This involves a meta approach of how to discuss questions of justice that reminds us in certain aspects of Habermas' (1996) discourse theory. I will, however, resist the temptation to go into these subjects.

More importantly, this book marks another shift in Daniels' work as his theoretical focus moves from the distribution of health *care* as the major concern of justice to a much broader view of the social determinants of *health*. This change of focus is also seen as a move towards a more fundamental layer of causality because the distribution of health is now seen as more important than the distribution of health care. Now, medical care is pictured as 'the ambulance waiting at the bottom of the cliff': it comes into play when the damage has already been done (Daniels 2008, p. 79). This shift does not mean that health care ceases to be important: even in an ideally just distribution of the social determinants of health people will still encounter disease, injury or disability. Consequently, healthcare remains of special moral importance; moreover, Daniels fears that its costs can easily lead society into a bottomless pit, making limits on health care inevitable (see Ch.7).

Surprisingly, Daniels' more recent theoretical extensions and innovations do not change his approach to aging as going through a uniform natural sequence of age stages. He continues to call his approach to aging the *Prudential Lifespan Account* (cf. 2008, pp. 171–174) without any indication of a possible change since his *Am I my Parents' Keeper?* His extensive discussion of social determinants of health does not lead to an investigation of the ways in which these social determinants of health – that he does connect with 'health inequalities' – lead to inequalities in aging which would undermine the uniformity of his age stages. His programmatic statement at the beginning of the chapter about 'Global Aging and Intergenerational Equity' announcing the integration of knowledge about the importance of the social determinants of health with an 'account of equity between age groups' (2008, p. 162) already makes it clear that he is not going to pay attention to inequities *within* age groups.

The Prudential Lifespan Account: three basic problems

The point of Daniels' *Prudential Lifespan Account* is to make life 'as a whole' better through a prudential distribution of resources over the subsequent life stages. There are some layers of problems that need to be discussed. Although aging is indeed inherent in human life, it is also part of the interhuman condition that each individual does not know how long she will live. This is a crucial problem for *Complete Life Egalitarianism* as it proposes working with fixed budgets for a 'complete life', inviting problems in planning for an adequate income (1) and for adequate access to health care (2). Meanwhile (3), problems of social inequality over the life course that lead to unequal aging trajectories in terms of (healthy) life expectancies are neglected and assumed away in favor of an intra-personal model of distribution. In *Just Health* Daniels repeats his conviction about just aging: 'The basic idea is that, since we all age, we should take as a model for what is fair between age groups what is prudent for us to do for ourselves at each stage of life' (2008, p. 162). As a result of this rudimentary theory of aging as going through identical age stages, combined with a neglect of ageism, the result of the *Prudential Lifespan Account* remains a tendency to depreciate 'old age' and to create problems for older citizens in spite of Daniels' intention to solve them.

(1) Prudentially planned income and the risk of longevity

Daniels warns that resources should not be wasted on projects of youth, leaving little for old age (Daniels 1988, p. 120; 1996, p. 120ff). He assumes that the result of prudential planning would be that incomes remain roughly equal over the lifespan. This *Income Preservation Principle* would ensure that people have enough resources at every stage of their lives to realize their particular plans (Daniels 1988, p. 121).

However, this outcome of the prudential planning process is not very likely because information about average life expectancies may be available for the prudential planners but such statistical prognoses offer no certainty to individuals, although they do inform us that the chances of living much longer than average are per definition slim. Will the prudential planner not be inclined to reserve less for the risk or fortune – depending on how one would value such a prospect – of living very long? This is all the more likely because the total amount that can be prudentially distributed over the lifespan is assumed – as in Dworkin's constructions – to be fixed, so that resources that are reserved for old age would directly diminish the opportunities that earlier stages of life would have: 'Inequalities in income levels between stages of life work only as a zero-sum game, making one period of life better at the expense of another period or stage of life' (Daniels 1988, p. 121).

Even if the age of the prudential planner remains hidden behind the veil of ignorance, the whole point of planning is that it should take place at a relatively young age. It seems farfetched, however, to ask young adults to make such important decisions over a possibly very long future with great uncertainty and major unpredictable changes. To propose a situation in which they will be held responsible in 40, 60 or 80 years time for their autonomous decisions appears to overburden the individual. Moreover, life expectancies may continue to rise, implying that life lasts longer than imagined at the moment of prudential planning. Nevertheless, for most young adults the possibility of living a very long life (say, until 95 or a 100 years), will probably not put much weight in the balance. For most young adults 'old age' is just an abstract possibility and in an ageist culture beset by negative associations. Providing for an uncertain old age would hardly seem worthwhile because it might seem nothing more than living a life of disease, disability, uselessness and terminal decline. What would be the use of investing in such a future when they can freely take from the money at their hands to drive that Porsche now?

While Dworkin assumes that the exemplary planner would be 25 years old, Daniels proposes that the prudential planner is ignorant of her age so she may be much older but even then, planning remains per definition confronted with an uncertain future. Even in planning for the future at the age of 50 years, when ageist denigration of older people may still run high, it is not unlikely that the resources that would enable one to continue to live well into a much higher age will be scaled down because the likelihood of being still alive at such ages remains per definition small. Therefore, in his later work Daniels ponders the question whether rationally prudent individuals should not discount their later years as a result of a diminishing fecundity of the benefits they can expect from them. In such cases, 'other things being equal, a later year is worth less than an earlier one because whatever opportunities for generating further benefits from activities pursued in a later year are less than those generated at an earlier year' (Daniels 1996, p. 282).

However, although the existential uncertainty remains, it does happen that people live very long: how are these very old people supposed to have the resources they need? What if life turns out to be much longer than prudentially expected? Would it be prudential to plan for such an unlikely event, continuing to 'benefit from our own … prudent savings'? (Daniels 1988, p. 45). This uncertainty is not faced in Daniels' *Prudential Lifespan Account*. It is assumed to be solved through a merely postulated *Income Preservation Principle* which would coincide with the choices of the prudential planner for his own future. If the *Prudential Lifespan Account* were put into practice, the result would be that those who do live relatively long might end up in dire situations. This would put them at serious risk. Moreover, they would be held responsible for their predicament because they didn't provide for their longevity. In a discussion of this problem Daniels (1996) proposes *ad hoc* that people should buy annuity, which is another illustration of his tendency to introduce, much like Dworkin, economic models of market oriented prudential planning.

(2) Restricted Access To Health Care For Older People

We don't know how long we will live but we also don't know what our health status will be. Here, Daniels changes his approach: future income and health care needs are treated differently. In contrast to Daniels' (unrealistic) expectation that a prudential planner would decide that income would remain roughly equal throughout life, health care resources would be distributed in such a way that they protect and restore the '*age-relative normal opportunity range*' of a particular stage of life (Daniels 1988, p. 74; 1991, p. 239). The result is that old age would receive a larger share of the total health care budget that can be used during a 'whole life'. This may sound attractive but it will be difficult to establish such an opportunity range. In case this should succeed and it were to be implemented it would create problems for those who deviate from the presupposed 'normality', such as young people who suffer from chronic illness or older people who live very long and in good health but with insufficient resources because these have been reserved for health care they don't need. Moreover, people who live for very long will run the risk of being denied medical attention because this might not be included in the age related distribution of resources. Although Daniels tends to think that his approach would bring justice for older persons, we have reasons to protest with McKerlie (2012, p. 41) against the harsh consequences of the *Prudential Lifespan Account*.

(3) The reduction of interpersonal distribution to an intra-personal task

Another layer of problems concerns the relationship between interpersonal and intrapersonal distributions. Daniels proposes at the very beginning a strict separation between them: 'We have put interpersonal issues of justice outside the frame of our problem by assuming we already have solutions for them...' (1988, p. 53). However, it remains doubtful whether such a separation is possible in designing institutions that must distribute resources over the whole life of a population.

Daniels' proposal is to trust the individual rational planner who puts his self-interest first and plans his life prudently, distributing his resources over the life stages. It remains unclear, however, how distributions within individual lives could be separated from interpersonal distributions. Daniels does not just propose an analytical distinction between, on the one hand, distributions *between* individuals and, on the other hand, *within* their lives, but tends to *reduce* problems of interpersonal distribution to intrapersonal ones (cf. McKerlie 2012): '*We must view the prudent allocation of resources through the stages of life as our guide to justice between groups*' (Daniels 1988, p. 74).

This reflects back on Daniels' claim that he would give an answer or even a solution to the *Generational Equity* debate;

> We must not look at the problem as one of justice between distinct groups in competition with each other, for example, between working adults who pay high premiums and the frail elderly who consume many services. Rather, we must see that each group *represents* a stage in our lives. We must view the prudent allocation of resources through the stages of life as our guide to justice between groups.
>
> (Daniels 1988, p. 45)

Neither his individualistic perspective nor his stage theory appear to be adequate to give an answer to the macro problems that were posed, be it sometimes awkwardly, in this debate. Problems of interpersonal or 'inter-generational' justice such as the ones that may arise when birthrates are dropping and populations are aging can hardly be solved by or reduced to intra-personal prudence; to planning issues that would arise inside individual lives because of the differences between 'natural' age stages. The appeal to prudence pretends to solve problems between age groups while at the same time pretending that the prudential allocation remains merely intra-personal. McKerlie (2012) rightly observes that the relation between institutions and individual responsibility remains problematic in Daniels' theory.

In later publications such as the chapter on the 'Prudential Life-span account of justice between generations' in *Justice and Justification* (1996, pp. 257–283) Daniels has tried to present solutions for several problems of distribution between age groups, but these tend to be utilitarian, such as flexible, part-time employment of older workers and pleas for active aging. Such mixtures of contradictory theoretical models, stemming from Rawlsian theories, prudential economics, and utilitarian pragmatism, do not help to clarify the issues Daniels wants to solve.

The lonely planner oversees the stages of life

In accord with *Complete Life Egalitarianism* Daniels is looking for a prudent distribution of resources over stages of life that will maximize the quality of a whole life. He appears to have found a natural, quasi trans-historical hold in the idea that aging is a process of going though subsequent natural 'stages' that follow each other according to the same basic pattern. The prudential planner may not know what age he might have in the projected life course, but he knows what each age would mean in terms of this stage theory (see Ch.7 about life stages).

The basic pattern of human life would consist of a sequence of stages that naturally follow each other, unifying people from different cohorts as age groups. Daniels' basic concept of an *'age-relative normal opportunity range'* (1988, p. 74; 2008, p. 185) presupposes a life course – or life span, as he calls this – consisting of a few homogeneous stages that are only different from each other. He therefore suggests approaching questions of 'intergenerational justice' not as a conflict between the young and the old but as negotiating differences between life stages.

Daniels, however, develops his theory of aging mainly from the perspective of a lonely planner who has to distribute his savings over his life. This gives the impression that the prudential planner is a productive and well-off investor in his future opportunities, somebody who is well positioned to answer the call that 'we need to see ourselves at other stages of our lives, *benefiting from our own … prudent savings'* (Daniels 1988, p. 45). However, unexpected life course events such as unemployment, chronic disease or longevity cannot always be addressed by drawing on 'our own prudent savings'. Savings may not be enough and too many people end up in situations where they are unable to save because they need all their income to survive. Daniels has put such 'interpersonal issues of justice outside the frame of our problem by assuming we already have solutions to them' (Daniels 1988, p. 52). It is hard to see, however, how someone could plan for a 'complete life' and leave out institutions, interpersonal relations, such as mutual support between family members and friends or intergenerational transactions and inheritance between (grand)parents, children and grandchildren. During long lives individuals will be confronted with largely unforeseeable macro-developments such as large-scale conflicts, wars, economic and social crises. They need to be able to trust more enduring social entities that will take care of their basic needs and rights as citizens in times of crisis: interpersonal constellations at different levels such as partners, friends, family, community, society are much better able to adapt to unforeseen developments or crises and are crucial for mutual support and recognition. Of course, one can 'put interpersonal issues of justice outside the frame of our problem by assuming we already have solutions for them' (Daniels 1988, p. 53) but then the question arises what the relevance of such an intrapersonal exploration might be for a reorganization of the life course that even pretends to solve problems that were posed in the Generational Equity debate.

A stage theory of aging is not only a rudimentary approach to contemporary forms of aging with their impressive diversities of 'old age', but is especially unsuited to approach questions of social inequality. Daniels' theory of aging and social justice begins with putting the most pressing problems of social justice outside his field of study: 'Specifically, I assume that *fair shares* of health care or income are being distributed over the life-span' (Daniels 1988, p. 118). This basic neglect leads to the impression that the prudential planner wants to address social justice but assumes that 'the problem of achieving equitable treatment of distinct cohorts' can be solved by assuming 'an otherwise just society' (Daniels 1988, p. 137). Questions of social inequality leading to differences *within* age groups – in more technical terms, intra-age and intra-cohort differentiation – are completely neglected. This assumes that aging would be a purely natural process that takes place without any constitutive influence of differentiated and changing social contexts. Problems of *in*equitable treatment *within* these cohorts that develop from early life on in interaction with the main drivers of social inequality (see Ch.3) are placed outside his perspective on 'Justice between the Young and the Old'. Moreover, there is no discussion of ageism although it is very likely that this would influence planning for a future old age.

As we have seen, problems of unequal distribution of social determinants of health are acknowledged in his later work *Just Health* but with no implications for his view on aging. Aging remains a process of moving though age stages; the only tensions that are discussed are those between these stages, especially between the young and the old, not between groups within the same age stage. As is the case with the Luck Egalitarians, constructs of equality push actually existing social inequality – which may have been the original motivation to develop egalitarian theories – out of sight: 'important principles of distributive justice prohibit our using "morally irrelevant" traits of individuals, like race, religion, or sex, as a basis for differential treatment in distribution of important social goods, such as educational or job opportunities, civil liberties, health care, income and wealth' (1988, p. 40). It is a strange ambition for a theory of distributive justice to avoid – like the proponents of 'color blindness' – speaking about actually existing inequalities between citizens because these would be 'morally irrelevant'. Daniels' discussions of health inequalities are not really integrated in his theory of distributive justice, leading to a theory that aims at constructing an ideal world of equality without critical interaction with actually existing forms of inequality.

McKerlie's Priority View

With his *Justice between the Young and the Old* (2012) the Canadian philosopher Dennis McKerlie represents the priority perspective that is also part of the egalitarian platform (Parfit 2002; see Ch.7). McKerlie distances himself from *Complete Lives Egalitarianism* that was shared by the authors who were discussed above, from Rawls to Daniels; with the possible exception of Sen. For the priority view the moral ground for helping is not based on comparison of complete lives but on the urgency of the situation people find themselves in. McKerlie argues for an independent moral importance of suffering:

> Unlike the concern for equality, it (the priority view J.B.) does not focus on the relationship between the lives of different people. It considers the absolute condition of the person who is badly off and holds that, in virtue of that condition, it is especially important to help that person.
>
> (2012: 54)

Therefore, he opposes Nagel's idea that more favorable earlier or later phases in life can compensate present suffering because the past does not really matter if somebody is starving now. Even when older people have had a splendid life but run into serious trouble in old age, there will still be a moral appeal to help them. For the same reasons Daniels is criticized by McKerlie because he would neglect pressing problems of older people here and now (a 'synchronic' concern) in favor of his prudent distribution of resources over age groups (a 'diachronic' concern). McKerlie protests that people who are suffering *now* cannot be helped through diachronic planning. According to McKerlie, misery would remain objectionable even if it were to be compensated in the context of a complete life. For him this doesn't mean that principles of justice for complete lives should be discarded but that it would be problematic if these principles were to become the dominant perspective: 'I grant that we also need to apply the egalitarian values at the level of complete lives, but I think that a view that exclusively uses complete lives as the relevant temporal unit will be incomplete and unable to account for some of our strongest judgments' (McKerlie 2012, p. 17).

McKerlie also disagrees with the luck egalitarians on the issue of individual responsibility. Arneson (2000) with his 'responsibility catering prioritarianism' may seem to come close to McKerlie's position but Arneson first demands proof that individuals are not responsible for their problems: irresponsible persons cannot be allowed to swallow up public resources. This may appear to make sense but, in reality it is usually extremely difficult to prove that people are responsible for the dire situations they find themselves in; hence, Rawls' caution at this point. McKerlie's answer is that in his account of priority 'a benefit received by someone badly off has special value even if she is responsible for her own suffering'; he objects to egalitarians 'who make the wrongness of inequality depend on responsibility' (p. 104).

According to McKerlie the major concern of the priority view is helping the worst off and those in acute need: the worse off they are, the more important a benefit will be for them. This so-called leximin version of prioritarianism implies that we ought, as a first priority, maximally to improve the condition of the worst-off individuals, then as a second priority, maximally to improve the condition of the second worst-off, and so on up to the best-off. As in Sen's capability approach, there should be no equality of benefits but a differentiation according to need.

In principle the priority view has no special connection with age; it is only committed to helping those who are badly off. In McKerlie's book *Justice between the Young and the Old*, however, the priority view is developed with a strong concern for 'old age' because as people move through the stages of youth, maturity and old age, they enter a life stage of suffering: 'the misery that the people feel when they are old can itself provide us with a reason, and a reason of justice, to help them' (2012, p. 55). Sometimes McKerlie seems to be more nuanced in his characterizations of old people but they figure mainly as distressed and miserable. The 'elderly', especially those older than 75 years (p. 6) form an 'age group' (p. 3) that goes through the 'life stage' (p. 53) of 'great misery' (p. 30) in which they are 'distressed' (p. 9). They are living in terrible retirement homes that are also old, over-crowded and badly managed, where they get adequate health care, but little opportunity for dignity and for anything approaching happiness (p. 7). Against all utilitarian calculi that reign supreme in social policy for senior citizens, including Callahan's age limits, Dworkin's residualist view of old age, and Daniels' Prudential Lifespan Account, McKerlie maintains that old people have a moral claim: their miserable situation should be improved. This claim would still hold even if the improvement of their conditions were not to be cost effective so that the required investments might give more wellbeing if directed at young people.

Clearly McKerlie has been shocked by certain conditions that older people have to live in and he should be credited for bringing such situations to the attention of those who assume that older people are well of compared to younger adults. He assumes, however, that these miserable conditions are representative for the life stage of 'old age', as if all older people are patients who are struggling to survive in terminal conditions. Such a hospitalization of older people does not lead to an acknowledgement of their participation as adult citizens in society; as if older people should not be taken seriously in public debate, politics, work or education. This amounts to what Bob Binstock (2010) has called 'compassionate ageism'. Moreover, this view of old age as a life stage of misery neglects societal inequalities in which disadvantaged people have a much greater chance to end up in terrible conditions and underfunded nursing homes than those who are well off. This is a way to naturalize social inequality by making misery a defining characteristic of 'old age': if old people are miserable that would only be natural – they are 'old'! – and, therefore, no reason to question why this may be so. Helping those who live in miserable circumstances is vitally important but this should not hide from view that society treats certain groups of older people with neglect and denigration and others as respected customers of prime services.

Although McKerlie's priority view goes beyond the individualistic pre-occupations of the other approaches to aging that were discussed above, its interpersonal perspective is too limited as it neglects the way in which miserable situations for older people are constituted by societal structures of inequality. Of course, in situations of acute need there should be immediate relief but as long as many such situations do not occur at random it is crucial to target the structural dynamics that are causing them. Distributive justice cannot be reduced to immediate relief: McKerlie's priority view remains within the short time perspective of charity organizations without attention for the origins of the problems he wants to alleviate.

Without doubt, charity and immediate help can be urgently important and it makes no sense to tell those who suffer that they must wait and be patient until social inequalities have been mitigated. However, besides the individual responsiveness and compassion there is also the question what kind of society we owe each other? An important *raison d'être* of the social sciences in a broad sense, including sociology, economics, history and social psychology is that we can learn about the complicated ways in which problems on a large scale are reproduced in specific situations, without being directly caused by the individuals who suffer from them. Such problems differ between societies and some societies have found better ways to address problems than others. Such learning processes require the ability to look beyond the pressures that come from the need to help here and now.

Conclusion

As most readers will be unfamiliar with the theories that were discussed in this chapter I will give a brief concluding overview. For the *Generational Equity* and the *Fair Innings* advocates the problem of social justice and the life course is, first, that the older 'generation' has been unfairly advantaged by the entitlements they have been granted during the build up of the supportive life course. Secondly, there is a fear that older people are kept alive by advanced medical technology which will deplete public resources with disastrous consequences for other age groups. As soon as people have achieved a relatively high age, such as 75 years, they should be ready to die so that they will no longer be a burden to society. The main problem with this approach is that the drastic reduction of public funds will hit especially disadvantaged citizens who have already fewer chances of reaching old age in good health. The opposition of the 'older' versus the 'younger', 'active' or 'working' generation neglects the inequalities within these 'generations'. If their proposals were put into practice, these inequalities would be deepened.

Dworkin's version of *Complete Life Egalitarianism* is not to put a maximum age on the claims for justice but to lay the risks in the hands of young adults whose life budgets should be distributed in such a way that the inequality of their talents has been evened out by monetary transfers among them. In *Luck Egalitarianism* we find a superficial acknowledgement that social inequality has deep roots in pre-adult life. There is, however, hardly an egalitarian interest in exploring the consequences of what Rawls had called the 'deep inequalities' into which people are born and by which they are formed during their pre-adult lives. There is much more interest in integrating the libertarian principle of individual responsibility into constructs of social equality. Moreover, the monetarized equalization of resources betrays an idealization of market mechanisms as a vehicle of social justice (see also Ch.7). After the equalization of resources at the beginning of adulthood, the only justified claim for support would arise from being hit by brute bad luck. However, as such 'bad luck' would only come from uncontrollable natural events there is no room to acknowledge that harmful events or processes can also have structural or cultural sources without being caused in any way by the individual victims. The conclusion must be that luck egalitarianism gravely underestimates the consequences of pre-adult inequality and neglects the harmful effects of social inequality along the life course. Moreover, although not as bad as in the *Generational Equity* advocacy, there is an ageist neglect of the value of later life.

With his *Prudential Lifespan Account* Daniels tries to give an answer to the opposition between 'the old' and 'the young' as seen, for instance in the *Generational Equity* debate. His version of *Complete Life Egalitarianism* is to propose that the life course consists of three stages: youth, adulthood and old age that should each be seen as qualitatively different in needs. His theorem of an 'age-relative normal opportunity range' implies that his 'life stages' are actually age groups (see Ch.4 and Ch.7). As these age groups would only differ from each other without internal differences Daniels avoids all problems of social inequality.

McKerlie wrote his *Justice between the Young and the Old* out of protest against those who claim that suffering in old age should be seen in the context of a 'complete life' as being compensated by better times. He advocates helping 'the elderly' even when this is not cost effective because helping has priority over other considerations. However, McKerlie not only neglects the differences and inequalities among 'the elderly', he also assumes that miserable conditions are representative for the life stage of 'old age' as a whole, neglecting that many problems of older people are consequences of social inequalities that grow in intensity along the life course.

These responses from egalitarian theorists of social justice to the neoliberal turn of capitalism with its huge implications for the organization of the life course are either irrelevant or highly problematic and worrisome. To avoid the illusion that the neoliberal turn of capitalism was only the work of dominant political and economic elites, we need to face the reality that an important part of the cultural elite of whom one might hope that they would follow societal developments critically from an egalitarian perspective of social justice, actually looked the other way, covering up the consequences of social inequality.

Notes

1 https://data.worldbank.org/indicator/SP.POP.65UP.TO.ZS?
2 https://www.youtube.com/watch?v=FLOH3aYb2Ic

Chapter 7

Social inequality and social justice over the life course

Overview

The first half of this last chapter draws some conclusions from the confrontation between the empirical data of a sharpening of social inequality and egalitarian theories about social justice over the life course. The first section questions the relevance of constructing theories of social equality without empirical information about social inequalities and the societal context in which these inequalities are produced and reproduced. This is followed by a critique of a tendency in these theories to obscure health inequalities by focusing on 'the bottomless pit of health care costs', especially with regard to older people. These ageist approaches are supported by theories that portray 'old age' as a homogeneous life stage; particularly one of stagnation and decline. I will delve a bit deeper into the 'naturalizing' presuppositions of such theories, also because the oppositions between 'the young' and 'the old' only aggravate the problems that would supposedly be solved. These considerations lead to the issue of a prevention which includes the organization of the life course and its infrastructure as these play a major role in the reproduction of society, including its inequalities. Such social preconditions are crucially important because human beings are not per definition but potentially autonomous. Society plays an important role in safeguarding the preconditions of individual autonomy, including the autonomy of older people. This section forms a kind of transition from the critically oriented sections to the more constructively oriented sections. A much needed reconstruction of the life course and its infrastructure might be guided by a capability approach modified by a concept of 'equal citizenship'. In this context it will be argued that striving for 'equality' is not inspired by ideals of 'the same' or the absence of differences: the basic problem is a hierarchical structuring of diversity. This is not merely a problem of identity politics (mutual respect) but also one of political struggles for an more equal distribution of resources. The final section sums up some of the costs of public indifference. The unfounded slogans of 'self regulatory wholesome markets', 'equal opportunities' and 'individual responsibility' function to protect those in power as long as the chronically disadvantaged

DOI: 10.4324/9781003392590-8

remain willing to put all the blame on themselves for their lack of success. Their exploding rancor, however, is skilfully manipulated by the same elite who abandoned them. The only way forward is to invest in the life course of the most important resource of the country: its population – in all its diversity.

Ideal theories of equality and social inequalities. The need for critical approaches

'For justice is best defined by its opposites'

John Stuart Mill[1]

Although we may assume that the motivation to think about equality has something to do with experiences of inequality, we have seen a strong preference among prominent egalitarians for constructs of 'equality'. For example the equality of 'fair innings'; the luck egalitarian construct of equal starting positions at early adulthood, followed by equal individual responsibility with public provisions for bad brute luck, and Norman Daniels' 'age relative normal opportunity range' that would equally apply to all people. These different constructions of *Complete Life Egalitarianism* have in common that they neglect the social inequalities that speak so clearly from the research that has been gathered in the first chapters. The tendency of luck egalitarians to construct principles that are so abstract that they are supposed to apply to all possible past and future situations, illustrated by abstract examples with *ceteris paribus* assumptions, leave us with theories that fail to get a grip on empirical evidence of actually existing forms of inequality. It must be with a sigh of relief that these theorists can finally point to individual responsibility and marketed distributions as a way to make their theoretical constructs more easily acceptable.

As a defense one might say that any criticism of inequality presupposes an implicit idea of equality so that, first of all, we need to try to clarify what might be meant by this idea because without it, we would have no ground to criticize inequality. This may be necessary to a certain extent and later in this chapter I will even propose a concept of equal citizenship, but in close contact with experiences and evidence of social inequalities. It would be farfetched to claim that we must first have a perfect theory for all times and places, before we can acknowledge or calibrate experiences of social inequality. It is doubtful whether we can derive all possible situations of inequality from a concept of equality. Anyway, we have seen that in the course of constructing such an ideal universe of equality, the connections with problematic situations that we wanted to clarify or improve to begin with are easily lost.

An important motivation for egalitarian critique remains a compassionate concern about social inequality as forms of suffering that are inflicted by structurally and culturally imposed oppression and exclusion from what counts in a society as acceptable living conditions. Such concern may translate into trying to understand how these problems come about and trying to change them for the better in full awareness that this will be an ongoing learning process. It may need some experience of suffering and indignation to step out of the dominant neoliberal narratives to begin to see or suspect that certain situations fly in the face of everything that we have learned to associate with social justice or equality. Adorno and Margalit, especially, have emphasized that criticizing inflicted suffering does neither need a perfect empirical understanding of its causes nor a fully developed theory of justice to be uttered in criticism: 'The requirement of eradicating all cruelty, including humiliation, does not require any moral justification in its turn, since the paradigm example of moral behaviour is behaviour that prevents cruelty. This is where justification comes to an end' (Margalit 1996, p. 88; cf. Baars 1987).

Egalitarian concern for social inequalities requires an openness to the possibility that seemingly unproblematic general rules or equal rights can become very problematic in certain situations. Equality before the law may seem to be quite straightforward as everyone whose car gets towed in a parking offence will have to pay the same fine. For a wealthy person, however, this may hardly be noticed whereas it will create a financial crisis for somebody with lesser means who had to park there in an emergency. Generally, wealthy persons tend to be less equal before the law because they can afford to have expensive law firms defend their cases in court whereas somebody who does not have the necessary resources will have no other possibility than to accept whatever pseudo-legal bullying comes their way. Such simple examples demonstrate the necessity to investigate how abstract principles function in specific contexts and how frequently returning problems may be traced back to societal structures (Baars 2012; Baars & Phillipson 2013).

The confrontation between libertarians and egalitarians typically results in an opposition of uncontextualized 'individual responsibility' or 'liberty' versus uncontextualized 'equality'. Both individual responsibility and equality have important roles to play in a democratic society but they become problematic when they remain abstract, uncontextualized principles that should be followed in deciding about claims citizens may have regarding, for instance, support or opportunities. Parfit (2002) has proposed distinguishing between three basic egalitarian values or principles that give some possibilities to opening up the abstract principle of equality to the social contexts in which it is used. The *first* principle is (strict) *equality*: it is in itself bad that some people are worse off than others. In this strict form, the principle of equality raises many questions as it comes close to saying that the goal of equality would be that everyone should be the same. As we have seen in Chapter 5, this comes close to the caricature that libertarians love to make of egalitarianism. Such a strict version of equality would indeed lead to absurd implications: as if it would be better to blind a whole population than to tolerate people among them who can see. Equality for its own sake is clearly too abstract; therefore, this basic concept needs further interpretation and contextualization, for instance in relation to empirical forms of inequality as discussed in the first three chapters. *Priority*, Parfit's *second* egalitarian principle gives more possibilities to include contextual factors: this is the principle or idea that benefiting people matters more the worse off people are. This goes a step further in recognizing inequality and why this can be an urgent problem, apart from the mere fact that people are not 'equal' in many ways. We have encountered this principle in discussing Rawls' Difference Principle and in McKerlie's priority theory of 'elderly needs'. The *third* egalitarian principle is that of *sufficiency*: no-one should fall below a certain minimum threshold. As Harry Frankfurt has put it: 'what is important from a moral point of view is not that everyone should have the same, but that everyone should have enough' (Frankfurt 1988, p. 134). This principle emphasizes the moral duty to improve the situation of the worst off to a minimal level of decent living. Below I will explore this further, connecting Sen's capability approach with citizenship rights.

It appears that all of these three egalitarian principles can be used to address social inequality over the life course. Equality, for instance, remains vital for legal and political equality such as equality before the law or equal voting rights but, as said before, this formal principle has to be put in context. Whereas prioritarian approaches emphasize the need to improve the lot of the worst off, such as giving the poorest soup and shelter, they tend to neglect the necessity to improve such situations more structurally. Sufficiency theories tend to approach inequality more broadly and insist that citizens must decide by democratic negotiation what should be made available to all citizens so that they are able to stand as equals and lead a decent life in their society. A much used but very rudimentary example of sufficient income is 60% of average income. What acceptable living conditions would be in given situations will ultimately have to be decided in a democratic political process. This does not mean that we have to wait with critical or constructive assessments until all citizens have come to a final decision. Citizens can with arguments and evidence criticize certain situations as unacceptable and propose improvements that are based on their experience and expertise. These proposals are part of a broader discussion about what acceptable living conditions might be in a society that citizens would like to call theirs. It should be noted that in the discussion about equality, priority and sufficiency, all attention tends to go to the distribution of material resources. In a later section I will continue to try to redress this imbalance and underline the basic importance of resources *and* respect, as has been done before in discussing the main sources of social inequality.

Trying to ground 'acceptable living conditions' in an ideal theory can easily block a clear view of problems that are experienced by people who live in situations that are drastically different from those who construct these theories.

If there is a lack of openness for the experiences of people in their specific situations such problems can become invisible for experts although they are a reality for disadvantaged groups. This implies the need to be open to the work of investigative journalists or to citizens who are protesting that their living situations are unacceptable or that their citizen rights are being offended. Without such mutual confrontations between theory and practice, social movements and research on social inequality will lack conceptual and argumentative clarity while consistent theories of justice or equality for all times and places will remain parallel moral universes that can be admired for their sophistication but remain isolated from the societies they are supposed to serve. Or worse: they may result in neglecting or covering up injustice or inequality because certain problematic situations don't fit or show up in their constructs.

The critical constructive approach that I am advocating has solid roots in both American pragmatism and in continental traditions of practical philosophy. The American pragmatist John Dewey has emphasized that we don't live by well established clear theories that give answers to all situations but that we only begin to think critically about our conduct when we are confronted with a problem that stops us from behaving unreflectively (Dewey 1910). This reflects our daily experience: we recognize the reality of a problem before we know how to solve it. It is even essential for our survival to acknowledge the reality of a problem, such as a fire that is breaking out, although we don't know how it started or how to put it out, but we try. We can try to improve a situation without knowing what would be 'perfect equality'; without being able to 'settle all possible claims on our conduct in all possible worlds or in the best of all possible worlds' (Anderson 2010, p. 3).

In thinking about what *kind* of inequalities would deserve critical attention one obvious starting point would be to look at what a specific society proclaims as being crucially important and what it therefore pretends or assumes to offer equally to all its citizens. In this way a critique does not apply criticism from outside but takes the ideals of a particular society seriously and uses them as criteria for critical questioning. An example would be 'equality of opportunity'.

Being stuck in the land of equal opportunity

Egalitarian thinkers have been fiercely criticized by libertarians because they are pleading for equal *outcomes* for everybody, so that hard working people and lazy profiteers would get the same, with the eventual result that no one will want to work anymore and everybody will be worse off in the end. The remedy would be equality of opportunities and this would, indeed, be realized in the US, and be the main reason for its overwhelming success in the accumulation of wealth. One of countless examples has been given by Paul Ryan, Republican speaker of the House of Representatives, in a tweet of September 2nd 2017: 'In our country, the condition of your birth does not determine the outcome of your life. This is what makes America so great.' Equality of opportunity is seen as fair, while equality of outcome – which Milton Friedman called socialism –would be unfair and not merito-cratic. Protesting social inequality would only be an easy way to avoid full commitment to the flourishing of people's potentials, leading to dependency on others, asking from them what everybody should secure for himself or herself. Therefore, social inequality would not be a problem but a blessing in disguise as it brings out the best in those who are prepared to work hard for their families and save for their well-earned retirement. Social inequality is seen as a rich source of incentives: if even the poorest people were to put their backs into it and work harder their situation would improve. Reducing social inequality would only lead to a leveling down: a situation in which a few lazy persons would be better off, but everyone else worse off. Another libertarian strategy that seemingly appeals to the 'common good' emphasizes that free markets are essential for wealth creation: the profits that are made will *eventually* benefit all citizens as they trickle down and raise all the boats.

This appeal to individual responsibility presupposes that there would be, indeed, equality of opportunities. The question of how opportunities *are* actually distributed in any given society is, however, an empirical question. We have seen evidence of how unequally opportunities are distributed even before birth, and how initial advantages and, especially, disadvantages tend to accumulate along the life course during education, working life and old age, if people live long enough to reach that at all. The assumption of 'equal opportunity', the idea that everyone can get ahead, and even become rich if they only work hard enough, has become an ideological construct that leads to self-satisfaction and self-conceit for the advantaged, and to demotivation and depression for the disadvantaged. This ideology leads to a neglect of persistent inequalities that can only become worse under the rule of familiar but ultimately divisive slogans.

There remains an impressive gap between, on the one hand, the claim of a society that it offers its citizens equal opportunities, and on the other hand the realistic or feasible opportunities that seriously disadvantaged people have to participate in society. This is a gap of social injustice and inequality that is neglected and leaped over when individuals are held responsible for their fate, because they would have failed to work hard enough to become successful. This unequal distribution of opportunities results in a mixture of formally equal citizen rights and materially unequal conditions under which these rights are put into practice. Such as the equal right of children to go to a school, but with huge inequalities between these schools and within the whole educational system in terms of material and professional resources. In spite of all good intentions of schoolteachers, this will remain a challenging reality as long as the educational system continues to play a central role in the reproduction of a severely unequal society.

Rawls tried to address the problem by developing a *fair* instead of a *formal* equality of opportunity. A *formal* equality would imply that advantaged positions would not be filled according to prejudice, nepotism or favoritism, but also not with indifference. Only relevant qualities of a candidate would count: 'those who are at the same level of talent and ability, and have the same willingness to use them, should have the same prospects of success regardless of their initial place in the social system, that is, irrespective of the income class into which they are born' (Rawls 1971, p. 73). A *fair* equality of opportunity, however, would imply that all citizens have an equal chance to *develop* the capacities to become a serious candidate for these positions. At this point Rawls warns, however, that 'It is impossible in practice to secure equal chances of achievement and culture' even for those who have the same talents because the 'willingness to use' their talents and to make an effort depend on 'happy family and social circumstances' (1971, p. 74). At least as long as the institution of the family exists this would be impossible.

Rawls capitulates too soon: he may have been afraid of authoritarian policies that would disrupt families. But giving more attention and more support for families in difficult situations does neither mean that the state would have to break down the front door and force their way into the family home nor that children from disadvantaged families would have to be separated from their parents and put in large education camps. Another option would be to give all children high quality education at all levels instead of giving them equal rights to be picked up by a school bus. There are many possibilities to support disadvantaged families, such as giving them sufficient resources: on a *Unicef* scale of indicators of national child care policies, the wealthiest country of the planet comes at place 40 out of 41. The US is the only OECD country without nationwide, statutory, paid maternity leave, although some states offer paid parental leave insurance programs to eligible workers.[2]

There is another important aspect of the principle of equal opportunity that has been largely ignored as Rawls focused primarily on the advantages that offices are supposed to bring to their occupants such as prestige, income, interesting and challenging work, while ignoring questions of justice regarding the good that occupants of higher office are supposed to do for those whom they serve (Anderson 2010). In racially pluriform societies, it is often seen as important that offices are occupied by members from different groups to distribute influential public positions or offices equally over these different groups. A crucial additional reason for such a policy would be to counteract the tendency of members of advantaged groups to be uninformed and prejudiced about the situations and problems of the disadvantaged they are also supposed to serve. The standard perspectives within their own bubbles remain easily unquestioned and uncritically supported by equally advantaged colleagues, making them less competent for office. Diversity, therefore, is important, not because ways of looking at the world would be determined by culture, race, gender or age, but because diversity gives access to informal norms and specific situational experiences that are relevant to facing social policy challenges.

The eclipse of society

Rawls was deeply concerned about what he called 'deep inequalities': inequalities arising from unequal starting positions in life. Because such deep inequalities originate from societal structures instead of individual actions he saw them as a fundamental problem for a society that he would like to understand as a fair system of social cooperation. Therefore, he was keen on addressing deep inequalities with his difference principle and, especially, with his principle of fair equality of opportunity. Putting aside the problematic way Rawls proposed to address these problems, we can still appreciate that he acknowledged social inequality as being structurally constituted and evolving over the life course with deep roots in early life.

Whereas Rawls sought to convince citizens that they would be responsible for their society as a fair system of social cooperation, the luck egalitarians focus on individual responsibility as a way to disarm the libertarian approach by incorporating its main principle in their theories of equality. This leads to a first luck egalitarian critique of Rawls: in his concern for the worst off he failed to ask whether they might be individually responsible for their dire situation. In an attempt to implement a fair theory of individual responsibility that might even silence libertarian critique, the luck egalitarians construct arguments to deny citizens crucial basic resources, going after 'the undeserving', and threaten to harm the most vulnerable. Secondly, in not making individuals responsible for their situation, Rawls failed to distinguish clearly between 'choice' and 'circumstance'. According to the peculiar interpretation of the luck egalitarians the circumstances that overrule, as bad brute luck, individual choice are grounded in nature, both inside (genetic determination) or outside (natural disasters). In this way Rawls' insight that deep inequalities develop from the very start of the life course as a result of basic societal inequalities gets discarded. One wonders, with critics such as Elizabeth Anderson (1999), what has become of egalitarian concerns for oppression and exploitation? Cohen seems to rescue these concerns as he argues that 'the primary egalitarian impulse is to extinguish the influence on distribution of both exploitation and brute luck', but he goes on to define the specific egalitarian view of exploitation as 'brute-luck-derived asset differences which skew distributive outcomes' (1989, p. 908).

These disputes illustrate the division between Rawls' egalitarianism and that of the luck egalitarians. For Rawls there is an important difference between responsibility for a shared society and responsibility for your own actions, career or family:

This conception [of justice] includes what we may call a social division of responsibility: society, the citizens as a collective body, accepts the responsibility for maintaining the equal basic liberties and fair equality of opportunity, and for providing a fair share of the other primary goods for everyone within this framework, while citizens (as individuals) and associations accept the responsibility for revising and adjusting their ends and aspirations in view of the all-purpose means they can expect, given their present and foreseeable situation.

(1999b, pp. 371, 407)

Because Rawls' primary objective is to construct a theory of social justice in terms of a cooperative system which advantages all citizens, his concern is not whether the individual is responsible for his preferences, but whether his claims can be justified to others (Blake & Risse 2008). For Rawls social justice is more than distributive justice in terms of who should have what; it is primarily about explicating a system of fair cooperation that needs adequately functioning institutions. He does not begin with an idea of individualized moral responsibility which must then be adapted to politics at a societal level; instead, he begins with a political notion of what can be justified to free and equal citizens within a system of social cooperation, after which he develops a conception of responsibility that can work within this societal system. As Rawls explains in his *Political Liberalism* (1993) a society cannot be built on individual preferences.

After the neoliberal turn we see a transition in post-Rawlsian egalitarianism from Rawls' perspective of a just society, be it of a rather functionalist, harmonistic and almost transhistorical kind, to an eclipse of society. The luck egalitarians break away from Rawls' proposal that institutions, not individuals, should absorb market risks such as unemployment, workplace accidents or a devaluation of property in a recession which puts people up with large debts. Society disappears from view as it is 'microfied', as Hagestad and Dannefer (2011) would say, into a handful of people.

To clarify his critique of theorists who plead for equality over a complete life McKerlie, for instance, uses examples of A who is prosperous and B who is miserable during one year, while the other year the roles are reversed. Or he invites us to imagine a society in which half of the population is well off and the other half badly off, while they change places every few years. Such examples are not really helpful to clarify social inequality. Philosophers of social justice may decide to leave this to the social scientists but this merely continues a situation where experts from both sides of the aisle find the others' publications irrelevant. Jonathan Wolff characterizes the luck egalitarian concept of society as follows:

Where differential conditions of production are mentioned we are given examples of individual rural entrepreneurs (the hard-working market-gardener) rather than the multi-national joint-stock company owned by a combination of other institutions managing money on behalf of investment funds, pension funds, and a small number of wealthy individuals, which is the dominant ownership pattern of modern capitalism.

(Wolff 2010, p. 338)

Cohen even suggests in his book *Why Not Socialism?* (2009) that we should organize society on camping trip principles.

Examples that are given are usually comparisons between A and B, including invitations to imagine a universe consisting of two persons. This may occasionally be useful for conceptual clarification but the problem is that, in luck egalitarian thought, examples of social inequality rarely extend beyond such comparisons between Smith and Jones. Wolff and De-Shalit (2007, pp. 10 ff.) criticize 'much of contemporary political philosophy' (especially luck egalitarianism) for its aspiration to a level of theoretical abstraction which detaches it from the empirical world. Being inspired by anti-egalitarian authors such as Nozick (1974), bizarre examples and surprising counter-examples have become popular with the result that this dominant paradigm in political philosophy has become 'oddly disengaged from the real world' (Wolff & De-Shalit 2007, p. 11). It appears that the disinterest in pressing societal problems should be compensated by constructing principles to legislate how the world should be. However, in looking away from the urgent problems that are increasingly dividing the neoliberal society luck egalitarianism has developed into an ideology in which the philosophers are not even trying to interpret the world.

The idealization of market mechanisms

This ideological role of contemporary political philosophy becomes even more embarrassing in its uncritical acclaim for markets as vehicles for social equality. At a historical moment when unregulated markets are idealized for their inherent blessings by rich elites who are shamelessly profiting from an increasingly unequal society, the luck egalitarians join them in praising the blessings of market mechanisms for their capacity to produce equal distributions. In the writings of Dworkin, the leading author of post-Rawlsian egalitarianism, there is a staggering idealization of market mechanisms, auctions and insurance. Especially insurance plays a crucial role in his thoughts because it offers opportunities to transform brute bad luck into option luck and thus into individual responsibility. According to Fleurbaey (2002) the idea that hypothetical insurance markets should play an important role in determining what equality is, grows in importance in Dworkin's later work. It remains hard to understand how insurance would produce social justice under market conditions. According to Colin Macleod (1998) one of the most problematic aspects of Dworkin's theory is his claim that 'perfect markets are intrinsic to the best interpretation of equality' and his recommendation 'that we build a theory of equality around ideal markets' (p. 224). That all citizens should buy insurance for the risks they expect to run over the life course may be the dream of those governments that would prefer to get away from public responsibilities such as education, health care or pensions. However, would this be in the interest of their citizens and, especially, would this reduce social inequalities among them?

In spite of the imagined blessings of marketed justice in Dworkin's egalitarian constructions, it is most likely that insurance companies which operate in competitive markets will try to reduce their liabilities. In cases of conflict, the burden of evidence will most probably be shifted to those who are already in vulnerable situations and unlikely to be able to afford the assistance of expensive lawyers who also work under market conditions. You don't have to be a fan of Michael Moore's *Sicko* to have doubts about the chances of victims of bad brute luck being adequately compensated if they are not able to afford effective legal assistance.

The responsibility for bad option luck ('bad choices') that is central for the luck egalitarian view on social equality over the life course implies that there will be no support for those who are *held* responsible for their situation of need. John Roemer (1993), a luck egalitarian who had, just like Jerry Cohen (1991), more reservations about the blessings of the market than Dworkin, proposed reducing assistance for health care costs to the degree that people can be held responsible for their illness. However, even in cases where the epidemiological evidence seems robust, seemingly straightforward verdicts may turn out to be complicated. People do get lung cancer without having been a smoker. There are other factors that may cause this disease such as the interaction of genetic predispositions with environmental conditions such as fine dust or otherwise polluted air. It may be better to improve the quality of the air that people have no choice but to breathe in, and to increase the taxes on tobacco. In that way the public load of health care costs of diseases, that have statistically been shown to be connected to specific lifestyles, can be reduced without moralizing approaches that offer a seemingly fair assessment of personal responsibilities but are morally problematic. Moreover, as the proposed personal assessments of individual responsibility for disease will be extremely complicated and expensive to implement, it is most likely that standardized bureaucratic procedures will take their place with all the risks that were referred to above. Every sufferer from lung cancer, or any other typical 'life style disease', may be held individually responsible for his condition.

The idealization of market mechanisms as the solution to problems of inequality goes together with a simplification and easy harmonization of their possible negative consequences. In Dworkin's theory, market risks are portrayed as relatively harmless; a kind of gambling with money that you do not really need. Dworkin actually uses the example of buying a lottery ticket to illustrate how individuals must be held responsible for the outcomes of their decisions (Dworkin 1981, p. 294). But lottery gambling is not a necessity of life: you can do this or not. And if you lose you can't lose more than the price of the ticket. The structural force of market risks are cut to the size of his idea of option luck: 'a matter of how deliberate and calculated gambles turn out – whether someone gains or loses through accepting an isolated risk he or she should have anticipated and might have declined' (Dworkin 2000, p. 73).

It is surprising to see how such a simple transaction as buying a lottery ticket, a relatively small short term risk that can precisely be determined, can be presented as an example of how prudent people should be able to manage their lives under unregulated market conditions. The decisions that people have to make in their lives with far reaching consequences over the life course are reduced to the simplicity that, if things go wrong, it must be because someone has made irresponsible choices. Dworkin appears to theorize from the perspective of somebody who has enough financial reserves not to have to worry and who can afford to take 'deliberate and calculated gambles'. It seems as if the market of option luck would be a blessing for all prudent citizens as it would filter out those who are responsible for their own misfortune. It is astonishing that those who claim to be egalitarians are so reluctant to offer protection against the downside risks of unregulated markets (Anderson 2008).

Even a welfare oriented luck egalitarian such as Richard Arneson, who doubts that the brute luck/option luck distinction can bear the weight of justifying grave inequalities, only offers a self declared impotent alternative. With his 'responsibility-catering prioritarianism' Arneson (2000a) emphasizes the crucial role of inner merit or individual authenticity in being responsible. If persons have been truly responsible and prudent, they should be compensated if things go wrong. Although he concedes that such reward according to inner merit poses insuperable epistemic obstacles and that implementing such schemes would even be disastrous, this would still be the only way to justice. As we have seen, Rawls had severe doubts about such an approach to social inequality: 'the ideas of individual deservingness and responsibility and individual well-being, even if they could be made clear in principle, cannot conceivably be measured by any institutions we could devise' (1971, p. 106). But Arneson maintains that such criticism would confuse the ultimate standard of justice with the policies that might implement it. The standard of inner merit must be used to evaluate the justice of the world, even when we are unable to put this into practice.

Those who are successful and wealthy are, however, not likely to be confronted with intense questioning of their innermost sincere intentions and actions. John Roemer (1993) even suggests classifying people into socioeconomic types, with a corresponding standard of conduct that can be reasonably expected from them, based on political estimates of the kinds of societal pressures and disadvantages they are likely to encounter and should be excused to some degree for succumbing to. In trying to avoid the *Scylla* of invading the privacy of individuals he slams into the *Charybdis* of prejudicial group stereotypes in terms of racial, ethnic, gender, or religious backgrounds. Although the luck egalitarian paradigm of social justice is supposed to develop an egalitarian perspective on social inequality it appears to be completely isolated from empirical research about this subject. This results, at best, in practically irrelevant constructs of social equality; at worst, in intellectual legitimation of neoliberal policies which promote unregulated markets and uncontextualized individual responsibility.

Justice, ageism, and the 'bottomless pit of health care'

When would health inequalities be unjust?

In confrontation with the impressive health inequalities that have been discussed above, the question arises of when do health differences become inequalities or, as it has usually been phrased: what kind of health inequalities would be unjust? An influential answer has been that health inequalities should be seen as inequitable if they are avoidable, unnecessary and unfair (Whitehead 1999). We need to be cautious not to interpret this matter in the narrow frame of individual responsibility. Such an approach may seem straightforward in holding individuals accountable for their health behavior but evades the impressive inequalities in health and life expectancies between stratified groups in society that cannot merely be seen as caused by individual irresponsibility. Most of these are primarily the results of circumstances that could be avoided or importantly improved by adequate policies: such as a lack of sufficient income, adequate housing, safe work, health care, clean water, adequate sanitation, or vaccination.

In his 2008 book *Just Health* Daniels agrees with Amartya Sen (2004) that health equity must be seen in the broader context of social justice and underlines that health is morally important because it protects the range of opportunities that are open in a given society: not being held back by disease or disability is a crucial factor in being able to participate in society. He claims, therefore, that health inequality would be unjust 'when it results from an unjust distribution of the socially controllable determinants of population health' (Daniels 2008, pp. 140, 101). To determine whether such a distribution would be just or unjust he falls back on Rawls' justice as fairness, including Rawls' preference in solving problems by constructing principles. Especially the principles of *Fair Equality of Opportunity* and the *Difference Principle* – together leading to what Rawls calls 'democratic equality' –would be decisive in determining whether distributions would be just or unjust. Daniels' question 'When are health inequalities unjust?' is answered by appealing to these abstract principles. If they were to be followed unjust inequalities would disappear: 'The residual inequalities that emerge with conformance to the principles are not a compromise with what justice ideally requires; they are acceptable as just' (Daniels 2008, p. 99).

In his further elaboration, however, Daniels emphasizes, *first*, the limited possibilities of changing or even challenging the ways in which society is actually distributing the determinants of population health, although this distribution is clearly unjust given the existence of major health inequalities. Of course, possibilities for change are always limited but the question remains how far these limitations can be stretched in a more just direction and that is an open political question; not something that can be decided on moral grounds unless one were convinced that the present situation in a society is the only one that is morally justifiable.

Moreover, Daniels appeals to the limitations of our knowledge: if we don't know how to avoid health inequalities they cannot be considered unjust. Such a judgment would depend on our understanding of basic mechanisms of health inequalities and the practical possibilities of avoiding them. One would think that Daniels had just presented a clear perspective on both as he wrote that unjust health inequality 'results from an unjust distribution of the socially controllable determinants of population health'(-Daniels 2008, pp. 140, 101). When the causal pathways and biological mechanisms behind pervasive associations between health indicators and measures of social advantage are not yet clear, the goal of equity would dictate to give high priority to research to uncover these pathways and mechanisms (Braveman et al. 2011). To illustrate his view, Daniels refers to the longer life expectancies of women compared to those of men: are they unjust? His answer is negative and he denies that this is a pressing question of justice: it would not be necessary to restrict the resources that go to women in order to reduce their life expectancies. To close the issue with such a bizarre argument presupposes that the longevity of women deserves no further attention because they are already in an excellent position as they live, on average, longer than men. This does not address the possibility that women still live much shorter than would be possible under more favorable circumstances (see Ch.3).

Secondly, in contrast to his emphasis on the limitations of knowledge, Daniels continues to work with his theory of a 'natural' and 'normal' 'age-relative opportunity range' which is not only far from modest in its pretensions but also is used to legitimate far reaching decisions. His approach to health and health care remains built on the assumption that the range of opportunities that should be made available to people is limited by the condition that such a range should be 'normal' in the sense of stage- and age-relativity. Improving population health and reducing health inequalities should strictly remain within these ranges. The goal of health care would therefore be 'protecting the age-relative opportunity range for individuals by promoting normal functioning at each stage of life' (Daniels 2008, p. 185). He insists that his application of Rawls' *Fair Equality of Opportunity* principle to health needs 'does not rectify or level all inequalities in function among people. It aims only to keep people functioning normally' (Daniels 2008, p. 58; cf. 36, 96). So, in his 2008 *Just Health* Daniels repeats the basic assumption from his 1988 book *Am I my Parents' Keeper?*: questions of justice or injustice regarding the organization of the life course can only be decided in the light of stage- and age related 'normality'. In his later book he tries to give this assumption a scientific foundation that remains, however, questionable. He assumes that fixed, biologically grounded developmental patterns determine the stages of life that all adults will go through in synchrony with their chronometric age. Certainly, processes of functional decline as people get older are a reality of human life, but such processes hardly develop according to a uniform age-related natural rhythm (see next section).

Daniels' theory of 'normal species functioning' and the 'age-relative normal opportunity range' would also make it possible for Daniels to distinguish between the *treatment* of pathology and the *enhancement* of otherwise normal traits such as trying to perfect somebody's nose or chin. 'The primary rationale ... for assisting someone medically is that we are preventing or treating a departure from normal functioning. Departure from the "natural baseline" of normal functioning is the primary eligibility condition for claiming assistance to meet health needs' (2008, p. 154).

Daniels claims that 'the prudential lifespan argument' would establish that under 'very special conditions of resource scarcity' – that remain unspecified – 'it is not unjust to ration life extending health-care resources purely by age'. He goes on to criticize 'the principle that health status, not age, is the morally relevant basis for distributing health-care resources'. (Daniels 1988, p. 98). Based on his theory of age-relative normality Daniels claims that the three stages of life strictly correspond with age groups, providing a seemingly clear hold for distributional justice over the life course. We have seen, however, that this approach to distributional justice neglects inequalities *within* the three age groups, which amounts to a drastic reduction of the problem of social justice over the life course. Moreover, it remains peculiar to build the justification of claims on 'normality'; whether this refers to what people feel to be 'normal' or to a 'natural order'. For a theory of health inequalities it may be better, at least in advanced postindustrial societies, to use the health scores of the socioeconomically most advantaged group as the reference for what would be possible for other groups as well (Braveman & Gruskin 2003; Marmot, 2010).

Thirdly, Daniels wants to guard against claims on public funds that are not necessary to maintain 'normal' functioning. Although he supports universal health care, he warns the reader to be careful and not to rush things, especially in the interest of the worst off. The admonition to restrain support of the worst off for their own good – a strange rhetorical twist – returns in several important concluding statements, such as:

> Our commitment to reducing health inequality should not require steps that threaten to make health worse off for those with less-than-equal health status. So the theoretical issue reduces to this: Would it ever be reasonable and rational for contractors to accept a trade-off in which some health inequality is allowed in order to produce some nonhealth benefits for those with the worst health prospects?
>
> (2008, p. 98)

The problematic motivation to allow health inequalities might be, however, that this situation produces nonhealth benefits for those with the best health prospects.

In Rawls' later work we can find a similar argumentative spin: he warns, for instance, that our design for a health care system should not drain resources in such a way that the overall prospects of those who are worst off are worsened further (2001, p. 173). His statement that 'economic and social inequalities are to be judged in terms of the long-run expectations of the least advantaged social group' (1978, p. 44) suggests that we should guard against the rising expectations of the worst off. This boils down to an authoritarian and patronizing attitude by which the just claims of severely disadvantaged citizens are silenced: 'You will have to wait patiently and if you want more, you will get even less…'. Similarly, Daniels begins with addressing the question 'When are health inequalities unjust?' but turns out to be primarily concerned in answering the question how health inequalities can be justified. It seems as if the sophisticated discourse of social justice must save us from foolish attempts to put an end to major health inequalities: 'Justice stops us from falling into a bottomless pit of health needs' (Daniels 2008, p. 63).

Daniels' work on health inequalities gives the impression that he sees the need to criticize health inequality which results from an unjust distribution of the socially controllable determinants of population health. However, he clearly shies away from such a criticism by constructing abstract principles, dwelling on the limitations of our knowledge (which does not prevent him from developing his theory of an 'age related opportunity range') and warning about 'limited resources' and the 'bottomless pit' of health care costs. These last two narratives have been popular for a long time and have primarily functioned as a pretext for avoiding discussing ways to improve public health and the quality of the health care system.

An ageist obsession with the 'bottomless pit' of health care costs

Rawls related justice and social inequality at least conceptually to the structure of society. Although this constitutive context is lost or left to the market in the main post-Rawlsian theories, Daniels occasionally includes societal backgrounds in his analyses. An example is his criticism of bioethics: its failure to look at the societal determinants of population health would not be a matter of conceptual rigidity or disciplinary blindness to social scientific or public health research. According to Daniels it is caused by powerful economic interests that have a profound influence on the agenda of bioethics, as the 'economic incentives to people in bioethics come largely from medicine and the scientific and policy institutions that interact with medical delivery' (2008, p. 102). Indeed, vast economic interests benefit from the conviction that health care alone can improve public health. Existential fear helps to sustain the fascination of the general public for technological developments in health care that might cure life threatening diseases and eventually even abolish death.

A simple basic pattern returns in many decision games and riddles regarding health care for older people that are presented in the *Generational Equity* and *Fair Innings* literature and, beyond that, in many bioethical publications. There is only one very costly life saving intervention available (representing anything from the arsenal of medical technology that would save a life or probably secure it for some years) but there are two or more competing candidates and the only difference between them is their age. The constructed age conflicts may be between 35 and 65, or 55 and 75, but the underlying agenda is usually that the older person should be denied treatment, and what the arguments might be to justify that. Of course, if an age could be found at which everybody would collapse into terminal decline this might make these choices easier. However, as Wicclair (1993, p. 97) states:

> even if it is the case generally that unpreventable death from natural causes of people over seventy-five or eighty is properly understood as 'an acceptable event', it does not follow that it is generally acceptable to withhold life-extending medical care from people over seventy-five or eighty. It also does not follow that it is generally improper for people over seventy-five or eighty to desire life-extending care that would enable them to continue to pursue their interests.

Whereas John Rawls had proposed a theory of justice that would protect citizens from utilitarian calculi of large-scale benefits that are carried out without considering the consequences for individual persons, Callahan and others propose utilitarian policies and seem to be proud of their firm neglect of individuals and their circumstances as soon as they have exceeded a certain age. Michael Rivlin (2000) has argued that this fixation on age, as for instance in the *Fair Innings Argument*, is superficially justified by appealing to a methodological *ceteris paribus* caveat which states that all other factors that might also be relevant are assumed to be the same and make no difference. This methodological caveat supports the superficial justification of 'age' as the decisive factor. However, as Rivlin has rightly argued, age is just one factor amongst many others because in practice all other things are never equal. Rivlin (2012) even qualifies such indifference as unethical. He illustrates his objection by the story of a doctor about an old patient 'who gazed around her cluttered poky Council Flat and mused that in her days in the Depression and the War, trodden down by a drunken husband and delinquent offspring, she never thought she would "end up in such comfort and happiness" as she was now enjoying' (p. 139). So much for age as a foundation of 'fair innings'.

Often the *Fair Innings Argument* is linked to *QALY* (*Quality Adjusted Life Year*) (cf. Williams 1997). This is probably the best known example of a series of utilitarian social choice theories that are aiming at maximal efficiency of health care resources. *QALY* is used to value a particular treatment of a person of a certain age considering its costs, the number of years that would be gained by the medical intervention, and the resulting quality of life. In principle, this approach broadens the perspective beyond age as a determinant of decisions. Algorithms such as *QALY* can still be seen as some form of egalitarian justice but the abbreviations already tell us that there is no time to lose. Of course, efficiency should be part of the considerations leading to a fair decision, but here the balance between fairness and efficiency is clearly tipping in the direction of efficiency. The many blossoming decision making algorithms such as CUA, QALY, QALE, CEA, CBA, COI or SAVE should not absorb thinking about health ethics. In applying them it is assumed that crucial assessments such as life expectancy of a particular person or the expected quality of life can be weighed rationally or even calculated precisely. This may produce impressive scientifically phrased and calculated legitimations of policies but prejudice, positive and negative evaluations of persons or the relevance of life stages can easily sneak in. Should we also allow prejudice about young people as irresponsible heavy drinkers and drug abusers who are mainly ruining their own lives and those of others? We may worry with John Harris (1985) whether *QALY* or its variations are not inevitably ageist? In the spirit of the *Fair Innings Argument* Lockwood (1988) insists that *QALY must* be ageist or otherwise face the unconstrained needs that will lead us all into the bottomless pit of health care costs. It seems that the highest form of bioethical expertise has become the capacity to make blind age-related decisions or to follow algorithms. John Harris (1985), however, denies the relevance of age in health care and holds that attacking age as a relevant criterion for distribution of health care resources may still be the best anti-ageist strategy. Against a background of wide spread ageism the fascination with highly expensive technological wonders, in combination with sophisticated algorithmic decision making, will probably have the effect of reducing health care for those older people who cannot afford expensive health insurance or to go to private clinics.

The more general inclination to gaze in admiration at new medical discoveries has its flipside in a broad concern about the costs of all these interventions that tend to draw attention away from the societal determinants of health. The tendency to regard health care as a bottomless pit, especially in the case of older people, has a long tradition in American history (cf. Fried 1978). It is kept alive not only by the *Generational Equity* advocates, but even by Dworkin who assumes, not only that a rational person would not buy life extending treatments if ill at advanced age and suffering from dementia, but also that he would decide against 'technology whose main results benefit people in relatively old age' (Dworkin 1993, p. 890). His 'rational person' is supposed to prefer buying insurance against other harms. Moreover, the young adults at Dworkin's imaginary auction have to plan for a 'complete life' of unknown length knowing that every resource that is reserved for old age cannot be used earlier in life.

> My point is rather that they would not want those additional months at the cost of the sacrifices in their earlier, vigorous life that would be necessary if they had to make that choice. They would think the money better spent, earlier, on job-training or education or investment or on something else that would benefit their lives as a whole more than just taking on a few months of very limited life at the end.
>
> (Dworkin 1993, p. 891)

Dworkin also comes up with the more general argument that over a quarter of medical expense in the US is spent on people in the last six months of their lives. 'Most young people on reflection would not think it prudent to buy insurance that could keep them alive, by expensive medical intervention, for more than four or five months at the most if they had already lived into old age' (Dworkin 2000, p. 314).

These stunning remarks deserve some critical comments. *First*, the last six months of someone's life are not strictly age-related: they may take place at any age. *Second*, many older people who experience a more or less prolonged terminal phase have been quite healthy for decades during which their health insurance premiums continued to be paid. The expenses during the 'last six months of their lives' may be a dent in the accumulated profits of health insurance corporations but hardly amount to a moral argument. *Third*, Dworkin's argumentation betrays a drastic ageist devaluation of 'old age'. According to age-related definitions of 'old age' this verdict would apply to everyone who has lived around 65 years or even shorter. This is relatively young compared to contemporary life expectancies in developed countries and betrays little appreciation for the worth and dignity of life in 'old age'. Moreover, the outcome of medical interventions is not always predictable; in some cases people die soon after having undergone an expensive medical intervention, in other cases they may have still decades of vitality before them. The doctrine of *Complete Life Egalitarianism* dominates Dworkin's approach to aging, prescribing that budgets should be fixed by young adults for their 'complete lives' while reproducing ageist denigration of the value of their future lives in 'old age'. Expensive medical interventions should not take place 'at the cost of sacrifices in their earlier, vigorous life'. He even plays the libertarian card of defending individual freedom: it would be 'a disservice to justice to force everyone to have such insurance through a mandatory scheme' (Dworkin 2000, p. 314ff.). This priority of a 'vigorous life' implies not only a demeaning of disabled life but also that an important, possibly very long phase of later life is reduced to a residual affair. To put it as crudely as the practical implications of such a policy would be: after having reached the expiration date of 'old age' people should be disposed of as soon as they become costly. Insofar as Dworkin's constructions are an ethical blueprint for an equal society this is very concerning: such an ideal society should heavily cut down resources for those who have already lived into old age. They would merely represent a bottomless pit of health care costs. Such reductions would, again, not hit the wealthy, who can take care of themselves by buying the necessary services, but the most vulnerable.

According to a more generally shared argument the main road into the bottomless pit of health care costs would be expensive, life extending interventions. To argue against this makes sense in terminal situations (that may arise at any age) when medical treatment continues to be delivered without any realistic perspective on improvement (Baars 2017). In such a case it becomes urgent to face and accept the finitude of life but health care in the 'life stage' of 'old age', that may last four decades or more, is not only confronted with such terminal situations.

The bottomless pit argument regarding healthcare is also built on the claim that it would be irresponsible to spend 'limitless amounts' on health care to reduce health inequalities while society has to spend its limited resources also on such things as education, the military, libraries, transportation infrastructure, or recreation. Indeed, resources are per definition finite and a just society must provide for more than health care, but delivering good quality universal health does not imply having to spend such extreme amounts of money per capita as the US does with results that are worse than those of much poorer countries. Daniels seemed to agree, by the way, with this last diagnosis in the volume he produced with Bruce Kennedy and Ichiro Kawachi (2000). There is no evidence that countries that do have universal health care don't sustain an active and productive workforce, that they stop educating children and adults, don't have publicly supported theatres and public libraries, or don't provide for retirement. The *Generational Equity* hawks appear to have highjacked the social justice debate about aging: it has predominantly become a debate about 'infinite' resources being spent on some 'thing' as residual, meaningless and irrelevant as older people.

The 'bottomless pit argument' focuses all attention on health care costs, avoiding the social inequalities that are behind the inequalities in health and life expectancies. Although the demographic pressure of the aging population in the US is relatively light it does pose major challenges; so, there are policy choices to make and these are exactly what matters. To suggest, however, that society as we know it will disappear in a black hole of public health care costs does not help to open the necessary discussion. Moreover, the bottomless pit argument presupposes that the only way to improve population health would be to spend 'unlimited amounts' on health care. The research on societal determinants of health demonstrates that we need a broader perspective of the factors that constitute social inequality in a broad sense (see Ch.3).

Speaking of a 'bottomless pit': Michael Marmot (2010) has presented some rather straightforward calculations of the avoidable human and economic costs that are the consequences of the differences in health and life expectancies of a population, in this case England, with a population that is six times smaller than that of the US (cf. for the US Preston & Vierboom 2021).

1   If the mortality rates of all classes in the working age group of 30–59 years had been the same as those of the 'higher managerial and professional' class in England and Wales in 2003, around 67,000 fewer deaths in this age group would have taken place and a total of 2.3 million years of life potentially saved.

2   A similar analysis of mortality can be based on educational qualification: if the mortality level of all people were the same as for those with degree-level qualifications, 202,000 premature deaths would be avoided at ages 30 and over each year and 2.6 million years of life potentially saved for England.

3   The third estimate focuses on the quality of neighborhoods: the extra years that would be lived if all those born in 2010 experienced the current death rates of the 10 percent of least deprived areas (1.3 million years) or if everyone currently alive experienced these more favorable death rates (98 million extra years).

4   If all those born in 2010 experienced the current rates of illness, disability and death seen in the 10 percent of least deprived areas they would enjoy some 4.1 million extra years of healthy life. The comparable gain for everyone currently alive is 285 million years of healthy life.

5   By comparing the current situation, with its considerable levels of inequality, with one in which everyone had the same health outcomes as the richest 10 percent of the population in England, it is estimated that there are currently productivity losses of £31–33 billion per year, while lost taxes and higher welfare payments would amount to £20–32 billion per year.

6   Direct NHS healthcare costs in England associated with treating the consequences of inequality amount to £5.5 billion per year for treating illness and mental illness and prescriptions. These activities represent

approximately one third of the NHS budget and the full impact of health inequalities on direct healthcare costs is considerably greater than this.

7   Inequalities in obesity currently cost £2 billion per year, predicted to rise to nearly £5 billion per year in 2025.

The 'bottomless pit' argument appears to be dominant not only in explicitly ageist perspectives on *Generational Equity* or the *Fair Innings Argument* but also in more reflected egalitarian perspectives on social justice and aging. Obviously, the extreme health care costs in the US are a legitimate concern, especially in relation to its poor outcomes. But the interpretation that growing health care costs would be caused by treating older people with expensive but fruitless life extending technology and, especially, to conclude that access to health care should be restricted for older people is problematically shortsighted. This interpretation neglects not only the profit oriented organization of health care in a broad sense, including Big Pharma and other sectors, that are clearly interested in maximizing returns and profits (see Ch.2). It also reproduces stereotypes or narratives about older people that are inadequate and denigrating.

Predominant among these appears to be the assumption that spending major sums of money on older people is a waste because such practices keep old, unproductive people alive although they are going to die anyway. While the last remark points to the ultimate certainty for all people, regardless of their ages, it has become an easy excuse for those who should be held accountable for the death of many older people in challenging situations such as the Chicago Heat wave or the Covid-19 pandemic. In a historical perspective the idea that those who are officially defined as 'old' are frail and struggle with bad health can be seen as a residue of the deplorable situation of older people during the early stages of national retirement policies in the late 19th and early 20th century. A window on the way in which old age was seen in Bismarck's Germany at the time of the first national pensions can be found in Jacob Grimm's 1860 speech about old age. He emphasized that old people should be grateful to have reached this stage, looking back in silent melancholy on their lives, as they sit quietly on a bench in the soft evening sun (Baars & Dohmen, forthcoming). Such images of older people, in which their participation in society is reduced to sitting on a bench and being cared for, still appear to be widely held.

In these stereotypes 'old age' figures as a stage of life without internal differentiation in terms of, for instance, class, gender or race. What appears to unify these people is that they are 'old'. Of course, the finitude and increasing vulnerability of life must be accepted as part of our 'interhuman condition' (Baars 2012). But there is no reason to continue to entertain the idea of a homogeneous 'old age' that is filled with nostalgia, chronic disease or disability. Although there has been some stagnation and even decline of health expectancies during the last years, presently many citizens from developed countries live much longer than their ancestors in the 19th and early 20th century (Oeppen & Vaupel 2000). It has often been observed that older people are extremely diverse. But we should be cautious to interpret this diversity as the result of a life stage of autonomous choice that is only limited by the finitude of life. From life course research we can learn that inequality within each birth cohort becomes stronger as the cohort members get older (Dannefer 2022). As we have seen, social inequalities lead to health inequalities, including dramatically unequal chances to live long and relatively healthy lives.

Another problem that results from the assumption that 'old age' is a brief residual phase of life is that little thought has been given to the opportunities older people have to participate in society. Some decades into the 21st century there is still too little attention to the opportunities of older people; moreover, whatever respect for them that may have existed has largely been lost in an idealizing commodification of what is 'young' and 'new' (see Ch.4). Age related restrictions of opportunities conflict with older people's social needs, abilities and interests. Although they are labeled as 'old' because they have lived beyond a certain age, they can still live for some decades and to deny them opportunities to participate in society is to leave them to boredom, meaninglessness or a 'sick role'. Opening up opportunities for older people requires foremost that they are respected as equal citizens. Besides their intrinsic worth as a person with interests and activities they should also be encouraged and welcomed to share their experience, expertise and memories. A great diversity and creativity of life styles demonstrate that many older people are not held back by conventions surrounding 'old age' but also that they are not mere pawns in a political economic field of power (Gilleard & Higgs 2000). Such emphasis on pluralization, however, has to be balanced with an analysis of the underlying social inequalities (Formosa & Higgs 2015; Hyde & Higgs 2016).

Participation in society should not be identified with entrepreneurial activities or employment but should also not exclude these, enlarging the possibilities of doing work that is materially rewarding and personally gratifying. Regarding work and retirement it appears necessary to find a better balance between policies that may be intended to protect but also have restrictive implications on the one hand and exposing older people to the free play of the labor market on the other hand. In some countries of the EU retirement is still mandatory which protects those who have become unable to work but for others presents the problem that they have to retire from work at relatively young ages. Much of their productive potential is lost while they run the risk of being unable to build up sufficient retirement income. Moreover, they are prematurely excluded from the central domains of society and from interactions with younger people outside their families. The US, by contrast, had early laws against age discrimination, but many senior citizens have to work as long as they possibly can because otherwise they wouldn't have sufficient income.

The neoliberal exploitation of the 'dependency ratio' between 'the young' and 'the old'

It appears that the debates about social justice over the life course have become dominated by concerns about towering pressures on 'the young' because the public burden of 'the old' would become unbearable. This diagnosis follows the way in which most early pension systems have been developed: taxes on young workers finance the pensions of older people. In many countries workers' incomes are still taxed according to this so-called *Pay As You Go* system. But even when they are not, and the distribution of health care or pensions has largely been left to markets, the problems of aging populations still tend to be diagnosed in terms of a dependency ratio, with the productive adult population on one side and older people as their burden on the other side. This dependency ratio has been rising as a result of lowering birth rates leading to relatively large proportions of older people in comparison to the numbers of younger adults.

Although there are hardly sustainable alternatives to population aging this does pose serious challenges for societies. But to continue to portray these developments in terms of unbearable dependency ratios is inadequate and ideologically biased. Demographic reports need to be seen in relation to the structural changes in productivity, the generation of wealth and the distribution of income during the last four decades. Although corporation profits and returns on capital have risen since the neoliberal turn and income from labor has stagnated, the usual parameters of discussions about the social contract between 'generations' have remained the same. Dependency rates are still calculated in terms of a relation between the active or working population and the older population, while tax reductions or even tax evasions have become common practice for corporations in a neoliberal race to the bottom. Given this situation, it would make sense to increase the taxes on the excessive profits that are being generated by multinational corporations, strengthening the public resources that are necessary to maintain and improve the social and moral infrastructure of the life course. Of course, the opposite has happened as neoliberal policies have been embraced by most governments of developed countries and supported by transnational agents such as the OECD (1988a, 1988b) or the World Bank (1994). Most governments have been cutting back on care and support for vulnerable groups and have drastically reduced the entitlements of senior citizens, such as public pensions.

The bitter irony of the neoliberal exploitation of the 'dependency rate' is that such policies suggest protecting the working population from being overwhelmed and exhausted by a gray tsunami of older people. This diverts attention away from the fact that the pressure on the working population has been intensified with each reduction of their social rights and pensions so that the bottom 50% of the working population is pressed into chronic precarious situations. Such policies may properly be called 'neoliberal' as they transfer problems that are generated at a structural or population level to 'the individual', neglecting the unequal positions and opportunities of different groups of individuals.

It is astonishing to watch how a broad variety of problems, such as mounting health care costs, pensions or even a pandemic, continue to be framed as a conflict between 'the young' and 'the old'. However, as we have seen in the *Generational Equity* debates, the complaints about the tsunami of expensive redundant older people did not lead to supporting the children who were so dramatically portrayed as victims of the older population. It appears that the political target has been to reduce entitlements, health care and other expenditure on older people; a strategy that will hit especially the disadvantaged among them as the wealthy will find their way in the market. Daniels tried to appease these debates by pointing out that the interests of the young and the old are not opposed; they boil down to differences between life stages. I have argued against this view because the supposed homogeneity of 'the young' and 'the old' breaks down when confronted with major inequalities which begin in early life and tend to continue, given the decline of upward social mobility.

The problem is that deep inequalities tend to grow as cohorts get older, leading to increasing health inequalities as these processes interact with aging processes in a broad sense. The generalizing assumption that problems in later life occur because people have become 'old' hides these constitutive inequalities. That life expectancies have continued to rise, until recently, may add pressure to the dependency ratio but also increases the opportunities of older people to continue to participate in their societies. Moreover, the empirical evidence, for instance on the 'social gradient' that has been discussed in Chapter 2, has shown that stratified resources and respect have a much stronger impact on health than health care. So the 'bottomless pit' argument of health care costs begins at the wrong end of the causation and hits especially disadvantaged citizens while at the same time neglecting the possibilities of developing their potential so that the burden of health care costs becomes much bigger by focusing on the effects rather than the causes. If conditions were to be improved over the life course this would not only be beneficial for individual citizens but also for society by lowering the burden of disease in a population and, consequently, also the collective costs of health care. Especially the selective mortality of relatively young adults with a high productive potential, together with many years of chronic health problems or disability lead to an impressive loss for society, both in human and economic perspectives.

Naturalization: reframing of socially generated problems as 'natural'

> 'Nature and teaching are nearly alike. For teaching also reforms the person, and by reforming it produces a nature'
>
> Democritus (died 370 BC)

Arguments about the 'bottomless pit' of health care costs for 'old age' have much to do with traditional but inadequate ideas about the 'natural' stages of human life. Such naturalization of socially constituted problems is a popular way to gloss over profoundly problematic societal developments. It is even a common phenomenon in social scientific research, especially on subjects such as development, age and aging (Dannefer 2022). The millennia old philosophical idea that education or customs create a 'second nature' was applied to society by the post-Hegelians of the 19th century. Critical theorists of society such as Marx, Lukács and Adorno have argued that the forces dominating society have been falsely interpreted as 'natural' ('naturwüchsig') and not criticized on the basis of an understanding of their social origins (Baars 1987). This critical idea has been used to interrogate ideologies that existing situations or practices are 'natural' and therefore impossible to change (Baars 1991; Dannefer 2022).

The naturalization of social inequality has been known to exist in many societies: strangers, people with disabilities, people of different color or sexual orientation and even women have often been – and too often still are – regarded as naturally inferior. Their supposedly inferior nature served to legitimate discriminatory practices: because innate characteristics do not change there is nothing wrong with keeping everybody 'in their proper place'. On the contrary, this would lead to more harmony in society as such social relations would be more in tune with the way they were meant to be according to an 'original natural order'. These practices appealed to seemingly self-evident feelings and the 'foundation' of the assumed inferiority in natural causes usually tolerates little questioning.

Such naturalizing ideas and practices have left brutal scars in the lives of Jews, Blacks or Native Americans. But women or gay people have also been receiving their unfair share and even poor or less successful people have been seen as naturally lacking in talent, ambition, energy or effort. This naturalization of social inequality is a cultural strategy of responding to diversity that is used by dominant groups to turn differences between people into oppressive hierarchies. The ideological effect is that its structural and cultural sources disappear behind natural metaphors so that the processes that actually constitute discrimination are hidden from sight.

Since the discovery of the human genome an important contemporary form of naturalization has been to reframe socially constituted problems, such as depression resulting from chronic unemployment or ageist exclusion, as caused by the genetic constitution of the individual. As if biological programs operated independently of social contexts. Such reframing has proven to be efficient and profitable (in the short run) through pharmaceutical interventions. Prescribing drugs saves time and it is most profitable for Big Pharma, enlarging and extending its power over professionals and professional organizations. Meanwhile, attention is diverted away from the actual causes to the individual who will be charged if she or he seeks treatment or has already become dependent on medical pit-stop services.

The naturalizing reframing serves the interests of dominant societal forces. It has the effect of hiding basic societal problems that should be acknowledged as public responsibilities. This means that modifiable pathogenic social circumstances are ignored, kept intact or allowed to expand. Both their causes and their consequences are privatized and shifted to individuals, especially to those who are hardest hit by them. As a by product the powerful enterprise of pharmaceutical pit stop services has created a self destructive culture of using drugs to try to change one's situation. It looks like a conditioned response when the problems are, again, reframed as those of the individual users, spending billions in going after them with great force, boosting the profits and power of the drug lords, while trying to satisfy moral prejudice without even facing the underlying problems.

A strong example of the ways in which ageist naturalization has been used by authorities to evade their responsibility can be found in the events surrounding the Chicago *Heat Wave* of 1995. In the few days between the 14th and 20th of July 740 people died and, as citizens began to ask questions, authorities began to spin away their responsibilities. In his 'social autopsy' of this public disaster Eric Klinenberg (2002) distinguished a few phases. The first phase was to deny that there was any problem but as the frenzied *Cook County Morgue* got overburdened with hundreds of dead bodies and its parking lot filled up with refrigerated trucks containing even more corpses, the media inevitably began to inform the public about the ongoing catastrophe. The official narrative then turned to naturalization: the people who died 'were about to die anyway'; a characterization of older people that has remained popular among authorities during the Covid-19 pandemic in their urge to rid themselves of their responsibilities in case of death by neglect. However, mortality rates did not drop below normal in the following months which would have been the case if it had been a matter of accelerated dying.

For those cases where this explanation was not convincing the strategy was to make the victims responsible: those who died would have rejected any help and chose to neglect themselves. Consequently, the 80 people strong evaluation task force from the US *Centers for Disease Control and Prevention* focused their investigation on the '*personal* characteristics that proved most consequential during the catastrophe' (p. 79). The half truth that there had been victims from all over the city and from every social class was used to cover up the fact that most of the dead had been people from the poor black South Side. That the *Heat Wave* deaths were also caused by austerity cuts on programs to help the poor with their energy costs and by a drastic reduction of the city's social workers who might have reached out to isolated people was conveniently hidden. The Mayor ordered an inquiry by a *'Commission on Extreme Weather Conditions'*; a title that invites the interpretation that social processes and public responsibilities were evaded again by pointing to the *force majeure* of being hit by an overwhelming natural disaster. This pattern of evasion of responsibility has, alas, been observed in other disasters such as Katrina and has become typical for many approaches to the Covid-19 pandemic.

Throughout history cultures have differed in their respect for older people but usually the disadvantaged, poor or disabled among them have not been treated well. Generally the status of older people in Western societies has been precarious, even in historic societies with strong gerontocratic elements such as ancient Greece and Rome (Troyansky 2015; Parkin 2003). The discussions on the apocalyptic burden of aging populations by the advocates of *Generational Equity* or *Fair Innings* demonstrate that the status of older people is increasingly under threat. In the wealthiest country of the world people above a certain age are bluntly told that their lives are behind them and that they should ready themselves to die because they would be taking resources away from children who are unable to vote. Older people are positioned outside society, as if they don't belong there any longer; their only connection with society is that they are its burden.

'Old Age': a homogeneous and residual stage of life?

As we have seen, leading egalitarian theorists of social justice have approached the life course as a constellation of three life stages. This is a forceful reduction of, especially, 'old age' as it is the longest, the most differentiated and the most unequal of the three 'stages', if we want to use these terms at all. To regard aging as a natural process which takes place in stages that are basically the same for everyone neglects the diversity and social inequality that co-constitute aging processes.

Contemporary ageism preferably uses demographic projections of the costs of an aging population to demonstrate that older people are a fatal burden to society. That life expectancies for the wealthy part of the US population have been rising rapidly over the last decades is not seen as a challenge to improve the living conditions of those citizens who have remained behind. In a strange rhetorical spin this is seen as a danger to society because a life stage that is seen as *residual* and redundant would become longer and longer because 'unnaturally' prolonged through expensive medical interventions that would be paid for by the young. The *Generational Equity* advocates indulge in a negative naturalization of aging as a hopeless decline so that for older people medical interventions would be futile: leading into a bottomless pit of senseless public expense. The bitter irony of this narrative is that relatively long healthy lives and expensive medical technologies have mainly remained privileges of the wealthy, so that the proposed reductions of public funds for the older population will hit especially those who have been disadvantaged all along.

Egalitarian theorists of social justice such as Dworkin or Daniels don't use the populist and overtly abusive ageist phraseology some advocates of *Generational Equity* or the *Fair Innings Argument* indulge in. Their ideas, however, also show important 'blind spots' regarding aging and one of them is the widespread idea that living is a process that leads to a rather uniform stage of 'old age' that is characterized by an age-relative 'normal' decline. While we all have to face a certain death, aging over the life course – as has been documented extensively in earlier chapters – is an extremely unequal process resulting in major health inequalities. Although these egalitarians might be expected to criticize social inequality, these structural processes and their culmination along the life course into old age remain out of sight.

For Dworkin and other luck egalitarians the life course consists of a first stage of inequality that could and should be equalized at the beginning of adulthood inaugurating the second stage of life in which citizens will be responsible for their own 'option luck'. In Chapter 6 I already discussed the naturalization of the inequalities of the first stage of life that should be compensated for by the equalizing auction at the beginning of adulthood. And the bad brute luck that the young adults should insure themselves against is again supposed to come merely from natural disasters, both outside and inside humans: floods, hurricanes and lightning as well as inborn disabilities or lack of marketable talents. Identifying all bad brute luck as caused by natural disasters hides the structural dynamics that may play a prominent role in them.

After the second stage of life there is 'old age'. Dworkin states that he does not expect that most young people would think it prudent 'to buy insurance that could keep them alive, by expensive medical intervention, for more than four or five months at the most if they had already lived into old age' (Dworkin 2000, p. 314). In other words: it would be foolish to invest in old age: the life time budget would be better spent on 'normal' adulthood than on this useless and residual stage of life. He basically identifies being ill in old age with being demented or terminally ill so that a few extra months would merely be an extension of senseless suffering that could only be bought at disproportionately high costs. This hides from sight that 'old age' may last as long as 'normal adulthood' and that the chances to live long and healthy are strongly influenced by cultural and structural inequalities. These inequalities are hidden from a perspective on the life course that pretends to be egalitarian but uses naturalizing perspectives that cover up structural causes of social inequality.

Probably, Dworkin did not think very much about old age so he just reproduced common ageist prejudice. By contrast, Daniels has devoted much attention to 'old age' and 'the elderly'. In a short autobiographical reflection Daniels (2009) stated that

> My initial goal in addressing questions of intergenerational justice was to rescue my opportunity-based account from the charge that it was age-biased (aren't the opportunities of older people in their past? If so, shouldn't we give less weight to meeting their health needs?)
>
> (p. 39)

However, in spite of his intentions to develop a theory that would be free from the charge of being age-biased he has introduced another form of age bias: a division of the life course in three stages resulting in broad generalizations about 'old age' as a uniform stage of life. This assumed homogeneity, however, is contradicted by increasing inequalities among those who would inhabit this age stage.

Daniels has claimed that the concept of 'age relativity' which plays a crucial role in his theory, has a solid scientific foundation. To answer the question what 'age-relativity' would mean for a phase of life that can be as long and differentiated as 'old age', Daniels seeks help in the biomedical sciences. He criticizes the broad definition of the WHO according to which health is 'a state of complete physical, mental, and social well-being or happiness, and not merely the absence of disease or infirmity' and argues that more biomedical 'conceptual narrowness' is required. Surprisingly, this leads to a definition of health as 'normal functioning for our species' (p. 37) which does not seem less broad.

For more precision he refers to studies of pathology: 'Health needs are objectively ascribable ... since we can ultimately rely on the scientific methods of the biomedical sciences to characterize pathology, as well as on our growing understanding of epidemiology, including social epidemiology, to clarify what we need to function normally' (p. 37). The 'non-normative (naturalistic) distinction between normal functioning and pathology' would make it possible that disputes about it can generally be resolved by the publicly accessible methods of the biomedical sciences' (p. 42). So, 'normal species functioning', Daniels' reference point to define health or departures from it, would be 'as objective and value-free as the biomedical sciences themselves' (p. 38) and allow 'avoidance of all normative judgments in identifying departures from normal functioning' (p. 38). These claims are built on the assumption that a clear definition of 'normal functioning for our species' for all times and places is possible; which seems unlikely. Moreover, such a scale of normal functioning for subsequent ages would include acceptable age-relative degrees of 'pathology'. It remains unclear how this could lead to the desired outcome: a basis for the precise assessment of 'age relativity' in the face of the impressive differences in health between persons with the same age. Apart from sound objections against these theoretical constructions it must be feared that their practical outcome would be that materially disadvantaged older people would have to content themselves with supposedly 'normal' forms of pathology, whereas the more advantaged will be able to get treatment whatever their age might be.

Daniels puts his trust also in scientific models such as the *Diagnostic and Statistical Manual of Mental Disorders* (p. 153). This in spite of all critical discussions of subsequent DSM versions that have proven far from value free in, for instance, approaches to homosexuality or in the 'presumption that all aspects and forms of suffering encountered late in life represent inevitable manifestations of the decline of aging' (Douthit 2006, p. 177). In spite of reasserting his claims it remains unclear how he might be backing them up.

As discussed above, Daniels has given much attention to 'health inequities', especially of gender and race (2008, p. 300ff.), but this has not changed his perspective on aging as a process of going through more or less homogeneous age-related stages. He transforms Rawls' assumption that all citizens would be 'fully functional over a complete life' (Rawls 1985, p. 234) into the assumption that all are aging according to 'natural' stages of life. The prudential contractors in Daniels' original situation are assumed to operate from a point where they can see beyond the uncertainties of future developments as their knowledge would be firmly grounded in unchanging natural cycles. The contractors do not know how old they might be in the hypothetical just society but they have no doubt regarding the distinctions between life stages. In that way Daniels tries to secure a natural, quasi transhistorical hold in the idea that aging is a process of going though natural 'stages' and that 'generations' follow each other but remain basically the same, as different cohorts subsequently flow through these stages. The next step is to suggest a prudent distribution of resources over stages of life that would respect the inherent differences between them so that the quality of complete lives would be maximized. According to his view of *Complete Life Egalitarianism* the life course would be a repetitive natural phenomenon, that can be overseen as a whole; much like Callahan's appeal to a 'natural life span'.

The 'stages' of human life that figure in the works of Callahan, McKerlie, Dworkin and Daniels are supposed to refer to objective differences between temporal parts of human lives that are age-related and grounded in nature. Without much reflection they reproduce conventional ideas and folklore about the 'stages' of life. From the early origins of Western civilization human life has been seen as an invariant sequence of life stages. In many cultures, we can find an interpretation of the universe as a harmonious and repetitive *cosmos* that is not only meaningfully connected with social formations such as families or social hierarchies, but also with rhythms of nature and the stages of a human life (Baars 2012). Stages of life are part of many pre-modern narratives or theories of the world that presuppose a fundamental *Logos*, as Heraclitus or the Stoic philosophers would call it: a harmonious order underlying the repetitive movements of the cosmos. In this context the human life cycle may be interpreted as deriving its meanings, for instance, from the influence of the planets as we see in the work of Ptolemy (Burrow 1986; Sears 1986). It is still a part of popular culture to compare stages of life with 'the seasons', especially the seasons of the Global North.

The stage theories that we encounter in the work of contemporary egalitarians fall back behind the level of research that we find, for instance in Rowntree's more than 120 years old study *Poverty. A Study of Town Life* (1901). Rowntree was faced with a similar neglect of poor and older people in his hometown York as we see in contemporary society with its idolization of success and fortune. For many of the inhabitants of York 'old age' was identical with poverty and misery without any perspective that this might change for the better. Meanwhile, provisions for old age such as pensions, Social Security or Medicare have improved the lives of most older people in Western societies; a sign that such policies can be effective. Nevertheless, easy phrases such as 'Old age comes with problems' have continued to be used to cover up the many problems older people are faced with that have nothing to do with aging processes per se. Such traditional folklore is still widely used to legitimize the idea that 'old age' is a residual 'stage' of life so that it would be useless and therefore, irresponsible to invest time, energy and money to try to help older people. Against such naturalization of poverty and misery Rowntree decided that he would 'throw some light upon the conditions which govern the life of the wage-earning classes in provincial towns, and especially upon the problem of poverty' (1901, p. vii). In his later work *The Human Needs of Labour* (1918) he summarized some of his findings in the form of a life cycle theory which represented the stages or 'periods' as he called them, that workers would go through:

> The life of a labourer is marked by five alternating periods of want and comparative plenty. During early childhood, unless his father is a skilled worker, he probably will be in poverty; this will last until he, or some of his brothers or sisters, begin to earn money and thus augment their father's wage sufficiently to raise the family above the poverty line. Then follows the period during which he is earning money and living under his parent's roof; for some portion of this period he will be earning more money than is required for lodging, food, and clothes. This is his chance to save money. If he has saved enough to pay for furnishing a cottage, this period of comparative prosperity may

continue after marriage until he has two or three children, when poverty will again overtake him. This period of poverty will last perhaps for ten years, i.e. until the first child is fourteen years old and begins to earn wages; but if there are more than three children it may last longer. While the children are earning, and before they leave home to marry, the man enjoys another period of prosperity – possibly, however, only to sink back again into poverty when his children have married and left him, and he himself is too old to work, for his income has never permitted his saving enough for him and his wife to live upon for more than a very short time. A labourer is thus in poverty, and therefore underfed – (a) in childhood – when his constitution is being built up; (b) in early middle life – when he should be in his prime; (c) in old age.

(Glennerster 2004, p. 24)

For many of the most disadvantaged citizens in the US this basic diagnosis still appears to be valid. Rowntree, however, insisted that these empirically existing 'periods' of poverty from childhood to 'old age' could be expected to materialize in the lives of 'labourers' because of their position in society. These periods would not be found in the lives of more advantaged people such as skilled workers. The typical circumstances of the 'labourers' were caused by extremely low – a contemporary economist might say 'market conform' – wages and by abandonment of poor older people in their misery. As he investigated the causes of poverty he was struck by their structural origin and consequently opposed the dominant view that the poor were responsible for their own plight or that such life cycles of poverty were natural for those born from poor working parents.

Another more recent example of the idea that even 'normal' adult life is determined by subsequent natural stages can be found in the popular book *The Seasons of a Man's Life* (1978) – translated into many languages – by the well-known psychologist Daniel Levinson in which he claimed to be able to develop a universal model of life stages on the basis of 40 interviews with American citizens (cf. Dannefer 1984). Following the international success of this book Levinson published later *The Seasons of a Woman's Life* (1994) built on a slightly broader basis of 45 interviews. For men, Levinson distinguished ten quasi natural 'Seasons of Life' in adulthood, beginning with the 'early adult transition' at the age of 22 and ending with the onset of 'late adulthood' at the age of 65 years. This last season is characterized by an absence of any development: it consists of accepting that one has become old including the stereotypes that come with this status such as being preoccupied with socially irrelevant personal pleasures.

Note that these stages of life – in contrast to Rowntree's theory – are supposed to be valid, in an empirical and normative sense, for all people. This is different from more personal 'phases' that people may construct as part of their biographies, where life events such as meeting partners, marriage, work, major illness, and death of a parent or partner usually play a major role. Such life events can be planned by the person concerned as in marriage or migration; they can be caused by tragic events but they can also have structural causes such as involuntary long term unemployment in economic recessions or as a result of outsourcing production. In contemporary developed societies an individual may go through diverse subsequent or overlapping phases such as a short or very long formal education, followed by work/career, marriage, parenthood, widowhood, grandparenthood, retirement, marriage, education, second career and retirement, without diminishing the quality of such a life as unnatural, abnormal or less worthy in a moral sense. Such phases undermine especially the distinction between the second stage of 'normal' adulthood and the third stage of 'old age'. To get a grip on this unclarity 'midlife' and its proverbial innate 'crisis' have become popular since the term was launched in the 1960s. Midlife would be characterized by feelings of depression, remorse, and anxiety, or the desire to display youthfulness and make drastic life style changes that would be not be in harmony with the natural wisdom and acceptance of the older person who has already been growing inside. However, according to studies on midlife crises such as Vaillant's (2012) 75-year longitudinal study on adult development midlife crises are actually rare experiences (cf. Lachman &Boone James 1997; Brim, Ryff &Kessler 2004). Rather than being caused by an innate inner crisis the years that precede the relative protection of Social Security and Medicare are vulnerable for socially generated crises such as 'older worker' unemployment, welfare retrenchment, production outsourcing, corporate layoffs or being dependent on insecure gigs. To inform people that structurally generated feelings of insecurity and abandonment should be accepted as resulting from an innate midlife crisis is just another way of shifting what should be a public burden to disadvantaged citizens.

In stage theories about 'old age' it is usually assumed that active life is completed when people have become 'old' which is usually set around 60 or 65 years. From that moment on, the active development of those old people is assumed to have stopped: they would naturally 'disengage' from society (Cumming & Henry 1961; cf. Baars 2012). Since the late 1960s, however, the idea that characteristics of older adults would be fixed and unlikely to change has been increasingly questioned, for instance by research from the 'life span perspective in developmental psychology' inspired by authors such as Paul Baltes and Warner Schaie. Their pioneering research has suggested that personal agency and environmental influences, rather than early life experiences, continue to have strong effects on adult characteristics. Moreover, they emphasize that consequences of early developmental experiences can be transformed by later experiences, and that the course of development remains malleable into old age. These findings form the basis for their thesis of the 'plasticity of old age' in the context of a lifelong process of psychological development (Baltes, Lindenberger &Staudinger 1998). In the light of this research paradigm, adulthood cannot be divided in a short vital and flexible young adulthood on the one hand, and a decades long stage of rigid 'old age'on the other. Rather, adulthood remains a long process of change that extends even into the terminal phase of life. Such malleability is, of course, also open to and possibly limited by the forces of social inequality.

In contrast, prominent thinkers about social justice and aging cling to rudimentary stage theories. Daniels has subtitled his book about aging *An Essay On Justice Between the Young and the Old* (1988); McKerlie's book is called *Justice between the Young and the Old* (2013). There is ample reason to doubt that such contrasts are helpful in addressing the changes that take place along the life course. In contemporary Western societies, being defined as 'old' or 'older worker' often begins when people 'turn fifty'; this definition has even been reproduced by organizations such as the AARP or their European equivalents that claim to represent the interests of older people. So, being a so-called normal adult may last for about 30 years, while being regarded as 'old' may take 50 years and even more. This is almost twice as long as being a 'normal' adult, and nevertheless this long period is still called, in stark generalizing terms, 'being old' or 'old age' as if it were a long process of stagnation. The usefulness of such age categorizations to provide a clear overview of, for instance, potential productivity or need for care is becoming increasingly problematic. The long and differentiated processes that are taking place during 'old age' defy static qualifications such as 'senescence,' 'old people', or 'the elderly'. Aging processes are a reality of life but they don't follow age-related stages. The popular belief that humans are like dogs and that you can't teach an old dog new tricks may well be an ageist projection that insults even smart old dogs.

Prevention and the infrastructure of the life course

In trying to prevent health problems in later life the usual target is adult behavior. This may well contain good advice but it is a narrow path to prevention; moreover, in many cases it will come too late. Prevention requires an understanding of the aggregate causes of the problems one would like to prevent from happening. Research from a macro oriented life course perspective appears to be indispensible to clarify the processes that will most likely lead to later problems; as such it might also contribute to society's self monitoring. Structurally caused social inequality plays an important role in the complex constitutive processes that constantly reproduce and change society.

In the empirical parts of this book we have seen overwhelming evidence for a basic trend that can be seen as the unfolding consequence of the neoliberal model for further development of developed countries: increasing social inequality. Wagner, the CEO of Shell who was quoted in the Preface, was right on target: 'Don't back the losers but pick the winners!' The worrisome results have been increasing income and wealth for a small minority, an increasing divide between the advantaged and the disadvantaged, leading to increasing socioeconomic insecurity for an increasing part of the middle class. Together this translates over time into increasing health inequalities, disastrous health consequences of modifiable circumstances over which especially disadvantaged individuals have little control. Such inequalities can have far reaching consequences for all citizens when they get out of hand and begin to tear societies apart. This neoliberal model has seen its most pronounced development in the US but it has also left its scars in other developed countries as they joined the neoliberal turn that promised to bring increasing income and wealth to their political and economic elites.

The life course as an instrument of power

'Social inequality' does not only refer to a situation at a particular moment but also to ongoing processes in which an unequal society is being reproduced over time. The organization of the life course plays a major role in this reproduction as it creates, protects, neglects or destroys the structural preconditions that are necessary for education, work, retirement or health care to function well for all citizens. The reference to an 'organization of the life course' does not imply that there is a clear plan behind such an organization. Much is just the effect of corporate strategies or of policies that are meant to address specific problems in education, the labor market or nursing homes politics. According to Daniels (2008) one of the major problems of the US health care system is precisely the absence of a life course perspective. This has important consequences for prevention policies: health care risks of children and so-called 'normal' adults are mostly covered by private insurance plans, which show little interest in prevention of health problems that often occur when people get older. And in the context of the – often poor – universal Medicare health care coverage for senior citizens there appears to be no motivation to invest in early prevention.

The way in which the life course turns out to be organized anyway serves to reproduce a society over time and if a society is unequal the life course will tend to be organized in such a way that this inequality is reproduced. Positive factors tend to support and enforce each other so that a positive start in life can make all the difference. The same is even more true, however, for a negative start as adverse conditions tend to enforce each other mutually and socioeconomic, personal and medical insults accumulate over the life course. Especially detrimental factors tend to strengthen each other: as Ben-Shlomo and Kuh remark 'it is far more common for adverse exposures to be clustered' (2002, p. 287). Just like negative clustering tends to aggravate the consequences of stressful life events (Evans &Kim 2007, 2010).

As we have seen, these processes tend to begin very early in life, even during gestation and are connected to stratified situations that tend to extend their influence along the life course into later life. This does not mean that situations in later life are straightforwardly determined by earlier situations or that the dice are definitively cast at birth. Negative and positive potentials are built up in early life and continue to have influence but their actualization also depends on the continuing interaction between behavior and social contexts. Although physical or mental insults can have cumulative effects over the life course, it is never too late to eliminate or mitigate burdening situations, or to prevent problems in the future lives of children, workers or older people. In adverse circumstances negative predispositions can lead to serious health problems – even at an early age – but in more favorable contexts such predispositions are more likely to remain latently in the background. Such a lack of strict environmental determination does not imply, however, that individuals are able to determine in freedom how their lives will evolve as soon as they reach the age of majority. The restrictive impact of the social environment, in a broad sense, is inversely proportional to the social vulnerability of citizens and continues to make itself felt, for better or for worse, throughout gestation, childhood, adolescence, young adulthood, and later life.

The dominant forces in any unequal society will try, however, to ensure that the life course is organized in such a way that their interests are being protected. In extreme cases, existing inequalities will be reproduced by sorting citizens at a young age into different structural trajectories that are very unequal in opportunities, constraints and risks. The highly consequential processes of unequal material and cultural endowment that take place from the earliest phases in life, are part of the reproduction of power and inequality in a particular society. Even if individuals ascend or descend in socioeconomic status the general pattern of inequality remains roughly the same, unless this happens in very large numbers changing basic patterns. We have seen this happening since the neoliberal turn: a small group has amassed enormous wealth, while large numbers of people have been sliding downwards into chronic insecurity.

Public neglect of the infrastructure of the life course

One of the apparently inspiring perspectives of the neoliberal turn was to break out of the restrictions of a stuffy welfare society with its bureaucratic rigidities and extended entitlements for citizens who were too lazy to venture out into the world of unlimited profits. Whereas before the neoliberal turn many small and large enterprises of all sorts showed – in spite of their capitalist aims – some responsibility for their communities, including paying more taxes than has become usual, neoliberal elites underlined the necessity to become 'lean and mean' in order to survive the cutthroat competition. Although there are still important differences between companies, and many of them are practicing some form of corporate social and environmental responsibility, there has also been an important trend to streamline *Corporate Social Responsibility* or *CSR* as a business discipline aiming at strengthening the brand and prestige of the company.

Continuing to chase targets to become even leaner and meaner leads to a sharpening of the distinction between the immediate interests of enterprises and anything beyond those interests, with the consequence that all social or ecological preconditions that are not directly translated into production costs are seen as irrelevant. As a consequence of the deregulation of markets, self-centered enterprises have been taking advantage of any loophole in national laws or evading them by going global: outsourcing production without protecting those who become the new workers abroad or compensating those who have become unemployed at home, exploiting their employees (Amazon, Walmart) and customers (Google), or pushing small middle class businesses out of the market (Amazon, Walmart). Other consequences of the unhinged entrepreneurial flight forward are the damages that are inflicted upon the environment throughout the whole production line in the form of a ruthless exploitation and pollution of natural resources. Natural environments are taken for granted as a never ending, self purifying source of energy and useful material, while the wider costs of their exhaustion or poisoning are not included in the company's calculations. These costs are externalized from the production process and become invisible, until they return on the balance sheets of society in the form of long term destructive effects that tend to become increasingly difficult to address, let alone restore. Even in confrontation with such consequences unregulated markets demand to wait for competitors to move first.

A typical example of how these strategies lead to long-term problems is the neglect of infrastructure. Small and large enterprises profit from local and national infrastructures that enable their productivity, but are not supported by these enterprises. When infrastructure is not maintained for lack of public funds, initial small cracks and breaks will eventually lead to a collapse. This is also the case with the infrastructure of the life course: *the institutions that protect and generate citizens' opportunities to participate in society from birth to death.* The ways in which these institutions operate are crucially important in two ways: in providing material and immaterial resources such as income and education, but also in interacting respectfully with citizens. Just like a society needs roads, bridges, tunnels or internet infrastructure to support and facilitate the production, transportation and communication that are vital for its functioning, its citizens need their lives along the life course to be supported by a secure and energizing infrastructure.

This is not merely a matter of targeted support for certain groups of disadvantaged citizens, although this does remain a prioritarian short term issue of help and support in situations of need. However, to stop running behind the accumulation of preventable problems and to begin to heal some of the deepening divisiveness, it would be a good idea to construct and maintain a life course infrastructure which supports all citizens. We recall Sen's criticism of Rawls that equal distribution of goods would reproduce and enlarge inequalities. But supplying goods to all citizens might also strengthen support for such policies and increase a feeling that there is something that binds citizens together. The wealthy would have to pay their share of taxes, which would be more than what less wealthy citizens would have to pay, but for all citizens education or health care, for instance, would be free. Other examples might be child benefits for all mothers, affordable or free transport or more protection of working conditions, income and pensions; or invigorating the relational infrastructure of the life course by subsidies to establish community centers, safe parks, opportunities for exercise and sports, where people can join activities, chat, share experiences, avoid boredom, feeling more secure or emotionally and practically supported. Although loneliness cannot always be prevented, the contextual conditions for living with it or overcoming it can be improved.

Such a provision of public goods is not merely a reproduction and enlargement of inequalities when it goes together with developing a tax system in which the most advantaged pay their fair share. When Warren Buffett observes that his secretary faces higher taxes than he has to pay this is clearly out of balance. It should be added that Buffett and other extremely wealthy people have tried to adjust the imbalance by forming an unusual pressure group of people who want to pay more taxes.[3] This is a promising but still minor diversion from the main stream. On top of being blessed with low taxes the extremely rich 1% profit from fiscal strategies which lead to absurd situations that are occasionally brought to light[4]: billionaires reward themselves, for instance, with a modest income that entitles them to tax cuts so that they pay effectively no taxes at all.

As a consequence of this culture of tax evasion public revenues are much lower than they should be in order for it to be possible to invest in the richest resource of a nation: its population. In that way, the infrastructure of the life course remains underfunded, preventing a more just and also a more productive distribution of resources over the life course. In this situation it appears urgent to restore and update the social and moral infrastructure of the life course so that talents can flourish and those who are directly threatened in their existence will be protected by systemic risk buffers, instead of being annihilated or forced to collectively bail out irresponsible elites who will resume their risky but profitable practices as soon as they can. Such an overhaul of the life course infrastructure might even gradually change the system in a more humane direction. When citizens can work in steady jobs with proper benefits and universal health care, adequate provisions that protect citizens from the effects of unemployment, poverty, disease or disability, even crises will not be as devastating as what we have witnessed in the shadows of the financial crisis. If, however, a majority (60%) of the US population works on an hourly basis with most of them having hardly any possibility to save for eventualities, even a short stagnation will lead to an acute crisis. In the richest economy of the 21st century only a minority of the population is immune from the possibility of falling into poverty as a result of events beyond their control. How can people be expected to save for retirement when they are living from paycheck to paycheck? Even small crises highlight the destructive effects of an extremely unequal society that tries to convince itself that it would be the country with the greatest opportunities for everybody who is determined to be successful.

Moreover, bubbles of extremely rich people not only acquire disproportionate political influence but also tend to undermine social cohesion. Instead of admiring or envying outrageous salaries and bonuses there is ample reason to suspect that society propagates questionable, superficial and destructive forms of success. Paying relatively small amounts of taxes may seem nice but the effects, such as impoverishing public goods in a broad sense, present a grave threat to society. It may take some time to see the benefits of paying (more) taxes. US citizens who come to work in European countries that have been relatively successful in deflecting the neoliberal regime may, at first, be shocked to learn about the tax rates. But gradually they find out that education, health care and many other forms of care, support or public transport, are still freely available or fairly affordable, although they are certainly not perfect and have come under increasing pressure from neoliberal marketization.

One of the basic problems of the neoliberal turn is that the market has taken over those parts of the life course infrastructure that provide services for which the wealthy are prepared to pay, such as optimal health care and high quality education. Such a marketization of institutions will work for the advantaged part of the population but not for those who need it most. Allowing markets to regulate citizens' opportunities to benefit from, for instance, education or health care implies a reduction of citizens to consumers who have to buy these services, referring those who cannot afford them to deteriorating public institutions. Those who can buy the services they need are structurally supported in their capacity to choose: where to live, in what house, what they prefer as diet, what education to give their children, which job to chose, where to travel to, or what hobbies to take up in retirement.

The neoliberal deconstruction of the life course has been effective in accumulating inequalities: the advantaged are welcomed, supported and cheered on as they grow up and older, whereas the disadvantaged encounter lack of support, degraded facilities and disrespect. Opportunities are not equally distributed; on the contrary, access to resources and rewards are stratified in segregated trajectories so that existing patterns of inequality are not mitigated but reproduced or even deepened. The school-to-prison pipeline is joined by the school-to-Ivy-League-leadership pipeline and other intermediate constructions, sorting citizens from the very start into trajectories with very unequal opportunities. This boils down to a fundamental objection to neoliberal policies: a society is not a market; markets function *within* societies. To restrict and regulate markets, citizens need to decide in the political arena where markets are useful and productive and where they are not. This will not be an easy process: the expensive marketed pipelines work so well for the economic and political elite so they may not feel the need to change any of this.

The social preconditions of autonomy and individual responsibility

One of the most troublesome implications of the neoliberal turn has been to hold individual citizens responsible for handling the consequences of large-scale societal changes such as outsourcing production or deregulating financial markets. We have seen that individual autonomy as *the capacity for individual responsibility and prudential choice* has even become the moral anchor of the life course in the dominant egalitarian paradigms of thinking about social justice over the life course, in complete neglect of such structural pressures. This criticism does not imply that individual responsibility and prudential choice are not important: they are. But they are also limited: somebody who as a young man in the 1960s made the prudential choice of taking a job in mining or shipbuilding may find out some decades later that his refined expertise has lost its value on the labor market where he is, moreover, seen as an older worker and becomes chronically unemployed like countless others in his community. We can hardly say that he has been irresponsible and should carry the full burden of his autonomous decision. Society – including micro levels of communities or social networks – is much better equipped to deal with sudden economic crises or transitions to other forms of production that may crush individuals and their families when left on their own.

In a life course perspective, the range of what can be chosen autonomously by an individual should not be overrated. This makes 'autonomous choice' in the context of the life course a concept that should be handled with care. Nevertheless, John Rawls insists that individuals should make a 'rational long-term plan of life' to express what a good life might be for them, and that they should stick to that plan because 'one feature of a rational plan is that in carrying it out the individual does not change his mind and wish that he had done something else instead' (1971 pp. 92, 421; cf. Baars 2012, Ch.5). In line with Rawls, Dworkin and Daniels have also emphasized that autonomous individuals should be held responsible for a prudent determination of their future lives, even decades ahead. In the context of contemporary life courses this sounds quite unrealistic: as if the rational independent agent were able to foresee the hurdles, options and consequences of his choices over several decades in a society with an accelerating pace of change. Although people are often forced to choose and will be held responsible for their choices, the range of choice is limited by the particular alternatives they can choose from; moreover, even the consequences of optimally informed prudent decisions over a long period of time remain unpredictable.

These problems cannot be sufficiently addressed if human autonomy is approached in terms of fundamental questions such as 'What is it to be a human being?' and 'What is it to live a human life?'. Much of my work on aging as a process of learning to live a finite life (cf. Baars 2012, 2017a) aims to clarify what human beings may share. But these approaches are less adequate in finding out where their situations may be different. For wealthy people resources are also finite; their choices are also limited by available alternatives, and their futures also remain uncertain. But they have significantly more resources than poor people; institutions such as the educational system help them to a good start in life; their social networks and many marketed services will support and protect them in the future if things go wrong, and they will probably live much longer in good health. The ambition to construct a theory of social justice for all times and all places needs to be moderated and brought in a productive relation with the specific times and places in which people live. Moreover, the constitutive force of societal macro contexts should not be neglected.

To see what happens to individuals over the life course as a mere result of their choices neglects that the opportunities to thrive in life or to become chronically ill and even to die at a relatively young age are unequally distributed. An intellectually gifted person who grows up in a poor and heavily polluted environment with the genetic predisposition of a weak respiratory system can easily develop a chronic lung disease followed by an early death. Growing up in a more affluent neighborhood with the same talents and predispositions, however, presents much fewer obstacles to a fulfilling career and a long healthy life, privileged by an excellent education, having the resources to buy a house in a less polluted environment and to support a lifestyle that respects his bodily vulnerabilities. Of course such long and fulfilling living will also require responsible action and commitment, but the inequality in opportunities cannot be overlooked.

The underreflected overemphasis on individual responsibility harmonizes well with the neoliberal message that all citizens participate in society at their own risk, like the idealized entrepreneur who sees all problems as challenges and succeeds in the end (see Ch.1). Especially those citizens who do not have the resources to invest, compensate losses and navigate through crises may get the impression that this type of society is not really meant for them. To encourage them to participate in society, narratives such as the

'American Dream' are brushed off to give them an inspiring perspective and at the same time legitimate the harshness of the neoliberal society. Those who fail would have followed other people's opinions instead of remaining independent; they would have made the wrong choices or they would not have shared their authentic personality and motivation.

In discussions about social inequality and the problems that many people face in struggling through life with insufficient resources, a common but problematic answer is to point to those exceptional independent people who did make 'it', in spite of highly disadvantaged backgrounds. This does indeed demonstrate that people are not fully determined by their socio-economic background, yet this answer still remains too easy and unsatisfactory. Do we really want a society where only exceptionally fortunate or gifted individuals are able, not to reach 'the top', but to escape from their severely disadvantaged situations? It is a poor diagnosis of social inequality that remains dependent on worn out tokenistic arguments such as pointing to somebody who has 'made it successfully out of the slums'. When upward social mobility severely declines so that only a few of those born in families with the lowest incomes quintile make it to better positions this does not make the situation less unequal; it only confirms the inequality. Individual escapes do not change or justify structural inequality. Social inequality is not a matter of one person who gets richer or poorer; it concerns large segments of whole populations and the relations between those who do well, better and best, and those who do worse and worst. To imply that all those who remain stuck in bad neighborhoods have not put their backs into it, insults not only those who have worked hard during a long life without making any progress, but also those who remain unemployed against their will, and those who are chronically ill or need to care for others.

The predominant narratives of progress, equal opportunity, and success show little tolerance for reports about social inequality, systemic discrimination or the general wellbeing of the population, insisting instead on pressing forward. There is little consideration of the possibility that fundamental problems will be reproduced, even at a higher level, by insisting that the way forward is through developing individual characteristics such as character, internal locus of control, achievement motivation, resilience or prudence (Dannefer, Gilbert & Han 2020). Deeply rooted and complicated mechanisms of social inequality are present in all countries. But it appears that there is a stronger tendency in the US to frame these problems in terms of behavior or character, assuming that biological or cultural differences play a dominant role, while neglecting the effects of material hardship as well as policies that benefit those already advantaged.

In trying to address both urgent and structural problems constructively it is important to distinguish several levels of social policy. When people are caught in bad circumstances it makes little sense to tell them to wait for a more just society. They may urgently need food banks, donations from charity and other support to keep them alive; this is the point of priority in social justice. Although those who work in charity organizations will experience on a daily basis how vitally important their efforts are for those who rely on their help, there is also the sense of mopping up water while the fire hydrants are blasting: distressing situations will not improve or may even get worse if there are no structural changes of the factors that produce these situations.

Similarly, it may be good to help people to become more resilient so that they become better equipped to face the personal challenges they will encounter over the life course (Hayslip & Smith 2012). It remains crucial to distinguish between, on the one hand, encouraging and supporting people to get through difficult situations here and now and, on the other hand, the ideological use of a 'heroic independence' that can easily be used to play down or even legitimate damaging forms of social inequality. Even under terrible circumstances, some people can impress us with a remarkable autonomy but this does not in any way justify such circumstances or make them less harmful. Supporting and encouraging people in difficult situations should be kept free from self-help cultures which proclaim and commercially exploit the idea that you can become anything you like if you really commit yourself. For the large majority this will merely add the problem of being seen as a spineless failure to their list of challenges.

Individual autonomy and its social conditions

The relation between individual autonomy and its social conditions is complicated and precarious. But there is a problem with the way in which autonomy is generally understood or taken for granted in contemporary society: humans are not per definition but *potentially* autonomous. Autonomy and its active correlate agency cannot be seen as given with being human; it is a potential that has to be developed and protected over the life course. Glen Elder's (1974) classic study of the formative experiences of children of the Great Depression has, for instance, demonstrated the importance of *timing*: at what age experiences of deprivation are likely to have lasting negative consequences. His conclusion is also that some hardship can even have positive effects in later life, *given sufficient support and resources*.

With the proper material and immaterial resources, involving respect, care and education, children may develop into what we regard as autonomous persons. Regardless how informed adults may be, without the necessary material and immaterial preconditions, the ability or freedom to choose remains an empty word; when, for instance, the only choice is between a bad school or no school, a bad house or no house, a bad job or no job. Taking autonomy and individual responsibility seriously implies that the human potential for autonomy must be supported throughout the life course; for instance, by offering all citizens not only a sufficient level of material resources but also education and health care of high quality.

To solemnly proclaim – even out of sincere respect for the dignity of human beings – that all adults are autonomous persons who must assume full responsibility in deciding how they want to live, should not serve to neglect the social preconditions of autonomy. This highly problematic way of approaching the issue of autonomy is in line with a long tradition in Western thought in which this concept was forged. When the Enlightenment thinkers proclaimed that all humans were essentially autonomous they brought a message of freedom and emancipation from aristocrats who assumed that they alone would be autonomous by blood. But taken out of this context, the idea of human autonomy as rational self-determination raises more questions than answers. Sometimes we get the impression that this rational individual can create himself like the proverbial 'self made man' or, like Baron Munchhausen, pull himself from the mire of irrational nature by his own hair and take on a rational essence. This type of rationalist pretention is especially problematic when the time perspective of self-determination moves from simple actions to complicated decisions with unpredictable consequences over decades. Some limited forms of self-determination may be feasible, but although we must, as responsible individuals, choose and plan, there is often a lack of the most needed information, resources, influence, or power to make adequate decisions and realize life plans accordingly. Moreover, the fundamental uncertainty of the future limits the ability to plan ahead.

Other Enlightenment thinkers opposed the Kantian rationalistic idea that autonomy is given with being gifted with a rational consciousness. Rousseau, for instance, argued that autonomy is grounded in a pure human nature that would unfold spontaneously if only society would leave it alone. The late 18th century discovery of 12 year old Victor, the feral child of Aveyron, shocked both perspectives. The poor boy, who was portrayed in François Truffaut's 1970 film *L'Enfant Sauvage* (*The Wild Child*) had apparently lived for years in the woods with animals as his only companions. Victor was unmistakably human but didn't look anything like the autonomous embodiment of a rational consciousness or the romantic dream of a splendid pure natural being that still speaks from Hollywood's image of Tarzan. Victor was a suffering, abandoned boy who could not speak or grasp words as his hearing was especially developed to signal approaching danger or the fall of wild fruit (cf. Dannefer 2022). Victor, the 19th century German boy Kaspar Hauser, and the other feral children who have been found since, in different parts of the world, deliver a sobering message to many who assume that autonomy is readily given with being human and will be fully developed as soon as a person reaches a certain age so that each individual adult can be held fully responsible, not only for specific actions but for his societal fate. Moreover, many people who are mentally disabled will have insurmountable difficulties in achieving what is regarded as 'normal' autonomy, but they are still human beings who need support to maintain their own form of autonomy.

Although there is overwhelming evidence that human lives depend in many ways on interpersonal relations and broader social contexts, many discussions of autonomy still neglect these constitutive factors, and cling to limited notions in which the independence from others takes center stage, as if we would become more autonomous the less we have to depend on others and as if social bonds are per definition a limitation of our autonomy (Taylor 1991; Raz 1986). The concept of a 'relational autonomy' has been introduced in the last decades as an attempt to redefine autonomy by focusing on its social preconditions, freeing it from traditional ideas of rational independence and emphasizing the social embeddedness of the self and the social relations that make autonomy possible (Mackenzie & Stoljar 2000; Christman & Anderson 2005; Taylor 1985). In the next section I will explore these questions from a capability perspective on citizenship while maintaining a macro perspective that includes – but also goes beyond – the micro social context that is predominantly presupposed in theories of relational autonomy.

However, instead of guarding the preconditions of individual autonomy, the dominant focus has been on protecting individual autonomy from coercion: as a right to be protected from outside interference in one's choices and decisions. The problem is that this right of non-interference protects against only one form of threat to individual autonomy: being dominated by others. For libertarians the dominant threat is an authoritarian state; being free from such domination is certainly important but not sufficient to enable persons to lead an autonomous life. This defensive concept of autonomy is meant to protect individual citizens but too often it is propagated without concern for the question *how* they might be able to be autonomous, rationally choosing agents. The freedom to be left alone can work fine when somebody is healthy and well supplied with the resources he needs but can easily turn into a nightmare of being left without any help or support.

Autonomy and aging

Autonomy is already a precarious issue for 'normal' adults but it gets an extra problematic twist when people get older. In the context of aging studies autonomy usually becomes an issue as soon as an older person needs permanent rather than incidental help, as if the person were falling from a state of self evident and unproblematic adult 'independence'. Theories about the autonomy of older people typically assume that they figure in health care settings. Moreover, the instrumental context of interventions appears to dominate the ways in which autonomy is approached; the primary concern about 'autonomy' is that patients might not be able to make informed choices. A typical example can be found in an overview article by Lothian & Philp (2001) in the *BMJ* about 'Maintaining the Dignity and Autonomy of older people in the Healthcare Setting':

> Autonomy refers to individual control of decision making and other activities. The literature suggests that both the dignity and the autonomy of older people are often undermined in healthcare settings. Autonomy is threatened when patients (and their carers) are not given adequate information or the opportunity to understand fully their diagnosis and to make informed choices about their care.
>
> (p. 668; cf. Welford et al. 2012)

This gives the impression that for health professionals the problem of autonomy is primarily to protect patients from being misinformed so that they need to get their diagnosis and treatment options across. Autonomy is not approached in terms of what citizens – even when they are older – need in resources and respect to be able to function as an ill but equal citizen. Instead, autonomy is implicitly regarded as independence and, as such, as characteristic for the 'normal' adult and something that older people should try to maintain: they should try to *remain* independent like normal adults. The baseline of much thinking about autonomy over the life course is that children are assumed to *become* independent, 'normal adults' would *be* independent, and aging people should try to *remain* independent. This is without much questioning of what may be meant by these ideas or how they might be accomplished.

Given this approach, it is only logical that the ideal of an autonomous old age is the 'Third Age' with its vitality that is kept going in full productivity, maintained through health care in the form of efficient pit stop service (Baars 2006). However, equating autonomy with independence is already unrealistic for 'normal adults' but even more inadequate in situations of frailty and chronic dependence that have been typified as the 'Fourth Age' (Laslett 1989). Consequently, perspectives for autonomous agency in the Fourth Age remain elusive (Grenier & Phillipson 2013).

The confrontation with the daily realities of long-term care has already led to a decades long concern about autonomy of older patients in such institutional contexts (Kane & Caplan 1990), including some worrying reports (e.g. Lidz, Fischer & Arnold 1993) and critical reflections (Agich 1993). Several authors have used Goffman's (1961) model of the total institution to portray situations where patients seem practically deprived of their autonomy and even of their dignity as human beings. There are many differences in quality between, for instance, nursing homes, so there is no reason to condemn all of them. But too often the privacy of patients, the way they might dress, their diets, opportunities for meaningful relationships with other patients and staff appear to be muzzled in a regime in which they are merely seen as declining bodies, unworthy of anything other than to be subjugated to institutional schedules and even abused. The continuing problematic conditions in many nursing homes has led to much indignation but, fortunately, also to constructive action (Shura, Siders & Dannefer 2010; Thomas 1996). One example among many is *The Long Term Care Community Coalition*, an organization that published in 2020 an alarming report about the extent to which nursing home conditions fail to meet the standards of care for animals in zoos and other settings and has dedicated itself to advancing quality, dignity and justice in nursing homes and other residential care settings.[5]

There are many different approaches to and definitions of autonomy, also with regard to aging (cf. Laceulle 2018) and differences between persons and their situations are crucial ingredients of what autonomy will mean in reality. Human autonomy is a potential that comes in many different forms that develop through challenging processes that extend from early childhood into later life. Autonomy cannot be taken for granted in one specific form; it is, rather, a precarious quality of embodied persons, whose identities are formed, embedded and changed in cultural, linguistic and social practices.

The proclamation that human beings are per definition autonomous beings who can reflect on and control their actions and, therefore, who can be held responsible for the situations in which they find themselves does not quite settle the matter. The statement that 'all human beings are autonomous' cannot be taken as an empirical statement. It is a critical idea that calls for its optimal realization in society; a moral evocation to respect and support humans in developing their potential for autonomy along the life course so that citizens become and remain able to participate in society and enjoy mutual respect as an equal citizen. To ignore persistent structural mechanisms by making people fully responsible for the ways in which their lives evolve over several decades is a forceful reduction of the dynamics between individual agency and structural forces over the life course. To unfold, autonomy needs supportive, protective, inspiring and respectful institutions. In other words: it is a matter of citizenship.

Capabilities as feasible opportunities for equal citizenship

How to think from a perspective of social justice about ways to reduce social inequalities of resources and respect? Social problems as well as health problems change form and become more complicated as they develop. The research on cumulative disadvantage (see Ch.3) demonstrates that initial disadvantage tends to breed more misery further along the life course. Even when poverty has been the initial condition that has led to chronic disease or crime, such later clusters of problems cannot be solved by giving the monetary support that would have solved the initial poverty. As disadvantages accumulate, the initial cause of a disadvantaged situation cannot simply be reversed into its cure.

Is it possible to give some positive beacons of orientation that might guide a reconstruction of the life course infrastructure, instead of running behind the damages inflicted on large groups of the population? It may seem that we need concepts such as 'wellbeing' or 'happiness' because resources don't have much meaning if these don't improve the lives of their recipients. I have, however, evaded individualistic constructs like 'happiness', 'wellbeing' or a concept like 'satisfaction' which largely depends on levels of expectation, and have used instead health expectancies in a broad sense as more reliable indicators of the long term effects of social advantage or disadvantage. Searching for the probable causes of health inequalities has led me to social inequalities of resources and respect. Undoubtedly, the reduction of social inequality would be an important step but to improve the wellbeing of the population we need also to think about what might constitute or improve the lives of citizens without prescribing how they should live.

For this purpose it may be helpful to go back, behind the dominant post-Rawlsian constructions, to Sen's capability approach. As we have seen, capabilities are not what people aspire to achieve, such as having a family, a good job or a fulfilling retirement – Sen calls these *functionings* – but what *enables* them to achieve these goals if they want to. Capabilities refer to feasible opportunities to be and to do what people have reason to value. This rather loose and open approach has been further articulated by Martha Nussbaum (2001) in a more precise and restricted form resulting in a list of beings or doings that make a life fully human. This has again inspired Sabine Alkire (2002) to give an extensive overview of the lists of fundamental needs or functionings that have been drawn up by theorists from different disciplines. Although the prospect of making a definitive and exhaustive list seems not very promising there appears to be broad support for the following slightly adapted short-list (Wolff & De-Shalit 2007):

1 *Being able to live to the end of a human life of normal length; not dying prematurely.* I would qualify 'normal' as of reasonable length, in comparison with the (healthy) life expectancies of the most advantaged;

2 *Being able to have good health, nourishment, clothing and shelter.* These first two functionings correspond with the initial focus of this book on (healthy) life expectancies. I have used these as long-term indicators of the wellbeing of populations without going further into what might constitute such wellbeing but it is plausible that this would also require the following capabilities:

3 *Being able to socialize with others, with compassion, friendship, self respect and justice; feeling safe and connected with others in meaningful relations of mutual respect leading to a sense of control over one's life.* We have seen the crucial importance of these capabilities *ex negativo* in the research on the undermining   effects   of   broken   families,   low   social   status,

unemployment, denigrating and precarious forms of employment, racial and gender discrimination or exclusionary segregation.

4   *Being able to use the senses, to imagine, think and reason.* The importance of this capability has been corroborated in the discussed research on education as a main source or dimension of social inequality and as a way to escape disadvantage.

Two more general remarks are in order. *First,* negative scores on these capabilities tend to have more impact, because disadvantages tend to cluster with other disadvantages. So the major concerns are chronic *disability, bad* health, *early* death, *failing* social integration or a *lack* of education. So, the primary focus should be on actual or emerging inequalities, not on static constructions of equality among citizens. *Second,* the first three capabilities correspond with the main dimensions of social inequality (see Ch.3) as the presence of their absence, so to speak. Money and wealth, however, are absent because unlike life, health, education or mutual respect and contact, money only has instrumental value. In a society where services are marketed and food must be bought or rent paid it makes, of course, a huge difference not to have to worry about paying the bills for basic goods. Beyond a certain level, however, money and wealth will not add to further improvement. This is an important argument to include basic sufficiency in citizenship rights instead of focusing on accumulating wealth for a minority without much concern for the wellbeing of the population. Although a society without markets remains elusive, a society is still more than the sum of its markets; moreover, *unregulated* markets play a destructive role in the most vital domains of society such as public health, health care, education or social integration.

The distinction between capabilities on the one hand and functionings on the other hand clarifies a problematic assumption that plays a crucial role in the debated egalitarian theories of social justice, specifically, the assumption that every individual should be held responsible for their 'choices' and 'decisions' that have led to the situations they find themselves in over the life course. This presupposes that these individuals had the capabilities – as feasible opportunities – to chose better alternatives. Sen's example of the freedom not to eat in a hunger strike presupposes the opportunity to eat and this opportunity makes all the difference. Declaring that somebody's societal fate is generally the result of her choices or decisions neglects this crucial distinction. This does not imply a complete exoneration of the worst off: they are still taken seriously as citizens who remain responsible for the ways in which they, for instance, drive a car, treat their children and other people or are cautious not to put others at risk. However, uncontextualized principles of individual choice, decisions in connection to responsibility for their societal fate are of little use. Much depends on the question whether we can reasonably expect persons in disadvantaged situations to act in certain idealized ways.

On the one hand, the capability approach has great potential to develop a differentiated approach to developmental problems that are crucial for the reduction of social inequality. Its basic questions are clear: what would these specific people *value* being and doing (functionings)? What are they *able* to be and to do (capabilities)? What are the specific limitations, tensions and frictions that they face in realizing what they value most? On the other hand, a well known criticism of Sen's capability approach has been that his approach is too vague because he has refused to give a clear list of capabilities and functionings. However, Sen's emphasis on the crucial role of a situational specificity that cannot always be theoretically anticipated is not per definition a weakness, because people are not the same in their needs or in what they regard as most important in life, and they do live in specific situations. Some need more, others less or different resources to enjoy a reasonably equal level of opportunities to participate in society. As we have seen, such situational specificity has been Sen's major reason in criticizing Rawls' proposal of distributing resources equally because this would not result in more equality but would reproduce and amplify the already existing inequalities between people. Disabled people, for instance, need more resources to attain a reasonably equal level of opportunities to be mobile. The result will not be the same as being fully mobile but should, given the disability, be acceptable as a way to participate in society in equality with others.

This emphasis on enabling people in different situations also makes sense with regard to the need for adaptation to unforeseeable conditions along the life course. Although it is good to prepare for the future if you have the means to do so, it is also necessary to acknowledge that we don't live in a world of predictable and controllable linear developments. Instead of forcing young adults to plan their lives ahead and to face the consequences of their choices 50, 60 or 70 years later, as Dworkin suggests, or to approach the future like Daniels in terms of two or three coherent age stages, it is crucial to appreciate that citizens can continue to contribute to society much longer than they might expect but also that the resources they need to remain sufficiently equipped to face life's challenges can change very quickly. When somebody has an accident, is widowed or has a stroke, daily life and its needs may change drastically.

Because of this situational openness the capability approach still faces the question of how to prevent being highjacked by sheer endless personal preferences, falling in a bottomless pit of satisfying all kinds of needs individuals may have? What if they want all and everything as much as anyone else? Or if they insist on the satisfaction of any idiosyncratic need? How to answer the individualistic claims of vocal adults who behave like spoiled children? There must be a difference between the countless things that individuals may desire and what society is obligated to offer them. One way to structure and limit the legitimate claims that people may have, is to restrict what they can legitimately ask to what appears to be necessary to attain equal citizenship. The capabilities that should be secured by the state are those that would enable persons to participate in society as an equal citizen. The state, as the political embodiment of its citizens, ought to secure for all citizens those basic goods that members of society can agree on under conditions of pluralism regarding the question of what a good life would be. This implies limiting the range of goods that should be provided collectively, to feasible opportunities to satisfy basic needs in a dignified way and to stand as an equal citizen (Anderson 1999).

To substantially reduce social inequality beyond mopping up while the fire hydrants are blasting, it will be necessary to secure the social pre-conditions of equal citizenship. To share citizenship rights means that people are able to relate to each other as equals; that they enjoy equal legal, political and social rights so that they have feasible opportunities to function as equals in civil society and political decision making. This implies the promotion of a culture of mutual respect supported by laws against practices of discrimination or denigration of people because of their status, gender, race or age. Resources must be distributed with the aim of providing citizens with equal opportunities to live a respected, dignified life and participate as equals in society. This does not mean that these resources must be equal in the sense of 'the same': they must be *sufficient* to enable people to function as an equal citizen.

Linking capabilities to citizenship avoids artificial discussions about claims to satisfy extravagant needs (such as drinking outrageously expensive wine, eating caviar or staying in a luxury resort) that would be justified because certain people would be 'genetically determined' to have these needs. It is not the wishes or desires of any individual that would be decisive but what citizens decide, in a democratic process, should be made available to all citizens. To hang out on the beaches of the world, wear the most expensive suits or drive only Bentleys or Lamborghinis, living like the glossy jet set may be the ultimate dream of a perfectly happy life for many people but this is not necessary to participate as an equal citizen in society. The preconditions of citizenship do not include free face lifts or other interventions in the ongoing battle between gravity and bodily appearance. Citizens may chose to buy these products or services on the market but they do not need to be publicly funded. This distinction reminds us of Daniels' distinction between treatment and enhancement. It is, however, not 'naturalized' in the form of grounding the distinction in 'species-specific normality' as in Daniels' theory; it remains based on social and political processes of decision making.

Amartya Sen (1995) has argued that the capabilities to avoid premature mortality and to be free from avoidable morbidity have a particular moral and political importance. Health may not be the goal of life but being in good health helps to realize whatever is meaningful to be and do in life. Society has an obligation to safeguard the health status of its citizens as a condition of their flourishing: without health, agency is constrained. Inequitable health outcomes are systematically experienced by population subgroups that are disadvantaged as a result of a clustering of negative factors, such as low income, insufficient education, and/or being discriminated against because of race, ethnicity, gender or age. Such differences are constituted along the life course and they are unfair and unjust, because they mock any idea of equality or equal chances to live a long life that is not prematurely burdened by chronic disease or disability.

As discussed above, the critical norm that can be derived from these findings is the right of all social groups to attain the level of health, including health expectancies, that is enjoyed by the most privileged group in a specific society (Braveman & Gruskin 2003). In international comparison we might even assess premature death as a death that occurs before the average life expectancy at birth of the world's longest surviving populations, such as Japan or Hong Kong. The goal of health equity is not that every individual should have the 'same' health, but rather the elimination of the major socially constituted health inequalities that were demonstrated in Chapters 2 and 3.

Capabilities are positive beacons to reconstruct and improve the infrastructure of the life course, so that policies are not simply running after urgent problems that keep coming up because of underlying structural and cultural dynamics. Their feasibility for citizens must be secured by institutions, so that individual citizens are able to plan ahead, assuming responsibility for their situations in the knowledge that society will support them in times of crises instead of writing them off. Moreover, capabilities need to be secured for citizens of all ages, not only for instance for children, leaving 'normal' adults to the risks of the market so that large groups are faced with continuous stress from minimal control over their environments or are forced into deplorable working conditions leading to bad health and poverty as they get older.

Human rights should not only protect citizens from outside interference or domination but also include social rights. Moreover, to go beyond mere proclamations of human rights by transnational organizations it will be necessary to implement them within nation states, extending them subsequently to illegal immigrants, asylum seekers and the stateless. This will be a long-term complicated process but, much like the transformations that are necessary to respond to climate change, there are hardly sustainable alternatives.

What is the point of offering people resources if they are not going to use them? One answer would be that many citizens *will* be using them and consider them as basic for a good life. Moreover, securing capabilities for equal citizenship is important because these are crucial for the quality of a society and the general wellbeing of its population. Even if individuals never vote, never (need to) go to a hospital, never visit a museum or a theater it sets the tone for a society when a majority of citizens decide through their political institutions that equal access to education, the political process, to health care, museums or theaters belong to a society they would like to call theirs. Moreover, this does not imply that markets would disappear or that the economy would fall into the grip of centralized planning. Markets still have important roles to play, for instance, in the efficient allocation of goods. However, a society is not the same as and indeed is much more than a collection of markets. The publicly shared responsibility of taking care of all citizens leads to different results from what unregulated markets would offer them, such as excellent conditions for the wealthy but bad schools, bad houses, underfunded health care, and neglected infrastructure for those who live in poor neighborhoods.

Public goods are an important part of the capabilities or feasible opportunities to participate in society in a broad sense: such as schools, theaters, museums, public buildings, safe public spaces, ramps, Braille signs, benches, exercise facilities in safe and healthy places or reliable means of transportation and communication. Public spaces should be inviting and safe; not commodified, for instance, by restaurants and bars that occupy public space by banning out public toilets and monopolizing places to sit. Inviting public spaces include what the WHO (2007) has called 'age friendly cities and communities' (Buffel, Handler & Phillipson 2019; Van Hoof & Marston 2021). It is strange, however, to think that only senior citizens would have such demands because they would all be disabled. Well maintained public spaces are also good for younger citizens, who prefer safe areas or need facilities when they are disabled or just not feeling well.

A criticism that can be expected to come from libertarians is that implementing such proposals amounts to a plea for a *nanny state* where the lives of citizens are controlled by the state which would suppress the individual freedom to buy what is needed or wanted on the market. This presupposes, however, that everybody is *able* to buy what they need on the market and that they have equal opportunities to acquire the necessary resources to do that. Moreover, securing capabilities for citizens does not mean that their lives are programmed by others so that they had no freedom to decide what they would like to be or to do. The non-identity of capabilities or feasible opportunities and actual functionings opens a domain of agency and responsibility: citizens should be capable of going out, meeting other people, to vote or receive adequate health care, but should have the freedom to do this or not. The point is to protect, for instance, the quality of education or working conditions, not to determine what kind work people should do or how they should live. Moreover, opportunities are necessary preconditions that do not come instead of personal efforts: completing a good education, finding or creating fulfilling work, grounding and sustaining a happy family still require personal commitment.

The access to a basic but dignified income can be conditional because not only should individuals be able to function in a more equal society, this society must also be able to support the preconditions of equal citizenship. So, as long as robots are not taking over all possible work incentives, to be productive remains necessary (Anderson 1999). Even a basic income can be conditional upon working for it, provided that there are opportunities to work, one is able to work, and this can be balanced with care obligations. Moreover, most people will want to work and save to obtain goods above the basic level of sufficiency. Not actively participating in society will have many consequences for the persons concerned, so they have enough to lose. Maybe, a supportive life course, citizenship, individual responsibility, and incentives for social participation and contributions to societal tasks such as care, productivity and innovation are not irreconcilable after all.

Poverty, disadvantage and the marginal effects of wealth

Real poverty does not always fit models of income distribution; for instance, a family may have a good income but still face bankruptcy because the health care costs of a child or a parent are not covered by the health insurance. Social inequality cannot be identified with poverty, but poverty remains an important marker of social inequality and signals its acute relevance and urgency because it represents an existential threat. This answers the popular remark that social inequality is inevitable because every society will have citizens who are worse off than others. Social inequality, however, is not merely a matter of relative positions on a continuous scale but basically a problem of *insufficiency* of resources and/or respect that may, in the worst situations, threaten mere survival and, more generally, prevent people from participating in society as an equal citizen. Without this urgency, social inequality tends to be reduced to mere relative differences in income or wealth or any other indicator. The substance of debates and analyses of social inequality is not the inequality that exists between wealthy people or between millionaires and billionaires. The problem of social inequality refers to situations that remain below the standards that a society should set for its citizens and enshrine in citizenship rights.

The priority of poverty and disadvantage was highlighted, for instance, in the study of Makaroun and colleagues (2017; see Ch.2) demonstrating that those in the lowest wealth quintile had a much higher hazard of death and disability than those in the second quintile. They concluded from their own and others' research that relatively small increases in wealth for the poorest would contribute to substantial gains in life expectancy and function. For those in the other quintiles, increases in wealth led to much flatter rates of health gain. This relationship between income/wealth and health has also been noticed at a macro level in the so-called *Preston curve*: individuals born in richer countries, on average, can expect to live longer than those born in poor countries but this link flattens out. At low levels of per capita income, increases in income are associated with large gains in life expectancy, but at high levels of income there are diminishing returns so that increased income has little associated change in life expectancy. These results clearly suggest that social policy interventions to decrease social inequality will have the highest impact by focusing on society's most disadvantaged members. This is not only a matter of giving them sufficient food, clothes or shelter but especially of improving their opportunities to participate in society. Poor families have limited options, which is one of the defining elements of poverty, so they also have little opportunity to improve their prospects through their own efforts.

From the research reviewed in earlier chapters it has become clear that poverty is not merely the fate of a more or less static group of 'the worst off'. Poverty can also hit those who are 'off benefits' and are working in multiple jobs. Moreover, people who used to see themselves as members of the middle can find themselves quite suddenly on the edge of poverty when an economic stagnation, recession or crisis hits them, although they have done nothing to cause or provoke this. During the Covid-19 crisis we saw media reports of thousands of people lining up for groceries at food banks. Most of them never expected they would have to do this. This widespread vulnerability, caused by a drastic deterioration of the position of the lower middle class in the distribution of wealth (see Ch.1), has led to feelings of insecurity and fear of sliding down into temporary or more permanent poverty with all the health effects that were documented in the earlier chapters of this book.

With the interpretation of equality as sufficiency for equal citizenship I also want to question the idealized aspiration to accumulate as much material resources as you can and to regard this as a sign of a good life, in spite of all the suffering, damage and garbage that are left behind on the way to the top. In a sustainability or a social-existential perspective it may well be argued that this is not the way to a fulfilling life (cf. Baars 2012, 2017). It would be good to revitalize a socially engaged tradition of writers such as William Morris, George Orwell or Richard Tawney who sought a good life of dignity in modesty and sufficiency (Wolff 2010). More recent examples of such criticism are Robert Frank's (1999) *Luxury Fever: Why Money Fails to Satisfy in an Era of Success* and Robert Lane's (2000) *The Loss of Happiness in Market Democracies*.

Rawls also honored this tradition:

It is a mistake to believe that a just and good society must wait upon a high material standard of life. What men want is meaningful work in free association with others, these associations regulating their relations to one another within a framework of just basic institutions. To achieve this state of things great wealth is not necessary. In fact, beyond some point it is more likely to be a positive hindrance, a meaningless distraction at best if not a temptation to indulgence and emptiness.

(Rawls 1971, p. 290)

In an economy that is assumed to thrive on consumer spending it may be especially difficult, although certainly not impossible, for those who enjoy the endless stream of commodities that they don't really need, to try to transcend the interest in unnecessary and even harmful material goods and turn towards art, culture, conversation, and shared personal and spiritual development; towards goods arising out of community, friendship, companionship. Such immaterial goods must not be divided or become less when others get more of them, so that whatever I have you cannot have: they become more when they are shared.

At a certain level of prosperity it becomes a sign of corrupted values and priorities to want more and even more. Noble Prize laureates such as Joseph Stiglitz (2015) and Angus Deaton (Case & Deaton 2020) have extensively demonstrated that an overemphasis on financial growth leads to an unproductive economy of rent seeking shareholders. A case in point would be the observation that the US has per capita the most expensive health care system in the world but its results are much worse than those of other, sometimes much poorer nations. Of course, more money is gained by those at the top of the US health care system, including health insurance companies and Big Pharma, but is this the ultimate goal of health care?

Inequalities of resources and respect

As we have seen, there has been much discussion amongst egalitarians about *what* it is that should be equally distributed: resources, outcomes, opportunities, or welfare. At this point they appear to agree with a libertarian like Nozick for whom equality is nothing more than a pattern of distribution. The main difference between them would be that Nozick opposes such an equal distribution, whereas the egalitarians argue in favor of it. In the debates about social justice and aging, the focus has been on material resources, especially health care costs. This is true for the *Fair Innings Argument* and for its opposite, the priority theory of McKerlie. Daniels' *Prudential Life Span Account* includes income besides health care costs, but this confirms the observation that the distribution of material resources would be all that matters. As we have seen, Dworkin has even gone so far that all talents, abilities and disabilities should be marketed and monetarized at the auction for young adults, where equality is merely seen in terms of a financial redistribution. This one-sided approach to equality is aptly expressed in the title of one of Cohen's best known essays 'On the Currency of Egalitarian Justice' (1989).

In their theories about aging and social justice most, if not all, of the discussed theorists join the ageist alarmism about the bottomless pit of health care costs for those who have already reached 'old age', although they live in the richest country of the world with a relatively young population. Their proposals will hit the most vulnerable among the older population, whereas the advantaged will find their way on the market. All attention for the distribution of material resources, however justified in itself, should not neglect the crucial significance of relations of mutual respect between citizens, including older citizens. Social inequality is not only a matter of distribution: ideologies and practices of respect and disrespect in the form of superiority/inclusion or inferiority/exclusion constitute an important part of the problem of social inequality.

The social bases of self respect

The French philosopher Paul Ricoeur writes: 'the recognition of myself as responsible agent or of my capacities anticipates recognition of others but does not realize this' (Ricoeur 2005, p. 255). In other words, it is still possible to retain self respect in the sense of seeing oneself as a dignified human being and as an autonomous source of moral claims, even in situations of constant humiliation or disrespect. There are impressive stories of people in concentration camps or about citizens who have been confronted with repressive regimes but remained unshattered in their self respect (Frankl 2006). But such stories are no proof that respect from others would not be crucial for one's wellbeing: these stories also relate the pain and suffering of *not* being respected.

Rawls fully acknowledged the importance of self respect and its social basis. Without self respect 'nothing may seem worth doing, or if some things have value for us, we lack the will to strive for them. All desire and activity becomes empty and vain, and we sink into apathy and cynicism' (Rawls 1971, p. 440). For him the main issue of justice remained the distribution of primary goods: these are the goods that everybody needs and wants but he insisted that the most important primary good would be self respect which would depend on the basic structure of society: its social bases (Rawls 1971, pp. 246, 440). In *A Theory of Justice* Rawls still treats self-respect as a primary good that can be distributed, but this changes in his later work. In *Political Liberalism* (1993, p. 82) he emphasizes that primary goods such as 'equal basic rights and liberties' and 'fair equality of opportunity' count among social bases of self-respect but can no longer be viewed as goods that could be distributed. Sen also underlines the crucial role of the social bases of self-respect; in that spirit he recalls the statement of the 18th century moral economist Adam Smith on the right to stand up in public without fear of being disrespected (see Ch.1). Both Rawls and Sen approach equality in terms of a distribution; respectively, of primary goods and capabilities, but they also acknowledge a relational dimension of egalitarianism that does not easily fit distributive theories.

Michael Marmot's pioneering work has consistently demonstrated the significance of social status in predicting health outcomes. Negative health effects are not only plausibly caused by having to follow orders from superiors in daily life but also by daily experiences of discrimination, denigration and exclusionary segregation (Ch.3). Although being in full control over your life is an illusion (Baars 2012) a feeling of being secure and in charge of your life is important for wellbeing. This can also be gathered from research on the effects of situations where these aspects are under pressure such as in unemployment or in precarious forms of employment: a low sense of control infringes one's sense of autonomy and increases the risks for heart disease. But this is also a matter of social cohesion. A sense of belonging to one's community and larger society where one feels respected appears to be crucial: strong social networks keep people alive longer and in better health (Marmot 2004). A corrosion of social control in the community can easily lead to more criminal activity or increasing fear of this, so that the advantaged may begin to leave the community and conditions spiral down. One of the reasons behind the high mortality among poor older citizens during the *Chicago Heat Wave* is that they didn't feel secure enough to open the windows and didn't have safe air-conditioned public places to go to (Klinenberg 2002).

Self respect is not a static inborn quality of humans; it is rather an intersubjective process of challenges and support. An extensive body of research documents that the development of self respect and related qualities, such as self-esteem or self-confidence, require that others show respect. As we have seen in the discussion of ageism, this will not become less important when adults get older. Developing and protecting mutual respect amongst citizens requires that institutions serving crucial processes in education, labor market, housing, courts, health care or income protection operate respectfully in relating to citizens of different class, color, gender or ages.

Respect is a proper concern of social justice: self respect implies seeing oneself as a dignified human being, deserving of equal moral concern, and as an autonomous source of moral claims, which presupposes respect for others, treating them as dignified human beings deserving of equal moral concern. This includes seeing others as persons one could identify with when they are in trouble. In the context of social inequality this is particularly relevant when lack of respect is not an isolated incident of irritation or anger, but the result of firmly established patterns of discrimination. Movements of people who are struggling against inequalities of race, age and gender in a broad sense demonstrate that social inequality is not just a matter of material resources.

Does the call for respect lead away from a more equal distribution of resources? According to Nancy Fraser (1997) the Civil Rights Movement already began to shift priorities from redistribution to recognition after the late 1960s. Brian Barry (2001) has noted that in the US there has been a strong tendency to focus on identity politics; much less on distribution issues as in most European countries, although the more recent immigration crises have unfortunately ignited identity politics in many European regions. In the context of the theoretical eclipse of social inequality during the 1980s and 1990s (Ch.5), Charles Taylor even argued in his essay 'The Politics of Recognition' (1992) that the struggle for equality belonged to a past that was still free from demands for the recognition of cultural difference. Indeed, the 'new social movements' (Calhoun 1994) that have dominated much of public politics since the neoliberal turn, have crystallized around what Inglehart (1977) called 'post materialist' issues such as peace, ecology, race or ethnicity, age and gender in a broad sense.

However, historical research on labor movements, for instance by Barrington Moore (1978), has shown that in the past − contrary to Taylor's opinion − struggles for equality have also been motivated and ignited by violations of locally transmitted claims to honor. Similarly, sociological research on class struggle, for instance by Sennett and Cobb (1972) has demonstrated that what members of the lower social class have seen as their major oppression and injustice was often a lack of respect for their way of life and cultural heritage. Struggles for equality have also ignited in protest against the assumed superiority of certain elites who tended to treat others as 'naturally' inferior. But generally, emancipatory struggles have been fought for mutual respect *and* material redistribution. Moreover, as demonstrated by the empirical evidence that was discussed in earlier chapters, we can hardly say that problems of inequality that form the substance of Taylor's 'struggle for equality' have ended and that a struggle for recognition of cultural difference has taken or should take its place.

Identity political struggles for mutual respect need not be opposed to the distribution of sufficient resources. Tearing both dimensions apart with the aim of questioning which is the most important does not tend to lead to fruitful discussions as can be seen in the *Redistribution or Recognition* discussion between Nancy Fraser and Axel Honneth (2003). One of the reasons why identity struggles for respect have continued to gain momentum is that ethnic and gender minorities continue to be discriminated against, even if they are relatively wealthy. We hear the continuing stories of successful black people who are pulled over because their car does not fit their ethnic profile; of the prominent black Harvard professor Henry Louis Gates who was arrested − and fortunate not to be shot − for trying to open the jammed door to his own house, or even Obama's story of the humiliating experience of hearing clicking car locks as a black man approaches on the side walk. The highly educated and well off among discriminated groups are usually the most vocal and influential in public discourse, but for them a lack of material resources may seem less urgent. However, for many black citizens the situation is dramatically different. Police brutality, such as that protested against in the *Black Lives Matter* movements, reinforces the tendency to focus on identity issues instead of on a more equal distribution of resources.

The basic problem is not that there are differences between people, but that some differences are met with practices of oppression, which unmask a society that would like to see itself as protecting the equal opportunities and mutual respect of its citizens. Clearly, trying to overcome social inequalities that persist and even accumulate over the life course is a matter of resources *and* respect. It would not really help if people are personally respected but left without necessary material resources, nor would it help if people are given sufficient resources but have to endure continued denigration or are not taken seriously.

Even in destitute situations, people will try not just to survive but to live their lives in mutually supportive and respectful relationships with others they can trust. When such forms of social cohesion in clusters of disadvantage are neglected, even well intended attempts to improve their situation may fail to succeed. When people are removed from slum-like habitats to more hygienic and comfortable housing in tower-blocks, they may lose their social networks and a shared sense of community. Citizens need to be included in the planning of their future situations, so that they can feel they are taken seriously and can assume some responsibility for the decisions that are made. Improving people's situations with material resources such as better housing needs to go together with mutual respect.

Another long term improvement, both in terms of resources and identity, would be to intensify efforts to integrate the education of children from different racial and ethnic backgrounds; something that has been at the core of the civil rights movement since racial segregation in schools was deemed unconstitutional in 1954. Attempts to reduce school segregation by busing black students into white neighborhoods began in the 1960s and were extended in the early 1970s. Towards the end of the 1970s these efforts were paralyzed in the face of massive resistance from white parents. This is regrettable because black children who were able to attend integrated schools benefited greatly from the experience as Rucker Johnson, an economist at the University of California, Berkeley, shows in his 2019 book *Children of the Dream: Why School Integration Works*. Integrated schooling increased wages by 30% and reduced the chance of incarceration by 22 percentage points. As he writes, there is nothing magic about sitting next to white children; one thing, however, that remains consistent in the history of American schooling is that resources follow white children.

The enormous resources that go into the punitive system would be much better spent in trying to avoid situations that easily lead to criminal behavior; trying to put people on tracks that lead to more constructive contributions to society. Even if this were only modestly successful it could mark a major difference in going from a harsh and indifferent society to a caring and supportive society. This does not deny the importance of personal responsibility and, indeed, not everybody in desperate or tempting situations will become a criminal. But instead of placing all bets on the punitive system scaring badly influenced young kids into the rational and moral autonomy of law abiding citizens, this situation calls for public responsibility to support people in their struggle for an even moderately better life. The US society as a whole carries a great responsibility, for instance, for its racial policies of the past and the present, in creating and deepening inequalities.

Denigration and discrimination because of class, ethnicity, gender, age or abilities, result in servility, resentment, bitterness on one side, and patronage and arrogance on the other. These highly emotional demarcations silence the fact that all people are different in their DNA as well as in their biographical experiences. As said before: both genetically and historically we are all migrants. Because all people are inevitably different from each other, there is no other way than to include and respect differences, avoiding the exploitation of certain types of differences to advance a hopeless agenda of societal division and deepening inequalities. Striving for 'equality' is not inspired by ideals of 'the same' or the *absence* of differences; the problems begin with a hierarchical structuring of diversity between persons who are segregated into separate groups, based on race, ethnicity, gender, class or age.

The most fundamental test that any egalitarian theory must meet is that its principles express equal respect and concern for *all* persons. In spite of Kant's limitations in the development of this principle, he clearly pointed out that equal moral worth is not a matter of talent, virtue, merit or success: equal moral worth is an inherent quality of human beings. Such normative principles have a critical edge; they are not meant to harmonize or gloss over existing inequality or injustice. Color-blind formalism, for example, according to which 'all lives matter' neglects the problem that specific groups in society *are* treated differently depending on their color. Equal citizenship does not imply that citizens have to be, or to get, the *same*, but instead that, in recognition of all the differences between them, at a basic level they accept each other as equals, and are recognized by institutions as equal citizens, having equal rights, including social rights. Equal citizenship includes mutual *respect*, as well as a distribution of sufficient material and immaterial *resources*, so that citizens can relate to each other as equals.

The costs of public indifference: growing inequality and resentment

At the beginning of the discussion about libertarianism versus egalitarianism (Ch.5), we encountered a widespread libertarian fear that the implementation of equal citizenship in a more comprehensive social sense would mean that 'all would be worse off, instead of some being worse off. However, less unequal societies are not less productive than those with greater inequalities. Several countries in North Western Europe, and Asian countries like Japan, are doing equally well or not much worse than the US in terms of GDP, but much better in taking care of their populations, as indicated by health expectancies. GDP per capita is around $60,000 in the US, while Germany and Japan have to contend with $45,000 and $38,000 respectively. Such high scores for GDP *per capita* in a country with so much poverty illustrates how badly wealth has been distributed amongst citizens. Even in terms of capitalist competitiveness, the leading role of the US is dubious. In fact, the *Global Competitiveness Report 2017–2018* published by *The World Economic Forum*, a solid capitalist institution, puts countries like Switzerland (1st), Singapore, The Netherlands, Germany, Hong Kong, Sweden, Japan and Finland in the top ten of the most competitive economies. The US has asserted its (2nd) place in this list, but at the expense of extraordinary high levels of income inequality. The other countries in the top ten are among the world's least unequal countries, in spite of a general decline in egalitarian politics since the 1980s.[6] Sweden and Finland are two of the world's countries with the highest labor union density: 66% and 64% respectively in 2016.[7] More recently, major international institutions such as the OECD, the World Bank, and the IMF have acknowledged that extreme inequalities in wealth and income are economically inefficient. Also, prominent US economists such as Nobel Prize laureates Joseph Stiglitz (2015, 2019) and Angus Deaton (Case & Deaton 2020) have presented ample arguments that drastic changes are not only necessary but realistically possible, and have debunked the idea that the US cannot afford more equality of income, education and health care. It has been and still is a political choice whether to invest in the life course infrastructure of society or to leave this to the market, with the result that inequalities will become even deeper than they already are. It is an illusion to assume that this would not also harm the advantaged or extremely rich. Should we settle for the apparent ideal of the neoliberal elite in which rich people have to hide, with all their 'freedom', in fenced communities, with barbed wire, armed bodyguards, panic rooms, and armored cars to take their children to a fortified school?

The one-sided emphasis on individual freedom and individual responsibility – that has even been adopted by the egalitarian theories of social justice and the life course, as has been discussed – has the effect of protecting those in power. There is too little concern for those who are structurally disadvantaged or discriminated against because of race, ethnicity, gender or age. The libertarian conception of defensive freedom emphasizes protection from an authoritarian state, without acknowledging its public responsibilities beyond such elementary tasks as protecting property. In her extensive study *Freedom: An Unruly History* De Dijn (2020) has recently investigated the origins of this type of thinking about freedom in terms of the limitation of state power. This has been a deliberate and dramatic rupture with long-established ways of thinking about liberty. For centuries people in Western societies identified freedom, not with being left alone by the state, but with the ability to exercise control over the way in which they were governed. In contrast to what many think, the defensive conception of freedom was not invented by the revolutionaries of the 17th and 18th centuries who created the modern democracies. It was propelled, rather, by their critics and opponents in an antidemocratic backlash following the Atlantic Revolutions. De Dijn argues convincingly that we owe this view of freedom not to the liberty lovers of the Age of Revolution but to the enemies of democracy.

Moreover, many big corporations monitor and control consumers in ways that are far more sneaky and effective than what has been typical of the government's arsenal. Powerful corporations like Google, Facebook and Amazon flourish by the illusion that their services only benefit personal or professional expression and choice, but it is not so easy to evade the intrusive services of these dominant companies. These and other large internet based corporations are keen to give consumers the impression that they have a special personal relationship with them, while they are surveyed over the life course. The neoliberal individual wants to free himself from the state, but surrenders to large multinational corporations that aim to optimize control over their customers. With every contact the manipulative algorithms are refined and the digital tentacles are sucking more information out of customers who may still think they are personally appreciated by these giant octopuses.

We need to look at the social preconditions of freedom. As has been argued above, a society is free to the extent that its citizens are *able* to function as free citizens. To be free requires the opportunities to be *able* to chose or decide, otherwise it does not make sense to speak of a free choice or a free decision. Without securing such pre-conditions, the equality of citizens before the law, or the political equality as the right to vote cannot come to fruition. This vital connection between equality and freedom should only be broken in specific situations when, for instance, people are imprisoned because they have committed a crime.

We might think of citizenship rights as composed of different layers that have been formed subsequently in a historical process that has been sketched by Marshall (1950). A first layer contains civil liberties that secure individual freedom such as freedom of speech, freedom of thought or the right to own property. A second layer contains political participation rights, such as legislations against discrimination, the right to participate in the exercise of political power as a member of a body invested with political authority or as an elector of the members of such a body. These political participation rights were meant to ensure that the civil liberties, mentioned in the first layer, did not remain the privilege of the wealthy bourgeois, but that all citizens would be included in the political process. The third layer refers to social status rights that would guarantee sufficient material resources to ensure that the political participation rights from the second layer could be realized for all. If a majority of the citizens has to struggle to survive without feeling secure even about their immediate future, they will have other things on their mind than participating in political debates or even voting. Marshall emphasized that these three-layered rights presuppose each other and only together would make equal citizen status possible (cf. Pettit 1997).

Citizens' social rights suffer from a commercial idealization of the autonomous consumer who makes rational choices on the markets so that deregulated markets can function optimally in developing and distributing what these citizens need. However, high quality education, good working conditions, optimal public health, social protection along the life course, humane forms of cure and care, can hardly be expected from unregulated markets; they do not count among the proud achievements of the decades that have passed since the neoliberal turn. Strengthening the preconditions of equal citizenship implies not only a formal acknowledgement, but the practical implementation of social rights. These rights are meant to protect the lives of citizens but also to open opportunities to get an optimal education, permitting full social participation, including participation in the workforce and political activities, as well as receiving respect as an equal citizen. In order to implement these rights, so that they don't remain abstract ideals, they have to be supported by institutions which take care of generating and distributing opportunities to all citizens over the entire life course.

Freedom and equality need not be regarded as opposites. This may seem to be the case when equality is identified with an equal distribution of property, and freedom with the individual right to acquire, own, use and dispose of property in unregulated markets. It has become, however, scandalous to define freedom in terms of property rights since slavery was defended with reference to property rights. This underlines once more the need for egalitarian perspectives that oppose oppression, investigating the origin, functions and remedies for inequalities, instead of being satisfied with sophisticated constructions of 'equality'.

Meritocracy as ideology

When a society is unequal it need stories to legitimate these inequalities; especially stories about how superior positions grounded in nature have been very effective. Important examples of such naturalization are stories about the superiority of noble blood, racial characteristics, masculinity, vital adulthood, intelligence, or other talents. According to such ideological stories it is 'natural' for aristocrats of noble blood to rule over common people; for men to dominate women; for young adults to ridicule and residualize older people and for talented people to look down on those who are not as gifted. Belief in the natural order of social inequality has gradually become more contested as modern egalitarian narratives have discarded 'noble blood' as a natural ground for superiority in favor of a work ethic of merit. As we have seen, this does not mean that legitimations of social inequality as flowing naturally from racial characteristics, masculinity or young adulthood have vanished.

As long as people believe in naturalizing ideologies of superiority and inferiority they have little reason to think about the social backgrounds of (dis)advantage. The ideology of meritocracy denies natural foundations of inequality but equally suppresses thinking about the inequality of *opportunities* to attain positions with prestige and income. These positions would exclusively be based on individual merit within the system of a just hierarchy that controls and endorses individual accomplishments (Sandel 2020). Because of this assumption there was much indignation when the FBI discovered that wealthy people like television actress Lori Loughlin and her husband had paid large sums, up to $500,000, to get their children admitted to elite colleges that would provide genuine certificates of merit. This spectacular cleansing operation, however, cannot save meritocracy: the meritocratic ideology can only convince citizens that inequalities of resources and respect would be acceptable, if every citizen did indeed have the same chance to live in advantaged positions. The neoliberal organization of the life course favors those who are already advantaged. There are ideological cheers for the exceptional cases where disadvantaged individuals have 'made it', using them as proof that everyone can achieve this, so that it is unnecessary or even harmful to change the opportunity structures that bring out the best in people.

But it is simply not true that everybody who works hard will make significant progress; not to mention reaching the proverbial 'top'. 'Merit' can only function to legitimate social inequality if there were indeed a level playing field from early childhood on. Otherwise, meritocracy is merely an ideology that covers up social inequalities, not only in starting positions but also in further support along the life course to develop talents and abilities as people grow up and older. Many of those who have been working hard until retirement have been confronted with the bitter reality that they have not been able to improve their situation: they just managed to survive, and their children are not doing any better.

Moreover, the appreciation and respect for work has shifted away from vitally important tasks such as cleaning, transporting and providing food, caregiving or providing security in the community. A sluggish and mediocre performance of a banker will be more highly rewarded and respected than the hard work of a truck driver or home caregiver. During a pandemic these workers may be praised for their 'essential work', but this does little to change their situation in the long run. From an individual perspective it might have been better for the income of the care worker to change profession and specialize in creating spam email, but from a broader perspective it is a fundamental mistake to disrespect and undervalue the skills and commitment that are intrinsic in caregiving. It is an illusion that a wealthy democratic society can prosper without adequate care or the contributions of other essential workers. As if their problems, in the words of Wilbur Ross (see Ch.1), would barely be 'a blip on the U.S. economy's radar'. The ideology of meritocracy becomes especially toxic, adding insult to injury, with its narratives of 'success' versus 'failure' and 'winners' versus 'losers' and the conspicuous consumption which underlines the difference. This easily leads to arrogance on one side and resentment on the side of those who suffer from the collateral damage of neoliberal progress.

Unequal distribution of resources and destruction of habitats are, however, not necessarily caused by discriminatory intentions. Unmitigated market forces just as easily turn against white workers and their families, who saw their futures being crushed as society transferred the burdens of the transition to new forms of productivity to those who were committed to its previous forms, such as coal mining and steel production. As a mobster would say: 'this is nothing personal, just business'. Markets are not driven by respect for people; therefore, they need political monitoring and interventions to protect and support citizens. Failing to do this has led to a destructive transformation of old identity politics, when those who used to think of themselves as somehow superior to others, suddenly realize that they are treated like useless tools.

At a certain moment chronically disadvantaged citizens are no longer inclined to believe the ideologies of the powerful; they are no longer willing to put all the blame on themselves for their lack of success. They don't believe anymore in the mantra of individual responsibility for their fate, because they know that they have not been lazy or irresponsible. The result is a strong distrust in the political elite and, especially, in the precarious and time consuming processes of democratic decision making or the checks and balances of a democracy. Disillusionment can turn easily into indignation and anger that are, unfortunately, skillfully manipulated by the same leaders who have abandoned those they represent. Unfortunately, this frustration is not always translated into constructive political action but tends to be exploited in another form of identity politics, lamenting or praising the suffering of discarded builders of the nation and promising them a future in which they will no longer be forgotten but get little more than cheerful caps.

The advertised strong man revitalizes the old narrative of the superior leader who promises to save his followers but gets helplessly stuck in blaming others for causing their problems: other countries, international treaties, migrants, minorities, or even older people. Consequently, the resulting political programs tend to become resentful forms of nostalgic nationalism: closing the borders and pushing 'the others' out because they are said to be responsible for the decline into a continuing struggle for survival. Amidst their hardship, people are longing back to the days when the world seemed safer – at least for white men – which may actually mean that their socio-economic existence was safer, and prospects to better one's situation by working hard were more realistic. They want their voices to be heard, but they appear to be easily manipulated by empty promises that they will be heard and won't be forgotten. The risk is that rising inequality, lower social mobility, and the disenfranchisement of younger generations could result in even more polarized and short-sighted politics, creating a populist trap.

In his book *The Tyranny of Merit* (2020) the Harvard philosopher Michael Sandel has investigated the causes of recent discontent in American politics. With good reason he emphasizes the disruptive effect of the persistent neglect of moral questions such as the meaning of human rights, the common good, and what we owe each other as citizens. It is also true that political debates have become increasingly technocratic and uninspiring for most citizens, which does not help to invigorate the democratic debate. It can be doubted, however, that populist revolts erupt because of a lack of rich normative discussion, or because most citizens are not able to follow the debates between experts who disagree with each other or are politically divided. Sandel even insists that the main problem is not that the losers of neoliberal politics have not been compensated. There is a tendency in his meritocracy critique to disconnect the mutual respect between citizens from the necessary resources to live a decent life. As if the neoliberal undermining of socioeconomic stability for large parts of the population is less important than the declining respect for their work or person. Humility and appreciation from above or respect without sufficient resources will do little to improve situations. Such a hierarchy of respect above resources may be evident for moral philosophers but it tears apart fundamental pillars of a democracy that can only give strong support if they stand together. Marshall's understanding of social status rights contains the warning that if citizens have to struggle to survive without feeling secure, they will have other things on their mind than participating in political debates.

Without a reduction of social inequality of opportunities, chronically disadvantaged citizens will continue to live in deplorable situations and create dynasties of poverty as the counter image of the dynasties of extreme wealth and influence. Moreover, large parts of the middle class will continue to be pressed into situations of socioeconomic survival stress with the constant risk of sliding down into poverty. If kept in close connection to actually existing inequality the ideal of equal opportunities may still have an important role to play: not to reach 'the top' but to participate in society as a respected citizen with sufficient resources.

The costs of public indifference

Indeed, long lives are for the rich. An abundance of empirical research about the populations of developed countries shows that disadvantaged people are likely to die sooner than those who fare better and have sufficient resources to live well. Those who live shorter lives have to suffer through more years of disease than the most advantaged. This perverse longevity gap captures in a nutshell the grave injustice of the ways in which the life course has been organized. While the rich get richer and live longer to enjoy this, more people are living with socioeconomic survival stress and suffer longer although they live shorter. However, the evidence is mounting that this comes at considerable cost for the advantaged and, most of all, for the quality of society as a place where citizens can live well. As I already discussed in the Introduction and in Chapter 2, the dynamics of inequality in the countries with the most strict neoliberal regime have taken a course where we can no longer see any winners. Recent mortality rates in the US are showing that *all* Americans, *including the rich*, are unhealthier and dying earlier than citizens of other developed countries. For a long time, the US did well in life expectancy at age 85 – generally, an age category populated by the most advantaged – but since 2010 things have gone further downhill so that the US was in 2018 worst off at just about every age (Barbieri 2022; Ho 2022). That *Long Lives should* only be for *the Rich* has turned out to be a self destructive program, raising urgent questions of social inequality and social justice over the life course. Since the neoliberal turn of capitalism at the beginning of the 1980s, life expectancies of the US populations have been falling dramatically behind those of their peer nations. Even if these life expectancies and mortality rates were to improve drastically, it will still take decades to catch up with other OECD countries.

Even when the rich – short for the most materially and immaterially advantaged citizens – improve their life expectancies, there is a price to be paid for the extreme inequalities that will continue to divide the nation. Finally, being a hundred or a thousand times richer than the average citizen does not even mean that you will live twice as long. To live long and healthily requires *sufficiency*, not abundant wealth.

Insofar as the social and moral infrastructure of the life course is not functioning adequately, it will generate too few opportunities and too many problems for too many people. In the event of emergencies, attention goes to immediate help, but preventing them would be better, both from a perspective of human wellbeing as well as financial costs. Although communities may try to respond to pressing needs, they tend to be structurally overwhelmed, especially in situations where they are needed most. They need more support from governments than the admonition to wait for the moment when this or that particular crisis will be over. Neglected structural problems will continue to create larger problems and will inevitably force themselves onto the agenda.

The political elites of the most developed countries have irresponsibly welcomed the neoliberal degrading of society to a complex of self-correcting markets which culminate in a profitable shopping paradise for individual consumers, without adequate monitoring of sectors where markets might be helpful and sectors where they are disruptive. Neoliberal flexible opportunism and its policy offshoots have failed. Promoting self-correcting markets and uncontextualized individual responsibility as the solution for all social problems is self-defeating, because it covers up and increases the inequalities which are pushing an already deeply divided society into more conflict and instability. The cost of sharing opportunity and wealth may seem high for today's elites, but the alternative may be far worse, having to live with luxury forms of survival stress, trying to find shelter by living in fenced communities, protected by small private armies with armored cars.

It will be crucial to try to convince the wealthy and powerful that they will also benefit from a more equal society. The citizens of wealthy countries need inspiring perspectives based on sustainable growth and a fair sharing of resources and respect, avoiding the reproduction or deepening of inequalities, so that all citizens may thrive in a society that has learned to share its enormous wealth. The citizens of the US and of those countries whose elites have chosen to follow – some more, some less – the neoliberal turn of capitalism have to assume responsibility for their societies. They can no longer wait patiently for the moment when wealth begins to trickle down, creating a more egalitarian distribution of opportunities to participate in society, when the dominant forces in these societies are geared to increase inequalities. A crucial part of the way forward, breaking out of the loop of rising inequality, political polarization and short-sighted politics is to safeguard the preconditions of equal citizenship from birth to death. Beyond granting citizens formal equalities which actually depend on one's resources it is crucial to upgrade the social and moral infrastructure of the life course, attending to the needs of people who are trying to raise their children, improving schools, working conditions, health care, and the living situations of those who have to live with disability or frailty in old age. The time has come for the US to abandon its proliferation of policies which aim at enlarging wealth for a few to invest this in its most precious resource: its population – in all its diversity.

Notes

1 Mill, J.S. (1968) *Utilitarianism* and *On Liberty*. Including Mill's 'Essays on Bentham'. Cleveland: Meridian Books.
2 https://www.unicef-irc.org/publications/pdf/Family-Friendly-Policies-Research_UNICEF_%202019.pdf
3 See Patrioticmillionaires.org
4 https://www.propublica.org/article/the-secret-irs-files-trove-of-never-before-seen-records-reveal-how-the-wealthiest-avoid-income-tax
5 https://nursinghome411.org/ltccc-report-animal-care-vs-nursing-home-care/
6 http://www.lisdatacenter.org
7 https://stats.oecd.org/Index.aspx?DataSetCode=TUD

References

Abel-Smith, B. & Townsend, P. (1965) *The Poor and the Poorest*. London: Bell.

Abramson, C.M. (2015) *The End Game: How Inequality Shapes our Final Years*. Cambridge, MA: Harvard University Press.

Achenbaum, W.A. (1995) Images of Old Age in America, 1790–1970. In Featherstone, M. & Wernick, A. (Eds.) *Images of Aging: Cultural Representations of Later Life*. New York, NY:Routledge, 17–26.

Adler, N. & Newman, K. (2002) Socioeconomic Disparities in Health: Pathways and Policies. *Health Affairs*: 60–76.

Agich, G.A. (1993) *Autonomy and Long-Term Care*. New York, NY:Oxford University Press.

Alexander, K.L., Entwisle, D.R. & Olson, L.S. (2014) *The Long Shadow: Family Background, Disadvantaged Urban Youth, and the Transition to Adulthood*. New York, NY:Russell Sage Foundation.

Alkire, S. (2002) *Valuing Freedoms. Sen's Capability Approach and Poverty Reduction*. Oxford: Oxford University Press.

Allport, G.W. (1958) *The Nature of Prejudice*. Garden City, NY: Addison-Wesley.

Alston, P. (2017) *Statement on Visit to the USA, by Professor Philip Alston, United Nations Special Rapporteur on Extreme Poverty and Human Rights*. OHCHR. https://www.ohchr.org/en/statements/2017/12/statement-visit-usa-professor-philip-alston-united-nations-special-rapporteur.

Altman, N. & Kingson, E. (2015) *Social Security Works! Why Social Security Isn't Going Broke and How Expanding It Will Help Us All*. New York, NY: Oxford University Press.

Alwin, D.F. (2003) Generations, Cohorts, and Social Change. In Mortimer, M. & Shanahan, J. (Eds.) *Handbook of the Life Course*. New York, NY:Kluwer, 23–49.

Alwin, D. & McCammon, R. (2007) Rethinking Generations. *Research in Human Development*: 219–237.

Anand, S. & Sen, A.(1994)Human Development Index: Methodology and Measurement. Human Development Report Office Occasional Papers. New York.

Anderson, E. (1999a) Towards a Non-Ideal, Relational Methodology for Political Philosophy. *Hypatia* 24 (4): 130–145.

Anderson, E. (1999b) What is the Point of Equality? *Ethics*: 287–337.

Anderson, E. (2008) How Should Egalitarians Cope with Market Risks? *Theoretical Inquiries in Law* 9: 239–270.

Anderson, E. (2010) *The Imperative of Integration*. Princeton. NJ:Princeton University Press.

Andersen, K. (2020) *Evil Geniuses. The Unmaking of America*. New York, NY: Random House.

Applewhite, A. (2016) *This Chair Rocks: A Manifesto Against Ageism*. Networked Books.

Arber, S. & Attias-Donfut, C. (Eds.) (2000) *The Myth of Generational Conflict: The Family and State in Ageing Societies*. London: Routledge.

Arber, S. et al. (2004) Influence of Patient Characteristics on Doctors' Questioning and Lifestyle Advice for Coronary Heart Disease: A US/UK Video Experiment. *British Journal of General Practice*: 673–678.

Arias, E. et al. (2021) NVSS Vital Statistics Rapid Release Report No. 015 Provisional Life Expectancy Estimates for 2020. https://www.cdc.gov/nchs/data/vsrr/vsrr015-508.pdf.

Arneson, R. (1990a) Is Work Special? Justice and the Distribution of Employment. *American Political Science Review* 84: 1127–1147.

Arneson, R. (1990b) Liberalism, Distributive Subjectivism, and Equal Opportunity for Welfare. *Philosophy and Public Affairs* 19: 158–194.

Arneson, R. (1997) Rawls, Responsibility, and Distributive Justice. In Fleurbaey, M., Salles, M. & Weymark, J. (Eds.) *Justice, Political Liberalism, and Utilitarianism: Themes from Harsanyi and Rawls*. Cambridge: Cambridge University Press: 80–108.

Arneson, R. (2000) Luck Egalitarianism and Prioritarianism. *Ethics*: 339–349.

Arneson, R. (2012) Rethinking Luck Egalitarianism and Unacceptable Inequalities. *Philosophical Topics* 40:153–169.

Aronson, L. (2019) *Elderhood: Redefining Aging, Transforming Medicine, Reimagining Life*. London:Bloomsbury.

Arrow, K.J. (1963) Uncertainty and the Welfare Economics of Medical Care. *The American Economic Review*. 941–973.

Avendano, M. et al. (2010) Do Americans Have Higher Mortality than Europeans at all Levels of the Education Distribution? A Comparison of the United States and 14 European Countries. In Crimmins, E.M., Preston, S.H. & Cohen, B. (Eds.) *National Research Council (US) Panel on Understanding Divergent Trends in Longevity in High-Income Countries*. Washington: National Academies Press.

Ayalon, L. & Tesch-Römer, C. (Eds.) (2018) *Contemporary Perspectives on Ageism: International Perspectives on Aging*. Cham, Switzerland: Springer Nature.

Baars, J. (1987) De mythe van de totale beheersing. Adorno, Horkheimer en de dialektiek van de vooruitgang. (The Myth of Total Domination. Adorno, Horkheimer and the Dialectics of Progress). Amsterdam: SUA.

Baars, J. (1990) Review of *Ageing Populations. The Social Policy Implications*, OECD: Paris 1988. *Ageing & Society*: 241–422.

Baars, J. (1991) The Challenge of Critical Gerontology: The Problem of Social Constitution. *Journal of Aging Studies* 5: 219–243.

Baars, J. (2006) *Het Nieuwe Ouder Worden*. Amsterdam: Humanistics University Press.

Baars, J. (2010a) Philosophy of Aging, Time, and Finitude. In Cole, T.R., Ray, R. & Kastenbaum, R. (Eds.) *A Guide to Humanistic Studies in Aging*. Baltimore, MD: Johns Hopkins University Press, 10–20.

Baars, J. (2010b) Time and Aging: Enduring and Emerging Issues. In Dannefer, D. & Phillipson, C. (Eds.) *International Handbook of Social Gerontology*. New York, NY:Sage, 367–376.

Baars, J. (2012a) *Aging and the Art of Living*. Baltimore, MD: Johns Hopkins University Press.

Baars, J. (2012b) Critical Turns of Aging, Narrative and Time. *International Journal of Ageing and Later Life* 7: 143–165.

Baars, J. (2016) Concepts of Time in Age and Ageing. In Scarre, G. (Ed.) *The Palgrave Handbook of the Philosophy of Aging*. London: Palgrave, 69–86.

Baars, J. (2017a) Aging: Learning to Live a Finite Life. *The Gerontologist*: 969–976.

Baars, J. (2017b) Human Aging, Finite Lives and the Idealization of Clocks. *Biogerontology*: 285–292.

Baars, J. (2020) Living in a Temporal Perspective. Aging Between Metric and Narrative Time. In Schweda, M., Coors, M. & Bozzaro, C. (Eds.) *Aging and Human Nature. Perspectives from Philosophical, Theological, and Historical Anthropology*. Zurich: Springer, 113–128.

Baars, J. (2021) Narrative Configurations of Ageing and Time. In Skagen, M. (Ed.) *Cultural Histories of Ageing: Plots, Myths and Metaphors of the Senescent Self*. Abingdon: Routledge, 21–41.

Baars, J. & Dohmen, J. (forthcoming) *Towards an Art of Aging: A Rediscovery of Forgotten Texts*. Baltimore: Johns Hopkins University Press.

Baars, J. & Phillipson, C. (2013) Connecting Meaning with Social Structure: Theoretical Foundations. In Baars, J., Dohmen, J., Grenier, A. & Phillipson, C. (Eds.) *Ageing. Meaning and Social Structure. Connecting Critical and Humanistic Gerontology*. Chicago: University of Chicago Press.

Baars, J. & Visser, H. (Eds.) (2007) *Aging and Time: Multidisciplinary Perspectives*. Amityville, NY: Baywood.

Baars, J., Dannefer, D., Phillipson, C. & Walker, A. (Eds.) (2006) *Aging, Globalization, and Inequality: The New Critical Gerontology*. Amityville, NY:Baywood.

Baars, J., Dohmen, J., Grenier, A. & Phillipsons, C. (2013) *Aging, Meaning and Social Structure: Connecting Critical and Humanistic Gerontology*. Policy Press.

Baars, J., Knipscheer, C.P.M. & Breebaart, E. (1993) *Older People in Europe. National Report on the Netherlands*. Research Report on behalf of the European Community. EU, Brussels.

Baier, A. (1994) *Moral Prejudices*. Cambridge: Cambridge University Press.

Baltes P.B., Lindenberger, U.& Staudinger, U.M. (1998) Life-span Theory in Developmental Psychology. In Damon, W. & Lerner, R.M. (Eds) *Handbook of Child Psychology. Vol. 1: Theoretical Models of Human Development*. New York, NY: John Wiley & Sons, 1029–1043.

Banks, J., Marmot, M., Oldfield, Z. & Smith, J. (2006) Disease and Disadvantage in the United States and in England. *JAMA*, 2037–2045.

Barbieri, M. (2022) Socioeconomic Disparities Do Not Explain the U.S. International Disadvantage in Mortality. *The Journals of Gerontology: Series B*: 158–166.

Barker, D., Osmond, C., Golding, J., Kuh, D. & Wadsworth, M. (1989) Growth in Utero, Blood Pressure in Childhood and Adult Life, and Mortality from Cardiovascular Disease. *BMJ*: 564–567.

Barnes, J. (Ed.) (1995) *The Complete Works of Aristotle: The Revised Oxford Translation*. 2 vols. Princeton, NJ:Princeton University Press.

Barr, B., Bambra, C. & Whitehead, M. (2014) The Impact of NHS Resource Allocation Policy on Health Inequalities in England 2001–11: Longitudinal Ecological Study. *BMJ*: 348g3231.

Barry, B. (2001)*Culture and Equality*. Cambridge, MA:Harvard University Press.

Barry, B. (2005) *Why Social Justice Matters*. Oxford: Polity.

Bartley, M. & Plewis, I. (2002) Accumulated Labour Market Disadvantage and Limiting Long-term Illness: Data from the 1971–1991 Office for National Statistics' Longitudinal Study. *International Journal of Epidemiology* 31: 336–341.

Bateson, P., Barker, D., Clutton-Brock, T. et al. (2004) Developmental Plasticity and Human Health. *Nature*: 419–421.

Bauer, P. (1981) *Equality, the Third World, and Economic Delusion*. Cambridge, MA: Harvard University Press.

Bauman, Z. (2000) *Liquid Modernity*. New York: Wiley.

Beauvoir, S.de (1972) *Coming of Age*. London: Putnam.

Beck, U. (1992) *Risk Society: Towards a New Modernity*. London: Sage.

Beck, U. & Beck-Gernsheim, E. (2002) *Individualization: Institutionalized Individualism and Its Social and Political Consequences*. London: Sage.

Bell, D. (1972) On Equality: I. Meritocracy and Equality. *Public Interest* 29: 29–68.

Bell, D. (1976) *The Cultural Contradictions of Capitalism*. New York, NY: Basic Books.

Ben-Shlomo, Y. & Kuh, D. (2002)A Life Course Approach to Chronic Disease Epidemiology: Conceptual Models, Empirical Challenges and Interdisciplinary Perspectives. *International Journal of Epidemiology* 31: 85–293.

Bengtson, V. & Achenbaum, W.A. (Eds.) (1993) *The Changing Contract Across Generations*. New York, NY:Aldine de Gruyter.

Bieler, A.S. & Morton, A.D. (2001) *Social Forces in the Making of the New Europe. The Restructuring of European Social Relations in the Global Political Economy*. New York, NY:Palgrave.

Biggs, S. & Lowenstein, A. (2011)*Generational Intelligence: A Critical Approach to Age Relations*. London: Routledge.

Bytheway, B. (1995) *Ageism*. Buckingham: Open University Press.

Binstock, B. (1983) The Aged as Scapegoat. *The Gerontologist*:136–143.

Binstock, R.H. (2010) From Compassionate Ageism to Intergenerational Conflict? *The Gerontologist*: 574–585.

Birren, J. (1959) Principles of Research on Aging. In Birren, J. (Ed.) *Handbook of Aging and the Individual: Psychological and Biological Aspects*. Chicago: University of Chicago Press, 2–242.

Birren, J. (1999) Theories of Aging: A Personal Perspective. In Vern, L.Bengtson, V. & Warner Schaie, K. (Eds.) *Handbook of Theories of Aging*. New York, NY: Springer, 459–471.

Black, T. (2009) *When a Heart Turns Rock Solid: The Lives of Three Puerto Rican Brothers On and Off the Streets*. New York, NY:Vintage.

Blackburn, R. (2004) *Banking on Death: Or Investing in Life: The History and Future of Pensions*. London: Verso.

Blake, M. & Risse, M. (2008) Two Models of Equality and Responsibility. *Canadian Journal of Philosophy*: 165–199.

Blanchard, O. (2006) European Unemployment: The Evolution of Facts and Ideas. *Economic Policy*: 5–59.

Bloch, E. (1995) *The Principle of Hope.* Cambridge, MA: MIT Press.

Blue Cross Blue Shield (2019) *The Health of Millennials.* https://www.bcbs.com/the-health-of-america/reports/the-health-of-millennials.

Boardman, J.D. et al. (2001) Neighborhood Disadvantage, Stress, and Drug Use Among Adults. *Journal of Health and Social Behavior:*151–165.

Bognar, G & Hriose, I. (2014) *The Ethics of Health Care Rationing. An Introduction.* Abingdon:Routledge.

Bognar, G. (2015) Fair Innings. *Bioethics* 29: 251–261. doi:10.1111/bioe.12101.

Bond Huie, S.A., Krueger, P.M., Rogers, R.G. & Hummer, R.A. (2003) Wealth, Race, and Mortality. *Social Science Quarterly:* 667–684.

Bond, M.J. & Herman, A.A. (2016) Lagging Life Expectancy for Black Men: A Public Health Imperative. *American Journal of Public Health:*1167–1169.

Bosworth, B., Burtless, G. & Zhang, K. (2016) *Later Retirement, Inequality in Old Age, and the Growing Gap in Longevity Between Rich and Poor.* Washington, DC: The Brookings Institution/George Washington University.

Boudiny, K. (2013) Active Ageing: From Empty Rhetoric to Effective Policy Tool. *Ageing & Society:*1077–1098.

Bourdieu, P. (1984 [1979]) *Distinction. A Social Critique of the Judgment of Taste.* London: Routledge.

Brandmeir, K., Grimm, M., & Holzhausen, A. (2015). *Allianz Global Wealth Report 2015.* Munich, Germany: Allianz SE.

Braveman, P. & Barclay, C. (2009) Health Disparities Beginning in Childhood: A Life-Course Perspective. *Pediatrics:*163–175.

Braveman, P. & Gruskin, S. (2003) Defining Equity in Health. *Journal of Epidemiology Community Health* 57: 254–258.

Braveman, P., Egerter, S. & Williams, D. (2011) The Social Determinants of Health: Coming of Age. *Annual Review of Public Health:* 381–398.

Braveman, P.A., Cubbin, C., Egerter, S., Williams, D.R. & Pamuk, E. (2010) Socioeconomic Disparities in Health in the United States: What the Patterns Tell Us. *American Journal of Public Health:* 20–35.

Braveman, P.A., Kumanyika, S., Fielding, J., Laveist, T., Borrell, L.N., Manderscheid, R. & Troutman, A. (2011) Health Disparities and Health Equity: The Issue Is Justice. *American Journal of Public Health.* Suppl 1: 149–155.

Kotlikoff, J. & Burns, S. (2005) *The Coming Generational Storm.* Cambridge, MA: MIT Press.

Brim, O., Ryff, C. & Kessler, R. (2004) *How Healthy Are We? A National Study of Well-Being at Midlife.* Chicago: University of Chicago Press.

Brock, D. (1989) Justice, Health Care, and the Elderly. *Philosophy and Public Affairs:* 297–312.

Brogden, M. (2001) *Geronticide. Killing the Elderly.* Philadelphia, PA: Jessica Kingsley Publishers.

Buffel, T., Handler, S. & Phillipson, C. (Eds.) 2019*Age-Friendly Cities and Communities. A Global Perspective.* Bristol: Polity.

Bui, C.N., Peng, C., Mutchler, J.E. & Burr, J.A. (2021) Race and Ethnic Group Disparities in Emotional Distress Among Older Adults During the COVID-19 Pandemic. *The Gerontologist* 61 (2): 262–272.

Burdorf, A. (2006) The Effect of High Physical Load at Work on Physical Function at Old Age. *Occupational and Environmental Medicine* 63: 437.

Burrow, J.A. (1986) *The Ages of Man: A Study in Medieval Writing and Thought.* Oxford: Oxford University Press.

Burton, L. & Whitfield, K. (2006) Health, Aging, and America's Poor: Ethnographic Insights on Family, Co-Morbidity, and Cumulative Disadvantage. In Baars, J., Dannefer, D., Phillipson, C. & Walker, A. (Eds.) *Aging, Globalization and Inequality: The New Critical Gerontology.* Amityville, NY: Baywood, 215–230.

Butler, R. (1980) Ageism: A Foreword. *Journal of Social Issues* 36. doi:10.1111/j.1540-4560.1980.tb02018.x.

Butler, R. (1969)Age-ism: Another Form of Bigotry. *The Gerontologist* 9 (4): 243–246.

Butler, R. (1975) *Why Survive? Being Old in America.* Baltimore and London: Johns Hopkins University Press.

Bytheway, B. (1995)*Ageism.* Buckingham: Open University Press.

Calasanti, T. (2015) Combating Ageism: How Successful Is Successful Aging? *The Gerontologist* 56 (6): 1093–1101.

Calhoun, C. (Ed.) (1994) *Social Theory and the Politics of Identity.* Oxford: Blackwell.

Callahan, D. (1987) *Setting Limits: Medical Goals in an Aging Society.* New York, NY: Simon and Schuster.

Callahan, D. (1994) Setting Limits: A Response. *The Gerontologist*: 393–398.

Callahan, D. (2012) *In Search of the Good: A Life in Bioethics. A Memoir.* Cambridge, MA: MIT Press.

Caplan, L. (2014) The Boomer Fallacy: Why Greedy Geezers Aren't Destroying our Financial Future. *American Scholar*, Summer. https://encore.org/blogs/debunking-the-greedy-geezer-meme/.

Carstensen, L. (2009) *A Long and Bright Future.* New York, NY: Broadway.

Case, A. and Deaton, A. (2000)*Deaths of Despair and the Future of Capitalism.* Princeton, NJ: Princeton University Press.

Case, A. & Deaton, A. (2015) Rising Morbidity and Mortality in Midlife Among White Non-Hispanic Americans in the 21st Century. *PNAS*: 15078–15083.

Case, A. & Deaton, A. (2017)Mortality and Morbidity in the 21st Century. *Brookings Papers on Economic Activities*: 397–476.

Case, A., Fertig, A. & Paxson, C. (2005) The Lasting Impact of Childhood Health and Circumstance. *Journal of Health Economics* 24: 365–389.

Chandra, A. et al. (2010) Understanding Community Resilience in the Context of National Health Security: A Literature Review. RAND Working Paper. doi:10.7249/WR737.

Cherlin, A.J. (2018) Psychological Health and Socioeconomic Status Among Non-Hispanic Whites. *Proceedings of National Academy of Sciences USA*: 7176–7178.

Chetty, R., Stepner, M., Abraham, S., et al. 2016The Association Between Income and Life Expectancy in the United States, 2000–2014. *JAMA*: 1750–1766.

Chetty, R., Hendren, N., Kline, P. & Saez, E. (2014) Where Is the Land of Opportunity? The Geography of Intergenerational Mobility in the United States. *The Quarterly Journal of Economics*: 1553–1623.

Chetty, R., Friedman, J., Saez, E., Turner, N. & Yagan, D. (2017) Mobility Report Cards: The Role of Colleges in Intergenerational Mobility. Working Paper, National Bureau of Economic Research. https://www.nber.org/papers/w23618.

Chetty, R., Grusky, D., Hell, M., Hendren, N., Manduca, R. & Narang, J. (2016) The Fading American Dream: Trends in Absolute Income Mobility Since 1940. https://inequality.stanford.edu/sites/default/files/fading-american-dream.pdf.

Choi, H., Steptoe, A., Heisler, M., et al. (2020) Comparison of Health Outcomes Among High- and Low-Income Adults Aged 55 to 64 Years in the US vs England. *JAMA Internal Medicine*: 1185–1193.

Christakis, N. (2020) *Apollo's Arrow: The Profound and Enduring Impact of Coronavirus on the Way We Live*. New York, NY:Little, Brown Spark.

Christman, J. & Anderson, J. (2005)*Autonomy and the Challenges to Liberalism: New Essays*. Cambridge: Cambridge University Press.

Chudacoff, H.P. (1989) *How Old Are You? Age Consciousness in American Culture*. Princeton, NJ: Princeton University Press.

Clark, M. (1973) Contributions of Cultural Anthropology to the Study of the Aged. In Nader, L. & Maretzki, T. (Eds.) *Cultural Illness and Health*. Washington, DC: American Anthropological Society.

Clingan, N. (2012) *The Actuality of Critical Theory in the Netherlands, 1931–1994*. Dissertation. Berkeley, CA: University of California. https://digitalassets.lib.berke ley.edu/etd/ucb/text/BarrClingan_berkeley_0028E_12550.pdf.

Coburn, D. (2015) Income Inequality, Welfare, Class and Health: A Comment on Pickett and Wilkinson, 2015. *Social Science & Medicine*: 228–232.

Cohen, G. (1989) On the Currency of Egalitarian Justice. *Ethics*: 906–944.

Cohen, G. (1991) *Incentives, Inequality, and Community*.Tanner Lecture 1991, Stanford University.

Cohen, G. (1993) Equality of What? On Welfare, Goods, and Capabilities. In Nussbaum, M. & Sen, A. (Eds.) *The Quality of Life*. Oxford: Clarendon.

Cohen, G. (2009) *Why Not Socialism?*Princeton, NJ/Oxford: Princeton University Press.

Cohen, L.M. (1993)*Justice Across Generations: What Does it Mean?*Public Policy Institute AARP.

Cole, T.R. (1992) *The Journey of Life: A Cultural History of Aging in America*. New York, NY:Cambridge University Press.

Coleman, K.A. (1995) The Value of Productive Activities of Older Americans. In Bass, S. (Ed.) *Older and Active: How Americans over 55 Are Contributing to Society*. London: Yale University Press, 169–203.

Conley, D. (2002) Forty Acres and a Mule: What if America Pays Reparations? *Contexts*: 13–20.

Connell, R. (2005) *Masculinities*. Cambridge: Polity Press.

Corak, M. & Heisz, A. (1998) The Intergenerational Earnings and Income Mobility of Canadian Men: Evidence from Longitudinal Income Tax Data (October 1998) Statistics Canada Working Paper No. 113. http://dx.doi.org/10.2139/ssrn. 139768.

Covinsky, K. & Katz, M. (2020) Editor's Note: Supplemental Nutrition Assistance Program—Do Not Take the Food Out of Patients' Mouths, *JAMA Internal Medicine*: 605–606.

Crenshaw, K. (2019) *On Intersectionality: Essential Writings*. New York: New Press.

Crimmins, E.M. & Cambois, E. (2003)Social Inequalities in Health Expectancy In Robine, J., Jagger, C., Mathers C.D. et al. (Eds.) *Determining Health Expectancies*. Chichester: John Wiley & Sons, 111–126.

Crimmins, E.M. & Saito, Y. (2001) Trends in Healthy Life Expectancy in the United States, 1970–1990: Gender, Racial, and Educational Differences. *Social Science & Medicine*: 1629–1641.

Crimmins, E., Jung Ki Kim, & Aïda Solé-Auró (2011) Gender Differences in Health: Results from SHARE, ELSA and HRS. *European Journal of Public Health*: 81–91.

Critser, G. (2003) *Fat Land. How Americans became the Fattest People in the World*. Boston:, MA:Hoghton Mifflin.

Cruikshank, M. (2009) *Learning to Be Old: Gender, Culture, and Aging*. Washington DC: Rowman & Littlefield.

Crystal, S. (2006) Dynamics of Late-Life Inequality: Modeling the Interplay of Health Disparities, Economic Resources and Public Policies. In Baars, J., Dannefer, D., Phillipson, C. & Walker, A. (Eds.) *Ageing, Globalization and Inequality*. Amityville NY: Baywood, 205–213.

Crystal, S. (2018) Cumulative Advantage and the Retirement Prospects of the Hollowed-out Generation: A Tale of Two Cohorts. *Public Policy & Aging Report*: 14–18.

Crystal, S. & Shea, D. (2003) Cumulative Advantage, Public Policy, and Late-Life Inequality. In Crystal, S. & Shea, D. (Eds.) *Economic Outcomes in Later Life: Public Policy, Health, and Cumulative Advantage. Annual Review of Gerontology and Geriatrics* 22: 1–13.

Crystal, S. & Waehrer, K. (1996) Later-life Economic Inequality in Longitudinal Perspective. *The Journals of Gerontology, Series B* 51: 307–318.

Crystal, S., Shea, D. & Reyes, A.M.(2017)Cumulative Advantage, Cumulative Disadvantage, and Evolving Patterns of Late-Life Inequality. *Gerontologist* 57: 910–920.

Cumming, E. & Henry, W. (1961)*Growing Old: The Process of Disengagement*. New York, NY:Basic Books.

Cupit, G. (1998) Justice, Age, and Veneration. *Ethics* 108: 702–718.

Daly, M.C., Duncan, G.J, McDonough, P. & Williams, D.R. (2002) Optimal Indicators of Socioeconomic Status for Health Research. *American Journal of Public Health* 92: 1151–1157.

Daniels, N. (1985) *Just Health Care*. New York, NY:Cambridge University Press.

Daniels, N. (1988)*Am I My Parents' Keeper? An Essay on Justice Between the Young and the Old*. Oxford: Oxford University Press.

Daniels, N. (1991) A Lifespan Approach to Healthcare. In Jecker, N. (Ed.) *Ageing and Ethics*New York, NY:Springer, 227–246.

Daniels, N. (2003) Democratic Equality: Rawls's Complex Egalitarianism. In Samuel Freeman, R. (Ed.), *The Cambridge Companion to Rawls*. Cambridge University Press, 241–276.

Daniels, N. (1996)*Justice and Justification: Reflective Equilibrium in Theory and Practice*. Cambridge:Cambridge University Press.

Daniels, N. (2008) *Just Health. Meeting Health Needs Fairly*. New York, NY:Cambridge University Press.

Daniels, N. (2009)Just Health: Replies and Further Thoughts. *Journal of Medical Ethics* 35: 36–41.

Daniels, N. & Sabin, J.E. (2002)*Setting Limits Fairly: Learning to Share Resources for Health*. New York, NY: Oxford University Press.

Daniels, N., Kennedy, B. & Kawachi, I. (2000) *Is Inequality bad for our Health?* Boston, MA: Beacon Press.

Dannefer, D. (1984) Adult Development and Social Theory: A Paradigmatic Reappraisal. *American Sociological Review*: 100–116.

Dannefer, D. (1987) Aging as Intracohort Differentiation: Accentuation, the Matthew Effect, and the Life Course. *Sociological Forum*: 211–237.

Dannefer, D. (2003) Cumulative Advantage and the Life Course: Cross-fertilizing Age and Social Science Knowledge. *Journals of Gerontology, Series B*: 327–337.

Dannefer, D. (2020) Systemic and Reflexive: Foundations of Cumulative Dis/advantage and Life Course Processes. *Journals of Gerontology B*:1249–1263.

Dannefer, D. (2022) *Age and the Reach of Sociological Imagination: Power, Ideology and the Life Course*. New York, NY:Routledge.

Dannefer, D., Kelley-Moore, J. & Huang, W. (2016) Opening the Social: Sociological imagination in life course studies. In *Handbook of the Life Course*. New York, NY:Springer, 87–110.

Dannefer, D., Gilbert, M. & Han, C. (2020) With the Wind at Their Backs. *Annual Review of Gerontology and Geriatrics: Economic Inequality in Later Life*: 105–126.

Darity, W., Jr. (2008) Forty Acres and a Mule in the 21st Century. *Social Science Quarterly*, 89 (3), 656–664.

Davey Smith, G. (Ed.) (2003) *Health Inequalities. Lifecourse Approaches*. Bristol: Polity.

Davey Smith, G., Harding, S. & Rosato, M. (2000) Relation between Infants' Birthweight and Mothers' Mortality: Prospective Observational Study. *BMJ* 320: 839–840.

Davey Smith, G., Whitley, E., Gissler, M. & Hemminki, E. (2000) Birth Dimensions of Offspring, Premature Births, and the Mortality of Mothers. *Lancet* 56: 2066–2067.

Davey Smith, G., Harding, S. & Rosato, M. (2000) Relation Between Infants' Birthweight and Mothers' Mortality: Prospective Observational Study. *BMJ* 320: 839–840.

Dawson, M. (2016) Hidden in Plain Sight: A Note on Legitimation Crises and the Racial Order. *Critical Historical Studies* 3: 143–161.

De Dijn, A. (2020) *Freedom: An Unruly History*. Boston, MA:Harvard University Press.

Deater-Deckard, K. et al. (1998) Multiple Risk Factors in the Development of Externalizing Behavior Problems: Group and Individual Differences. *Development and Psychopathology*: 469–493.

Demetriou, D. (2001) Connell's Concept of Hegemonic Masculinity: A Critique. *Theory & Society*: 337–361.

Derrida, J. (1998) *Of Grammatology*. Baltimore, MD: Johns Hopkins University Press.

Desmond, M. (2016) *Evicted: Poverty and Profit in the American City*. New York, NY: Broadway Books.

Dewey, J. (1910) *How We Think*. Boston, MA:Heath.

DiPrete, T.A., & Eirich, G.M. (2006) Cumulative Advantage as a Mechanism for Inequality: A Review of Theoretical and Empirical Developments. *Annual Review of Sociology*: 271–297.

Dolk, D. (1998) Risk of Congenital Anomalies Near Hazardous-Waste Landfill Sites in Europe: the EUROHAZCON Study. *The Lancet*: 422–427.

Dominguez, T.P., Dunkel-Schetter, C., Glynn L.M. et al. (2008) Racial Differences in Birth Outcomes: The Role of General, Pregnancy, and Racism Stress. *Health Psychology*: 194–203.

Douthit, K. (2006) Dementia in the Iron Cage: The Biopsychiatric Construction of Alzheimer's Dementia. In Baars, J., Dannefer, D., Phillipson, C. & Walker, A.

(Eds.) *Aging, Globalization, and Inequality: The New Critical Gerontology*. Amityville, NY: Baywood, 159–182.

Dunn, C. (2012) The Effect of Ageing on Autonomy. In H. Lesser (ed.) *Justice for Older People*. Amsterdam: Rodopi: 51–64.

Dworkin, R. (1981a) What is Equality? Part 1: Equality of Welfare. *Philosophy And Public Affairs*: 185–426.

Dworkin, R. (1981b) What is Equality? Part 2: Equality of Resources. *Philosophy And Public Affairs* 10: 283–345.

Dworkin, R. (1993) Justice in the Distribution of Health Care. *McGill Law Journal*: 882–898.

Dworkin, R. (2000) *Sovereign Virtue. The Theory and Practice of Equality*. Boston, MA: Harvard University Press.

Dworkin, R. (2003a) Equality, Luck and Hierarchy. *Philosophy and Public Affairs*: 190–198.

Dworkin, R. (2003b) Sovereign Virtue Revisited. *Ethics*: 106–143.

Dwyer-Lindgren, L. et al. (2017) Inequalities in Life Expectancy Among US Counties, 1980 to 2014. Temporal Trends and Key Drivers. *JAMA Internal Medicine*: 1003–1011.

Easterlin, R.A, (1987) The New Age Structure of Poverty in America: Permanent or Transient? *Population and Development Review*: 195–208.

Ehrenreich, B. (2001)*Nickel and Dimed: On (Not) Getting By in America*. New York, NY: Henry Holt.

Eckert, D.J. (1986) The Busy Ethic: Moral Continuity between Work and Retirement. *The Gerontologist* 26 (3): 239–244.

Elder, G. (1974) *Children of the Great Depression*. Chicago: University of Chicago Press.

Elo, J. (2009) Social Class Differentials in Health and Mortality: Patterns and Explanations in Comparative Perspective. *Annual Review of Sociology* 35: 553–572.

Emanuel, E.J., Gudbranson, E., Van Parys, J., Gørtz, M., Helgeland, J. & Skinner, J. (2020) Comparing Health Outcomes of Privileged US Citizens With Those of Average Residents of Other Developed Countries. *JAMA Internal Medicine*. Published online December 28, 2020.

Erikson, R. (2001) Why Do Graduates Live Longer? In Jonsson, J.O. & Mills, C. (Eds.) *Cradle to Grave: Life-Course Change in Modern Sweden*. Durham: Sociology Press.

Erikson, E.H. & Erikson, J.M. (1997) *The Life Cycle Completed: Extended Version*. New York, NY:W.W. Norton.

Espey, D. (2014) American Indian and Alaska Native Mortality. *American Journal of Public Health*: 251–506.

Esping-Andersen, G. (1999) *Social Foundations of Postindustrial Economies*. New York, NY:Oxford University Press.

Estes, C. (1979) *The Aging Enterprise*. San Francisco, CA:Jossey-Bass Publishers.

Estes, C. & DiCarlo, N. (2019) *Aging A-Z. Concepts Toward Emancipatory Gerontology*. New York, NY:Routledge.

Estes, C. & Wallace, S. (2005) Older People. In Levy, B.S. & Sidel, V.W. (Eds.) *Social Injustice and Public Health*. New York, NY:Oxford University Press, 106–122.

Etzioni, A. (2006) A Neo-Communitarian Approach to International Relations: Rights and the Good. *Human Rights Review*: 69–80.

European Commission (2009) *Dealing with the Impact of an Ageing Population in the EU*. Brussels.

Evans, G.W. (2003) A Multimethodological Analysis of Cumulative Risk and Allostatic Load Among Rural Children. *Developmental Psychology* 39: 924–933.

Evans, R.G. (2008) Thomas McKeown, Meet Fidel Castro: Physicians, Population Health and the Cuban Paradox. *Healthcare Policy*: 21–32.

Evans, G. & English, K. (2002) The Environment of Poverty: Multiple Stressor Exposure, Psychophysiological Stress, and Socioemotional Adjustment. *Child Development*: 1238–1248.

Evans, G. & Kim, P. (2007) Childhood Poverty and Health. Cumulative Risk Exposure and Stress Dysregulation. *Psychological Science*: 953–957.

Evans, G. & Kim, P. (2010) Multiple Risk Exposure as a Potential Explanatory Mechanism for the Socioeconomic Status–Health Gradient. *Annals of the New York Academy of Sciences*: 174–189.

Evans, W., Wolfe, B. & Adler, N. (2012) The SES and the Health Gradient: A Brief Review of the Literature. In Wolfe, B., Evans, W. & Seeman, T. (Eds.) *The Biological Consequences of Socioeconomic Inequalities*. New York, NY: Russell Sage.

Ezzati, M. et al. (2008) The Reversal of Fortunes: Trends in County Mortality and Cross-County Mortality Disparities in the United States. *PLOS Medicine* 5 (4): e66. https://doi.org/10.1371/journal.pmed.0050066.

Facebook (2012) *Facebook Community Standards*. Retrieved on May 7, 2012. http://facebook.com/communitystandards.

Fairlie, H. (1988) Greedy Geezers: Talkin' 'Bout My Generation. *New Republic* 18.

Fernandez, R. & Klinge, T. (2020) *Private Gains We Can Ill Afford. The Financialisation of Big Pharma*. Amsterdam: SOMO.

Ferraro, K.F. & Kelley-Moore, J.A. (2003) Cumulative Disadvantage and Health: Long-term Consequences of Obesity? *American Sociological Review* 68: 707–729.

Ferraro, K.F., Shippee, T.P. & Schafer, M.H. (2009) Cumulative Inequality Theory for Research on Aging and the Life Course. In Bengtson, V.L., Silverstein, M., Putney, M. & Gans, D. (Eds.) *Handbook of Theories of Aging*, Second Edition. New York, NY:Springer, 414–433.

Fishkin, J. (1983) *Justice, Equal Opportunity, and the Family*. New Haven, CT: Yale University Press.

Fishman, T. (2012) *A Shock of Gray: The Aging of the World's Population and How it Pits Young Against Old, Child Against Parent, Worker Against Boss, Company Against Rival, and Nation Against Nation*. New York, NY:Scribner.

Fleurbaey, M. (2008) *Fairness, Responsibility, and Welfare*. New York, NY:Oxford University Press.

Flew, A. (1980) *The Politics of Procrustes. Contradictions of Enforced Equality*. London: Prometheus.

Formosa, M. & Higgs, P. (2015) *Social Class in Later Life: Power, Identity and Lifestyle*. Bristol: Polity.

Foster, L. & Walker, A. (2015) Active and Successful Aging: A European Policy Perspective. *The Gerontologist*: 83–90.

Foucault, M. (1965) *Madness and Civilization: A History of Insanity in the Age of Reason*. London: Tavistock

Foucault, M. (1978)*Discipline and Punish. The Birth of the Prison*. New York, NY: Pantheon.

Foucault, M. (1990) *The History of Sexuality. Volume 1. An Introduction.* New York, NY:Vintage.

Foucault, M. (1990) *The History of Sexuality. Volume 2. The Use of Pleasure.* New York, NY:Vintage.

Foucault, M. (1990) *The History of Sexuality. Volume 3. The Care of the Self.* New York, NY:Vintage.

Frank, R. (1999) *Luxury Fever: Why Money Fails to Satisfy in an Era of Success.* New York, NY:Free Press.

Frankfurt, Harry (1988) *The Importance of What We Care About.* Cambridge: Cambridge University Press.

Frankl, V. (2006) *Man's Search for Meaning.* Boston, MA:Beacon.

Fraser, N. (1997) *Justice Interruptus.* New York, NY:Routledge.

Fraser, N. (2016) Expropriation and Exploitation in Racialized Capitalism. *Critical Historical Studies* 3: 163–178.

Fraser, N. & Honneth, A. (2003) *Redistribution or Recognition?* London: Verso.

Freeman, H. & Gonos, G (2009) Taming the Employment Sharks: The Case for Regulating Profit-driven Labor Market Intermediaries in High Mobility Labor Markets. *Employee Rights and Employment Policy Journal*: 101–176.

Fried, C. (1978) *Right and Wrong.* Cambridge, MA: Harvard University Press.

Friedman, L. (2003) Age Discrimination Law: Some Remarks on the American Experience. In Fredman, S. & Spencer, S. (Eds.) *Age as an Equality Issue.* London: Bloomsbury, 175–190.

Fukuyama, F. (1992) *The End of History and the Last Man.* London: Penguin.

Galbraith, J.K. (1952/2017) *American Capitalism. The Concept of Countervailing Power.* New York, NY:Routledge.

Galea, S. & Vlahov, D. (2002) Social Determinants and the Health of Drug Users: Socioeconomic Status, Homelessness, and Incarceration. *Public Health Reports (Suppl 1)*: S 135–145.

Gandal, N., Yonas, M., Feldman, M., Pauzner, A. & Tabbach, A. (2020) Long-Term Care Facilities as a Risk Factor in Death Due from COVID-19. VOX EU–CEPR. https://cepr.org/voxeu/columns/long-term-care-facilities-risk-factor-death-covid-19.

Gavrilov, L. & Gavrilova, N. (2006) Reliability Theory of Aging and Longevity. In Masoro, E. & Austad, S. (Eds.). *Handbook of the Biology of Aging*, 6th edition. San Diego, CA: Elsevier, 3–42.

Gerdtham, U. & Johannesson, M. (2003) A Note on the Effect of Unemployment on Mortality. *Journal of Health Economics*: 505–518.

Geronimus, A.T. (1992) The Weathering Hypothesis and the Health of African-American Women and Infants: Evidence and Speculations. *Ethnicity & Disease*: 207–221.

Geronimus, A.T. (1996) Black/White Differences in the Relationship of Maternal Age to Birthweight: A Population-based Test of the Weathering Hypothesis. *Social Science and Medicine*: 589–577.

Geronimus, A. et al. (2015) Race/Ethnicity, Poverty, Urban Stressors and Telomere Length in a Detroit Community-Based Sample. *Journal of Health and Social Behaviour*: 199–224.

Giddens, A. (1991) *Modernity and Self-Identity: Self and Society in the Late Modern Age.* Cambridge: Polity Press.

Gilbert, S.F. & Epel, D. (2009) *Ecological Developmental Biology.* Sunderland: Sinauer Associates.

Gilder, G. (1981) *Wealth and Poverty.* New York, NY:Basic Books.

Gilleard, C. & Higgs, P. (2000) *Cultures of Ageing. Self, Citizen and the Body.* Harlow: Pearson.

Gilleard, C. & Higgs, P. (2011) Ageing Abjection and Embodiment in the Fourth Age. *Journal of Aging Studies*: 135–142.

Gilleard, C. & Higgs, P. (2014) *Ageing, Corporeality and Embodiment.* London: Anthem Press.

Ginn, J. & Arber, S. (1993) Pension Penalties: The Gendered Division of Occupational Welfare. *Work, Employment and Society*: 47–70.

Glendon, M.A. (1991) *Rights Talk: The Impoverishment of American Political Discourse.* New York, NY:Free Press.

Glenn, N.D. (2004a) Distinguishing Age, Period, and Cohort Effects. In Mortimer, J. & Shanahan, M. (Eds.) *Handbook of the Life Course.* New York, NY: Springer, 465–476.

Glenn, N.D. (2004b) *Cohort Analysis.* Thousand Oaks, CA: Sage.

Glennerster, H. (2004)The Context for Rowntree's Contribution. In Glennerster, H., Hills, J., Piachaud, D. & Webb, J. *One Hundred Years of Poverty and Policy.* York: Rowntree Foundation, 1–8.

Gluckman, P.D. & Hanson, M.A. (2005) *Mismatch: The Lifestyle Diseases Timebomb.* New York, NY:Oxford University Press.

Gluckman, P. & Hanson, M. (Eds.) (2006) *Developmental Origins of Health and Disease.* New York, NY:Cambridge University Press.

Goffman, E. (1961) *Asylums.* New York, NY:Anchor Books.

Gold, R., Kennedy, B., Connell, F. & Kawachi, I. (2002) Teen Births, Income Inequality, and Social Capital: Developing an Understanding of the Causal Pathway. *Health and Place*: 77–83.

Gopinath, M. (2018) Thinking about Later Life: Insights from the Capability Approach. *Ageing Internatinal*: 254–264.

Gottfredson, L.S. (2004) Intelligence: Is it the Epidemiologists' Elusive "Fundamental Cause" of Social Class Inequalities in Health? *Journal of Persona lity and Social Psychology*: 17–99.

Gould, R. (2002) The Origin of Status Hierarchies: A Formal Theory and Empirical Test. *American Journal of Sociology*:1143–1178.

Graeber, D. (2019) *Bullshit Jobs: The Rise of Pointless Work, and What We Can Do About It.* London: Penguin.

Grandjean, P. & Landrigan, P. (2014) Neurobehavioural Effects of Developmental Toxicity. *The Lancet Neurology*:330–338.

Grenier, A. & Phillipson, C. (2013) *Rethinking Agency in Late Life: Structural And Interpretive Approaches.* In Baars, J., Dohmen, J., Grenier, A. & Phillipson, C. (Eds.) *Ageing. Meaning and Social Structure. Connecting Critical and Humanistic Gerontology.* Chicago: University of Chicago Press, 55–80.

Grenier, A., Phillipson, C. & Settersten, R. (2021) *Precarity and Ageing. Understanding Insecurity and Risk in Later Life.* Bristol: Polity.

Gruenewald, T. et al. (2012) History of Socioeconomic Disadvantage and Allostatic Load in Later Life. *Social Science & Medicine*: 75–83.

Gullette, M. (2018) The Monument and the Wrecking Crew. Ageism in the Academy. https://www.aaup.org/article/monument-and-wrecking-crew#.WxU7Jy2s3OR.

Gurland, B.J., Page, W.F. & Plassman, B.L. (2004) A Twin Study of the Genetic Contribution to Age-related Functional Impairment. *Journals of Gerontology (A)*: 859–863.

Gutman, L.M., Sameroff, A.J. & Cole, R. (2003) Academic Growth Curve Trajectories from 1st Grade to 12th Grade: Effects of Multiple Social Risk Factors and Preschool Child Factors. *Developmental Psychology*: 777–790.

Habermas, J. (1987a) *The Theory of Communicative Action. Volume Two: Lifeworld and System: A Critique of Functionalist Reason*. Cambridge: Polity.

Habermas, J. (1987b) *The Philosophical Discourse of Modernity*. Cambridge: Polity.

Habermas, J. (1996) *Between Facts and Norms: Contributions to a Discourse Theory of Law and Democracy*. Cambridge, MA: MIT Press.

Hadbavna, A. & O'Neill, D. (2013) Ageism in Interventional Stroke Studies. *Journal of the American Geriatrics Society*: 2054–2055.

Hagestad, G. & Dannefer, D. (2011). Age, the Life Course, and the Sociological Imagination: Prospects for Theory. In Binstock, R.H. & George, L.K. (Eds.), *Handbook of Aging and the Social Sciences*. Elsevier Academic Press, 3–16.

Hagestad, G. & Uhlenberg, P. (2005) The Social Separation of Old and Young: A Root of Ageism. *Social Issues*: 343–360.

Hainey, K. & Katikireddi, S. (2020) The Inverse Care Law in Critical Care During the COVID-19 Pandemic. *The Lancet Regional Health Europe*. doi: https://doi.org/10.1016/j.lanepe.2020.100008.

Hales, C.N. & Barker, D. (2001) The Thrifty Phenotype Hypothesis. *British Medical Bulletin*: 5–20.

Hamler, T. et al. (2022) COVID-19 and Psychological Distress: Racial Differences Among Middle-Aged and Older Adults. *The Gerontologist*: 780–791.

Hao, Y. & Farah, M.J. (2020) The Affective Neuroscience of Socioeconomic Status: Implications for Mental Health. *British Journal Psychological Bulletin*: 202–207.

Harris, J. (1985) *The Value of Life. An Introduction to Medical Ethics*. London: Routledge & Kegan Paul.

Harrington, M. (1962) *The Other America. Poverty in the United States*. New York, NY:MacMillan.

Hart, J.T. (1971) The Inverse Care Law. *The Lancet*:405–412.

Harvey, D. (2005) *A Brief History of Neo-liberalism*. Oxford: Oxford University Press.

Haskins, R., Isaacs, J. & Sawhill, I. (2008) Getting Ahead or Losing Ground: Economic Mobility in America. https://www.brookings.edu/wpcontent/uploads/2016/06/02_economic_mobility_sawhill.pdf.

Hayflick, L. (2007a) Biological Aging is No Longer an Unresolved Problem . *Annals of the New York Academy of Sciences*: 1–13.

Hayflick, L. (2007b) Entropy Explains Aging, Genetic Determinism Explains Longevity, and Undefined Terminology Explains Misunderstanding Both. *PLoS Genetics*: 2351–2354.

Hayslip, B. & Smith, G. (Eds.) (2012) Emerging Perspectives on Resilience in Adulthood and Later Life. *Annual Review of Gerontology and Geriatrics* 32 (1): 211–230.

Hayward, M.D. & Gorman, B.K. (2004) The Long Arm of Childhood: The Influence of Early-Life Social Conditions on Men's Mortality. *Demography*: 87–107.

Head, J. et al. (2019) Socioeconomic Differences in Healthy and Disease-free Life Expectancy between Ages 50 and 75: A Multi-cohort Study. *European Journal of Public Health*:267–272.

Hearst, M.O., Oakes, J.M. & Johnson, P.J. (2008) The Effect of Racial Residential Segregation on Black Infant Mortality. *American Journal of Epidemiology*: 1247–1254.

Hendi, A.S. (2015) Trends in U.S. Life Expectancy Gradients: The Role of Changing Educational Composition. *International Journal of Epidemiology*: 946–955.

Hendi, A.S. (2017) Trends in Education-Specific Life Expectancy, Data Quality, and Shifting Education Distributions: A Note on Recent Research. *Demography*: 1203–1213.

Herd, P., Goesling, B. & House, J.S. (2007) Socioeconomic Position and Health: The Differential Effects of Education Versus Income on the Onset Versus Progression of Health Problems. *Journal of Health and Social Behavior*:223–238.

Hershey, D. (2010) *Entropy Theory of Aging Systems: Humans, Corporations, and the Universe*. London: Imperial College Press.

Hershey, D. & Wang, H. (1980)*A New Age Scale for Humans*. Toronto: Lexington Books.

Heuveline P. & Tzen, M. (2021) Beyond Deaths per Capita: Comparative COVID-19 Mortality Indicators *BMJ Open 2021*. doi:10.1136/bmjopen-202-42934.

Higgs, P. & Gilleard, C. (2014) Frailty, Abjection and the 'Othering' of the Fourth Age. *Health Sociology Review*: 10–19.

Hill, K.A. et al. (2020) Assessment of the Prevalence of Medical Student Mistreatment by Sex, Race/Ethnicity, and Sexual Orientation. *JAMA Internal Medicine*.: 655–665.

Hill, K.A., Gross, C.P. & Boatright, D. (2020) Combating Discrimination in Medical Education – Reply . *JAMA Internal Medicine*. Published online June 01, 2020. doi:10.1001/jamainternmed.2020.1590.

Himmelstein, D.U., Warren, E., Thorne, D. & Woolhandler, S. (2005) Illness and Injury as Contributors to Bankruptcy. *Health Affairs*. https://www.healthaffairs.org/doi/10.1377/hlthaff.W5.63

Ho, J. (2017) The Contribution of Drug Overdose to Educational Gradients in Life Expectancy in the United States, 1992–2011. *Demography*: 1157–1202.

Ho, J. (2022) Causes of America's Lagging Life Expectancy: An International Comparative Perspective. *The Journals of Gerontology: Series B*: 117–126.

Hoffmann, R. (2011) Illness, Not Age, Is the Leveler of Social Mortality Differences in Old Age. *The Journals of Gerontology: Series B*: 374–379.

Hogan, D. (1981) *Transitions and Social Change. The Early Lives of American Men*. New York, NY:Academic Press.

Honneth, A. (2012)Organized Self-Realization: Paradoxes of Individualization. In Honneth, A. *The I in We. Studies in the Theory of Recognition*. Cambridge: Polity, 15–68.

Horton, R. (2020) *The COVID-19 Catastrophe: What's Gone Wrong and How to Stop It Happening Again*. Cambridge: Polity.

House, J. & Williams, D. (2003)Understanding and Reducing Socioeconomic and Racial/Ethnic Disparities in Health. In Hofrichter, R. *Health and Social Justice: Politics, Ideology, and Inequity in the Distribution of Disease*. San Francisco, CA: Jossey-Bass, 89–131.

Huang, W. (2021)*Individualized Choice or Expanded Inequality A Cohort Comparison of the Transition to Adulthood between Late Baby Boomers and Early Millennials*. Doctoral dissertation, Case Western Reserve University.

Hudson, R. & Gonyea, J. (2012) Baby Boomers and the Shifting Political Construction of Old Age. *The Gerontologist*: 272–282.

Hyde, M. & Higgs, P. (2016) *Ageing and Globalisation*. Bristol: Polity.

INEGI (2017) *Encuesta nacional sobre discriminación (ENADIS) 2017*. https://www. inegi.org.mx/programas/enadis/2017/.

Inglehart, R. (1977) *The Silent Revolution: Changing Values and Political Styles Among Western Publics*. Princeton, NJ: Princeton University Press.

Institute of Medicine (2012) *For the Public's Health: Investing in a Healthier Future*. Washington, DC: National Academies Press.

Islam, N. et al. (2021) Effects of Covid-19 Pandemic on Life Expectancy and Premature Mortality in 2020: Time Series Analysis in 37 Countries. *BMJ*: e066768.

Iyengar, S. (1991) *Is Anyone Responsible? How Television Frames Political Issues*. Chicago, IL: University of Chicago Press.

Jacobs, M. (2017) *Panic at the Pump: The Energy Crisis and the Transformation of American Politics in the 1970s*. New York, NY: Hill & Wang.

Jemal, A. et al. (2008) Widening of Socioeconomic Inequalities in US Death Rates, 1993–. *PLoS One* 3 (5): e2181.

Jha, P. et al (2006) Social Inequalities in Male Mortality, and in Male Mortality from Smoking: Indirect Estimates from National Death Rates in England and Wales, Poland and North America. *Lancet*: 367–370.

Johnson, R. (2019) *Children of the Dream: Why School Integration Works*. New York, NY:Basic Books.

Kaa, D. van de (1987) Europe's Second Demographic Transition. *Population Bulletin*: 1–59.

Kamm, F. (1993) *Morality, Mortality: Death and Whom to Save from It: Vol. 1*, Oxford: Oxford University Press.

Kane, R.A. & Caplan, A.L. (Ed.) (1990) *Everyday Ethics: Resolving Dilemmas in Nursing Home Life*. New York, NY:Springer.

Kant, I. (1993) [1785]. *Grounding for the Metaphysics of Morals*. Translated by J. Ellington. London: Hackett.

Katz, S. (1996)*Disciplining Old Age*. Charlottesville, VA: University of Virginia Press.

Katz, S. (2000) Busy Bodies: Activity, Aging, and the Management of Everyday Life. *Journal of Aging Studies*: 135–152.

Katznelson, I. (2005) *When Affirmative Action Was White: An Untold History of Racial Inequality in Twentieth-century America*. New York, NY:Norton.

Kawachi, I., Adler, N.E. & Dow, W.H. (2010) Money, Schooling, and Health: Mechanisms and Causal Evidence. *Annals of the New York Academy of Sciences* 1186: 56–68.

Keating, D. & Hertzman, C. (1999) *Developmental Health and the Wealth of Nations: Social, Biological and Educational Dynamics*. New York, NY:The Guilford Press.

Keefe, P. (2021) *Empire of Pain: The Secret History of the Sackler Dynasty*. New York, NY:MacMillan

Kelley, J. & Huang, W. (2017) The "Good Times" Cohort in Later-Life: Black–White Differences in Pathways to Functional Limitations. *Research on Aging*: 526–548.

Kertzer, D. (1983) Generation as a Sociological Problem. *Annual Review of Sociology*: 125–149.

Kingson, E.R., Hirshorn, B.A. & Cornman, J.M. (1986) *Ties that Bind: The Interdependence of Generations*. Santa Ana, CA: Seven Locks Press.

Kirkwood, T. (1999) *Time of Our Lives: The Science of Human Ageing*. London: Phoenix.

Kirkwood, T.B.L. (2005) *Understanding the Odd Science of Ageing*. *Cell 120*: 437–447.

Klinenberg, E. (2002) *Heat Wave: A Social Autopsy of Disaster in Chicago*. Chicago: University of Chicago Press.

Kohli, M. (1986) The World we Forgot: A Historical Review of the Life Course. In Marshall, V. (Ed.) *Later Life. The Social Psychology of Aging*. London: Sage, 271–303.

Kohli, M. (Ed.) (1991) *Time for Retirement. Comparative Studies of Early Exit from the Labor Force*. Cambridge: Cambridge University Press.

Kohli, M. (2002) Generationengerechtigkeit ist mehr als Rentenfinanzierung . *Zeitschrift für Gerontologie und Geriatrie* 35: 12–38.

Kohli, M. (2004) Intergenerational Transfers and Inheritance: A Comparative View. In Siverstein, M. (Ed.) *Intergenerational Relations across Time and Place. Annual Review of Gerontology and Geriatrics* 24: 265–289.

Kohli, M. (2006) Aging and Justice. In Binstock, R.H. & George, L.K. (Eds.) *Handbook of Aging and the Social Sciences*. 6th edition. San Diego, CA: Academic Press, 456–478.

Kontopantelis, E. et al (2018) Disparities in Mortality among 25–44-year-olds in England: A Longitudinal, Population-Based Study. *Lancet Public Health*: e567–e575.

Kotlikoff, L.J. (1992) *Generational Accounting: Knowing Who Pays, and When, for What We Spend*. New York, NY: The Free Press.

Kröger, H., Pakpahan, E. & Hoffmann, R. (2015) What Causes Health Inequality? A Systematic Review on the Relative Importance of Social Causation and Health Selection. *European Journal of Public Health*, 25: 951–960.

Krugman, P. (2015) The Austerity Delusion, *The Guardian*, 29 April. https://www.theguardian.com/business/ng-interactive/2015/apr/29/the-austerity-delusion.

Kuypers, J. & Bengtson, V. (1973) Social Breakdown and Competence. A Model of Normal Aging. *Human Development* 16: 181–201.

Laceulle, H. (2018) *Aging and Self-Realization*. Bielefeld: Transcript.

Laceulle, H. & Baars, J. (2014) Self-realization and Cultural Narratives about Later Life. *Journal of Aging Studies*: 34–44.

Lacey, H., Smith, D. & Ubel, P. (2006) 'Hope I die before I get old': Mispredicting Happines across the Adult Lifespan. *Journal of Happiness Studies*: 167–182.

Lachman, M. & Boone James, J. (1997) *Multiple Paths of Midlife Development*. Chicago: University of Chicago Press.

Lane, C., Barnes, J. et al. (2019) Association between Vascular Risks across Adulthood and Brain Pathology in Late Life: Evidence from a British Cohort. *JAMA Neurology*. doi: https://doi.org/10.1001/jamaneurol.2019.3774.

Lane, R. (2000) *The Loss of Happiness in Market Democracies*. New Haven, CT: Yale University Press.

Lareau, A. (2003) *Unequal Childhoods: Class, Race and Family Life*. Berkeley, CA: University of California Press,

Laslett, P. (1988) *The World We Have Lost: Further Explored*. London: Routledge.

Laslett, P. (1989) *A Fresh Map of Life: The Emergence of the Third Age*. London: Weidenfeld.

Laslett, P. (1991) *The Emergence of the Third Age: A Fresh Map of Life*. Cambridge, MA: Harvard University Press.

Last, B.S., Lawson, G.M., Breiner, K., Steinberg, L. & Farah, M.J. (2018) Childhood Socioeconomic Status and Executive Function in Childhood and Beyond. *PLoS ONE* 13 (8): e0202964. https://doi.org/10.1371/journal.pone.0202964.

LaVeist, T.A., Gaskin, D.J., Richard, P. (2009) *The Economic Burden of Health Inequalities in the United States*. Washington, DC: Joint Center for Political and Economic Studies.

Lee, C. & Ryff, C. (2019) Pathways Linking Combinations of Early-Life Adversities to Adult Mortality: Tales that Vary by Gender. *Social Science & Medicine* 240, art. 112566. https://doi.org/10.1016/j.socscimed.2019.112566.

Lee, C., Tsenkova, V., Boylan, J. & Ryff, C. (2018) Gender Differences in the Pathways from Childhood Disadvantage to Metabolic Syndrome in Adulthood: An Examination of Health Lifestyles. *SSM–Population Health*: 216–224.

Levenson, A.J. (1981) Ageism: A Major Deterrent to the Introduction of Curricula in Aging. *Gerontology & Geriatrics Education* 1:161–162.

Leventhal, A., Bello, M., Galstyan, E., Higgins, S. & Barrington-Trimis, J. (2019) Association of Cumulative Socioeconomic and Health-Related Disadvantage With Disparities in Smoking Prevalence in the United States, 2008 to 2017. *JAMA Internal Medicine*. doi:10.1001/jamainternmed.2019.0192

Levine R.S. et al. (2001) Black-White Inequalities in Mortality and Life Expectancy, 1933–1999. *Public Health Reports*: 474–483.

Levinson, D. (1978) *The Seasons of a Man's Life*. London: Random House.

Levinson, D. (1994) *The Seasons of a Woman's Life*. New York: Ballantine.

Levitsky, S. & Ziblatt, D. (2018) *How Democracies Die*. New York, NY: Crown.

Levy, B. & Sidel, V.W. (Eds.) (2005) *Social Injustice and Public Health*. New York, NY:Oxford University Press.

Levy, B.R. (2003) Mind Matters: Cognitive and Physical Effects of Aging Self-Stereotypes. *Journal of Gerontology: Psychological Sciences* 58: 203–211.

Levy, B. (2009) Stereotype Embodiment: A Psychosocial Approach to Aging. *Current Directions in Psychological Science* 18: 332–336.

Levy, B. (2017) Age-Stereotype Paradox: Opportunity for Social Change. *The Gerontologist*: 118–126.

Levy, B. (2022) *Breaking the Age Code: How Your Beliefs About Aging Determine How Long and Well You Live*. New York:William Morrow.

Levy, B.R., Chung, P.H., Bedford, T. & Navrazhina, K. (2014) Facebook as a Site for Negative Age Stereotypes. *Gerontologist*:172–176.

Levy, B.R., Ferrucci, L., Zonderman, A.B., Slade, M.D., Troncoso, J. & Resnick, S. M. (2016) A Culture–Brain Link: Negative Age Stereotypes Predict Alzheimer's Disease Biomarkers. *Psychology and Aging* 31: 82–88.

Levy, B.R., Zonderman, A.B., Slade, M.D., & Ferrucci, L. (2009) Age Stereotypes Held Earlier in Life Predict Cardiovascular Events in Later Life. *Psychological Science* 20: 296–298.

Levy, B.R., Slade, M.D., Kunkel, S.R. & Kasl, S.V. (2002) Longevity Increased by Positive Self-perceptions of Aging. *Journal of Personality and Social Psychology* 83: 261–270.

Lewis, O. (1966) The Culture of Poverty. *Scientific American*.

Lewis, T.T., Cogburn, C.D. & Williams, D.R. (2015) Self-reported Experiences of Discrimination and Health. *Annual Review of Clinical Psycho*logy: 407–440.

Liang, J. & Luo, B. (2012) Toward a Discourse Shift in Social Gerontology: From Successful Aging to Harmonious Aging. *Journal of Aging Studies*: 327–334.

Liaw, F. & Brooks-Gunn, J. (1994) Cumulative Familial Risks and Low Birth Weight: Children's Cognitive and Behavioral Development. *Journal of Clinical Child Psychology*: 360–372.

Lidz, C.W., Fischer, L. & Arnold, R.A. (1993) *The Erosion of Autonomy in Long-Term Care*. New York, NY:Oxford University Press.

Lindland, E., Fond, M., Haydon, A. & Kendall-Taylor, N. (2015) *Gauging Aging: Mapping the Gaps between Expert and Public Understandings of Aging in America*. Washington, DC: FrameWorks Institute.

Livingston, G. (2013) *At Grandmother's House We Stay*. http://www.pewsocialtrends. org/2013/09/04/at-grandmothers-house-we-stay/.

Locke, J. (1690/1970) *Two Treatises of Government*. Edited. by P. Laslett. Cambridge: Cambridge University Press.

Löckenhoff, C.E. et al. (2009) Perceptions of Aging across 26 Cultures and their Culture-level Associates. *Psychology and Aging*:941–954.

Lockwood, M. (1988) Quality of Life and Resource Allocation. In Bell, J.M. & Mendus, S. (Eds.) *Philosophy and Medical Welfare*. Cambridge: Cambridge University Press.

Lohan, M. (2007) How Might we Understand Men's Health Better? Integrating Explanations from Critical Studies on Men and Inequalities in Health. *Social Science & Medicine*:494–504.

Longman, P. (1987) *Born to Pay: The New Politics of Aging in America*. Boston. MA: Houghton Mifflin Harcourt.

Longman, P. (2004) *The Empty Cradle: How Falling Birthrates Threaten World Prosperity and What to Do About It*. New York, NY:Basic Books.

Loopstra, R., McKee, M., Katikireddi, S.V., Taylor-Robinson, D., Barr, B. & Stuckler, D. (2016a) Austerity and Old-age Mortality in England: A Longitudinal Cross-Local Area Analysis, 2007–2013. *Journal of the Royal Society of Medicine*: 109–116.

Loopstra, R., Reeves, A., Barr, B., Taylor-Robinson, D., McKee, M. & Stuckler, D. (2016) The Impact of Economic Downturns and Budget Cuts on Homelessness Claim Rates across 323 Local Authorities in England, 2004–12. *Journal of Public Health*: 417–425.

Loopstra, R., Reeves, A., Taylor-Robinson, D., Barr, B., McKee, M & Stuckler, D. (2015) Austerity, Sanctions, and the Rise of Food Banks in the UK. *BMJ*. 350h1775.

Lothian, K. & Philp, I. (2001) Maintaining the Dignity and Autonomy of Older People in the Healthcare Setting. *BMJ*: 668–670.

Lu, M.C. & Halfon, N. (2003) Racial and Ethnic Disparities in Birth Outcomes: A Life-course Perspective . *Maternal and Child Health Journal*: 13–30.

Lucas, J.R. (1965) Against Equality. *Philosophy*:296–307.

Lutfey, K. & Freese, J. (2005) Toward Some Fundamentals of Fundamental Causality: Socioeconomic Status and Health in the Routine Clinic Visit for Diabetes. *American Journal of Sociology*: 1326–1372.

Luyendijk, J. (2015) *Swimming with Sharks: My Journey into the World of the Bankers*. London: Guardian Faber.

Lynch, J., Davey Smith, G., Harper, S. & Hillemeier, M. (2004) Is Income Inequality a Determinant of Population Health? Part 2. U.S. National and

Regional Trends in Income Inequality and Age- and Cause-specific Mortality. *Milbank Quarterly*: 355–400.

Lyons, D. (2016) *Disrupted: My Misadventure in the Startup Bubble*. New York, NY: Hachette.

Lyotard, F. (1984) *The Postmodern Condition. A Report on Knowledge*. Minneapolis, MN: University of Minnesota Press.

Lyotard, J. (1988) *Differend: Phrases in Dispute*. Minneapolis, MN: University of Minnesota Press.

MacIntyre, A. (1981) *After Virtue: A Study in Moral Theory*. Notre Dame: Notre Dame Press.

Mackenbach, J. et al. (2003) Widening Socioeconomic Inequalities in Mortality in Six Western European Countries. *International Journal of Epidemiology*: 830–837.

Mackenbach, J. (2012) The Persistence of Health Inequalities in Modern Welfare States: The Explanation of a Paradox. *Social Science and Medicine*: 761–769.

Mackenbach, J. et al. (2018) Trends in Health Inequalities in 27 European Countries. *Proceedings of the National Academy of Sciences*: 6440–6445.

Mackenzie, C. & Stoljar, N. (Eds.) (2000) *Relational Autonomy: Feminist Perspectives on Autonomy, Agency, and the Social Self*. Oxford: Oxford University Press.

Macleod, C. (1998) *Liberalism, Justice and the Market*. Oxford: Clarendon Press.

Macnicol, J. (2015) *Neoliberalising Old Age*. Cambridge: Cambridge University Press.

Madon, S. et al. (2001) Ethnic and National Stereotypes: The Princeton Trilogy Revisited and Revised. *Personality and Social Psychology Bulletin*: 996–1010.

Makaroun L.K. et al. (2017) Wealth-Associated Disparities in Death and Disability in the United States and England. *JAMA Internal Medicine*:1745–1753.

Mannheim, K. (1952) The Problem of Generations. In Kecskemeti, P.(Ed.) *Essays on the Sociology of Knowledge: Collected Works*. Volume 5.New York, NY:Routledge, 276–322.

Fleurbaey, M. (2002) Equality of Resources Revisited. *Ethics 113 (1)*: 82–105.

Margalit, A. (1996) *The Decent Society*. Cambridge: Harvard University Press.

Markovits, D. (2008) *A Modern Legal Ethics: Adversary Advocacy in a Democratic Age*. Princeton, NJ: Princeton University Press.

Marmot, M. (2001) Inequalities in Health. *New England Journal of Medicine*: 135–136.

Marmot, M. (2004) *The Status Syndrome: How Social Standing Affects our Health and Longevity*. New York, NY:MacMillan.

Marmot, M. (2010) *Fair Society Healthy Lives (The Marmot Review)*. Institute of Health Equity. http://www.instituteofhealthequity.org/resources-reports/fair-society-healthy-lives-the-marmot-review/fair-society-healthy-lives-full-report-pdf.pdf.

Marmot, M. (2006) Status Syndrome: A Challenge to Medicine. *JAMA*:1304–1307.

Marmot, M. & Shipley, M. (1996) Do Socioeconomic Differences in Mortality Persist After Retirement? A 25 year Follow-up of Civil Servants from the First Whitehall Study. *British Medical Journal*: 1177–1180.

Marmot, M. & Wilkinson, R. (Eds.) (1999) *Social Determinants of Health*. Oxford: Oxford University Press.

Marshall, T.H. (1950) *Citizenship and Social Class*. Cambridge: Cambridge University Press.

Marshall, V.W. & Tindale, J.A. (1978) Notes for a Radical Gerontology. *International Journal for Aging and Human Development 9*: 163–175.

Marx, K. (1867/1967) *Capital. A Critique of Political Economy*. New York, NY: International Publishers.

Mason, S.E., Kuntz, C.V. & Mcgill, C.M. (2015) Oldsters and Ngrams: Age Stereotypes across Time. *Psychological Reports: Sociocultural Issues in Psychology*: 324–329.

McCartin, J. (2011) *Collision Course: Ronald Reagan, the Air Traffic Controllers, and the Strike that Changed America*. New York, NY:Oxford University Press.

McGinnis, J.M., Williams-Russo, P., Knickman, J.R. (2002) The Case for More Active Policy Attention to Health Promotion. *Health Affairs*: 78–93.

McKee, M., Karanikolos, M., Belcher, P. & Stuckler, D. (2012) Austerity: A Failed Experiment on the People of Europe. *Clinical Medicine:* 346–350.

McKerlie, D. (1989) Equality and Time. *Ethics*:492–450.

McKerlie, D. (2012) *Justice between the Young and the Old*. Oxford: Oxford University Press, 2012,

Mead, L. (1986) *Beyond Entitlement: The Social Obligations of Citizenship*. New York, NY:Free Press.

Meara, E., Richards, S. & Cutler, D. (2008) The Gap Gets Bigger: Changes in Mortality and Life Expectancy, by Education, 1981–2000. *Health Affairs* 27 (2): 350–360.

Menchik, P.L. (1993)Economic Status as a Determinant of Mortality among Black and White Older Men: Does Poverty Kill? *Population Studies*: 427–436.

Merton, R.K. (1968) The Matthew Effect in Science. *Science* 199:55–63.

Mill, J.S. (1861/1998) *Utilitarianism*. Oxford: Oxford University Press.

Ministerio de Sanidad, Servicios Sociales e Igualdad (2013) *Estudio diagnóstico de fuentes secundarias sobre la discriminación en España*. https://sid.usal.es/idocs/F8/FDO27095/estudio_discrim_espana.pdf.

Minkler, M. Fuller-Thomson, E. & Guralnik, J.M. (2006) Gradient of Disability across the Socioeconomic Spectrum in the United States. *New England Journal of Medicine*: 695–703.

Minkler, M. (1986) Generational Equity and the New Victim Blaming. *International Journal of Health Services*:539–551.

Mirowsky, J, and Ross, C. (2003) *Education, Social Status, and Health*. New York, NY:Aldine de Gruyter.

Modell, J. (1991) *Into One's Own: From Youth to Adulthood in the United States, 1920–1975*. San Francisco: University of California Press.

Moody, H. (1988) Toward a Critical Gerontology: The Contribution of the Humanities to Theories of Aging. In Birren, J. & Bengtson, V. (Eds.) *Emergent Theories of Aging*. New York, NY:Springer, 19–40.

Moody, R. (1996) *Ethics in an Aging Society*. Baltimore: Johns Hopkins University Press.

Moore, B. Jr (1978) *Injustice: The Social Bases of Obedience and Control*. New York, NY: Palgrave.

Morrissey, M. (2016) *The State of. American Retirement: How 401(k)s Have Failed Most American Workers*. Washington, DC: Economic Policy Institute.

Morse, R. (2008) *Environmental Justice Through the Eye of Hurricane Katrina*. Washington, DC: Joint Center for Political and Economic Studies. https://inequality.stanford.edu/sites/default/files/media/_media/pdf/key_issues/Environment_policy.pdf.

Moss, N.E. (2002) Gender Equity and Socioeconomic Inequality: A Framework for the Patterning of Women's Health. *Social Science and Medicine* 54: 649–661.

Mullan, P. (2002) *The Imaginary Time Bomb: Why an Ageing Population is Not a Social Problem.* London: IB Taurus.

Murray, C. (1984) *Losing Ground: American Social Policy, 1950–1980.* New York, NY:Basic Books.

Murray, C. (2012) *Coming Apart: The State of White America 1960–2010.* New York, NY:Crown.

Myrdal, G. (1944) *An American Dilemma: The Negro Problem And Modern Democracy.* New York, NY; London: Harper and Brothers.

Nagel, T. (1979) The Policy of Preference. In *Mortal Questions.* Cambridge: Cambridge University Press, 91–105.

Nagel, T. (1991) *Equality and Partiality.* Oxford:Oxford University Press.

National Academies of Sciences, Engineering, and Medicine (2021) *High and Rising Mortality Rates Among Working-Age Adults.* Washington, DC: The National Academies Press.

National Academies of Sciences, Engineering, and Medicine (2019) *A Roadmap to Reducing Child Poverty.* Washington, DC: The National Academies Press.

Neugarten, B (1982) *Age or Need? Public Policies for Older People.* London: Sage.

Neugarten, B. & Havighurst, R. (Eds.) (1976) *Social Policy, Social Ethics, and the Aging Society.* Washington, DC: National Science Foundation.

Ng, R., Allore, H.G., Trentalange, M., Monin, J.K. & Levy, B.R. (2015) Increasing Negativity of Age Stereotypes across 200 Years: Evidence from a Database of 400 Million Words. *PLOS ONE* 10.

Nielsen, L. & Axelsen, D. (2017) Capabilitarian Sufficiency: Capabilities and Social Justice. *Journal of Human Development and Capabilities*: 46–59.

Nord, E. (2005) Concerns for the Worse Off: Fair Innings Versus Severity. *Social Science & Medicine:* 257–263.

Nozick, R. (1974) *Anarchy, State and Utopia.* New York, NY:Basic Books.

Nozick, R. (1981) *Philosophical Explanations.* Oxford: Oxford University Press.

Nussbaum, M. (1988) Nature, Function and Capability: Aristotle on Political Distribution. In Annas, J. and Grimm, R.H. (Eds.), *Oxford Studies in Ancient Philosophy.* Oxford: Clarendon, 145–184.

Nussbaum, M. (2000). *Women and Human Development. The Capabilities Approach.* New York: Cambridge University Press.

Nussbaum, M. (2001) *Women and Human Development: The Capability Approach.* Cambridge: Cambridge University Press.

Nussbaum, M. (2006) *Frontiers of Justice: Disability, Nationality, and Species Membership.* Cambridge, MA: Harvard University Press.

Nussbaum, M. (2007) *Frontiers of Justice: Disability, Nationality, Species Membership* (Tanner Lectures of Human Values). Harvard: Harvard University Press.

Nussbaum, M. & Levmore, S. (2017) *Aging Thoughtfully: Conversations about Retirement, Romance, Wrinkles, and Regret.* New York: Oxford University Press.

O'Cinneide, C. (2003) Comparative European Perspectives on Age Discrimination Legislation. In Fredman, S. & Spencer, S. (Eds.) *Age as an Equality Issue.* Oxford/ Portland, OR: Hart Publishing.

O'Neil, M. & Haydon, A. (2015) *Aging, Agency and Attribution of Responsibility: Shifting Public Discourse about Older Adults.* Washington, DC: FrameWorks Institute.

O'Rand, A. (2002) Cumulative Advantage Theory in Life Course Research. *Annual Review of Gerontology and Geriatrics*:14–30.

O'Reilly, P. & Caro, F. (1995) Productive Aging. *Journal of Aging & Social Policy*: 39–71.

OECD (1988a) *Ageing Populations. The Social Policy Implications*. Geneva:OECD.

OECD (1988b) *Reforming Public Pensions*. Geneva:OECD.

OECD (2018) Inequalities in Household Wealth across OECD Countries: Evidence from the OECD Wealth Distribution Database. Working Paper 88. Geneva: OECD.

Oeppen, J. & Vaupel, J. (2002) Broken Limits to Life Expectancy. *Science*: 1029–1031.

Okonkwo, N.E., Aguwa, U.T., Jang, M., et al. (2021) COVID-19 and the US Response: Accelerating Health Inequities. *BMJ Evidence-Based Medicine*: 176–179.

Oliver, M.L. & Shapiro, T.M. (1995). *Black Wealth/White Wealth: A New Perspective on Racial Inequality*. New York: Routledge.

Olshansky, J. et al. (2012) Differences in Life Expectancy Due to Race and Educational Differences Are Widening and May Not Catch Up. *Health Affairs* 31: 1803–1810.

Osnos, E. (2021) *Wildland. The Making of America's Fury*. London: Bloomsbury.

Pager, D. & Shepherd, H. (2008) The Sociology of Discrimination. *Annual Review of Sociology*: 181–209.

Palmore, E.B. (2004) Ageism in Canada and the United States. *Journal of Cross-Cultural Gerontology* 19: 41–46.

Papanicolas, I.; Woskie, L. & Jha, A. (2018)Health Care Spending in the United States and Other High-Income Countries. *JAMA*: 1024–1039.

Parfit, D. (1984) *Reasons and Persons*. New York, NY:Oxford University Press.

Parfit, D. (2002) *Equality or Priority?* In Clayton, M. & Williams, A. (Eds.) *The Ideal of Equality*. New York, NY:Palgrave, 81–125.

Parkin, T. (2003) *Old Age in the Roman World*. Baltimore, MD: Johns Hopkins University Press.

Pearman, F.A. (2019) The Effect of Neighborhood Poverty on Math Achievement: Evidence From a Value-Added Design. *Education and Urban Society*: 289–307.

Pearman, F.A. (2020) The Moderating Effect of Neighborhood Poverty on Preschool Effectiveness: Evidence From the Tennessee Voluntary Prekindergarten Experiment. *American Educational Research Journal*: 1323–1357.

Perry, B. (2002) Childhood Experience and the Expression of Genetic Potential: What Childhood Neglect Tells Us About Nature and Nurture. *Brain and Mind* 3: 79–100.

Peterson, P. (1999) *Gray Dawn: How the Coming Age Wave Will Transform America – and the World*. New York, NY:Three Rivers Press.

Pettit, P. (1997) *Republicanism: A Theory of Freedom and Government*. New York, NY: Oxford University Press.

Pew Research Center (2013)*The American Middle Class Is Losing Ground*. Washington, DC: Pew Research Center.

Parijs, van, P. (1999) The Disenfranchisement of the Elderly, and Other Attempts to Secure Intergenerational Justice. *Philosophy and Public Affairs* 27: 29–33.

Phillips, K. (2006) *American Theocracy: The Peril and Politics of Radical Religion, Oil, and Borrowed Money in the 21st Century*. London: Penguin.

Phillipson, C. (1982) *Capitalism and the Construction of Old Age*. London: MacMillan.

Phillipson, C. (2002) The Challenge of Retirement. *Generations Review*: 4–5.

Phillipson, C. (2013) *Ageing*. Cambridge: Polity Press.

Phillipson, C. (2018) 'Fuller' or 'Extended' Working Lives? Critical Perspectives on Changing Transitions from Work to Retirement. *Ageing & Society*:629–650.

Phillipson, C. & Walker, A. (1987) The Case for a Critical Gerontology. In Di Gregorio, S. (Ed.) *Social Gerontology: New Directions*. London: Croom Helm.

Pickett, K. & Wilkinson, R. (2015) Income Inequality and Health: A Causal Review. *Social Science & Medicine*: 316–326.

Piketty, T. (2014) *Capital in the Twenty-First Century*. Cambridge, MA: Harvard University.

Piketty, T. & Saez, E. (2014) Inequality in the Long Run. *Science* 344 (6186): 838–843.

Piketty, T., Saez, E., & Zucman, G. (2016) Distributional National Accounts: Methods and Estimates for the United States WID World. Working Paper Series N° 2016/3. https://wid.world/document/t-piketty-e-saez-g-zucman-distributional-national-a ccounts-methods-and-estimates-for-the-united-states-2016/.

Pimpare, S. (2008) *A People's History of Poverty in America*. New York, NY:Free Press.

Pinker, S. (2012) *The Better Angels of our Nature: Why Violence Has Declined*. New York, NY:Penguin.

Pongiglione, B., De Stavola, B.L. & Ploubidis, G.B. (2015) A Systematic Literature Review of Studies Analyzing Inequalities in Health Expectancy among the Older Population. *PloS one* 10 (6): e0130747.

Poole, M. (2006) *The Segregated Origins of Social Security: African Americans and the Welfare State*. Chapel Hill, NC:University of North Carolina Press.

Posner, R. (1995) *Aging and Old Age*. Chicago/London: The University of Chicago Press.

Powers, M. & Faden, R. (2006) *Social Justice: The Moral Foundations of Public Health and Health Policy*. Oxford:Oxford University Press.

Preston, S.H. & Vierboom, Y.C. (2021) Excess Mortality in the United States in the 21st Century. *Proceedings of the National Academy of Sciences* 118 (16): 1–3.

Preston, S.H. (1984) Children and the Elderly: Divergent Paths for America's dependents. *Demography*:435–557.

Quadagno, J. (1988) Generational Equity and the Politics of the Welfare State. *Politics and Society*: 353–376.

Quadagno, J. (1996) Social Security and the Myth of the Entitlement "Crisis". *The Gerontologist*: 392–499.

Rabito, F.A., Shorter, C., & White, L.E. (2003) Lead Levels among Children Who Live in Public Housing. *Epidemiology*: 263–268.

Ragonese, C., Shand, T. & Barker, G. (2019) *Masculine Norms and Men's Health: Making the Connections*. Washington, DC: Promundo-US.

Rakowski, E. (1991)*Equal Justice*. New York, NY:Oxford University Press.

Ralph, M. & Singhal, M. (2019) Racial Capitalism. *Theory and Society* 48: 851–881.

Rawls, J. (1971) *A Theory of Justice*. Cambridge, MA: Harvard University Press.

Rawls, J. (1978) The Basic Structure as Subject. In Goldman, A.I. & Kim, J. (Eds.) *Values and Morals*. Dordrecht: Springer, 47–78.

Rawls, J. (1980) Kantian Constructivism in Moral Theory . *Journal of Philosophy*.

Rawls, J. (1985) Justice as Fairness: Political not Metaphysical. *Philosophy and Public Affairs*: 22–51.

Rawls, J. (1993) *Political Liberalism*. New York, NY:Columbia University Press.

Rawls, J. (1995) Political Liberalism: Reply to Habermas. *The Journal of Philosophy*: 132–180.

Rawls, J. (1999a) *The Law of Peoples*. Cambridge, MA: Harvard University Press.

Rawls, J. (1999b) *Collected Papers*. Edited by S. Freeman. Cambridge, MA: Harvard University Press.

Rawls, J. (2001) *Justice as Fairness: A Restatement*. Cambridge, MA: Harvard University Press.

Raz, J. (1986)*The Morality of Freedom*. Oxford: Clarendon Press.

Reich, M. & Shibuya, K. (2015) The Future of Japan's Health System: Sustaining Good Health with Equity at Low Cost. *New England Journal of Medicine*: 1793–1797. doi:10.1056/NEJMp1410676.

Resnick, B. & Zimmerman, S. (2021) COVID-19 Recommendations for Research from the Gerontological Society of America COVID-19 Task Force, *The Gerontologist*: 137–140.

Reuben, D.B., Fullerton, J.T., Tschann, J.M. & Croughan-Minihane, M. (1995) Attitudes of Beginning Medical Students Towards Older People: A Five-Campus Study. *Journal of American Geriatric Society*: 1430–1436.

Reynolds, C. et al. (2019) A Decade of Epigenetic Change in Aging Twins: Genetic and Environmental Contributions to Longitudinal DNA Methylation. *Ageing Cell*. doi:10.1111/acel.13197.

Richardson, I.W. & Rosen, R.J. (1979) Aging and the Metrics of Time. *Journal of Theoretical Biology*: 415–423.

Ricoeur, P. (2005) *The Course of Recognition*. Cambridge, MA: Harvard University Press.

Rigney, D. (2010) *The Matthew Effect: How Advantage Begets Further Advantage*. New York, NY:Columbia University Press.

Riley, M.W., Kahn, R.L & Foner, A. (1994) *Age and Structural Lag: Society's Failure to Provide Meaningful Opportunities in Work, Family, and Leisure*. New York, NY: Wiley.

Rivlin, M. (2000) Why the Fair Innings Argument Is Not Persuasive . *BMC Medical Ethics*. doi:10.1186/147-93-1.

Rivlin, M. (2012) Setting Limits Fairly: A Critique of Some of Daniel Callahan's views. In Lesser, H. (Ed.) *Justice for Older People*. Amsterdam/New York, NY: Rodopi, 133–142.

Robertson, A. (1990) The Politics of Alzheimer's Disease: A Case Study in Apocalyptic Demography. *International Journal of Health Services*: 429–442.

Robertson, A. (1997) Beyond Apocalyptic Demography: Towards a Moral Economy of Interdependence. *Ageing and Society*:425–446.

Robinson, R.V. & Jackson, E.F. (2001) Is Trust in Others Declining in America? An Age-Period-Cohort Analysis. *Social Science Research* 30: 117–415.

Robinson, C. (1983) *Black Marxism: The Making of the Black Radical Tradition*. Chapel Hill, NC: University of North Carolina Press.

Roemer, J. (1993) A Pragmatic Theory of Responsibility for the Egalitarian Planner. *Philosophy & Public Affairs*:146–166.

Roncarati, J. et al. (2018) Mortality Among Unsheltered Homeless Adults in Boston, Massachusetts, 2000–2009. *JAMA Internal Medicine*: 1242–1248.

Rosen, S. (1981) The Economics of Superstars. *American Economic Review*: 845–858.

Rosengren A, et al. (2004) Association of Psychosocial Risk Factors with Risk of Acute Myocardial Infarction in 11119 Cases and 13648 Controls from 52 Countries (the INTERHEART Study): A Case-Control Study. *Lancet*: 953–962.

Rossignol, M., Leclerc, A., Allaert, F.A. et al. (2005) Primary Osteoarthritis of Hip, Knee, and Hand in Relation to Occupational Exposure. *Occupational and Environmental Medicine*: 772–777.

Rowe, J. & Kahn, R. (1998)*Successful Aging*. New York, NY:Dell.

Rowntree, B. (1901) *Poverty. A Study of Town Life*. London: McMillan.

Rowntree, B. (1918) *The Human Needs of Labour*. London: Nelson.

Rozanova, J. (2010) Discourse of Successful Aging in the Globe & Mail: Insights from Critical Gerontology. *Journal of Aging Studies*: 213–222.

Ruger, J.P. (2004) Health and Social Justice. *The Lancet*: 1075–1080.

Ruger, J. (2012) *Health and Social Justice*. New York, NY:Oxford University Press.

Ruhm, C. (2019) Drivers of the Fatal Drug Epidemic. *Journal of Health Economics*: 25–42.

Russell, J. (2015) *Social Insecurity: 401(k)s and the Retirement Crisis*. Boston:, MA: Beacon Press.

Saad-Filho, A. & Johnston, D. (Eds) (2005) *Neoliberalism: A Critical Reader*. London: Pluto Press.

Salazar-García, F. et al. (2004) Reproductive Effects of Occupational DDT Exposure among Male Malaria Control Workers. *Environmental Health Perspectives*: 542–547.

Sampson, R. (2012) *Great American City: Chicago and the Enduring Neighborhood Effect*. Chicago: University of Chicago Press.

Samra, R. et al. (2015) Medical Students' and Doctors' Attitudes towards Older Patients and their Care in Hospital Settings: A Conceptualisation. *Age and Ageing*: 776–783.

Sandel, M. (2005) *Public Philosophy: Essays on Morality in Politics*. Harvard: Harvard University Press.

Sandel, M. (1982) *Liberalism and the Limits of Justice*. Cambridge: Cambridge University Press.

Sandel, M. (2012) *What Money Can't Buy*. London: Allen Lane.

Sandel, M. (2020) *The Tyranny of Merit*. New York, NY:MacMillan.

Schaie, K. (2013) *Developmental Influences on Adult Intelligence: The Seattle Longitudinal Study*. 2nd edition. New York, NY:Oxford University Press.

Schaie, K. (2005) *Developmental Influences on Adult Intelligence: The Seattle Longitudinal Study*. New York, NY:Cambridge University Press.

Scheffler, S. (2003) What is Egalitarianism? *Philosophy and Public Affairs* 31: 5–39.

Schneider, D & Harknett, K. (2020) *It's about time: How Work Schedule Instability Matters for Workers, Families, and Racial Inequality*. https://shift.berkeley.edu/its-about-time-how-work-schedule-instability-matters-for-workers-families-and-racial-inequality/.

Schroots, J. & Birren, J. (1988) The Nature of Time: Implications for Research on Aging. *Comprehensive Gerontology*: 1–29.

Scrutton, S. (1990) The Foundations of Age Discrimination. In McEwen, E. (Ed.) *Age: The Unrecognized Discrimination*. London: Age Concern, 12–27.

Sears, E. (1986) *The Ages of Man: Medieval Interpretations of the Life Cycle*. Princeton, NJ: Princeton University Press.

Sen, A. (1970) *Collective Choice and Social Welfare*. 1st edition. San Francisco, CA: Holden-Day.

Sen, A. (1979) *Equality of What? Tanner Lecture on Human Values.* Stanford, CA: Stanford University Press.

Sen, A. (1985) *Capabilities and Commodities.* Amsterdam: Oxford University Press.

Sen. A. (1992a) *Inequality Re-examined.* Oxford: Oxford University Press.

Sen. A. (1992b) Missing Women. *British Medical Journal:* 587–588.

Sen, A. (1995) *Inequality Reexamined.* Cambridge: Harvard University Press.

Sen, A. (1999) *Development as Freedom.* Oxford: Oxford University Press.

Sen. A. (2003) Missing Women Revisited. *British Medical Journal:* 1297–1298.

Sen, A. (2004) Why Health Equity? In Anand, S., Peter, F. & Sen, A. (Eds.) *Public Health, Ethics, and Equity.* New York: Oxford University Press, 21–34.

Sen, A. (2005) Human Rights and Capabilities. *Journal of Human Development:* 151–166.

Sen, A. (2010) *The Idea of Justice.* London: Penguin.

Segall, S. (2010) *Health, Luck, and Justice.* Princeton: Princeton University Press.

Sennett, R. & Cobb, J. (1972) *The Hidden Injuries of Class.* Cambridge: Cambridge University Press.

Seshadri, S. (2019) Prevention of Dementia—Thinking Beyond the Age and Amyloid Boxes . *JAMA Neurology.* https://doi.org/10.1001/jamaneurol.2019.3785.

Settersten, R. & Ray, B. (2010)*Not Quite Adults: Why 20-Somethings Are Choosing a Slower Path to Adulthood, and Why It's Good for Everyone.* New York, NY:Bantam.

Shaikh, F., Kjølllesdal, M.K., Carslake, D., Stoltenberg, C., Davey Smith, G. & Næss, Ø. (2019) Birthweight in Offspring and Cardiovascular Mortality in their Parents, Aunts and Uncles: A Family-based Cohort Study of 1.35 million births. *International Journal of Epidemiology* 49 (1): 205–215.

Shapiro, T., Meschede, T., & Osoro, S. (2013) *The Roots of the Widening Racial Wealth Gap: Explaining the Black–White Economic Divide.* Washington, DC: Pew Research Center.

Sharkey, P. (2014) *Stuck in Place: Urban Neighborhoods and the End of Progress Toward Racial Equality.* Chicago: University of Chicago Press.

Shaw, A. (1994) In Defence of Ageism. *British Medical Journal:* 188–191.

Shuey, K.M. & O'Rand, A.M. (2004) New Risks for Workers: Pensions, Labor Markets, and Gender. *Annual Review of Sociology* 30: 453–477.

Shuey, K. and Wilson, A. (2008) Cumulative Disadvantage and Black–White Disparities in Life Course Health Trajectories. *Research on Aging*:200–225.

Shura, R., Siders, R.A. & Dannefer, D. (2010) Culture Change in Long-term Care: Participatory Action Research and the Role of the Resident. *The Gerontologist:* 212–225.

Silverstein, M. et al. (2012) *Symposium: Reconsidering the Life Course as a Key Concept in Social Gerontology.* Journals of Gerontology. *Social Sciences:* 205–237.

Silverstein, M., Hsu, H.E & Bell, A. (2019)Addressing Social Determinants to Improve Population Health: The Balance Between Clinical Care and Public Health. *JAMA:* 2379–2380.

Singer, P. (2020) Is Age Discrimination Acceptable? *Project Syndicate,* 10 June. https://www.project-syndicate.org/commentary/when-is-age-discrimination-acceptable-by-peter-singer-202–6?barrier=accesspaylog.

Singh, G.K., Kogan, M.D. (2007) Widening Socioeconomic Disparities in US Childhood Mortality, 1969–2000. *American Journal of Public Health:* 1658–1665.

Singh, G.K. & Siahpush, M. (2006) Widening Socioeconomic Inequalities in US Life Expectancy, 1908–2000. *International Journal of Epidemiology*: 969–979.

Sirey, J. et al. (2015) Adult Protection and Elder Abuse. Integrating Evidence-Based Mental Health into Elder Abuse Services to Serve Vulnerable Older Adults. *The Gerontologist*:160.

Smedley, B., Stith, A. & Nelson, A. (Eds.) (2003) *Unequal Treatment: Confronting Racial and Ethnic Disparities in Health Care*. Washington, DC: National Academic Press.

Smith, A. (1776/1976) *The Wealth of Nations*. London: Penguin.

Smith, A. (1759/1982) *The Theory of Moral Sentiments*. Cambridge: Cambridge University Press.

Soederberg, S., Menz, G. & Cerny, P. (2005) *Internalizing Globalization: The Rise of Neoliberalism and the Decline of National Varieties of Capitalism*. New York, NY: Palgrave MacMillan.

Sorenson, C., Drummond, M. & Khan, B. (2013) Medical Technology as a Key Driver of Rising Health Expenditure: Disentangling the Relationship. *ClinicoEconomics and Outcomes Research*: 223–234.

Soto-Perez-de-Celis, E. (2020) Social Media, Ageism, and Older Adults during the COVID-19 Pandemic. *EClinicalMedicine*. https://www.thelancet.com/journals/eclinm/article/PIIS2589-5370(20)30378-3/fulltext

Stafford, M., Cummins, S., Macintyre, S., Ellaway, A. & Marmot, M. (2005) Gender Differences in the Associations between Health and Neighbourhood Environment. *Social Science and Medicine*: 1681–1692.

Standing, G. (2012) *The Precariat: The New Dangerous Class*. London: Bloomsbury.

Starr, P. (2017) *The Social Transformation of American Medicine: The Rise of a Sovereign Profession and the Making of a Vast Industry*. New York, NY:Basic Books.

Steel, N., Ford, J.A., Newton, J.N. et al. (2018) Changes in Health in the Countries of the UK and 150 English Local Authority Areas 1990–2016: A Systematic Analysis for the Global Burden of Disease Study 2016. *Lancet*: 1647–1661.

Stein, E.M., Gennuso, K.P., Ugboaja, D.C. & Remington, P.L. (2017) The Epidemic of Despair among White Americans: Trends in the Leading Causes of Premature Death, 1990–2015. *American Journal of Public Health*: 1541–1547.

Stephens, C. & Breheny, M. (2018) *Healthy Ageing: A Capability Approach to Inclusive Policy and Practice*. London: Routledge.

Stiglitz, J. (2015) *The Great Divide: Unequal Societies and What We Can Do About Them*. New York, NY:Norton.

Stiglitz, J. (2019) *People, Power, and Profits: Progressive Capitalism for an Age of Discontent*. New York, NY: Norton.

Taylor, C. (1985) What is Human Agency? In *Human Agency and Language: Philosophical Papers*. Cambridge: Cambridge University Press, 15–44.

Taylor, C. (1991) *The Ethics of Authenticity*. Cambridge, MA: Harvard University Press.

Taylor, C. (1992) The Politics of Recognition. In Gutmann, A. (Ed.) *Multiculturalism and 'The Politics of Recognition'*. Princeton, NJ:University Press, 25–73.

Taylor, P. (2010) Cross-National Trends in Work and Retirement. In Dannefer, D., & Phillipson, C. (Eds.) *International Handbook of Social Gerontology*. New York: SAGE, 540–550.

Taylor-Robinson, D. et al. (2019a) Assessing the Impact of Rising Child Poverty on the Unprecedented Rise in Infant Mortality in England, 2000–2017: Time Trend Analysis. *BMJ Open*: 9e029424.

Taylor-Robinson, D., Lai, E.T., Whitehead, M. & Barr, B. (2019b) Child Health Unraveling in UK. *BMJ*: 1963.

Temkin, L. (1993) *Inequality*. New York/Oxford: Oxford University Press.

Tepper, J. & Hearn. D. (2018) *The Myth of Capitalism: Monopolies and the Death of Competition*. New York, NY:Wiley.

Thane, P. (Ed.) (2005) *A History of Old Age*. London: Thames & Hudson.

The Gerontologist (2015) *The Gerontologist Special Issue: Successful Aging* 55: 5–168.

Thomas, W. (1996) *Life Worth Living: How Someone You Love Can Still Enjoy Life in a Nursing Home*. Acton: VanderWijk & Burnham.

Tilly, C. (1999) *Durable Inequality*. Berkeley, CA: University of California Press.

Troyansky, D. (2015) *Aging in World History*. London: Routledge.

Uffink, J. (2007) Time and Aging: A Physicist's Look at Gerontology. In Baars, J. & Visser, H. *Aging and Time: Multidisciplinary Perspectives*. Amityville, NY: Baywood.

Uhlenberg, P. & Mueller, M. (2003) Family Context and Individual Well-Being: Patterns and Mechanisms in Life Course Perspective. In Mortimer, J.T. & Shanahan, M.J. (Eds.) *Handbook of the Life Course*. New York: Kluwer Academic/Plenum Publishers, 123–148.

Vaillant, G.E. (2012) *Triumphs of Experience: The Men of the Harvard Grant Study*. Cambridge, MA:The Belknap Press of Harvard University Press.

Van Hoof, J. & Marston, H. (Eds.) (2021) Special Issue :Age-Friendly Cities & Communities: State of the Art and Future Perspectives. *International Journal of Environmental Research and Public Health*.

Van Parijs, P. (1995) *Real Freedom for All*. Oxford: Clarendon.

Vaupel, J. (2010) Biodemography of Human Aging. *Nature*:536–542.

Veatch, R. (1988) Justice and the Economics of Terminal Illness. *Hastings Center Report* 18 (4): 33–40.

Verhaeghen, P., Aikman, S.N., Van Gulick, A.E. (2011) Prime and Prejudice. *British Journal of Social Psychology*: 501–518.

Verina, T., Rohde, C.A., Guilarte, T.R. (2007) Environmental Lead Exposure During Early Life Alters Granule Cell Neurogenesis and Morphology in the Hippocampus of Young Adult Rats. *Neuroscience*: 1037–1047.

Vincent, J. (1995) *Inequality and Old Age*. London: UCL Press.

Vincent, J. (2006) Globalization and Critical Theory: Political Economy of World Population Issues. In Baars, J., Dannefer, D., Phillipson, C. & Walker, A. (Eds.) *Aging, Globalization and Inequality: The New Critical Gerontology*. Amityville, NY: Baywood, 245–272.

Vincent, J.G., Patterson, & Wale, K. (2002) *Politics and Old Age: Older Citizens and Political Processes in Britain*. Aldershot: Ashgate.

Von Hayek, F. (1960) *The Constitution of Liberty*. Chicago: University of Chicago Press.

Wacquant, L. (2009) *Punishing the Poor: The Neoliberal Government of Social Insecurity*. Durham, NC:Duke University Press.

Wadhwa, P. et al. (2001) Stress, Infection and Preterm Birth: A Biobehavioural Perspective. *Paediatric Perinatal Epidemiology*: 17–29.

Wagland, R. (2004) *Age, Equality, and Cultural Oppression: An Argument against Ageism*. Doctoral Thesis, Brunel University.

Walker, A. (1981) Towards a Political Economy of Old Age. *Ageing & Society:* 73–94.

Walker, A. (2009a) The Emergence and Application of Active Aging in Europe. *Journal of Aging & Social Policy* 21: 75–93.

Walker, A. (2009b) Commentary: The Emergence and Application of Active Aging in Europe. *Journal of Aging & Social Policy*: 75–93.

Walker, A. (2018) Ageing and Social Justice. In Dowding, K. (Ed.) *Handbook on Global Social Justice*. Northampton, MA: Edward Elgar, 213–227.

Walker, A. & Walker, C. (Eds.) (1997)*Divided Britain: The Growth of Social Exclusion in the 1980s and 1990s*. London: CPAG.

Walker, M. (1999) *Mother Time: Women, Aging, and Ethics*. Lanham, MD: Rowman & Littlefield.

Wallace, P. 1999*Agequake: Riding the Demographic Rollercoaster Shaking Business, Finance and Our World*. London: Nicholas Brealey.

Welford, C., Murphy, K., Rodgers, V. & Frauenlob, T. (2012) Autonomy for Older People in Residential Care: A Selective Literature Review. *International Journal of Older People Nursing*: 65–69.

Werner, R., Hoffman, A., & Coe, N.B. (2020) Long-Term Care Policy after Covid-19: Solving the Nursing Home Crisis. *The New England Journal of Medicine* 383: 903–905.

White, K., Haas, J.S. &Williams, D.R. (2012) Elucidating the Role of Place in Health Care Disparities: The Example of Racial/Ethnic Residential Segregation. *Health Services Research*: 1278–1299.

Whitehead, M. (1999) *Principles and Basic Concepts of Equity in Health*. Division of Health and Human Services. World Health Organization. http://www1.paho.org/english/hdp/hdd/pahowho.pdf.

WHO (2002)*Active Ageing. A Policy Framework*. Geneva: WHO.

WHO (2007) *Global Age-Friendly Cities: A Guide*. Geneva: WHO. https://www.who.int/ageing/publications/Global_age_friendly_cities_Guide_English.pdf.

WHO (2021) *Global Report on Ageism*. Geneva: WHO.

Wicclair, M. (1993) *Ethics and the Elderly*. New York, NY:Oxford University Press.

Wilkinson, R.G. (1992) Income Distribution And Life Expectancy. *BMJ*: 165–268.

Wilkinson, R.G. (1996) *Unhealthy Societies: The Afflictions of Inequality*. London: Routledge.

Wilkinson, R. (2006) *The Impact of Inequality: How to Make Sick Societies Healthier*. New York, NY:Free Press.

Wilkinson, J. & Ferraro, K. (2002) Thirty Years of Ageism Research. In Nelson, T. (Ed.) *Ageism: Stereotyping and Prejudice Against Older Persons*. Boston, MA: Massachusetts Institute of Technology, 339–365.

Wilkinson, R.G. & Pickett, K.E. (2015) Reply to Coburn's Income Inequality, Welfare, Class and Health. *Social Science & Medicine*: 233–234.

Wilkinson, R.G. & Pickett, K.E. (2006) Income Inequality and Population Health: A Review and Explanation of the Evidence. *Social Science and Medicine*: 1768–1784.

Williams, A. (1995) The Revisionist Difference Principle. *Canadian Journal of Philosophy*: 257–282.

Williams, A. (1997) Intergenerational Equity: An Exploration of the 'Fair Innings' Argument. *Health Economics*: 117–132.

Williams, D.R. & Wyatt, R. (2015) Racial Bias in Health Care and Health: Challenges and Opportunities. *JAMA*: 555–556.

Williams, D.R. & Mohammed, S.A., Leavell, J. & Collins, C. (2010) Race, Socio-economic Status, and Health. *Annual NY Academy of Sciences*: 69–101.

Williamson, J., Watts-Roy, D. & Kingston, E. (Eds.) (1999) *The Generational Equity Debate*. New York, NY:Columbia University Press.

Williamson, J.B., McNamara, T.K & Howling, S.H. (2003) Generational Equity, Generational Interdependence, and the Framing of the Debate over Social Security Reform. *Journal of Sociology & Social Welfare*: 3–14.

Wilmoth, J., Boe, C., & Barbieri, M. (2010) Geographic Differences in Life Expectancy at Age 50 in the United States Compared with Other High-Income Countries. In Crimmins, E.M., Preston, S.H., Cohen, B. (Eds.) *International Differences in Mortality at Older Ages: Dimensions and Sources*. Washington, DC: National Academies Press. https://www.ncbi.nlm.nih.gov/books/NBK62591/.

Wilson, M., Kurrle, S. & Wilson, I. (2018) Medical Student Attitudes Towards Older People: A Critical Review of Quantitative Measures . *BMC Research Notes*. https://doi.org/10.1186/s13104-018-3186-z.

Winship, S. et al. (2022) *Long Shadows: The Black-White Gap In Multigenerational Poverty*. The Brookings Institution/George Washington University.

Witham, M.D. & McMurdo, M.E. (2007) How to Get Older People Included in Clinical Studies. *Drugs Aging*: 187–196.

Wolch, J. & Dear, M. (1993) *Malign Neglect: Homelessness in an American City*. San Francisco: Jossey Bass.

Wolff, E. (2002) *Top Heavy. The Increasing Inequality of Wealth in America and What Can Be Done About It*. New York: New Press.

Wolff, J. (1998) Fairness, Respect, and the Egalitarian Ethos. *Philosophy and Public Affairs* 27 (2): 97–122.

Wolff, J. (2010) Fairness, Respect and the Egalitarian Ethos Revisited. *Journal of Ethics* 14: 335–350.

Wolff, J. & De-Shalit, A. (2007) *Disadvantage*. Oxford: Oxford University Press.

Wolfson, M., Rowe, G., Gentleman, J.F. & Tomiak, M. (1993) Career Earnings and Death: A Longitudinal Analysis of Older Canadian Men. *Journal of Gerontology*: S167–S179.

Woolf, S.H. & Schoomaker, H. (2019) Life Expectancy and Mortality Rates in the United States, 1959–2017. *JAMA*: 1996–2016.

World Economic Forum (2020) *The Decline of Upward Mobility*. Geneva: World Economic Forum. https://www.weforum.org/agenda/2020/09/social-mobili ty-upwards-decline-usa-us-america-economics/.

World Bank (1994) *Averting the Old Age Crisis Policies to Protect the Old and Promote Growth*. Oxford: Oxford University Press.

World Health Organization (WHO) (2002) *Active Ageing. A Policy Framework*. Geneva: World Health Organization.

World Health Organization (WHO) (2021) *Global Report on Ageism*. Geneva: WHO.

Wouters, O.J. (2020) Lobbying Expenditures and Campaign Contributions by the Pharmaceutical and Health Product Industry in the United States, 1999–2018. *JAMA Internal Medicine*: 688–697.

Wyman, M., Shiovitz-Ezra, S. & Bengel, J. (2018) Ageism in the Health Care System: Providers, Patients, and Systems. In Ayalon, L. & Tesch-Römer, C. (Eds.), *Contemporary Perspectives on Ageism*. Cham, Switzerland: Springer Nature, 193–212.

Xiang X., Lu X., Halavanau, A., Xue J., Sun Y., Lai P.H.L., & Wu Z. (2021) Modern Senicide in the Face of a Pandemic: An Examination of Public Discourse and Sentiment About Older Adults and COVID-19 Using Machine Learning. *Journals of Gerontology. Series B, Psychological Sciences and Social Sciences* 76 (4): 190–200.

Yang, Y. & Land, K.C. (2013) *Age-Period-Cohort Analysis: New Models, Methods, and Empirical Applications.* New York, NY:Routledge.

Yates, E. (1988) The Dynamics of Aging and Time: How Physical Action Implies Social Action. In Birren, J. & Bengtson, V. (Eds.) *Emergent Theories of Aging.* New York, NY:Springer, 90–217.

Yates, E. (2007) Further Conjectures on the Nature of Time in Living Systems: Causes of Senescence. In Baars, J. & Visser, H. (Eds.) *Aging and Time: Multi-disciplinary Perspectives.* Amityville, NY: Baywood, 177–186.

Yekkala, R. et al. (2006) Racemization of Aspartic Acid from Human Dentin in the Estimation of Chronological Age. *Forensic Science International*: 89–94.

Young, I.M. (1990) *Justice and the Politics of Difference.* Princeton, NJ: Princeton University Press.

Yu J. et al. (2022) Adverse Childhood Experiences and Premature Mortality through Mid-adulthood: A Five-Decade Prospective Study. *The Lancet Regional Health – Americas.* https://doi.org/10.1016/j.lana.2022.100349.

Zuckerberg, M. (2012) Letter from Mark Zuckerberg. Form S-1: Registration Statement. Washington, DC: United States Securities and Exchange Commission.

Index

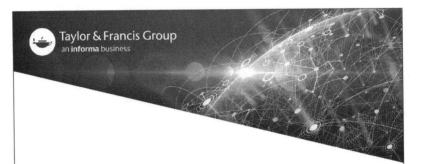